THE LAW OF THE EUROPEAN CENTRAL BANK

The Law of
the European Central Bank

by
CHIARA ZILIOLI
and
MARTIN SELMAYR

·HART·
PUBLISHING

OXFORD – PORTLAND OREGON
2001

Hart Publishing
Oxford and Portland, Oregon

Published in North America (US and Canada) by
Hart Publishing c/o
International Specialized Book Services
5804 NE Hassalo Street
Portland, Oregon
97213-3644
USA

Distributed in the Netherlands, Belgium and Luxembourg by
Intersentia, Churchillaan 108
B2900 Schoten
Antwerpen
Belgium

Hart Publishing is a specialist legal publisher based in Oxford, England.
To order further copies of this book or to request a list of other
publications please write to:

Hart Publishing, Salter's Boatyard, Folly Bridge,
Abingdon Road, Oxford OX1 4LB
Telephone: +44 (0)1865 245533 or Fax: +44 (0)1865 794882
e-mail: mail@hartpub.co.uk
WEBSITE: http//www.hartpub.co.uk

British Library Cataloguing in Publication Data
Data Available
ISBN 1–84113–245–4

Typeset by Hope Services (Abingdon) Ltd.
Printed and bound in Great Britain on acid-free paper by
Biddles Ltd, www.biddles.co.uk

Foreword

The creation of the single European currency was one of the most prominent events that took place around the turn of the century. There is no historical precedent of a similar monetary union covering so many independent states and their citizens, and leading to the creation of one of the two most important currencies in the world. With the introduction of the euro, the consolidation of the European Union has taken a major step forward. From an economic perspective, the euro represents a great new stride towards the achievement of a true single market between the 12 countries which have adopted the single currency. From a political point of view, it gives all citizens the most concrete example of the construction of Europe that they have ever seen over the past 50 years. And it also opens a fundamental chapter in the European experience of sharing sovereignty on key issues, with the creation of the European Central Bank, the European System of Central Banks and the Eurosystem, which—unlike the ESCB—only includes the national central banks of those countries participating in the single currency.

As a new supranational organisation of a very specific nature, the European Central Bank is now at the heart of the integration process which has been under way for half a century. The establishment of the single currency has followed the method described by Robert Schuman in his famous declaration of 9 May 1950: "Europe will not be made all at once, or according to a single plan. It will be built through concrete achievements which first create a de facto solidarity". With Monetary Union, Europe has reached a crucial stage of this integration process, involving the transfer of a key element of political sovereignty. And this transfer has been made to an organisation which is granted independence both from the European governments and from the institutions of the European Community, with a clear mandate: to maintain price stability in the euro area. The legal set-up of this new organisation is therefore of fundamental importance.

Quite a lot of research has already been published on the economic, monetary and financial aspects of European Economic and Monetary Union, including the operational features of the Eurosystem. Conversely, the institutional and legal aspects of Monetary Union have received relatively little attention.

"The Law of the European Central Bank" by Chiara Zilioli and Martin Selmayr will therefore receive a great deal of attention. This is warranted, not only because the authors cover a wide range of issues in a clear and readable manner, but also because of the quality of their work. I am confident that the book's audience will not be restricted to legal experts. It deserves a wide readership.

Christian Noyer,
Vice-President of the European Central Bank

Preface

This book deals with central banking from a legal perspective. At first glance, this seems to be a daring undertaking. Does a legal approach to central banking not go against the well-known saying according to which "central banking is an art"?[1] Have not central bankers themselves argued for many years and, in the end, successfully, for discretion rather than rules[2] as regards their policy decisions in complex economic situations?[3] Did not even F. A. Mann, the very expert on the legal aspects of money, state very clearly: "Such problems as monetary policy, the management and the supply, the quantity and the soundness of money are of no concern to the lawyer"?[4]

It is true that central banking and monetary policy traditionally have been understood as being outside the scope of legal thinking. For many, in particular for the ordinary man in the street, the politics behind money still have a very mysterious, almost quasi-religious character. Even though people use money every day, they prefer not to know about the complex details and mechanisms behind this useful tool of their economic activities. A prime example for this understanding is the United States where every one-dollar bill issued by the Federal Reserve bears the inscription: "In God we trust"; and Germany, where, according to Jacques Delors, not everybody believes in God, but where all believe in the Bundesbank.[5] As a consequence of this exceptional reputation and

---

[1] Cf. Hawtrey, *The Art of Central Banking* (London, 1970), ch. IV; and Niehans, *The Theory of Money* (Baltimore, Mld., 1978), 294: "However, economists should be under no illusion that central banking will ever become a science. Academic critics love to chide central bankers for their lack of a fully articulated doctrine of monetary policy, based on testable—and perhaps even tested—hypotheses. These critics mistake central bankers for what they are themselves, namely teachers and intellectuals. In fact, a good central banker is a doer and a politician, for whom even ambiguity and inconsistency may sometimes serve his purpose . . . However far monetary theory may progress, central banking is likely to remain an art."

[2] On this debate cf. Barro and Gordon, "Rules, Discretion and Reputation in a Model of Monetary Policy" [1983] *Journal of Monetary Economics* 101; cf. also the famous rule-based proposal by Friedman, *A Program for Monetary Stability* (New York, 1960).

[3] Cf. Issing, "Geldpolitik im Spannungsfeld von Politik und Wissenschaft" in Albeck (ed.), *Wirtschaftsordnung und Geldverfassung. Symposium zum 65. Geburtstag von Norbert Kloten* (Göttingen, 1992), 46 (51): "*Nun wird es niemanden überraschen, daß die Idee einer mechanischen Regel in den Notenbanken nicht gerade auf positive Resonanz stößt, müßte doch ihre Etablierung die Verantwortlichen schlagartig der Aura von Experten berauben, die ständig mit großem Sachverstand und feinnervigem Fingerspitzengefühl ausgestattet, komplexe Entscheidungssituationen zu bewältigen haben, und sie statt dessen zum Status von Halbautomaten degradieren*".

[4] Mann, *The Legal Aspect of Money* (5th edn., Oxford, 1992), 5.

[5] "*Nicht alle Deutschen glauben an Gott, aber alle an die Bundesbank*", quoted by Issing, "Should we have faith in central banks?", St. Edmund's College Millenium Year Lecture, Cambridge, 26 October 2000, published at http://www.ecb.int/key/00/sp001026_2.htm, 9.

standing of central banks, their relationship with the financial markets and their respective government only rarely ever became an issue of *legal* dispute.[6]

However, what once was true for central banking at the national level—the reduced importance of the law—is no longer necessarily true since 1 January 1999, the moment at which the European Central Bank (ECB) started fully to exercise its powers. The ECB is a unique central bank, and this chiefly for four reasons. First, it is not responsible for a national currency, but for the single currency of currently 12 Member States of the European Union (EU); the ECB therefore is the first central bank with a clearly supranational mandate. Secondly, the ECB is a central bank without a state, as its establishment has not been paralleled by the creation of a European federation with a central European government. Thirdly, the ECB is the creation of the Treaty establishing the European Community (the EC Treaty), which has been qualified by the European Court of Justice (ECJ) as a "constitutional charter";[7] it is thus a central bank the objectives, tasks, duties and competences of which do not stem simply from a piece of national legislation—as is the case of most central banks—but from supranational constitutional law. Fourthly, the ECB is, as a matter of law, the most independent central bank ever, as the EC Treaty itself lays down price stability as its primary objective (Articles 4(2), 105(1), first sentence EC) and entrenches, in Article 108 EC, its independence both from the Member States and from the Community institutions and bodies. Taken together, all these features suggest that the ECB is much more subject to the rule of law than central banks have been in the past. This new importance of the rule of law seems appropriate, if not necessary: the ECB's submission to the rule of Community law guarantees that, in spite of the present absence of a European government, the ECB does not operate in a vacuum, but is firmly embedded in a system of checks and control under the final authority of the ECJ.

It goes without saying that the integration of the ECB into the "Community governed by the rule of law" established by the EC Treaty does not mean that, today, every move of decision-makers in the "Eurotower" in Frankfurt am Main is likely to become litigated. As a matter of principle, the rule of law does not have as an automatic consequence increasing the number of controversies or requiring that conflicts arising always need to be resolved in a court case. Responsible decision-makers normally will be able to avoid appearance in court by observing legal rules in a transparent manner—a task which today is facilitated considerably as these rules are now clearly set out in the EC Treaty and in the Statute of the European System of Central Banks and of the European

---

[6] Smits, *The European Central Bank. Institutional Aspects* (The Hague/London/Boston, 1997), 106: "central banks have traditionally operated in an environment which is less than litigation-prone, and where the exact rules and competences were less important than the standing of the central bank and the weight of its advice".

[7] Case 294/83, *Parti écologiste "Les Verts"* v. *European Parliament*, [1986] ECR 1339, para. 23; *Opinion 1/91, EEA I* [1991] ECR I–6079, para. 21.

Central Bank (the Statute).[8] In addition, there is a long tradition in the case law of the ECJ which leaves substantial discretion for decisions which require a complex analysis of economic conditions;[9] the EC Treaty does not provide for a fundamental change in this approach as regards the policy of the ECB. It thus can be expected that only in the last resort will the ECJ be called to give a judgment in cases dealing with the technicalities of central banking operations to which the ECB could be a party.

However, one should also not overlook the fact that the legal principles which are to govern the activities of the new supranational bank—in particular the primacy of price stability and the far-reaching independence of the ECB—are unparalleled in central banking legislation throughout the world. As neither the Member States nor the Community institutions are yet used to this new degree of central bank independence, and as the ECB is still a rather young organisation, legal controversies are likely to arise around these principles which, though being written into the EC Treaty, will remain an issue of political debate in the years to come. Already today, a tendency may be observed for the supranational central bank responsible for the new single currency to be subject to more litigation than central banks have been in the past. For this, one does not need to refer to the staff cases which in the meantime have reached the Community judicature;[10] such cases, even though they may occasionally involve matters of principle,[11] are a typical phenomenon accompanying the work of every central bank and of all international or supranational organisations. Much more important in the present context is that, on 12 January 2000, a constitutional dispute has commenced in the ECJ involving the ECB and the Commission of the European Communities, started on the initiative of the latter.[12] This is an unprecedented step in the history of central banking: never before has a central bank been brought to court by the executive.

Against this background, the present book has legitimate reasons for focusing on "The Law of the European Central Bank", in particular on the legal principles which govern the organisation to which the responsibility for the single currency has been entrusted. For this purpose, the book is divided into five chapters. Chapter 1 deals with the legal nature of the ECB and its relationship with

---

[8] Inside the ECB, this importance of the rule of law is demonstrated by the responsibilities and tasks of its Directorate-General—Legal Services; cf. Sáinz de Vicuña, "The Lawyer at the ECB: A Description of the Legal Services of the European Central Bank" [1999] *Euredia* 591.

[9] On this, cf. Asso, "Le contrôle de l'opportunité de la décision économique devant la Cour européenne de justice" [1976] *RTDE* 21 and 177; Pache, "Die Kontrolldichte in der Rechtsprechung des Gerichtshofs der Europäischen Gemeinschaften" [1998] *DVBl* 380; Schmid-Lossberg, *Kontrolldichte im EG-Wirtschaftsrecht. Eine Untersuchung am Beispiel der Rechtsprechung des EuGH zu den Verordnungen im Währungsausgleich* (Frankfurt am Main, 1992).

[10] Two cases have already been declared inadmissible by the Court of First Instance (CFI): Case T–33/99, *Pinedo v. ECB* [2000] ECR Staff Cases, II–273; and Case T–27/00, *Staff Committee of the ECB and others v. ECB*, Judgment of 24 October 2000, not yet published.

[11] Cf. Selmayr, "Die Rechtssache T–33/99 und ihr gemeinschaftsverfassungsrechtlicher Hintergrund" [2001] *EWS* (in press).

[12] Cf. [2000] OJ C122/8.

the institutions and bodies of the European Communities. It analyses the controversial question to whom monetary sovereignty, originally belonging to the Member States, was surrendered by 11 Member States on 1 January 1999, and by Greece on 1 January 2001. Chapter 2 is dedicated to the European System of Central Banks (ESCB) through which the policies related to the single currency are implemented. As the ESCB is composed both of the ECB and of the central banks of the Member States, the question arises how competences and tasks are distributed and exercised within this system or, more precisely, who is the "governor" of this system. Chapter 3 analyses the making and the implementation of ECB law. Under the EC Treaty, the ECB has the power to adopt different types of legal instruments, including regulations, decisions, recommendations, opinions, guidelines, and instructions. The practical importance of these legal instruments requires a closer look at their characteristics and effects as well as at the way in which they are implemented through the ESCB. In chapter 4, the tasks and activities of the ECB are put in the context of differentiated integration. It is a fundamental characteristic of Economic and Monetary Union that its final stage does not take place with the full participation of all EU Member States, but that some of them have been given a derogation or special status as regards the introduction of the single currency. This chapter therefore attempts to give an overview of how the Community and the ECB cope with this still unusual experience of differentiated integration. Chapter 5 finally addresses the external aspects of the activities of the ECB: its scope of action under public international law and the relationship of the ECB's external competences with those of the Community institutions and the Member States.

The observations made in this book represent the result of two years of intensive joint academic work and publishing activities. During these two years, we approached the law of the ECB from different angles, thereby always answering legal questions which had arisen in the political and academic debate. We started, in spring 1999, with an article on the external relations of the "euro area",[13] which was followed, in summer 1999, by an article on the organisational structure of the ESCB and on the legal instruments of the ECB.[14] The series was completed in summer 2000 by an article on the legal nature of the ECB.[15] The present book is a compilation of all these articles, which now have been restructured, amended, updated, put in a systematic order, and accompanied by a Table of Cases, a Table of Legislation and a Bibliography. We hope thereby to give practitioners and academics alike a complete picture of the law of the ECB as it stands in the year 2001.

---

[13] Zilioli and Selmayr, "The External Relations of the Euro Area: Legal Aspects" (1999) *CML Rev.* 273.

[14] Zilioli and Selmayr, "The European Central Bank, its System and its Law" [1999] *Euredia* 187 and 307, republished in [1999–2000] *YEL* 348.

[15] Zilioli and Selmayr, "The European Central Bank: An Independent Specialized Organization of Community Law" (2000) *CML Rev.* 591.

This book would not have been possible without the constant exchange of thoughts with our colleagues at the European Central Bank and our academic friends. Even though the responsibility for the content of this book is entirely ours, we would nevertheless want to mention those who have contributed to it through numerous helpful comments and suggestions: Dr. José María Fernandez Martín, advisor to the Vice-President of the European Investment Bank (EIB), former Senior Legal Counsel in the Directorate-General Legal Services of the ECB; Professor Dr. Hugo Hahn, Würzburg; Pauline Koskelo, Justice at the Finnish Supreme Court, Helsinki, former Co-Director of the Legal Service of the EIB; Koen Lenaerts, Judge at the Court of First Instance of the European Communities and Professor in Leuven; Niall Lenihan, Senior Legal Counsel in the Directorate-General Legal Services of the ECB; Professor Dr. Carl-Otto Lenz, Brussels, former Advocate-General of the ECJ; Antonio Sáinz de Vicuña, General Counsel and Director-General of the Legal Services of the ECB; Hanspeter K. Scheller, Director-General for Administration and Personnel of the ECB; Professor Dr. Werner Schroeder, Leopold-Franzens-University, Innsbruck; Professor Dr. Michael Schweitzer, University of Passau; Professor Dr. Armin von Bogdandy, Johann-Wolfgang-Goethe-University, Frankfurt am Main; Professor Dr. Manfred Zuleeg, Johann-Wolfgang-Goethe-University, Frankfurt am Main, former judge of the ECJ.

We owe special thanks to Henrike Quast, Junior Research Fellow of the Centre for European Law at the University of Passau, for her invaluable help and assistance with all the technical aspects involved in the publication of this book.

It only remains to state that the views expressed in this book are our own and do not necessarily reflect those of the European Central Bank.

DR. CHIARA ZILIOLI

Deputy General Counsel and
Head of the Institutional Law Division
of the European Central Bank

DR. MARTIN SELMAYR

Director of the Centre for European Law
at the University of Passau and
Legal Advisor of Bertelsmann in Brussels

Frankfurt am Main, Passau and Brussels
August 2001

Contents

Table of Cases

EUROPEAN COURT OF JUSTICE

Judgments

Opinions

COURT OF FIRST INSTANCE

EUROPEAN COURT OF HUMAN RIGHTS

NATIONAL CASES

Austria

Germany

USA

Table of Legislation

Protocols annexed to the Treaties

Regulations

Recommendations

Opinions

ECB Guidelines

Community and ECB Agreements

Other Legal Instruments

NATIONAL LEGISLATION

Germany

Switzerland

United Kingdom

United States

PUBLIC INTERNATIONAL LAW

BIS

IMF

OECD

Vienna Convention of 21 March 1986 on the Law of the Treaties

WTO

Table of Figures

Abbreviations

AG	Advocate General
Am. J Comp. L	*American Journal of Comparative Law*
AöR	*Archiv des öffentlichen Rechts*
Art.	Article
BEAC	Banque des Etats de l'Afrique Centrale
BCE	Banque Centrale Européenne
BCEAO	Banque Centrale des Etats de l'Afrique de l'Ouest
BEI	Banque Européenne d'Investissement
BIS	Bank for International Settlements
CDE	*Cahiers de Droit Européen*
CE	Communauté européenne
cf.	compare
CFA-Franc	Franc de la Coopération financière en Afrique/Franc de la Communauté financière africaine
CFI	Court of First Instance of the European Communities
CFP-Franc	Franc de la Communauté financière du Pacifique
CFSP	Common Foreign and Security Policy
CML Rev.	*Common Market Law Review*
CON	Consultatio (= Consultation of the ECB)
DOM	Départements d'Outre Mer
DöV	*Die öffentliche Verwaltung*
DVBl	*Deutsches Verwaltungblatt*
EAEC	European Atomic Energy Community
EBRD	European Bank for Reconstruction and Development
EC	European Community/Treaty establishing the European Community
ECB	European Central Bank
ECHR	European Court of Human Rights
ECJ	European Court of Justice
ECOFIN	Council of Economic and Finance Ministers
ECR	European Court Reports
ECSC	European Coal and Steel Community/Treaty establishing the European Coal and Steel Community
ECU	European Currency Unit
EEA	European Economic Area
EEnA	European Environment Agency
EEC	European Economic Community
EIB	European Investment Bank

EIoP	*European Integration online Papers*
EL Rev.	*European Law Review*
EMCF	European Monetary Co-operation Fund
EMEA	European Agency for the Evaluation of Medicinal Product
EMU	Economic and Monetary Union
EONIA	European Overnight Indexed Average
EPM	ECB Payment Mechanism
ERM	Exchange Rate Mechanism
ESCB	European System of Central Banks
EU	European Union
EuR	*Europarecht*
EURATOM	Treaty establishing the European Atomic Energy Community
EuZW	*Europäische Zeitschrift für Wirtschaftsrecht*
EWS	*Europäisches Wirtschafts- und Steuerrecht*
ESZB	Europäisches System der Zentralbanken
EZB	Europäische Zentralbank
FAO	Food and Agriculture Organization of the United Nations
Fordham Int. LJ	*Fordham International Law Journal*
FRF	French Franc
GAB	General Arrangements to Borrow
GATS	General Agreement on Trade in Services
GATT	General Agreement on Tariffs and Trade
GG	Grundgesetz für die Bundesrepublik Deutschland (Basic Law of the Federal Republic of Germany)
IBRD	International Bank for Reconstruction and Development (the World Bank)
IEDOM	Institut d'Emission des Départements d'Outre Mer
IEOM	Institut d'Emission d'Outre-Mer
IMF	International Monetary Fund
Int. Soc. Sci. J	*International Social Science Journal*
IRCs	Independent Regulatory Commissions
JHA	Justice and Home Affairs
LIEI	*Legal Issues of European Integration*
MEP	Member of the European Parliament
MFI	Monetary and Financial Institutions
Michigan J Int L	*Michigan Journal of International Law*
NASCO	North Atlantic Salmon Conservation Organisation
NCB	National central bank
NEAFC	North-East Atlantic Fisheries Convention
NJW	*Neue Juristische Wochenzeitschrift*
OECD	Organisation for Economic Co-operation and Development
OHIM	Office for Harmonisation in the Internal Market
OJ	Official Journal of the European Communities

OLAF	Office européen pour la lutte anti-fraude (European Anti-Fraud Office)
PJCCM	Police and Judicial Co-operation in Criminal Matters
RMC	*Revue du Marché commun et de l'Union européenne*
RIW	*Recht der internationalen Wirtschaft*
Rs.	*Rechtssache*
RSC	Robert Schuman Centre
RTGS	Real-Time Gross-Settlement (System)
RTDE	*Revue trimestrielle du droit européen*
SEBC	Système européen des Banques centrales
TARGET	Trans-European Automated Real-time Gross-settlement Express Transfer (System)
TOM	Territoires Outre Mer
TRIPs	Trade Related Intellectual Property Rights
UEM	Union économique et monétaire
WM	*Wertpapier Mitteilungen*
YEL	*Yearbook of European Law*
ZEuS	*Zeitschrift für Europäische Studien*

1

What is the European Central Bank?

W HEN THE EUROPEAN Investment Bank (EIB) published a job vacancy in
Le Monde in 1979 in which it called itself an "independent institution",
Mr Dondelinger, then Member of the European Parliament, accused the EIB in
written questions addressed to the Council and to the Commission of waging "a
minor war of secession" inside the European Economic Community, and this
even before the latter had become a confederation.[1]

Today, the legal position of the European Central Bank (ECB) as an actor
independent of both the Member States *and* the institutions and bodies of the
European Communities[2] attracts similarily serious criticism. In 1999, in a contribution to the *Common Market Law Review*, Torrent, Professor of Political
Economy at the University of Barcelona and former member of the Legal Service
of the Council of the European Union, claims that this thesis could cause
"irreparable damage to the Community and to the whole institutional order of
the European Union (including to the ECB itself)".[3] Once again, the unity of the
Union is seen as being in danger.

Torrent's criticism reveals that the specific legal nature of the ECB is still quite
a new feature of Community law which is not yet generally known or accepted.
Of course, nobody will ever doubt the affiliation of the ECB to the organisational framework of the European Union or the fact that it forms an integral
part of what Advocate General Roemer once called "the unity of ideals" existing between the three European Communities and the EIB.[4] The real issue is the
position of the ECB *inside* this organisational framework and its relationship
with the Community institutions and bodies. In the debate thereon, one should
be extremely careful not to use the *political* concept of the unity of the Union as
an instrument to water down the *legal* principle of supranational central bank
independence which has been enshrined in Article 108 EC and thus in the

---

[1] Written question No 1104 and 1105/78 [1979] OJ C113/30 and C145/14.

[2] Cf. Selmayr, "Die Wirtschafts- und Währungsunion als Rechtsgemeinschaft" [1999] *AöR* 357
(369); "Die EZB als Neue Gemeinschaft—ein Fall für den EuGH?" [1999] *Europablätter* 170; and
Selmayr, "Wie unabhängig ist die Europäische Zentralbank? Eine Analyse anhand der ersten geldpolitischen Entscheidungen der EZB" [1999] *WM* 2429. On the impact of the ECB's legal nature on
external relations, cf. *infra*, Ch. 5, p. 171 *et seq.*

[3] Torrent, "Whom is the European Central Bank the Central Bank of?: Reaction to Zilioli and
Selmayr" (1999) *CML Rev.* 1229.

[4] Cf. Roemer AG's opinion in Joined Cases 27/59 and 39/59, *Campolongo* v. *High Authority of
the ECSC* [1960] ECR 391, at 418.

constitutional charter of a Community governed by the rule of law.[5] One should not disregard the fact that, with the start of Economic and Monetary Union (EMU) on 1 January 1999, the constitutional balance inside the European Union was modified considerably when the ECB as a new and independent legal person, established by primary Community law, started fully to exercise its powers. To point to these modifications of the Community legal order is thus not a sign of "secessionist tendencies", but an issue of fundamental importance for the proper functioning of EMU.

The following analysis will, first of all, outline the differentiated organisational structure of today's European Union (II.). It will then show where the ECB finds its place inside this structure (III.). After having discussed some practical consequences resulting from the new constitutional balance inside the European Union (IV.), the analysis will conclude with some remarks on what is sometimes called the "democratic deficit" of the ECB (V.).

II. THE ORGANISATIONAL STRUCTURE OF TODAY'S EUROPEAN UNION

Today, there are essentially two different views of the European Union. The first is a political view which is used by politicians in interviews and press conferences, and by journalists in articles and television reports. To make the ordinary citizen understand what happens at summits in Brussels or Lisbon, in meetings of the Commission or of the Council, they talk most of the time solely of "the European Union" or "the Union". We read about a "EU summit in Helsinki", about the "EU administration of the town of Mostar", or of a new "EU Directive" which has recently been adopted by the "EU Council" on a proposal from the "European Commission". Such terminology suggests that there is one entity called the European Union which can take political actions, legislate, or conclude international agreements through own institutions. It thus alludes to the existence of something that is "a kind of United States of Europe", in the tradition of the vision once expressed by Winston Churchill in his speech of 19 September 1946 at the University of Zürich.

Lawyers, and in particular Community lawyers, are aware that this political use of the notion European Union does not reflect with sufficient accuracy what is the perhaps most complex organisational structure of governance in the world. Even though there is growing recognition that also lawyers may—for presentational purposes—describe the European Union as a single organisation and a single legal system,[6] lawyers, in contrast to politicians and sociologists, in addition need to answer questions of competences, of legal responsibility, of contractual and non-contractual liability, and therefore they need to look more

---

[5] Cf. Case 294/83, *Parti écologiste "Les Verts'* v. *European Parliament* [1986] ECR 1339, para. 23; Opinion 1/91, *EEA I* [1991] ECR I–6079, para. 21.

[6] Cf. the approach chosen by A. von Bogdandy, "The Legal Case for Unity: The European Union as a Single Organisation with a Single Legal System" (1999) *CML Rev.* 887.

specifically for legal persons[7] to which they can impute responsibility and liability when they want to sue them or their institutions in court. Therefore, the
legal view—including that of Community lawyers who are, in their heart,
ardent supporters of an ever closer Union—cannot be satisfied with a unifying
(and simplifying) perspective of the European Union, but is obliged to analyse
the European Union more in detail.[8]

By doing this, lawyers soon find out that the European Union is far from being
a state-like organisational system; instead, they are facing a bewildering
"Europe of bits and pieces".[9] What is called "the European Union" seems itself
not even to be a legal person,[10] but just the common roof for a unique three-
pillar structure.[11] As is well known, the European Union unites under this roof
a first pillar within which the 15 Member States of the European Union have
pooled a number of sovereign rights as regards economic policy in a wide sense.
To this end, the first pillar contains a body of law generally characterised as
supranational and called "Community law". Alongside it is a second pillar in
the context of which the 15 Member States co-operate in an intergovernmental[12]

---

[7] With all respect, the concept of a legal person is certainly not just "a descriptive notion without normative content", as surprisingly claimed by Torrent, *supra*, n. 3, 1234. The ECJ itself mentions the legal personality of the EC as an essential element of its supranational nature, resulting
from the limitation of sovereign rights of the Member States and leading to the supremacy of
Community law; cf. Case 6/64, *Costa* v. *ENEL* [1964] ECR 585(593) and Case 22/70, *Commission*
v. *Council (ERTA)* [1971] ECR 263, paras. 13–14. Cf. von Bogdandy, *supra*, n. 6, 89 *et seq.*, who
talks of "the vexed question of legal personality", but nevertheless concludes (at 88) that in particular at the international plane, legal personality is vital for an organisation's capacity to interact with
other subjects of international law and that it determines the organisation's consequential liability.
On this, cf. *infra*, Ch. 5, p. 172 *et seq.*

[8] Such a differentiated legal approach—to be contrasted with a mere "social picture"—is also
favoured by Curtin and Dekker, "The EU as a 'Layered' International Organization: Institutional
Unity in Disguise" in P. Craig and G. de Búrca (eds.), *The Evolution of EU Law* (OUP, Oxford,
1999), 83 (83).

[9] Cf. Curtin, "The Constitutional Structure of the Union: A Europe of Bits and Pieces" (1993)
CML Rev. 17 (67), who even talks of "constitutional chaos". The new structure was also compared
to "a kind of a Gaudi structure", "a house which is half built, a work in progress, suddenly abandoned by its builders"; cf. "Editorial Comment" (1992) *CML Rev.* 199 (202). Dehousse, "European
Institutional Architecture after Amsterdam: Parliamentary System or Regulatory Structure?", RSC
Working Paper No 98/11, considers this wording to be applicable also to the Amsterdam Treaty the
"patchwork nature" of which he underlines at 596.

[10] On the controversy surrounding the Union's potential legal personality, cf. Curtin and Dekker,
supra, n. 8, 84 *et seq.* Today, only a progressive view concludes in favour of a legal merger of the
three Communities with the new European Union into a single legal person; cf. the "unity thesis" of
von Bogdandy and Nettesheim, "Die Verschmelzung der Europäischen Gemeinschaften in der
Europäischen Union" [1999] *NJW* 2324. The Commission had proposed to address again "the matter of the Union as a legal entity" at the Intergovernmental Conference 2000; cf. the Commission's
Opinion *Adapting the Institutions to Make a Success of Enlargement*, Brussels, 26 January 2000,
published at http://europa.eu.int/igc2000. However, the Treaty of Nice—the result of this intergovernmental conference—left this controversial issue undecided.

[11] Cf. Wellenstein, "Unity, Community, Union—What's in a Name?" (Guest Editorial) (1992)
CML Rev. 205 (207).

[12] Supranationalism and intergovernmentalism represent two fundamentally opposed organisational devices; cf. Virally, "Definition and Classification of International Organizations: a Legal
Approach" [1977] *Int. Soc. Sci. J.* 58 (62).

manner to achieve a common foreign and security policy; and by a third, and again mainly intergovernmental, pillar which relates to police and judicial co-operation in criminal matters among the 15 Member States. One may view this Union as a coherent[13] "temple",[14] but one also has to recognise that the powers of the institutions, the law-making procedures, the legal instruments available, the effects of these legal instruments in the Member States, and, most important, the scope of jurisdiction of the ECJ vary remarkably between the pillars of this temple.[15]

When further studying the first—and, as a matter of substance, central[16]—pillar of the European Union, the legal analyst inevitably encounters the "matriochka experience".[17] What at first glance looks like a monolithic entity called "the Community" consists in (legal) reality of a number of different legal persons of which each is called "Community": the European Coal and Steal Community (ECSC), already founded in 1951; the European Community (EC), which before Maastricht had been the European Economic Community (EEC); and the European Atomic Energy Community (EAEC). All these three Communities have their own legal personality (cf. Articles 281 EC; 6 ECSC; 184 Euratom) and are endowed with different, and in the case of the ECSC and the EAEC quite specialised, fields of activity, each described in the three Treaties which established them in 1951 and 1957 respectively.

It is true that the institutions of the three Communities were merged in 1957 and 1965,[18] as is recalled today by Article 9(2) of the Amsterdam Treaty. This institutional merger has led some writers to develop the concept of a

---

[13] Coherence inside the Union is promoted in particular by the existence of general provisions on membership (Art. 49 EU) and on the amendment procedure (Art. 48 EU), by common objectives (Art. 2 EU) and common principles (Art. 6 EU) of the Union, and by the so-called "single institutional framework" (Arts. 3 to 5 EU); on the latter, cf., however, "Editorial Comment", *supra*, n. 9, 202: "This is more an institutional 'géometrie variable' than a single framework"; and Wellenstein, *supra*, n. 11, 209: "a hybrid construction that is more singular than single".

[14] The metaphor of a "French gothic cathedral" is preferred to that of the temple by De Witte, "The Pillar Structure and the Nature of the European Union: Greek Temple or French Gothic Cathedral?" in Heukels, Blokker and Brus (eds.), *The European Union after Amsterdam. A Legal Analysis* (The Hague/London/Boston, 1998), 51. Cf. also Weiler, "Neither Unity nor Three Pillars—The Trinity Structure of the Treaty on European Union" in Monar, Ungerer and Wessels (eds.), *The Maastricht Treaty on European Union* (Brussels, 1993), 49, who favours the theological metaphor of "trinity" in which "oneness" and "separateness" coexist simultaneously.

[15] This has led the ECJ to look carefully at the boundaries between the supranational and the intergovernmental areas of the law of the European Union and to give, in the case of cross-pillar matters, a clear preference to the supranational first pillar on the basis of Art. 47 EU; cf. Case C–170/96, *Commission* v. *Council* [1998] ECR I–2763, paras. 14–17.

[16] Cf. the "Solemn Declaration on European Union", endorsed by the European Council at the Stuttgart Summit on 19 June 1983 which stressed the commitment "to strengthen and continue the development of the Communities which are the nucleus of European Union"; Bull.EC 6–1983, 24 (25), points 1.4 and 1.4.1.

[17] Matriochka is the famous Russian puppet which, when being opened, contains a smaller puppet which, again, contains several smaller dolls.

[18] By the Convention of 25 March 1957 on certain institutions common to the European Communities and by the so-called Merger Treaty of 8 April 1965 establishing a Single Council and a Single Commission of the European Communities.

"Community in the wide sense"[19] or to call the three Communities just "the Community" in political, but also in legal writings.[20] However, despite the close institutional and functional links existing between the three "twin" Communities, their legal separateness has been kept until today.[21] Even though the ECJ has underlined the aim to achieve a coherent and uniform interpretation of the EC, the ECSC and the EAEC Treaties, orientated at their common objectives,[22] and despite the similarities of their respective legal orders, the ECJ has never abandoned the legal distinction between the three Communities.[23] It has in particular seen the need to delimitate exactly whether a certain task requires action by this or that Community[24] because the powers of the Community institutions and the legislative procedures still vary between the EC, the EAEC[25] and in particular the ECSC Treaty.[26] The need for a distinction between the three legal persons EC, ECSC and EAEC becomes most apparent at the international

[19] Cf. Tizzano, "Contratti 'strumentali' e contratti d'impiego delle Comunità europee" [1978] *Rivista di diritto europeo*, 481 *et seq.*; and in his note on ECJ, Case 85/86, *Commission* v. *Board of Governors of the EIB* [1998] ECR 1281 in [1988] *Foro Italiano* 1281 *et seq.*

[20] As an example, cf. Ullricht and Donnelly, "The Group of Eight and the European Union", G7 Governance No 8 (November 1998), published at http://www.library.utoronto.ca/g7/governance/gov5, endn. 6, where they claim that the three Communities had become "the European Community (EC)" as a result of the Merger Treaty and then were transformed into "the European Union" by the Maastricht Treaty.

[21] Cf. Schermers and Blokker, *International Institutional Law. Unity within Diversity* (3rd edn., The Hague/London/Boston, 1995), § 1698: "Although the three pillars form part of the larger Union, the three Communities continue to exist as independent international organisations, based on separate treaties and with their own legal personality".

[22] Cf. Case 221/88, *ECSC* v. *Acciaierie Busseni SpA in liquidation* [1990] ECR I–495, paras. 10–16.

[23] Cf. Case 220/91 P, *Commission of the European Communities* v. *Stahlwerke Peine-Salzgitter AG* [1993] ECR I–2393, para. 27 *et seq.* In this case, the CFI had originally held that in spite of the differences between the liability regimes for the ECSC and the EC, the three Community Treaties would represent "a single legal order, albeit one established by three different Treaties", this would allow to interpret Art. 34 of the ECSC Treaty in the light of the criteria laid down by the ECJ in its case law on Art. 215(2) [now Art. 288(2)] EC; cf. Case T–120/89, *Stahlwerke Peine-Salzgitter AG* v. *Commission of the European Communities* [1991] ECR II–279, para. 78. The ECJ, however, stated on appeal that this reasoning is not correct when the liability of the ECSC is in issue: "Even though it is possible to point to similarities between the conditions for liability laid down by the ECSC and the EEC Treaties . . ., it is in the light of the criteria evolved for the application of Articles 34 and 40 of the ECSC Treaty that the Community judicature must define the facts and characterize the faults of such a nature as to render the Community liable".

[24] The need for delimiting clearly the tasks of the three Communities also results from Art. 305 EC according to which the provisions of the EC Treaty shall not affect the provisions of the ECSC Treaty and shall not derogate from the provisions of the EAEC Treaty.

[25] Cf. e.g. the *Chernobyl* case which concerned the adoption of a regulation on the basis of Art. 31 of the EAEC Treaty instead of Art. 100a of the EEC Treaty (now, as amended by Amsterdam, Art. 95 EC); cf. Case C–70/88, *European Parliament* v. *Council (Chernobyl)* [1990] ECR I–2041; and *Chernobyl II* [1991] ECR I–4529. See also Case C–327/91, *France* v. *Commission* [1994] ECR I–3641, paras. 31–39: no analogy to Art. 101 Euratom when an international agreement is concluded on the basis of the EC Treaty.

[26] Under the ECSC Treaty, the Commission enjoys very extensive powers of direct management of Community law. In addition, the ECSC Treaty will expire on 23 July 2002 (Art. 97 ECSC), in contrast to the EC and the EAEC Treaty, which are "concluded for an unlimited period" (Arts. 312 EC and 208 EA). Cf. also *Opinion 1/75*, *Local Cost Standard* [1975] ECR 1355, 1365: no bearing of Art. 71 ECSC in a prior reference procedure under the EEC Treaty.

level where so-called "Community agreements" are often concluded only by one or two of the three Communities. A prominent example is the Agreement on the European Economic Area[27] to which just the EC and the ECSC are parties, but not the EAEC.

Therefore, in addition to the distinction between the Union's three pillars, Community lawyers still need to distinguish between the three Communities inside the Union's first and central pillar.[28] From the point of view of legal precision, it is somewhat regrettable that this distinction has become more and more blurred in recent years by the terminology used by some of the Community institutions, in particular by the Council, which has decided to call itself the "Council *of the European Union*".[29] This new terminology is of course understandable against the background of the general programme of the Treaties heading towards further integration. However, in view of the different quality of the law created under the Union's supranational central pillar and under its intergovernmental pillars, one should not underestimate the danger of an intergovernmental "pollution" of the Community law method resulting from the politics behind such over-arching terminology.[30] Community lawyers should note in particular that the ECJ—which has the exclusive task to ensure that in the interpretation and application of the EC, the ECSC and the Euratom Treaty, the law is observed (Articles 220 EC; 31 ECSC; 136 EA)—continues to call itself correctly "the Court of Justice *of the European Communities*".

All this demonstrates that today we have still not reached a situation in which we can compare the Union to a state-like structure. This is in particular true after the amendments introduced by the Treaties of Amsterdam and Nice, which point rather to an increased flexibility and heterogeneity inside the European Union.[31] Today, one can therefore observe an enhanced need to dif-

---

[27] [1994] OJ L1/3.

[28] Cf. Blokker and Heukels, "The European Union: Historical Origins and Institutional Challenges" in Heukels, Blokker and Brus (eds.), *The European Union after Amsterdam—A Legal Analysis* (The Hague/London/Boston, 1999), 24: "the Amsterdam Treaty has preserved the 'three pillar structure' erected by the Treaty of Maastricht for an indeterminate period." Cf. also De Witte, supra, n. 14, 54: "the Member States . . ., while 'simplifying' and 'consolidating' with gusto in the Treaty of Amsterdam, have left in existence two separate Treaties, the EC Treaty and the EU Treaty, and have also confirmed the existence of three separate pillars". We would go even further and point to the existence of five Treaties altogether, including the ECSC Treaty, the Euratom Treaty, and the Treaty of Amsterdam itself.

[29] Council Decision 93/591/EU, Euratom, ECSC, EC of 8 November 1993 concerning the name to be given to the Council following the entry into force of the Treaty on European Union [1993] OJ L281/18, with corrigendum in [1993] OJ L285/41. More precise was "Editorial Comment", *supra*, n. 9, 202: "So it will be the Council *of the European Communities* that will enact the common foreign and security policy *of the Union* (which has no legal personality)" (original emphasis).

[30] A similar critical attitude in this respect is taken by Timmermans, "The Uneasy Relationship Between the Communities and the Second Union Pillar: Back to the 'Plan Fouchet' " [1996] *LIEI* 61.

[31] Cf. the analysis by Gaja, "How Flexible is Flexibility under the Amsterdam Treaty?" (1998) *CML Rev.* 855; Kortenberg, "Closer Cooperation in the Treaty of Amsterdam" (1998) *CML Rev.* 833; Koenig, "Die Europäische Union als bloßer materiellrechtlicher Verbundrahmen" [1998] *EuR* 139; see also the conclusion drawn by Blokker and Heukels, "The European Union: Historical Origins and Institutional Challenges" in Heukels, Blokker and Brus (eds.), *supra*, n. 28, 26: "In a

ferentiate carefully between the Union's pillars, the competences of the different legal persons therein as well as between the different types of "Union law" and their varying fields of application. This new degree of differentiation is taken into account by an increasing number of academics who prefer to view the European Union not through unifying glasses, but as a "Layered International Organization" in which a variety of sub-legal systems coexist, not only within the Union itself, but also within its three pillars.[32]

III. THE PLACE OF THE ECB INSIDE THE EUROPEAN UNION

Where is now the proper place for the ECB inside this heterogeneous organisational structure of the European Union? This is an issue which has, since Maastricht, triggered an impressive number of extremely divergent statements in legal writings. The ECB has already been classified as "Community institution"[33] or "Community organ",[34] as "quasi-institution",[35] as "a Community body",[36] but also as "a Community within the Community"[37] and even as "an independent actor within the European Union".[38] Of course, one should not

---

way, Maastricht has produced a paradox, which is consolidated by the Amsterdam Treaty: a Union has been established which appears not to be a union in a number of respects". On differentiated integration in the context of EMU, cf. *infra*, Ch. 4, p. 133 *et seq.*

[32] Cf. in particular Curtin and Dekker, *supra*, n. 8, 86. The understanding of the Union as a "Layered International Organization" was first developed by Dörr, "Zur Rechtsnatur der Europäischen Union" [1995] *EuR* 334 (347); cf. also Schroeder, "Die Rechtsnatur der Europäischen Union und verwandte Probleme" in Hummer and Schweitzer, *Österreich und das Recht der Europäischen Union* (Vienna, 1996), 3; Tizzano, "La personnalité internationale de l'Union européenne" [1998] *RMC* 11.

[33] In this sense cf. the original interpretation by Schweitzer and Hummer, *Europarecht* (5th edn., Neuwied/Kriftel/Berlin, 1996), para. 132; now modified by Schweitzer in Grabitz and Hilf, *Das Recht der Europäischen Union, Kommentar* (Munich, 1999), Art. 289, para. 9 *et seq.*; Art. 290, para. 14; Art. 291, para. 11 *et seq.*

[34] Of little help in the debate on the ECB's legal nature is its classification by some German authors as "*Gemeinschaftsinstitution*" instead of "*Gemeinschaftsorgan*"; cf. von Borries, "Die Europäische Zentralbank als Gemeinschaftsinstitution" [1999] *ZEuS* 281; M. Weber, "Das Europäische System der Zentralbanken" [1998] *WM* 1465 (1465). Because the German term "*Organ*" is the equivalent of what is called "institution" in the English and French text of the Treaties, "*institución*", "*istituzione*", and "*instituição*" in their Spanish, Italian and Portuguese versions. On the linguistic difficulties for the terminology used for describing the organisational structure of the Union, cf. Pipkorn in Starck (ed.), *Erledigung von Verwaltungsaufgaben durch Personalkörperschaften und Anstalten des öffentlichen Rechts* (Baden Baden, 1992), 227 (266 *et seq.*).

[35] Cf. Cloos, Reinesch, Vignes and Weyland, *Le Traité de Maastricht. Genèse, Analyse, Commentaires* (Brussels, 1994), 236.

[36] Cf. Pipkorn, "Der rechtliche Rahmen der Wirtschafts- und Währungsunion—Vorkehrungen für die Währungspolitik" [1994] *EuR* 85 (86); Weinbörner, *Die Stellung der Europäischen Zentralbank (EZB) und der nationalen Zentralbanken in der Wirtschafts- und Währungsunion nach dem Vertrag von Maastricht* (Frankfurt am Main, 1998), 387.

[37] Cf. Pernice, "Das Ende der währungspolitischen Souveränität Deutschlands und das Maastricht-Urteil des BVerfG" in Due, Lutter and Schwarze (eds.), *Festschrift für Ulrich Everling* (Baden Baden, 1995), ii 1057 (1059).

[38] Cf. Hahn, *Der Vertrag von Maastricht als völkerrechtliche Übereinkunft und Verfassung* (Baden-Baden, 1992), 42 and 73.

reduce the ECB's legal nature to just a terminological question. Nevertheless, we will try in the following lines to find an accurate notion to circumscribe most precisely the functions performed by the ECB within the general programme of the Treaties.

1. A false question

To start with, we first want to address the question which has recently been proposed in the doctrine as a possible starting point for discussing the legal nature of the ECB: "Whom is the European Central Bank the Central Bank of?".[39] By referring to "common sense", the answer given to this question is a seemingly easy analogy to the position of the Federal Reserve System in the United States of America and of the Bundesbank in the Federal Republic of Germany. Therefrom, one is indeed tempted to conclude automatically: the ECB must be "the Central Bank of the Community, no more, no less".[40]

Two short remarks need to be made on this. First, the brief analysis above has shown that the organisational structure of the European Union is not comparable with the existing organisational structures of the Member States.[41] Because of the peculiarities of the Union's legal system, the ECJ has always issued warnings against such analogies,[42] and recently, the European Court of Human Rights has also stressed "the *sui generis* nature of the Community which does not follow in every respect the pattern common in many States" as regards the separation of powers.[43] Therefore, we suggest extreme caution when using "common sense" arguments in the European Union's context. What sounds like common sense at the national level is quite often contradicted inside the *sui generis* framework of the European Union.

Secondly, it must be noted that the wording of the question, which is presented as conclusive for the legal nature of the ECB, reveals a somewhat incomplete view of the topic. Simply to ask "whom is the European Central Bank the Central Bank of?", reduces *a priori* too much the possible answers. The question suggests that, by definition, the ECB must legally *belong* to somebody—the Member States and the Community are mentioned as the only two possible alternatives—to whom its activities would be attributable or to whom the ECB would be attached by an institutional or even proprietary link. This excludes, from the beginning, a third option:[44] the establishment of the ECB as a new

---

[39]   By Torrent, *supra*, n. 3.

[40]   Cf. *ibid.*, 1231

[41]   This is even stressed by the defenders of the "unity thesis"; cf. von Bogdandy, *supra*, n. 6.

[42]   Cf. Case C–359/92, *Germany v. Council* [1994] ECR I–3681, para. 38.

[43]   Cf. ECHR, Judgment of 18 February 1999—24833/94, *Matthews v. United Kingdom*, para. 48.

[44]   Theoretically, a fourth possibility would be to classify the ECB as being the common bank (the "daughter") of the national central banks which are the shareholders of the ECB; cf. Seidel, "Die Wirtschafts- und Währungsunion im rechtlichen und politischen Gefüge der Europäischen Union" in Caesar and Scharrer (eds.), *Ökonomische und politische Dimensionen der Europäischen*

supranational organisation independent both of the Member States *and* of the Community institutions and bodies. The above analysis has shown that the European Union is very well capable of embracing several different supranational organisations under its common roof. In addition, it is common practice for states to establish international or even supranational banks as new international organisations, as is demonstrated by the example of the International Bank for Reconstruction and Development (the "World Bank"), of the European Bank for Reconstruction and Development (EBRD), of the Bank for International Settlements (BIS)—the members of which are not states, but central banks[45]—and, in the Community context, by the example of the EIB.[46]

We clearly agree that a general political classification of the ECB as "the Central bank of the European Union", as "the Central bank of the Community", or even as "Euro-Bank"[47] is possible in the language used by politicians and journalists. Such a lack of precision can be accepted by lawyers as a—harmless—*falsa demonstratio*,[48] which is perhaps necessary to convey the political message of the unity of the Union's political system. However, in the legal debate such politically inspired terminology should not create the slightest doubt about the true bearers of competences and legal responsibilities. A legal view must therefore start by scrutinising closely what really has happened in the already differentiated organisational structure of the European Union with the start of the third stage of EMU on 1 January 1999.

2. The "fourth pillar" proposal

A possible understanding of the ECB as "the European Union's central bank",[49] or as "an independent actor of the European Union"[50] has its origin in the history of the negotiations which ultimately led to the Maastricht Treaty. In an early stage of these negotiations, the idea was floated concluding a separate

Wirtschafts- und Währungsunion (Baden Baden, 1999), 215 (238). This is an interpretation which is probably based on earlier drafts of the EC Treaty and the Statute; in the present state of Community law, such a "company law analogy" does not at all match the relationship between the ECB and the national central banks; cf. von Borries, *supra*, n. 34, 294. This issue is also dealt with *infra*, Ch. 2, p. 63 *et seq.*

[45] On the international legal personality of the BIS, which is today undisputed, cf. Giovanoli, "The Role of the BIS in International Monetary Cooperation and its Tasks Relating to the ECU" in Effros (ed.), *Current Legal Issues Affecting Central Banks*, (Washington, 1992), i, 39 (42 *et seq.*).

[46] On the international legal personality of the EIB, cf. *infra*, Ch. 5, 000 *et seq.*

[47] Cf. Brand and Selmayr, "Die Euro-Bank", *Oberösterreichische Nachrichten*, 7 January 2000, 3.

[48] *Falsae demonstrationes* are a daily experience for the lawyer. While the man on the street, for example, does not bother to distinguish verbally between "property" and "possession", the lawyer even has to pay attention to such sophisticated differences as "legal ownership" and "beneficial ownership" in the Law of Trusts.

[49] Cf. von Bogdandy, "Organizational Proliferation and Centralisation under the Treaty on European Union" in Blokker and Schermers (eds.), *Proliferation of International Organizations. Legal Issues* (The Hague, 2001), 177, who thereby puts the ECB in the context of a European Union organised in accordance with his "unity thesis".

[50] Cf. Hahn, *supra*, n. 38, 42 and 73.

"Treaty on EMU" and thus to set up, inside the new temple called "the European Union", a fourth "monetary pillar"[51] in between the existing Community law structures and the new fields of intergovernmental co-operation in foreign and security policy matters and in justice and home affairs. At first glance, this concept appeared attractive to some Member States for a number of reasons. It would, first of all, have reflected the division of the Maastricht negotiations into two intergovernmental conferences,[52] one on EMU, the other on Political Union, which were kept separate until their very end. It should also not be forgotten that Member States had for a quite long time chosen traditional methods of inter-governmental co-operation in monetary matters within the context of the European Monetary System; a separate "Treaty on EMU" would have permitted them to continue this intergovernmental tradition. In addition, it seemed quite certain in the early 1990s that not all Member States would be able or willing to participate in the final stage of EMU: a separate "Treaty on EMU" or "monetary pillar" would have allowed for a structure flexible enough to take into account the divergent rights and obligations of participating and non-participating Member States; it would perhaps even have allowed the participation of third countries like Switzerland in the single currency, as favoured by some.[53] Finally, some Member States also showed a certain reluctance to "communautarise" the field of monetary policy so closely linked to the idea of national sovereignty; they understood very well that this would be equivalent to submitting it to a supra-national institutional framework, in particular to the jurisprudence of the ECJ; in contrast to this, the "fourth pillar" approach would have been compatible with giving the European Council—which is not an institution of the supranational Communities—a pivotal role as regards monetary policy and would thus have kept the ultimate control on monetary policy for the Member States.[54]

---

[51] On this concept, mainly originating from an early French proposal, cf. Louis, "Union moné-taire et Union politique, Le rôle du juge" in *La tutela giurisdizionale dei diritti nel sistema comuni-tario—Congresso di Venezia dell'U.A.E.* (Brussels, 1997), 585 (591), and *Commentaire Mégret, Le Droit de la CEE,* (1976), vi, 20; cf. also Di Bucci, "La corte di giustizia, l'unione economica e mone-taria ed il passaggio alla moneta unica" in *Scritti in onore di Giuseppe Federico Mancini, vol. II: Diritto dell'Unione Europea* (Milan, 1998), 307 (311); Selmayr, "Die Wirtschafts- und Währungsunion als Rechtsgemeinschaft", *supra*, n. 2, 360; von Borries, "Die Fortentwicklung der Europäischen Wirtschaftsgemeinschaft zur Wirtschafts- und Währungsunion" in Rengeling and von Borries, *Aktuelle Entwicklungen in der Europäischen Gemeinschaft* (Cologne, 1992), 105; Bailleix Banerjee, *La France et la Banque Centrale européenne* (Paris, 1999), 310, according to whom the "fourth pillar" concept originated in the French treasury.

[52] Both intergovernmental conferences were officially opened on 15 December 1990 in Rome; cf. Bull. EC 12–1990, 21, No 1.1.7. (Political Union) and 22, No 1.1.9. (Monetary Union). Cf. Louis, "Le lien entre les conférences intergouvernementales sur l'Union économique et monétaire et sur l'Union politique" in Monar, Ungerer and Wessels (eds.), *supra*, n. 14, 163.

[53] Cf. von Borries, *supra*, n. 51, 105.

[54] This idea was revitalised by the French proposals for establishing a kind of a "*gouvernement économique*" in parallel to the introduction of the single currency, which would have allowed the European Council to give instructions to the ECB; on this, cf. Chémain, *L'Union économique et monétaire. Aspects juridiques et institutionnels* (Paris, 1995), 317 *et seq.*; and the proposal of the President of the French Assemblée nationale, *Agence Europe* No 6655, 29–30 January 1996, 5.

Despite these arguments, the "fourth pillar" proposal quickly disappeared from the negotiating table. Obviously, there was a widespread will among most Member States to go one step further this time, to create not just an exchange rate mechanism, but a true *single* currency, thereby replacing the existing national currencies. The introduction of such a single currency among different states required, by definition, the setting up of a central authority to be responsible for the definition and implementation of the monetary policy for this single currency. It thus required a separation of monetary sovereignty from the context of national politics and its transfer to a supranational level. Soon it became clear at the intergovernmental conference that this revolutionary step of a complete *denationalisation* of monetary policy[55] could best be achieved by using the traditional Community law method which had been so successful in the past as regards the abolition of custom duties and the establishment of the common market.[56]

Therefore, in spite of the peculiarities of monetary policy, it was in the end decided to locate this new field of integrated policy not at the intergovernmental boundaries, but in the very heart of the European Union's temple: in its first and central pillar which is entirely governed by supranational Community law.[57] We therefore find today only one reference to EMU in the EU Treaty, in its Article 2, first indent, which mentions the establishment of EMU among the Union's objectives.[58] All the substantive, procedural and institutional provisions, in particular the provisions on the objectives, tasks and competences of the ECB, are to be found in the EC Treaty (Articles 2, 4, 8, 98 to 124 EC) and, as regards monetary policy, repeated and specified in the Statute of the European System of Central Banks and of the European Central Banks (the Statute), which

[55] Of course, this denationalisation is less radical than the one once suggested by Hayek; cf. Hayek, *Denationalisation of money—The Argument Refined. An Analysis of the Theory and Practice of Concurrent Currencies* (2nd edn., Lancing, 1978). Hayek suggested not only the abolition of national monopolies over money, but in addition the replacement of all public authority over money by private issuance. However, combined with the feature of central bank independence, the creation of the euro as supranational currency comes very close to putting Hayek's proposal into practice; cf. Issing, "Hayek—Currency Competition and European Monetary Union", Annual Hayek Memorial Lecture Hosted by the Institute of Economic Affairs (London, 27 May 1999), published at http://www.ecb.int/key/sp990527.pdf.

[56] On negative experiences with public international law concepts in European monetary co-operation (*Werner* resolution, the "snake" and ERM), cf. Selmayr, "Die Wirtschafts- und Währungsunion als Rechtsgemeinschaft", *supra*, n. 2, 361 *et seq.*

[57] A few traces of the original "fourth pillar"-proposal may still be detected in the EC Treaty; cf. the exclusion, by Art. 104(10) EC, of the possibility of starting infringement proceedings under Arts. 226, 227 EC in the context of the excessive deficit procedure; and the fact that in the Chapter on EMU, the European Council is mentioned for the first time in the EC Treaty; cf. Arts. 99(2) and 113(3) EC. This intrusion of the European Council into the domain of Community law is strongly criticised by Louis, "L'évolution du Conseil européen à la lumière de la réalisation de l'Union économique et monétaire" in Starace (ed.), *Divenire sociale e adeguamento del diritto. Studi in onore di Francesco Capotorti* (Milan, 1999) 253; cf. also Martenczuk, "Der Europäische Rat und die Wirtschafts- und Währungsunion" [1998] *EuR* 151; and Selmayr, "Die Wirtschafts- und Währungsunion als Rechtsgemeinschaft", *supra*, n. 2, 380 *et seq.*

[58] On the effect of Art. 2 EU in Community law, cf. *infra*, n. 158.

is attached as a Protocol to the EC Treaty (Articles 8 and 107(4) EC) and thus forms an integral part of primary Community law (cf. Article 311 EC).

As a consequence of the denationalisation of monetary policy, the decision-making process inside the ECB has been made legally immune to all kinds of national influence. As in the case of the Commission of the European Communities (cf. Article 213(2) EC), the "*caractère supranational*" of which had already been emphasised by the original Article 9(5) of the ECSC Treaty, Article 108 EC prohibits the ECB from seeking or taking instructions from any government of a Member State or any other national body. The ECB's independence from the Member States is further reflected in the organisational structure of the European System of Central Banks (ESCB) which has been established together with the ECB.[59] This system is composed of the ECB and 15 national central banks (Article 107(1) EC). However, the decision-making process inside the ESCB is centralised at its supranational level as it is governed exclusively by the decision-making bodies of the ECB (Article 107(3) EC).[60] The national central banks, which themselves have to be independent of the Member States by virtue of Article 108 EC and Article 14.1 of the Statute, are hence not representing national interests inside the ESCB, but are conceived as the operating arms of the ECB which have to act in accordance with its guidelines and instructions (Article 12.1 and 14.3 of the Statute).[61] This puts the ECB into a strong position for the fulfilment of its tasks in the Member States as it is not dependent on the support of national authorities, for instance, to require minimum reserves to be held by a credit institution,[62] to collect statistical information from economic agents[63] or to impose sanctions on undertakings which fail to comply with the ECB's regulations or decisions.[64]

Since 1 January 1999, 11 Member States have fully participated in the third stage of Economic and Monetary Union and have thus limited their sovereign rights in the field of monetary policy, have submitted their national central banks to the governance of the ECB and transferred national competences in this field entirely to a supranational level; on 1 January 2001, Greece followed their example. It is even questionable whether these Member States still have, in law, the power to revoke this step towards the single currency by an amendment to the Treaty in accordance with Article 48 of the Treaty on European Union.

---

[59] The organisational structure of the ESCB will be explained in more detail *infra*, Ch. 2, p. 53.

[60] Cf. *infra*, Ch. 3, p. 57 *et seq.*

[61] These provisions do not confer any rights or impose any obligations on the national central banks of Sweden, Denmark and the United Kingdom, which retained their powers in the field of monetary policy according to national law; cf. Art. 43.1 and 43.2 of the Statute; more extensively on differentiation as regards the ECB, cf. *infra*, Ch. 4, p. 155 *et seq.*

[62] Art. 19.1 of the Statute.

[63] Art. 5 of the Statute.

[64] Only when the ECB needs police powers to enforce its regulations and decisions, must it rely, like every public authority, on the support of the competent police authorities in the Member States; cf. Art. 3(2) of Council Regulation 2532/98 concerning the powers of the European Central Bank to impose sanctions [1998] OJ L318/4. On the details of the ECB's sanctioning regime cf. Ch. 3, *infra*, p. 122 *et seq.*

At least the wording of the EC Treaty seems to prohibit such a step backwards, as therein the process leading towards the single currency is called "irrevocable"[65] and "irreversible"[66]—the most far-reaching expression of the denationalisation of money as it has taken place with EMU.

As a first conclusion, we can state that monetary policy has been completely denationalised inside the European Union's first and central pillar so that it would be most inappropriate to view the ECB as "the Member States' central bank". It would also be legally not sufficiently precise to qualify the ECB as "the Union's central bank" as this would not answer the question about the intergovernmental or supranational nature of its tasks. As the ECB has been established by the EC Treaty and the Statute attached thereto, it is in any event a central bank within the first and central pillar of the Union, and hence a truly supranational central bank.

3. The bearer of monetary sovereignty since 1 January 1999

The complete denationalisation of monetary policy since 1 January 1999 is a well-known feature of EMU and practically undisputed in legal doctrine.[67] However, the denationalisation of monetary policy immediately leads to a further question: after having been completely separated from the national constitutional framework and after having been transferred to the supranational level, where exactly has monetary sovereignty passed inside the European Union's first pillar? In short: who is now—as regards the 12 Member States where the single currency has been introduced[68]—the bearer of monetary sovereignty, after the start of the final stage of EMU?[69]

---

[65] In Arts. 4(2), 118, 123(4) EC.

[66] In Protocol No 24 on the transition to the third stage of economic and monetary union.

[67] Torrent also follows our argument in this respect; cf. *supra*, n. 3, 1230.

[68] On the situation of Member States with a derogation and a special status, cf. *infra*, Ch. 4, p.134 *et seq*.

[69] This question is answered neither by Art. 2 nor by Art. 4(2) EC, as claimed by Torrent, *supra*, n. 3, 1232. These provisions make *the establishment* of EMU and *the introduction* of a single currency an objective of the European Community and a task of both the European Community and the Member States. They thus concern chiefly *the process* leading to the single currency and aim at submitting this process to the primary objective of price stability. However, they remain silent on the question to whom monetary sovereignty passes as soon as this process is completed. It is telling in this context that Art. 105 EC—which entrusts the responsibility for the single monetary policy to the ESCB, governed by the ECB—shall apply "from the beginning of the third stage", i.e. from 1 January 1999; cf. Art. 116(3), subpara. 2, EC. In view of the wording and the scheme of Arts. 2 and 4(2) EC, it thus appears quite daring to conclude that these provisions would attribute the responsibility for the definition and conduct of the single monetary policy and exchange-rate policy "to the Member States and to the Community *(and to nobody else)*", as suggested by Torrent (original emphasis). Torrent's view obviously has been inspired by the Spanish version of Art. 4(2), the wording of which—in contrast to in particular the English, the German, the French and the Italian versions—does not reflect the process-oriented nature of this provision sufficiently.

3.1. The three supranational legal persons established by the EC Treaty

At first glance, the logical answer seems to be: the EC. Inside the Union's central pillar, a transfer of sovereign rights not concerning the specific fields of coal and steel or atomic energy policies, but other economic policies in a broad sense necessarily falls under the EC Treaty. And the EC is the legal person by which supranational competences transferred by the Member States through the EC Treaty are normally exercised. To the legal person EC, the Member States have transferred the power to establish a customs union and a common market. It seems logical that the same must apply also to monetary policy, now freshly integrated in the first pillar.

However, a closer look reveals that the EC Treaty has established not one single bearer of sovereign rights, but three different supranational legal persons:

—According to Article 1 EC, the Member States "establish among themselves a EUROPEAN COMMUNITY"; and Article 281 EC reads: "The Community shall have legal personality".
—By virtue of Article 8 EC, "a European Central Bank (hereinafter referred to as 'ECB') shall be established in accordance with the procedures laid down in this Treaty"; and Article 107(2) EC reads: "The ECB shall have legal personality".
—By virtue of Article 9 EC, "A European Investment Bank is hereby established"; and Article 266(1) EC reads: "The European Investment Bank shall have legal personality".

The question arises: in what relationship do these three supranational legal persons stand to one another? Of course, they are all part of the "unity of ideals", of the "operational unity"[70] which links the EC, the ECSC and the EAEC Treaty, as well as of the coherent supranational legal system of Community law.[71] But is there, in addition to this conceptual link, also an institutional link between the EC, the EIB, and—most important for the present analysis—the ECB which, at the end of the day would allow all actions of the ECB to be imputed to the legal person EC? Is there a kind of organic or even proprietary connection between the EC and the ECB?

These important questions are unfortunately left open by Article 288(3) EC which addresses the issue of non-contractual liability. While Article 288(2) EC provides for a liability of the EC[72] for any damage caused by its institutions or by its servants in the performance of their duties, in accordance with the general

---

[70] Cf. Joined Cases 27/59 and 39/59, *Campolongo* v. *High Authority of the ECSC* [1960] ECR 391, 404.

[71] Cf. Case 221/88, *supra*, n. 22.

[72] In Community law, the question of the liability of the legal person EC must be clearly distinguished from the question of its representation in the courtroom in an action under Arts. 235 and 288(2) or (3) EC. Before the Community judicature, the EC is represented by the institutions which are alleged to be responsible for the matter giving rise to liability, as this is seen to be in the interests of a good administration of justice; cf. Joined Cases 63 to 69/72, *Wilhelm Werhahn Hansamühle and others* v. *Council of the European Communities* [1973] ECR 1229, para. 7; see recently Case

principles common to the laws of the Member States, Article 288(3) EC simply states that the preceding paragraph shall apply "under the same conditions" to damage caused by the ECB or by its servants in the performance of their duties. Does this mean that the EC is also liable for damage caused by the ECB? Or should this rather be understood as providing for a separate liability of the legal person ECB, in parallel to that of the legal person EC? Not much help on this question is offered by Article 35.3, first sentence, of the Statute which simply recalls that the ECB is subject to the liability regime provided for in Article 288 EC, but does not address the issue of the legal person which, at the end, has to pay for the damage incurred from its own financial resources.

3.2. The ECB—a Community institution?

The liability question and other problems would be easy to solve if one could qualify the ECB as a Community institution. The Community institutions are listed in Article 7(1) EC. Through them, the EC shall carry out the tasks entrusted to it by the EC Treaty. Whenever Community institutions act under the EC Treaty, they do not act for themselves, but always as representatives and thus in the name and on behalf of the legal person EC; they are the arms through which the EC is able to act and to achieve its political aims. This organic dependence of the Community institutions on the legal person for which they are acting has been stressed by the ECJ which once stated expressly that "only the Community has legal personality, and its institutions do not".[73] In line with this understanding of an institution, the ECJ has always attributed legal obligations entered into by the Community institutions to the legal person EC, and not to the institutions themselves.[74] Under Article 288(2) EC, all activities of the Community institutions under the EC Treaty are therefore imputable to the legal person EC.

Against this background, the ECB—unlike the Commission or the Council—cannot be qualified as an institution. The ECB itself has legal personality under Article 107(2) EC[75] and so-called "decision-making bodies"[76] to act in its name and on its behalf: the Governing Council of the ECB, the Executive Board of the

T–246/93, *Bühring* v. *Council of the European Union and Commission of the European Communities* [1998] ECR II–171, para. 26. On this case law, see Schmahl, "Ungereimtheiten und Rechtsschutzlücken bei der außervertraglichen Haftung der Europäischen Gemeinschaft" [1999] *ZEuS* 415 (416 *et seq.*). However, when she states (at 420) that there would be only one single budget at the Community level by which claims for damages could be satisfied, she ignores the financial resources of the ECB and of the EIB which do not form part of the Community budget, as will be explained *infra*, at p. 19 and 20.

[73] Cf. Joined Cases 7/56 and 74/57, *Algera* v. *Common Assembly of the ECSC* [1957] ECR 81 (57).

[74] Cf. Case C–327/91, *France* v. *Commission* [1994] ECR I–3641, para. 24 *et seq.*

[75] This is also stressed by Partsch in Léger (ed.), *Union européenne. Communauté européenne. Commentaire article par article des traités UE et CE* (Basel, 2000), Arts. 108, 109 CE: "*à la différence des institutions de la Communauté, elle [la BCE] dispose d'une personnalité juridique propre*".

[76] In the French text: "*organes de décisions*"; in German: "*Beschlußorgane*"; in Italian: "*organi decisionali*"; in Spanish: "*órganos rectores*".

ECB (Article 107(3) EC), and the General Council of the ECB as its third deci-sion-making body (Article 45 Statute). The ECB is also not listed in Article 7(1) EC among those institutions through which the EC carries out its tasks; and throughout the EC Treaty, the ECB is never referred to as a Community insti-tution, but always as something apart. According to Article 111(3), second subparagraph EC, Community agreements on monetary regime and foreign exchange regime matters shall be binding "on the institutions of the Community, *on the ECB* and on the Member States". Under Article 234, first subparagraph (b) EC, the ECJ has jurisdiction on the validity and interpretation of acts "of the institutions of the Community *and of the ECB*".[77] This can be understood only in the sense that the ECB is not a Community institution,[78] but that it must be something else.

3.3. The ECB—a decentralised Community body?

Sometimes, it is suggested[79] that the ECB would resemble such decentralised Community bodies as, to name but a few, the European Environment Agency (EEnA) in Copenhagen,[80] the European Agency for the Evaluation of Medicinal Products (EMEA)[81] in London, or the Office for Harmonisation in the Internal Market (OHIM) in Alicante.[82] In fact, the organisational structure of the Communities[83] consists not only of the three legal persons EC, ECSC and EAEC

---

[77] Cf. also Art. 51 of the Protocol on the Statute of the Court of Justice, annexed to the EU, EC and EAEC Treaties by the Nice Treaty, which, again, distinguishes between "the institutions of the Communities *and the ECB*."

[78] In this respect, the following statement of Mancini AG in para. 12 of his Opinion on Case 85/86, *Commission v. Board of Governors of the EIB* [1988] ECR 1281, regarding the EIB, can be applied also to the ECB: "the Bank lacks the fundamental characteristic of an organ, that is to say its acts are not directly imputable to the organisation—the EEC—of which, according to the propo-sition under consideration, it should be regarded as being an integral part. . . . So the Bank is neither an institution nor an organ."

[79] Cf. Torrent, *supra*, n. 3, 1233 and fn. 11. Cf. also Timmermans, "Editorial Comment: Executive Agencies within the EC: The European Central Bank—a Model?" (1996) *CML Rev.* 623 (626), where he however admits that the ECB is not really an executive agency, but rather "a fully-fledged regulatory agency". The difference between the ECB and the agencies is also shown by the way in which the question of the seat is treated: for the ECB (but not for the agencies) this is now laid down, together with that of the institutions of the European Communities and of Europol, in Protocol No 8 on the location of the seats of the institutions and certain bodies and departments of the European Communities and of Europol; on this, cf. Schweitzer, *supra*, n. 33, Art. 289, para. 10.

[80] Established by Council Regulation 1210/90 of 7 May 1990 on the establishment of the European Environment Agency and the European Environment Information and Observation Network (EEnA Regulation) [1990] OJ L120/1.

[81] Established by Council Regulation 2309/93 of 22 July 1993 laying down Community proce-dures for the authorization and supervision of medicinal products for human and veterinary use and establishing a European Agency for the Evaluation of Medicinal Products (EMEA Regulation) [1993] OJ L214/1.

[82] Established by Council Regulation 40/94 of 20 December 1993 on the Community trade mark (OHIM Regulation) [1994] OJ L11/1.

[83] On this and on the organisational diversity of Community law, cf. Hilf, *Die Organiations-struktur der Europäischen Gemeinschaften* (Berlin, 1982); Lenaerts, "Regulating the Regulatory Process: 'Delegation of Powers' in the European Community" (1993) *EL Rev.* 23; Craig and de

and their merged institutions, but in addition knows a number of separate, partially autonomous legal persons which have been set up by the Community institutions to achieve the objectives of the Treaties—which have been continuously expanded and intensified in the course of the last decades—in a decentralised manner. The Community institutions thereby have followed the example of the Member States which increasingly have chosen multi-level systems of governance by establishing agencies with varying degrees of independence.

Though having their own legal personality,[84] these decentralised bodies remain functionally closely linked to the Community institutions, their tasks and objectives.[85] As has been clearly underlined by the ECJ in its *Meroni* rulings,[86] the EC cannot, by creating such decentralised bodies with separate legal personality and by delegating powers to them, escape its responsibilities or liabilities under the EC Treaty. Today, the Community institutions try to counter potential reproaches for creating "irresponsible agencies" by always ascertaining a certain political supervision by the Community institutions over their decentralised bodies,[87] by linking them financially to the Community budget[88] and by providing for a specific—although often quite limited[89]—regime of legal

Búrca, *supra*, n. 8, 55, 69 *et seq*.; Berger, *Vertraglich nicht vorhergesehene Einrichtungen des Gemeinschaftsrechts mit eigener Rechtspersönlichkeit* (Baden Baden, 1999).

[84] Legal personality has been conferred to the EEnA by Art. 7, first sentence, EEnA Regulation; to the EMEA by Art. 59, first sentence, EMEA Regulation; and to OHIM by Art. 11(1), second sentence, OHIM Regulation.

[85] This is pointed out in the preamble to the EEnA Regulation, recital 8: "Whereas the Agency should co-operate with existing structures at Community level to enable the Commission to ensure the full application of Community legislation on the environment".

[86] Case 9/56, *Meroni & Co., Industrie Metallurgiche* v. *High Authority of the ECSC* [1958] ECR 133; Case 10/56, *Meroni & Co., Industrie Metallurgiche, società in accomandita semplice* v. *High Authority of the ECSC* [1958] ECR 157 (168 *et seq*.), where the ECJ annulled the High Authority's decision to delegate powers to the Brussels agencies on the applicant's complaint "that the High Authority has delegated to the Brussels Agencies powers conferred upon it by the Treaty, without subjecting their exercise to the conditions which the Treaty would have required if those powers had been exercised directly by it".

[87] Cf. Art. 8(1) EEnA Regulation: 2 Commission representatives and 2 qualified scientific personalities designated by the European Parliament in the EEnA's management board; cf. Art. 56(1) EMEA Regulation: 2 Commission representatives and 2 representatives appointed by the European Parliament on the EMEA's Management Board; cf. Art. 118 OHIM Regulation: Art. 122(1) OHIM Regulation: 1 Commission representative on the OHIM's Administrative Board.

[88] Cf. Art. 11(3) EEnA Regulation: the revenue of the EEnA consists, *inter alia*, of a subsidy from the Community entered in the general budget of the European Communities; cf. Art. 57(1) EMEA Regulation: the revenue of the EMEA consists, *inter alia*, of a contribution from the Community; cf. Art. 134(3) OHIM Regulation: OHIM's revenue comprises, *inter alia*, a subsidy entered against a specific heading of the general budget of the European Communities, Commission section. These direct financial links to the Community budget justify the general submission of all decentralised bodies to the full control of the Court of Auditors under Art. 248(1), second sentence EC.

[89] In some cases, the ECJ only has been given jurisdiction in disputes concerning the non-contractual liability of the decentralised bodies; cf. Arts. 18(2) EEnA Regulation; 60(2) EMEA Regulation. Cf. also Case T–148/97, *Keeling* v. *OHIM* [1998] ECR II–2217, where the CFI considered an action for annulment under Art. 173 of the Treaty (now Art. 230 EC) brought against a decision of the President of OHIM to be inadmissible because "acts emanating from Community bodies other than those listed in that provision may not be challenged on the basis of it. The Office for Harmonisation in the Internal Market is not one of the Community institutions listed in Art. 4 of the Treaty, nor is it mentioned in the first paragraph of Article 173 of the Treaty".

control for them, to be exercised by the ECJ.[90] The ECJ has not yet had an opportunity to rule on the legality of these new models of a delegation of powers in Community law. However, it seems to be guaranteed that it will not tolerate, as a result of the establishment of such decentralised bodies, any kind of *lacuna* in the complete system of legal remedies created by the Treaties.[91] Ultimately, the ECJ will therefore have to attribute the responsibility for the acts and omissions of decentralised bodies to the Community institutions which have created them.[92]

It is quite obvious that the ECB cannot be compared to such decentralised bodies. Most importantly, the ECB was not created by the Community institutions, but established directly by Article 8 EC in conjunction with Article 123(1), second subparagraph, EC.[93] The ECB thus has its roots not in secondary, but in primary Community law[94] and therefore exercises not powers *delegated* to it by the Community institutions, but *originary* powers given to it directly by the EC Treaty and the Statute.[95] A political supervision of the ECB by the Community

---

[90]   Art. 63 of the OHIM Regulation allows actions to be brought before the ECJ against decisions of OHIM's Board of Appeal on appeals in trade-mark cases. Cf. also Council Regulation 1035/97 of 2 June 1997 establishing a European Monitoring Centre on Racism and Xenophobia which provides, in Art. 15(3), for the ECJ's jurisdiction in actions for annulment under Article 230 EC brought directly against the Centre.

[91]   On this, cf. Case 294/83, *Parti écologiste "Les Verts'* v. *European Parliament* [1986] ECR 1339, para. 23.

[92]   Cf. de Búrca, *supra*, n. 83, 76 *et seq*. When Torrent, *supra*, n. 3, 1232 states in this context that it had never been argued that decentralised bodies were bodies "outside the Community", he misses Case 16/81, *Alaimo* v. *Commission* [1982] ECR 1559. Here, the Commission (!) in fact had argued that servants of the European Centre for the Development of Vocational Training were not employed by the European Communities (para. 5). The ECJ therefore had to analyse "whether the Centre is part of the 'European Communities' "(para. 7). In view of the principles governing the delegation of powers explained above, it is self-evident that the ECJ answered this question in the affirmative, as "the Centre was established by the Council, pursuant to Art. 235 of the EEC Treaty [now Art. 308 EC]" (para. 12).

[93]   Under these provisions, no act of secondary Community law was required for the establishment of the ECB; the ECB therefore could start with its work immediately after the Council of the European Union, meeting in the composition of the Heads of State or Government, had confirmed the 11 Member States which, in its view, fulfilled the necessary conditions for the adoption of the single currency, in accordance with Art. 109j(4) EC (now Art. 121(4) EC); cf. Council Decision (EC) 98/317 of 3 May 1998 [1998] OJ L139/30.

[94]   The establishment of the ECB through the means of primary Community law has its origins in Art. 102a(2) EEC, as inserted by the Single European Act: "insofar as further development in the field of economic and monetary policy necessitates institutional changes, the provisions of Art. 236 [now Art. 48 EU] shall be applicable". By this, the drafters of the Treaty wanted to prevent the establishment of a central monetary organisation by the Community institutions on the basis of Art. 235 EEC (now Art. 308 EC). Secondary Community law had already been used to establish the European Monetary Co-operation Fund (EMCF); cf. Regulation 907/73 of 3 April 1973 establishing a European Monetary Co-operation Fund [1973] OJ L89/2; on the EMCF and the problem of its legal basis see Louis, "Le Fonds européen de coopération monétaire" [1973] *CDE* 255.

[95]   Cf. also Lenaerts, *supra*, n. 83, 43: "To the extent that it appeared appropriate, in a given policy context, to create an internal body outside the Community institutional structure laid down in Art. 4 EEC, to take the necessary policy decisions in complete independence, it would be for the constitution itself to create such a body. Examples are the European Investment Bank . . . and the European Central Bank". This aspect was already stressed, as regards the EIB, by Mancini AG in Case 85/86, *supra*, n. 74, para. 8 of the AGs opinion. This is also the reason we did on purpose—and

institutions, as it takes place in the case of decentralised bodies, is not foreseen by the Treaty; Article 108 EC even prohibits explicitly any attempt by the Community institutions and bodies to influence the decision-making process the ECB. In addition, primary Community law does not provide for a budgetary link between the Community institutions and the ECB. On the contrary, the ECB has its own financial means for the fulfilment of its tasks—mainly the ECB's capital, paid up by the national central banks (Article 28 of the Statute), foreign reserves transferred to it by the national central banks (Article 30 of the Statute)[96] and monetary income accruing from the monetary policy function of the ESCB (Article 32 of the Statute)[97]—which do not form part of the budget of the European Communities[98] set up in accordance with Articles 268 EC *et seq.*,[99] but are administered exclusively by the ECB.

From this it follows that the acts or omissions of the ECB cannot, under the general principles governing a delegation of powers, be attributed to the EC and the Community institutions. The Member States have never, even for a juridical second, transferred their monetary sovereignty to the legal person EC—which then could have delegated the powers in this monetary field to the ECB—but have chosen to transfer it directly, without using the Community institutions as an intermediary, to the newly established ECB,[100] and thus to constitutionalise

not for lack of attention, as claimed by Torrent, *supra*, n. 3, 1233—not equate the ECB with decentralised bodies in (1999) *CML Rev.* 273; on the need to distinguish clearly between the ECB and decentralised bodies, cf. extensively Selmayr, "Die EZB als Neue Gemeinschaft—ein Fall für den EuGH?", *supra*, n. 2, 173 *et seq.*

[96] On the ECB's control over the foreign reserves of the Member States and its consequences for the exchange policy of the euro, cf. Selmayr, "Darf die EZB den Wechselkurs des Euro stützen?" [2000] *Europablätter* 209; and "Interventionen zwecks Preisstabilität. Die europarechtlichen Leitplanken für die EZB", *Neue Zürcher Zeitung*, No 237, 11 October 2000, 11.

[97] For the method of allocating monetary income during the transitional period from 1 January 1999 to 31 December 2001, where no euro banknotes are yet in circulation, cf. Decision ECB/2000/19 of 3 November 1998 as amended by Decision of 14 December 2000 on the allocation of monetary income of the national central banks of participating Member States and losses of the ECB for the financial years 1999 to 2001 [2000] OJ L336/119.

[98] Today, the budget covering EC, ECSC and EAEC is sometimes also called "general budget of the European Union" (cf. [1998] OJ L44/1). The reason seems to be that under Art. 28(2) and (3) and Art. 41(2) and (3) EU, all administrative expenditures of the Community institutions and, with some exceptions, operational expenditure resulting from second and third pillar activities "shall be charged to the budget *of the European Communities*". The emphasis added demonstrates that the language of the Treaties is, again, more accurate than the practice of some Community institutions.

[99] Not all financial resources used in the context of the Treaties are, by definition, part of the budget of the European Communities; cf., as an example, the expenditure necessary for the EEC's financial assistance under the Fourth ACP–EEC Lomé Convention, the implementation of which is shared by the EEC and its Member States. As, here, it is for the Member States to choose the source and methods of financing, the ECJ held that this expenditure was not Community expenditure, did not have to be entered in the Community budget and consequently was not subject to Art. 208 EC (now Art. 279 EC); cf. Case C–316/91, *European Parliament* v. *Council* [1994] ECR I–625, para. 39.

[100] This is in line with the language chosen already in *Convergence Report: Report required by Art. 109j of the Treaty establishing the European Community* of the European Monetary Institute (Frankfurt, 1998), at p. 2 of the Glossary as regards the definition of EMU: "Stage Three will start on 1 January 1999 in accordance with the decision pursuant to Art. 109j(4), with the transfer of monetary competence to the ESCB and the introduction of the euro". Such a direct transfer of sovereignty seems also to be the understanding of Louis, "Les relations internationales de l'Union

this (irreversible) transfer of sovereign power.[101] This makes it inappropriate to equate the ECB with decentralised bodies like the EEnA, EMEA or OHIM which stand, financially and organically, in a relationship of dependency *vis-à-vis* the Communities.

3.4. The example of the EIB

It seems very attractive to define the legal nature of the ECB by analogy to that of the EIB,[102] the third supranational legal person established under the EC Treaty. The advantage of such an analogy is that there already exists some very instructive case law of the ECJ as well as an impressive number of academic writings on the EIB's legal nature[103] so that one is tempted simply to transfer the arguments relating to the EIB to determine the legal nature of the ECB.

In fact, the ECB and EIB appear to be comparable for a number of reasons: they both have been established as legal persons directly by primary Community law, and not by the Community institutions; they both have been given their own financial resources, in the EIB's case mainly the capital paid up by the Member States; the EIB also has its own decision-making bodies—a Board of Governors, a Board of Directors, and a Managing Committee—through which it acts when it fulfils the tasks assigned to it under the EC Treaty and under the Protocol which contains the EIB's Statute; and both Banks are, by virtue of primary Community law (Article 291 EC), bearers of the same privileges and

économique et monétaire" in Société française de droit international (ed.), *Droit international et droit communautaire, perspectives actuelles* (Paris, 2000), 387 (388): "*la politique monétaire où les compétences nationales ont été transférées à un Système européen de banques centrales (SEBC), avec à son centre, une Banque centrale européenne (BCE)*". Such understanding has been criticised by Torrent, *Droit et pratique des relations économiques extérieurs dans l'Union européenne* (Brussels/Barcelona 1998), published at http://www.ub.es.depcp/ep/livreTorrent.html., Ch. VI, point 6.3. 1(a). But cf. Selmayr, "Die Wirtschafts- und Währungsunion als Rechtsgemeinschaft", *supra*, n. 2, 369; and Scheller, *Die Europäische Zentralbank* (Frankfurt am Main, 2000), 36. See also Issing, "European Integration at the Beginning of the New Millenium", http://www.ecb.int/key/00/sp000208.htm, 2: "The transfer of national currency sovereignty to the European Central Bank (sic!) represents a partial surrender of political sovereignty".

[101] In this context, it is interesting to see that the German Basic Law reflects very accurately the subtleties of the transfer of monetary sovereignty which has taken place with the establishment of the ECB and the introduction of the euro. It not only contains a general provision which enables the legislature, by way of a constitutional majority, to transfer sovereign rights *to the European Union* (Art. 23 of the Basic Law), but in addition knows a *lex specialis* in its Art. 88 which originally only dealt with the establishment of the Bundesbank. The second sentence of this provisions allows, since Maastricht, to transfer the tasks and competences of the Bundesbank directly to the ECB which has to be independent and committed to price stability as its primary objective. Art. 88, second sentence, also stresses the conceptual link between the ECB and the EU by requiring that this transfer has to take place "within the framework of the European Union". On this, cf. Janzen, *Der neue Artikel 88 Satz 2 des Grundgesetzes* (Berlin, 1996), in particular at 100.

[102] This is done by von Borries, *supra*, n. 34, 294 *et seq.*

[103] Cf., as an example, the former Director of the EIB's Legal Directorate Käser, "The European Investment Bank: its Role and Place within the European Community System" [1984] *YEL* 303; cf. also Dunnett (Head of Division at the EIB), "The European Investment Bank: Autonomous Instrument of Common Policy?" (1994) *CML Rev.* 721.

immunities as is the legal person EC (as well as the ECSC and the EAEC) itself. Furthermore, the case law of the ECJ on the EIB demonstrates how difficult it is to locate correctly an autonomous bank within the organisational system of the European Union and to determine its relationship with the Communities. It is telling that Advocate General Mancini needed almost 10 pages in one of his famous Opinions until he finally concluded, in his unparalleled words, that the EIB represents "a specific and autonomous segment of the organisational machinery of the Community".[104]

The ECJ was even more Solomonic in this respect. After having originally qualified the EIB as a "Community body established and with legal personality conferred by the Treaty",[105] it later stressed *"the ambivalent nature"* of the EIB. In this respect, the ECJ followed on the one hand the arguments put forward by the EIB which previously had underlined its special status within the Community legal order:

> It is true that under Article 129 of the Treaty [now Article 266 EC] the Bank has *legal personality distinct from that of the Community* and that it is administered and managed by organs of its own in accordance with its statute. In order to perform the tasks assigned to it by Article 130 of the Treaty [now Article 267 EC] the Bank must be able to act *in complete independence* on the financial markets, like any other bank. Indeed, the Bank is not financed out of the budget but from its own resources, which consist in particular of the capital subscribed by the Member States and funds borrowed on the financial markets. Lastly, the Bank draws up annual accounts and a profit and loss account which are audited annually by a committee appointed by the Board of Governors.[106]

On the other hand, the ECJ emphasised that there is still a certain functional link between the EIB and the Communities:

> Nevertheless, the fact that the Bank has that degree of operational and institutional autonomy does not mean that it is *totally* separated from the Communities and exempt from *every* rule of Community law. It is clear in particular from Article 120 of the Treaty [now Article 267 EC] that the Bank is intended to contribute towards the attainment of the Community's objectives and thus by virtue of the Treaty *forms part of the framework of the Community*.[107]

The ambivalent legal nature of the EIB becomes more understandable when one takes a closer look at the functions to be performed by the EIB. First of all, the Statute of the EIB has given it the character of a supranational bank with the

---

[104] Cf. Case 85/86, *supra*, n. 78, para. 13 of his Opinion.
[105] Case 110/75, *John Mills v. EIB* [1976] ECR 955, para. 14. The expression in the case's original language "*La Banque en tant qu'organisme communautaire*" first was somewhat unfortunately rendered in the English version as "the Bank as a Community *institution*". Cf. the more precise German translation: "*Gemeinschaftseinrichtung*". The ECJ later altered the English translation into "Community *body*" in Case 85/86, *supra*, n. 78, para. 24. On this translation problem, cf. Gulmann AG in Case C–370/89, *Société Générale d'Entreprises Electro-Mécaniques SA (SGEEM) and Etroy v. EIB* [1992] ECR I–6211, n. 6 of his Opinions.
[106] Case 85/86, *supra*, n. 78, para. 28, emphasis added.
[107] *Ibid.*, para. 29, emphasis added.

task of conducting lending operations. This lending is funded through the Bank's capital and, more important, through money borrowed by the EIB on the international capital market.[108] For this purpose, the Member States have established the EIB as *a legal person distinct from the Communities* which stands "on a footing of absolute equality"[109] with EC, ECSC and EAEC. The reason for this is quite obvious: as such an independent bank, the EIB appears to be free from government intervention, can be managed in accordance with the rules governing the activities of credit institutions and is thus capable both of winning the confidence of operators on the international capital market and of limiting the liability of its members only up to the amounts they have paid up for its capital.[110] These are also the main reasons why the EIB has been provided with own resources, separated from the budget of the European Communities, and why it is generally recognised that the EIB may act independently of the European Communities even at the international level, as is demonstrated, to mention a prominent example, by the membership of the EIB in the EBRD, in parallel to the EC[111] and the 15 Member States. Although the EIB, as such an independent bank, always remains a legal person established and bound by primary Community law, it is decisive that it will always act in its own name and on its own behalf during its lending operations.

However, the Treaty has not established the EIB merely to perform functions just "like any other bank". It has rather attributed to the EIB the role of *a financial instrument of the European Communities*, primarily of the EC, but also of the ECSC and the EAEC.[112] This second limb of the EIB's ambivalent nature is emphasised by Article 267 EC under which the EIB has the task of contributing, by having recourse to the capital market and utilising its own resources, "to the balanced and steady development of the common market *in the interest of the Community*". Conceptually, this creates a very strong link between the activities of the EIB and the policies defined by the Community institutions because it commits the organs of the EIB to the general objectives of the Community laid down in Article 2 EC in the same manner and to the same degree as the

---

[108] Cf. Arts. 22 and 23 of the EIB Statute.

[109] Cf. Mancini AG, *supra*, n. 78, para. 8.

[110] Cf. Minnaert, in Léger (ed.), *supra*, n. 75, Art. 266 CE, para. 9; see also Marchegiani, "La BEI et l'OLAF, un conflit de nature constitutionnelle" [2000] *RMC* 690 (691). Today, however, the EC sometimes guarantees part of the liability arising from EIB loans: cf. Council Decision 98/729/EC of 14 December 1998 amending Decision 97/256/EC so as to extend the Community guarantee granted to the European Investment Bank to cover loans for projects in Bosnia and Herzegovina [1998] OJ L346/54.

[111] Cf. Art. 3(1)(ii) of the Agreement establishing the European Bank for Reconstruction and Development [1990] OJ L372/4. The EIB joined the EBRD by the Decision of the Board of Governors of 11 June 1990 on the membership of the European Investment Bank in the European Bank for Reconstruction and Development [1990] OJ L377/3, while EC membership required a decision of the Council on a proposal from the Commission; cf. Council Decision 90/674/EEC of 19 November 1990 on the conclusion of the Agreement establishing the European Bank for Reconstruction and Development [1990] OJ L372/1.

[112] On the use of the EIB within the context of ECSC and in particular EAEC projects involving a need for credit, cf. Käser, *supra*, n. 103, 306.

Community institutions. In addition to this identity in objectives, the use of the EIB as financial instrument of the Communities is facilitated considerably by the specific institutional interconnection between the EIB and the Communities, even though there is no formal right of the Community institutions to instruct the EIB. In particular, the members of the EIB are always identical to the Member States of the European Communities by virtue of Article 266, second subparagraph, EC. As a consequence, the EIB's Board of Governors, which takes all the policy decisions for the Bank and is composed of one minister per Member State (Article 9(1) EIB Statute), is nothing but the EC's Council of Ministers acting under a different hat.[113] In addition, both the Member States and the Commission participate in the decision-making process inside the EIB: in particular, they have the right to nominate the members of the EIB's Board of Directors which has the sole power to take decisions on loans, guarantees and borrowing.[114] Against this background, it is most of the time merely a matter of form that policy decisions of the Community institutions are implemented accordingly through EIB decisions.

This role of the EIB as financial instrument of the Communities has been intensified from Treaty revision to Treaty revision. Today, the EIB is mentioned explicitly in Article 159 EC as one of the financial instruments of the Community, next to the three Structural Funds. Its financial resources may be activated by the Community institutions (by the intermediary of a decision of the EIB organs) in particular for purposes of the EC's development co-operation policy,[115] of its regional policy,[116] as regards its participation in sanctions imposed by the Council of the European Union on Member States which show a lack of discipline in fiscal policy,[117] and meanwhile also as an important instrument of employment policy in the context of the "Growth and Employment Pact".[118]

In addition, the EIB today is increasingly used by the Community institutions as an agent for the administration of Community funds, a function which today represents around 10 per cent of the EIB's activities and is now explicitly mentioned in Article 248(3), third subparagraph, EC. As such a *Community agent*, the EIB manages and operates Community funds in the name and on behalf of

---

[113] This was stressed already by Roemer AG, *supra*, n. 4, at 418. Cf. also Leanza, "Commento all'articolo 129" in *Commentario del Trattato CEE, vol. II* (Milan, 1965), 999.

[114] The Commission traditionally nominates its Director-General for Economic and Financial Affairs and its Director-General for Regional Policy for the EIB's Board of Directors; cf. Käser, *supra*, n. 103, 315.

[115] Cf. Art. 179(2) EC.

[116] Cf. Art. 159 EC and Protocol No 28 on economic and social cohesion.

[117] Cf. Art. 104(11), second indent, EC. Under this provision, the EIB will be "invited" by the Council "to reconsider its lending policy towards the Member State concerned".

[118] Cf. the Resolution of the European Council of 16 June 1997 on growth and employment [1997] OJ C236/3, para. 9, where the EIB is urged "to step up its activities" to contribute to the balanced and steady development of the common market in the interest of the Community, and where a number of concrete activities are listed for future EIB action.

the Communities and has to follow the directions of its respective principal—
the EC, the ECSC or the EAEC—the funds of which are involved.

Both the main function of the EIB as financial instrument of the Community
and its additional use as Community agent show that the EIB's "independence"—to which the ECJ refers in the decision quoted above, but which is
nowhere expressly mentioned in the EC Treaty—represents not more than *a
functional autonomy* which serves the purpose of enabling the EIB to operate
independently on the international capital markets. At the end of the day, the
EIB however has no choice but to support the regional, development or employment policies laid down by the Community institutions. Despite its separation
from the Communities by its own legal personality, the EIB therefore conducts
its lending operations always in close connection with the policies laid down by
the Community institutions which, ultimately, have the say on the political purpose of EIB operations. Since Maastricht, the scheme of the EC Treaty takes this
intimate functional and institutional relationship between the EIB and the
Communities into account, as the EIB—though not being a Community institution in the technical sense of Article 7(1) EC—is now mentioned in Part Five of
the EC Treaty entitled "Institutions of the Community".

The "quasi-institutional" nature of the EIB has an impact on the liability
regime of the EIB. In cases where the EIB acts as an autonomous bank on the
international capital markets, one might be inclined to conclude from the separate legal personality of the EIB and its autonomy as regards the technicalities
of its operations that the EIB itself, and not the Communities, would[119] be liable
for any damage incurred as a consequence of illegal activities, and would have
to remedy such damage by using its own financial resources,[120] although its
function as financial instrument of the Communities could also be used to support a different line of reasoning. The situation is clearer whenever the EIB
administers Community funds on behalf of one of the Communities in its capacity as Community agent. As the ECJ has already held, the activities performed
by the EIB in such a "principal–agent relationship"[121] are imputable to the

---

[119] The ECJ has not yet had the opportunity to deliver a judgment of principle on liability in such
a situation. If one takes the view that Art. 288(2) EC does not apply to such situations because of the
EIB's "independence", this question could only come to the ECJ by way of a preliminary reference
under Art. 234 EC because in this situation, liability questions have to be determined by the competent national courts. This would result from Art. 29, first subpara., of the EIB Statute, as—if Art.
288(2) EC does not apply—neither the EC Treaty nor the EIB Statute transfers jurisdiction in these
cases on the ECJ. On this, cf. Minnaert in Léger (ed.), *supra*, n. 75, Art. 266 CE, para. 25.

[120] This is the prevailing opinion in academic doctrine. Cf. Hilf, *supra*, n. 83, 40 *et seq*.; Hütz in
Grabitz and Hilf, *supra*, n. 33, Art. 9, para. 41. Cf. also the note of the EIB's Board of Governors of
4 December 1958 (quoted by Minnaert in Léger (ed.), *supra*, n. 75, Art. 266 CE, para. 9, according
to which the EIB "*assume l'entière responsabilité de sa gestion*".

[121] In the case in question, the EIB had financed a construction project in Mali by risk capital
from the resources of the Sixth European Development Fund. These resources were to be managed
by the EIB *on behalf of the Community*, while instruments giving effect to risk capital operations
were to be concluded by the EIB "*acting as the Community's authorized agent*", and to be managed
by the EIB "*acting for and on behalf of the Community*" and "*at the risk of the Community*". The
EEC had thus used the EIB as an agent in the context of its own development co-operation policy.

Communities, and any damage incurred therefrom has to be financed from their budget, in accordance with Article 288(2) EC:

> It would be contrary to the intentions of the authors of the Treaty if, when it acts *through* a Community body established by the Treaty and *authorized to act in its name and on its behalf*, the Community could escape the consequences of the provisions of Article 178 [now Article 235 EC] and the second paragraph of Article 215 of the Treaty [now Article 288(2) EC], the intention of which is to reserve for the Court's jurisdiction cases involving the non-contractual liability of the Community as a whole towards third parties.[122]

3.5. *Why an analogy between ECB and EIB is not appropriate*

What can we learn from the case law and practice regarding the EIB for the legal positioning of the ECB inside the European Union's central pillar? Does the ECB have a similarly ambivalent status under the EC Treaty as the EIB? Is it therefore appropriate to draw an analogy between the EIB and the ECB? Such an analogy would allow to view the ECB (at least partly) as being not in the possession and under the control of, but as a legal person distinct from, the European Communities.[123]

However, we suggest that such an analogy is not sufficient, because functionally and institutionally, the ECB is more remote from the Community institutions and their tasks than is the EIB. First of all, while it had been left to the case law of the ECJ to deduce, for the EIB, a certain degree of autonomy from its legal personality, the EC Treaty itself entrenches explicitly a far-reaching independence of the ECB in Article 108 EC. Here, the ECB is made immune not only to any national influence, as is also the case of Community institutions like the Commission; in addition, a general prohibition is established for all Community institutions and bodies to seek to influence the decision-making process of the ECB. Moreover, in contrast to the functional limitation of the EIB's autonomy to situations where it performs activities "like any other bank", the independence of the ECB encompasses, without any exception, all "the powers . . . tasks and duties" conferred on the ECB by the EC Treaty and the Statute.

This encompassing independence of the ECB reflects the different degree by which the EIB and ECB are conceptually linked to the Communities. While the objectives of the EIB are identical to those of the EC under Article 2 EC, among which figure both "a high level of employment" and "non-inflationary growth", the objectives of the ECB are laid down in Article 105(1) EC. This Article provides that the primary objective of the ESCB, through which the ECB carries out its tasks, shall be "to maintain price stability", while it shall only contribute to

---

[122] Case C–370/89, *supra*, n. 105, paras. 15 and 16, emphasis added.

[123] And therefore, it would already go one step further than what is considered to be admissible by Torrent, *supra*, n. 3, 1231.

the achievement of the general objectives of the Community, as laid down in Article 2 EC, if this is without prejudice to its primary objective. Article 105(1) EC thereby introduces a specific hierarchy of objectives for the policies to be pursued by the ECB and hence can be said to represent a *lex specialis* to Article 2 EC. This difference in objectives excludes, *a priori*, a use of the ECB as financial instrument of the Communities. The ECB is therefore not listed in the EC Treaty among the financial instruments of the Communities. On the contrary, in line with the general concept of neo-liberal economic thought, which underlies the provisions on EMU in the Maastricht Treaty,[124] Articles 101 EC and 21.1 of the Statute prohibit the ECB from giving any financial support to the European Communities as they exclude any type of credit facilities with the ECB, and thus any monetary financing, in favour of Community institutions or bodies. Moreover, by Article 108 EC, primary Community law itself prevents, as a general rule, the ECB becoming instrumentalised by the Communities.

The difference in objectives between the Communities and the ECB is also, as a matter of principle, incompatible with a "principal–agent relationship" between them: how could the principal put into practice policy objectives through its agent if this agent is, by law, required to give precedence to its own objectives whenever they conflict with those of its principal? How, in case of a conflict in objectives, could the Community institutions achieve their objectives through such an agent without infringing the prohibition of Article 108 EC not even to seek to influence the members of the decision-making bodies of the ECB and of the national central banks within the ESCB? Only in one case, and in a very limited and technical sense, could a sort of "principal–agent relationship" arise: Article 21.2 of the Statute allows the ECB to perform so-called "fiscal agent" functions for Community institutions or bodies. Under its fiscal agent function,[125] a central bank traditionally carries out various financial services as the government's central bank; it conducts banking accounts of government departments, boards and enterprises and carries out government transactions involving purchases or sales of foreign currency; it also makes temporary advances to the government in anticipation of taxes or the raising of loans from the public and extraordinary advances during a depression, war or other emergency. Under the Statute, the ECB could perform similar fiscal agent functions for Community institutions and bodies, albeit with the important exception that it may never make even temporary advances to them as this would conflict with the strict prohibition of any monetary financing in Articles 101 EC and 21.1 of the Statute.[126] For the ECB, there thus remain only technical fiscal agent functions—this may explain why the fiscal agent function of the

---

[124] Cf. Selmayr, "Die Wirtschafts- und Währungsunion als Rechtsgemeinschaft", *supra*, n. 2, 364 *et seq.* and 378 *et seq.*, where this is qualified as the end of the "Keynesian era".

[125] Cf. De Kock, *Central Banking* (Pretoria, 1954), 42 *et seq.*

[126] On the relationship between the prohibition of monetary financing and the fiscal agent-function, cf. extensively Smits, *The European Central Bank. Institutional Aspects* (The Hague/London/Boston, 1997), 75 and 288 *et seq.*

ECB is used by the Community institutions only under very exceptional circumstances.[127]

The functional separation of the ECB from the policies of the Communities through the diverging hierarchy of policy objectives is accompanied by a further distinction as regards its membership and institutional structure. In contrast to the Communities and the EIB, the "members" of the ECB are not the 15 Member States, but the national central banks[128] (Article 28.2 of the Statute), which are themselves independent of the Member States by virtue of Article 108 EC. Neither the Member States nor the Communities participate as such in the decision-making process of the ECB. The Presidency of the Council and a member of the Commission may only attend meetings of the Governing Council of the ECB, but are not allowed to vote there (Article 113(1) EC). It should also be noted that the decision-making bodies of the ECB—unlike those of the EIB—do not mirror the composition and functions of the Community institutions, but represent truly *sui generis* institutions.[129] In particular, the composition of the Governing Council of the ECB is not at all identical to that of the Council of Ministers. It rather comprises both the 12 governors of the independent national central banks of the Member States which today have the euro as their single currency, and the six members of the ECB's Executive Board (Article 10.1 of the Statute). Furthermore, the ECB's Executive Board is much more a supranational decision-making body than is the Commission of the European Communities. Member States are not only prohibited from instructing its members,[130] but

---

[127] Only temporarily, the ECB acted as "fiscal agent" as regards the administration of the Community facility providing medium-term financial assistance for Member States' balance of payments; cf. Council Regulation 1969/88 of 24 June 1988 establishing a single facility providing medium-term financial assistance for Member States' balances of payments [1988] OJ L178/1. Under this facility, there were, at the beginning of the third stage of EMU, still, two outstanding Community loans granted to Italy in 1993, originally administered by the EMCF, the administration of which passed to the EMI under Art. 6.1 of its Statute, and then to the ECB under Art. 47.1, first indent, of its Statute; cf. Decision 8/95 of the European Monetary Institute of 2 May 1995 concerning the administration of the borrowing and lending operations concluded by the European Community under the medium-term financial assistance mechanism [2001] OJ L55/77 (published *a posteriori*); and Decision ECB/1998/15 of 1 December 1998 concerning the performance by the European Central Bank of certain functions relating to medium-term financial assistance for Member States' balance of payments [2001] OJ L55/76 (published *a posteriori*). These loans expired at the end of 2000 and cannot be prolonged, as with the beginning of the third stage of EMU, the Treaty provisions allowing for balance of payment assistance have ceased to apply as regards Member States participating in the single currency; cf. Art. 119(4) EC. It seems that the Community legislator now wants to further restrict the scope of the ECB's fiscal agent-function by transferring the administration of loans under the medium-term financial assistance facility (which may become relevent again once current applicant countries have become members of the EU) from the ECB to the Commission; cf. Commission proposal of 7 March 2001 for a Council Regulation establishing a facility providing medium-term financial assistance for member states' balance of payments, COM (2001) 113 final; and ECB Opinion CON/2001/8 of 3 May 2001 [2001] OJ C151/18.

[128] This is not taken into account by von Borries, *supra*, n. 34, 294, who considers the Member States as members both of the EIB and of the ECB.

[129] On the role and composition of the ECB's decision-making bodies, cf. *infra*, Ch. 3, p. 83 et seq.

[130] The independence of the members of the Executive Board is reinforced by the fact that their term of office is not renewable, cf. Art. 11.2 of the Statute.

among the Executive Board members there is not even one national per Member State, as is the case with the Commission.[131] The legal criterion to become an Executive Board members is therefore not nationality, but "recognized standing and professional experience in monetary or banking matters" (Article 11.2 of the Statute). All this makes it impossible for the Community institutions or the Member States to implement their policy decisions through the ECB. In this context, it is interesting to note that in contrast to the EIB, the ECB is not even mentioned in the Fifth Part of the EC Treaty, entitled "Community institutions".

There is a final important difference which confirms that an analogy between the EIB and the ECB is not satisfactory. Unlike the EIB, which mostly carries out its tasks through contractual instruments, the ECB has a regulatory power of its own.[132] Under Article 110 EC and Article 34 of the Statute, the ECB, through its decision-making bodies, may adopt regulations, decisions, recommendations and opinions whenever this proves necessary for the fulfilment of its tasks.[133] The ECB is hence not meant to act on the financial markets "like any other bank", as is the EIB,[134] but has been given the power to control and steer unilaterally the amount of money in circulation and to confer rights or to impose obligations directly on economic agents in its field of competence. In view of this regulatory power of the ECB, the Court of First Instance has already refused to draw an analogy between the ECB and the EIB in its *Etienne Tête* case:

> In that context, it should further be considered that the future European Central Bank will be considerably different from the EIB. Article 108a of the EC Treaty [now Article 110 EC] provides for it to adopt regulations and decisions (which will be binding on the addressees), hence the necessity to allow for the possibility of natural or legal persons' bringing actions for annulment. In view of the different powers of the two banks, the analogy suggested by the applicants does not therefore appear to be justified.[135]

The existence of these considerable differences between the ECB and the EIB prevents, as a matter of legal reasoning, the definition of the legal nature of the ECB by analogy to that of the EIB. For the ECB, the main characteristic of the EIB—i.e. to act as financial instrument of the Community—is excluded by

---

[131] Cf. Art. 213(1) subpara. 4 EC, under which the Commission must include at least one national of each of the Member States. If the Nice Treaty enters into force, the Commission will enjoy a similar supranational status as the Executive Board of the ECB only from the moment "when the Union consists of 27 Member States". Only then, a new Art. 213(1) EC and a new Art. 126(1) Euratom will be inserted, the second subpara. of which will provide: "The number of Members of the Commission shall be less than the number of Member States"; cf. Art. 4(2) of the new Protocol on the enlargement of the European Union.

[132] On the ECB's regulatory power, cf. *infra*, Ch. 3, p. 91 *et seq.*

[133] On the application of the principle of conferred powers to the ECB's regulatory power through the *lex specialis* of Art. 8 EC, cf. *infra*, Ch. 3, p. 71.

[134] Cf. Case 85/86, *supra*, n. 78, para. 28.

[135] Case T–460/93, *Tête and others* v. *EIB* [1993] ECR II–1257, para. 19. The fundamental difference between the EIB and the ECB was already felt by Gulmann AG in his Opinion in Case C–370/89, *supra*, n. 105, para. 15 (thereby mentioning the ECB for the first time in the European Court Reports). He pointed to the fact that the ECB "has been given duties and powers by the new Treaty" and emphasised their "public-law nature", while the duties of the EIB would "only to a limited extent, if at all, involve the exercise of public authority in a restricted sense".

primary Community law under which the ECB enjoys not only a limited functional autonomy, but an encompassing independence as regards all its tasks, powers and duties. Even more than the EIB, the ECB is therefore a legal person distinct from the European Communities.

3.6. *Not a separate pillar of the Union, but an independent specialised organisation of Community law*

How can one reconcile the far-reaching functional, financial and institutional independence of the ECB with the fact that the ECB has been established as a supranational central bank by the EC Treaty and the Statute and therefore, from its very origin, is conceptually linked to the Communities?

It is telling that some of the authors which favour a unitary institutional view of the European Union nevertheless qualify the ECB, in view of its special status, as "an independent sub-organisation of the Union",[136] or even say that the whole EMU chapter "although inserted in the EC Treaty, is really a pillar itself, solitary and untouched by the recent intergovernmental conferences".[137] However, after the "fourth pillar" proposal was dropped so clearly during the negotiations leading to the Maastricht Treaty, the ECB has certainly *not* been a separate pillar within the Union, "detached" from the supranational structure of Community law, on the contrary: it rather represents, as shown above, the most supranational entity so far established by the means of Community law.

We therefore suggest viewing the ECB as *an independent specialised organisation of Community law*,[138] to demonstrate that it is at the same time a supranational organisation within the Union's first and central pillar, and independent from, albeit associated with, the existing three Communities. The special legal nature of the ECB may be summarised in the following three points.

First, the ECB is a supranational organisation which resembles in many respects the legal person EC, and even more the ECSC and the EAEC. Like the original three Communities themselves, the ECB has been given by the EC Treaty itself an exclusive task for a specific field of policy (monetary policy), and to this end a legal personality of its own, with own decision-making bodies, with an autonomous regulatory power, with its own financial resources, and with privileges and immunities. While the ECSC and the EAEC are, from their origin, specialised organisations for coal and steel and atomic energy policy, the ECB has been established by primary Community law as the specialised organisation for monetary policy. In this sense, one can even qualify the ECB, from a

---

[136] Von Bogdandy, *supra*, n. 6, 904: "because it is independent as regards its personnel, its finances and its legal personality".

[137] De Witte, *supra*, n. 14, 53.

[138] Cf. Selmayr, "Die Wirtschafts- und Währungsunion als Rechtsgemeinschaft", *supra*, n. 2, 372; this view is shared by Scheller in Glomb and Lauk (eds.), *Euro-Guide: Handbuch der Europäischen Wirtschafts- und Währungsunion* (Cologne, 1998), 2.

functional perspective, as a "new Community" within the European Union's central pillar which stands on an equal footing with the original three Communities.

Secondly, the ECB is a supranational organisation which is not dependent on the original Communities, as it has received its tasks, powers and duties directly from the EC Treaty and the Statute, not, by means of a delegation, from the Community institutions. In the performance of its tasks, the ECB is also not institutionally linked to the Communities, their institutions and bodies in a sense that its activities could be attributed to them; on the contrary, it never acts as financial instrument of the Community institutions or even for and on behalf of them (with the exception of technical fiscal agent functions), as this would be incompatible both with its independence and with its primary objective of price stability. Against this background, it would be inaccurate to consider the ECB as a "Community within the Community", since this could be interpreted as indicating its subordination to the legal person EC or to the Community institutions. Though having been established by the EC Treaty, the ECB is much more distinct from the EC than are the EC, ECSC and EAEC and also EIB from one another, as those all have identical members and a parallel or even merged institutional structure from which the ECB, its capital owners and its decision-making bodies can be clearly distinguished.[139] The relationship between the Communities and the ECB is therefore not one of subordination or of possession, but one of *association*.[140] The link of association is demonstrated by the fact that the provisions on the ECB and on monetary policy were inserted in Part Three of the EC Treaty under the title "*Community* policies", and that according to Article 105(2), first indent EC, the ECB shall, through the ESCB, define and implement the monetary policy *of*—although not for and on behalf of—*the Community*. All these provisions are evidence of the conceptual link between the activities of the ECB and the organisational system of Community law; however, they cannot be interpreted to subordinate the ECB to the original three Communities or even to their institutions, as none of them has the legal means at hands to transform the monetary policy laid down by the ECB into *their* policy, i.e. into a policy determined or directed by them; for that purpose, there exists neither a sufficient institutional nor a financial link between the

---

[139] In this direction cf. also Blokker and Heukels, *supra*, n. 28, 28 (n. 90), who consider that the provisions granting legal personality to the EIB and the ECB lead to a "*status aparte*" for both organisations; cf. also at 32, where it is mentioned that the European Union, without having legal personality, would be obliged to act "through the Communities and/or the Member States, or through legal persons such as the EIB and the ECB". Along the same lines, cf. Demaret, *Le Traité de Maastricht ou les voies diverses de l'Union* in Monar, Ungerer and Wessels (eds.), *supra*, n. 14, 37, at 39 *et seq.*: "*Du point de vue institutionnel, la matière monétaire occupe une place quelque peu à part dans le Traité instituant la Communauté européenne. Cela s'explique par sa spécificité ainsi que par le désir de rendre l'autorité monétaire pleinement indépendente.*"

[140] Already the EIB was said to be "associated" to the European Communities by the ECJ in Joined Cases 27/59 and 39/59, *supra*, n. 70, at 404. We suggest, however, that recent Treaty revisions have considerably intensified this link between the Communities and the EIB, which today represents their main financial instrument.

Communities and the ECB.[141] In this respect, the relationship between the Communities and the ECB resembles, at least to a certain extent, the relationship of the United Nations with the World Bank or the International Monetary Fund, which define themselves both as "specialised agencies *referred to in the UN Charter*", in contrast to "specialised agencies (or agents) *of* the United Nations".[142]

Thirdly, an understanding of the ECB as an independent specialised organisation *of Community law* rather than a separate pillar or even a "third party in relation to the Communities"[143] emphasises that despite its independence, the ECB undoubtedly forms part of the Community legal order by which it has been established; that it is an organisation within the European Union's first and central pillar; and that it is therefore fully subject to the principles of primary Community law and to the jurisdiction of the ECJ. This is demonstrated by the number of provisions in the EC Treaty and in the Statute, which confer

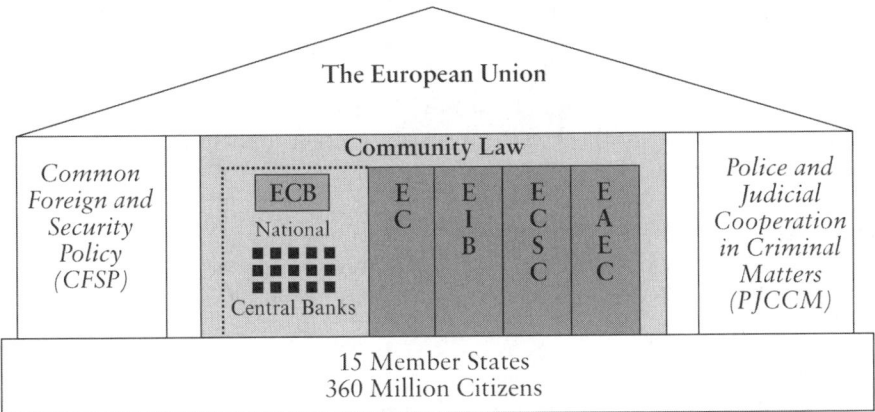

Fig. 1 *The European Central Bank as independent specialised organisation of Community law*

[141] Cf. Partsch, *supra*, n. 75, Arts.108, 109 EC, para. 4: "*la BCE n'est pas soumise à la tutelle d'aucune des institutions communautaires*". We would, however, mention the legal supervision by the ECJ as an exception to this far-reaching statement.

[142] On this, cf. Bleicher, "UN v IBRD: A Dilemma of Functionalism" [1970] *International Organization* 31; and Holder, "The Relationship Between the International Monetary Fund and the United Nations" in Effros (ed.), *Current Legal Issues Affecting Central Banks*, (Washington, 1997), iv 16 (18). See also the Committee on Negotiations with Specialised Agencies, *Report on Negotiations with the International Bank for Reconstruction and Development and the International Monetary Fund*, UN Economic and Social Council Doc. E/564 (16 August 1947), 3, where it is stressed that "the statement that the Bank (Fund) is a Specialized Agency . . . established by agreement among its member governments carries with it no implication that the relationship between the United Nations and the Bank (Fund) is one of principal and agent". The parallel between the situation of the World Bank and of the ECB is also seen by von Bodgandy, *supra*, n. 6, 904.

[143] Such a status was originally claimed by the EIB in Case 85/86, reported by Mancini AG, *supra*, n. 78, para. 5 of his Opinion.

jurisdiction upon the ECJ in ECB-related matters (cf. Articles 230, 232, 233, 234, 235 in conjunction with Articles 288(2), 237(d), 241 EC, and Articles 14.1, 35 and 36.2 of the Statute). The Court of Justice *of the European Communities* is therefore the only institution established under the Treaties which is competent throughout the entire supranational pillar of the Union; it exercises its jurisdiction over EC, ECSC, EAEC, EIB and likewise the ECB.[144] To view the ECB as an independent specialised organisation of Community law therefore expresses its subordination not to the political process within the European Union, but to the rule of Community law.

3.7. *A new degree of central bank independence*

Critics of the independent, though associated status of the ECB will perhaps argue that the idea of central bank independence never before has been stretched so far as to establish a central bank not inside, but only in association and on an equal footing with the entity the monetary policy of which it defines and implements. They may want to point to the example of the most independent central banks known so far—for example, to the German Bundesbank—which have always remained integrated into the constitutional structure of the state which originally had established them, although some of them were acting quite independently of their state at the international level.[145]

However, in our view these historic precedents are not authoritative for determining the legal position of the ECB within the *sui generis* organisational framework of the European Union's central pillar. When studying the legal features of central bank independence in Community law, as laid down in particular in

---

[144] This view is, again, shared by Timmermans, *supra*, n. 79, 628 *et seq.*: "The legal order of the ESCB ensures the respect of the rule of law by providing for an adequate system of legal protection through the European Court of Justice". Cf. also Louis, *supra*, n. 51, 591, where he emphasises *"l'insertion de la Banque centrale européenne dans l'ordre juridique communautaire et, en particulier, sa soumission au juge communautaire"*. Cf. also Selmayr, "Die Grenzen der Geldpolitik der Europäischen Zentralbank—eine Fallstudie" in Rohde and Köhler, *Geldpolitik ohne Grenzen* (Berlin, 2001—in press).

[145] Cf. the German IMF Act, [1978] *Bundesgesetzblatt II* 13, which reserves important rights to be exercised under the IMF Agreement for the Bundesbank. In the context of the IMF, one should also note the General Arrangements to Borrow (GAB), established in 1962, the original participants of which were 8 major industrial countries (USA, UK, France, Japan, Italy, Canada, Netherlands, Belgium), but also two independent central banks: the Deutsche Bundesbank and Sveriges Riksbank; cf. IMF, *Selected Decisions and Selected Documents of the International Monetary Fund* (24th edn., Washington, 1999), 423. In the view of Gold, "On the Difficulties of Defining International Agreements. Some Illustrations from the Experience of the International Monetary Fund" in Simha (ed.), *Economic and Social Developments. Essays in Honour of Dr. C. D. Deshmukh* (Bombay, 1972), 25 (30 *et seq.*), the participation of these central banks in the GAB represents participation "in their own right, and not as the fiscal agencies of Germany and Sweden". On the international legal personality of central banks cf. extensively Kramer, *Die Rechtsnatur der Geschäfte des Internationalen Währungsfonds* (Berlin, 1967), 35 *et seq.* Against this background, our proposition in (1999) *CML Rev.* 273 that national central banks may also exceptionally enjoy a (limited) international legal personality can hardly be qualified as "an extraordinary thesis" which would constitute "a kind of '*demonstratio ad absurdum*' ", as does Torrent, *supra*, n. 3, 1223.

Article 108 EC, one discovers that this new form of supranational central bank independence goes much further than that of any of the ECB's historic ancestors. First of all, while even the German Bundesbank's independence was just laid down in an ordinary statute which could at any time be amended by a simple majority of the Bundestag (the main legislative chamber of the German Parliament),[146] the ECB's independence is entrenched in the EC Treaty itself and thus in a document of constitutional quality which may only be amended by a unanimous decision of all Member States and the completion of—for the moment—15 national ratification procedures (cf. Article 48 EU).[147] Article 108 EC itself extends, at the supranational level, the idea of central bank independence to an independence from all Community institutions and bodies, thus including the Council and the European Parliament as the Community legislature. Furthermore, it should be noted that the central bank independence foreseen in Article 108 EC does not provide for any exceptions or restraints; the decision-making process inside the ECB is not even subject to a politician's suspensory right of veto, as was the case with the decisions of the Bundesbank's Central Bank Council which the German government could always delay for two weeks[148]—a possibility which had to be abrogated on the occasion of the Bundesbank's integration into the ESCB as it did not meet the stringent independence requirements of Articles 108 EC. This in itself shows that central bank independence is a more far-reaching principle now in Community law than it was before in national legal systems.

The new and higher degree of central bank independence is also demonstrated by Articles 237(d) EC and 35.6 of the Statute. Under these provisions, the ECB can directly sue a national central bank which has failed to fulfil its obligations under Community law. At first glance, this seems to contradict a well-known feature of Community law, which is that Member States are always liable for breaches of Community law whatever be the organ of the state whose act or omission was responsible for the breach, be it part of the legislature, the

---

[146] This is the view prevailing in German case law and academic writings; cf., as a representative example, Stern, *Das Staatsrecht der Bundesrepublik Deutschland* (Munich, 1988), ii, § 35 V 2. Art. 88, first sentence of the German Basic Law mentions only the existence of a "federal bank for currency and banknotes", but does not incorporate central bank independence as a legal principle; cf. BVerwGE 41, 334. A different position is taken by Seidel, *supra*, n. 44, 236, who takes the view that central bank independence as regards the legislature would result, in Germany, from the doctrine of separation of powers, as the central bank would form part of the executive. But see also the decision of the Federal Administrative Court (the *Bundesverwaltungsgericht*), BVerwGE 41, 334 where it is questioned whether the independent position of the Bundesbank is compatible with the doctrine of separation of powers and the democratic principle enshrined in Art. 20(1) of the German Basic Law.

[147] Cf. Timmermans, *supra*, n. 79, 630, who emphasises that the political institutions of the Community "cannot interfere or correct the monetary policy decisions made by the ECB. Art. 8 of the ESCB Statute states as a general principle: 'The ESCB shall be governed by the decision-making bodies of the ECB". The message is clear: and by no one else. The only authority to stop the system is the collectivity of Member States as '*Herren der Verträge*' (Art. N TEU [now Art. 48 EU])".

[148] Under the former para. 13, second para., third sentence of the Bundesbank Act.

executive or the judicature,[149] and including constitutionally independent officials[150] and autonomous regional entities[151]. A Member State thus can be sued by the Commission under Article 226 EC whenever a national entity—even if it enjoys independence under the respective Member State's constitution— infringes Community law; the Member State also bears liability for any damage incurred by individuals as a result of breaches of Community law by its author- ities, including independent agencies. This general premise of Community law, however, has been modified with the introduction of Article 108 EC. Member States today are prohibited from influencing any longer the acts or omissions of a national central bank which is fully integrated into the ESCB and therein sub- ject to the guidelines and instructions of the ECB. The original constitutional link between a Member State and "its" national central banks thus has been cut and replaced by a new supranational link to the ECB. This makes it impossible today for a Member States to be responsible for the compliance with Com- munity law by "their" national central bank when they fulfil functions within the ESCB.[152] It therefore appears to be appropriate that primary Community law no longer considers the acts and omissions of national central banks within the ESCB to be attributable to the respective Member State, but has introduced by Articles 237(d) EC and 35.6 of the Statute a direct line of responsibility between the ECB and the national central banks which enables the ECB itself to supervise the fulfilment of the obligations of national central banks imposed by Community law.[153]

Under Article 108 EC, the independent position of the national central banks as regards their Member State mirrors that of the ECB in its relationship to the EC, the monetary policy of which the ECB defines and implements through the ESCB without being subject to the control of the political Community institu- tions. The independent position of the ECB is even further accentuated by the fact that in parallel to monetary union, the Member States on purpose did not establish a central authority responsible for economic policy—as once sug- gested by the *Werner* Report—or even a new European "super-State". It is therefore possible to say that EMU has led, in parallel to its denationalisation, to a complete *depoliticisation* of monetary policy. Monetary policy has not been transferred by the Member States from their own control into the dependency

---

[149] Cf. Joined Cases C–46/93 and C–48/93, *Brasserie du Pêcheur SA* v. *Germany and The Queen* v. *Secretary of State for Transport, ex parte: Factortame Ltd and others* [1996] ECR I–1029, para. 32 *et seq.*

[150] Cf. Case 222/84, *Johnston* v. *Chief Constable of the Royal Ulster Constabulary* [1986] ECR 1651, para. 56.

[151] Cf. Case C–71/97, *Commission* v. *Spain* [1998] ECR I–5991, para. 17.

[152] When a national central bank fulfils functions outside the ESCB, Art. 14.4 of the Statute applies.

[153] See also Art. 14.2, second subpara., second sentence of the Statute which gives the governor of a national central bank standing in the ECJ to challenge decisions of Member States which relieve him or her from office for reasons other than those mentioned in the first sentence of the second sub- para. This is the first time that Community law allows a "national" official to challenge a national decision directly in the ECJ.

of Community policies, but has been entrusted to the ECB as a new supranational entity which is as independent in its relations to the Member States as it is as regards the European Communities.[154]

IV. PRACTICAL CONSEQUENCES OF THE NEW CONSTITUTIONAL BALANCE INSIDE THE EUROPEAN UNION

To view the ECB as an independent specialised organisation of Community law, which may even be compared to a "new Community", is a model that should help to understand better the attribution of functions and competences within the differentiated organisational framework of the European Union's first and central pillar. In this sense, it has been correctly emphasised[155] that the debate around the legal nature of the ECB is far from representing just an academic question, but has considerable practical implications.

1. Price stability as *"Grundnorm"* of the "new Community"

A first consequence has already been addressed in legal doctrine[156]: the question of the objectives which the ECB is legally obliged to pursue with its policy, in particular with the monetary policy it defines and implements. Article 2 EC talks only about the tasks of *the Community* and therefore is able directly to commit only the Community by diverse objectives such as "a high level of employment", "equality between men and women", "sustainable and non-inflationary growth" and "a high level of protection and improvement of the quality of the environment". As the ECB is an organisation independent of the Communities and their institutions, this provision cannot create a *direct* obligation for the ECB to promote all these objectives. Instead of the large number of objectives listed in Article 2 EC—and among which to choose is normally up to the discretion of the Community institutions—the ECB is committed, by its *lex specialis* Article 105(1), first sentence EC to price stability as its primary objective.

This does not mean, however, that Article 2 EC would have no significance at all for the ECB's policies. Here is where the "unity of ideals" between the ECB and the original Communities comes into play. Article 105(1), second

---

[154] This is also emphasised by the German Federal Constitutional Court in Cases 2 BvR 2134/92 & 2158/92, *Brunner et al.* v. *The European Union Treaty*, Judgment of 12 October 1993, *CML Rev.* (1994), 251 (261): "Placing most of the tasks of monetary policy on an autonomous basis in the hands of an independent central bank releases the exercise of sovereign powers of the state from direct national or supra-national control in order to withdraw monetary matters from the reach of interest groups and holders of political office concerned about re-election."

[155] By Torrent, *supra*, n. 3, 1240 *et seq.*

[156] Cf. on the one hand Torrent, *supra*, n. 3, 1229 *et seq.*; and, on the other hand, Selmayr, "Wie unabhängig ist die Europäische Zentralbank?", *supra*, n. 2, 2431 *et seq.*, 2438 *et seq.*

sentence, EC requires the ECB to contribute to the achievement of the objectives of the Community as laid down in Article 2 EC, if and as long as this is without prejudice to the ECB's primary objective of price stability. By this, the ECB is *indirectly* bound by the objectives listed in Article 2, including the objective of a high level of employment.[157] The Article 2 objectives, however, can be qualified only as the ECB's *secondary* objectives as, in case of conflict with its *primary* objective, the ECB is legally obliged to give precedence to price stability.[158]

Therefore, it seems appropriate to call price stability the *"Grundnorm"*[159] of the "new Community".[160] The way in which primary Community law emphasises this primary objective also shows that the independent nature of the ECB is not an end in itself, but has been created by the authors of the Treaties in order to secure freedom from inflation within the European Union. In this respect, the ECB's far-reaching independence is the result of the historic experience that the value of money can be kept stable only when those responsible for it are not directly influenced by the ups and downs of daily policy, by changing majorities in Parliament or by new, perhaps only short-term, policy lines adopted by a government.[161] In this sense, there is not necessarily a contradiction between the objective of price stability and employment policy, as in the long run, only a stable currency guarantees sustainable economic growth, and thus employment.

[157] Cf. Solans, "Should the ECB have Broader Objectives beyond Price Stability", speech of 24 May 1999, published at http://www.ecb.int.

[158] This primacy of price stability has not been affected by the amendment of Art. 2, first indent EU by the Amsterdam Treaty, which now lists at a prominent place among the Union's objectives "a high level of employment", but does not even mention the objective of price stability. As stated in Art. 47 EU, the provisions of the EU Treaty, other than those expressly amending the EC, the ECSC and the EAEC Treaty, shall not affect the existing *acquis communautaire*, on this, cf. Case C–170/96, *supra*, n. 15. This issue is, again, a clear demonstration of why it is important to qualify the ECB not generously as "the Union's central bank", but accurately as an organisation *of Community law*, as this means that for the ECB, the hierarchy of objectives as established by the EC Treaty always take precedence over a possibly divergent hierarchy now foreseen by the EU Treaty.

[159] In this see sense Herdegen, "Price Stability and Budgetary Restraints in the Economic and Monetary Union: The Law as Guardian of Economic Wisdom" (1998) *CML Rev.* 9 (21).

[160] Monetary policy therefore follows a different approach in Europe from in the USA where the Federal Reserve System has, under the Federal Reserve Act, a "dual mandate", i.e. to promote "maximum employment" and "stable prices". On the obligation of the Fed to strike a delicate balance between the two goals, cf. Blinder, "Central Banking in a Democracy" in Federal Reserve Bank of Richmond, *Economic Quarterly* (1996), 1 (5 *et seq.*).

[161] Cf. the dictum by the German Federal Constitutional Court in its *Maastricht* judgment, *supra*, n. 154, 262 *et seq.* In its view, the ECB's independence "takes account of the special characteristic (tested and proven—in scientific terms as well—in the German legal system) that an independent central bank is a better guarantee of the value of the currency, and thus of a generally sound economic basis for the state's budgetary policies and for private planning and transactions in the exercise of rights of economic freedom, than state bodies, which as regards their opportunities and means for action are essentially dependent on the supply and value of the currency, and rely on the short-term consent of political forces".

2. ECB law and its relationship with secondary law adopted by Community institutions

A second, important illustration of the new constitutional balance inside the EU is that, since the establishment of the ECB, there has existed a new type of secondary Community law: that is the secondary Community law produced by the decision-making bodies of the ECB. From the location of the ECB inside the first pillar and in parallel to EC, ECSC and EAEC, it follows that this secondary law—which one may call "ECB law", to be very precise[162]—is as much Community law as the law produced by the Council, the European Parliament and the Commission under the EC, the ECSC or the Euratom Treaty.

ECB Regulations, ECB Decisions, ECB Recommendations and ECB Opinions adopted under Articles 110 EC and 34 of the Statute mirror exactly the corresponding legal acts listed in Article 249 EC as regards their application, their effects and their supremacy within the legal orders of the Member States.[163] Thus, like regulations of the Community institutions under Article 249(2) EC, an ECB Regulation "shall have general application", "shall be binding in its entirety and directly applicable in all Member States" (Article 34.2, first subparagraph of the Statute).[164] According to Article 34.2, fourth subparagraph of the Statute in conjunction with Article 254 EC, ECB Regulations and ECB Decisions are also published in the Official Journal. And like other Community legal acts, ECB law is of course open to review or interpretation by the ECJ (Article 35.1 of the Statute).

Given the fact that there are no differences as regards the normative effect of ECB law and secondary Community law adopted by the Community institutions, the question arises in what relationship the regulatory powers of the ECB and of the Community institutions stand to one another. It has once been stated that "the ECB is the regulator *within* the system (Article 108A EC), and the Council the regulator *of* the system".[165] In our view, this statement is only partly in line with the attribution of regulatory competences to the ECB by the EC Treaty and the Statute.

Of course, the ECB is *the regulator of the ESCB*; it is the ECB which governs the ESCB (Article 107(2) EC), and it is within the exclusive responsibility of the

---

[162] The ECB makes the origin of its secondary law transparent by adding always an ECB number (instead of an EC, ECSC or Euratom number) to the title of a legal act adopted by its decision-making bodies. Thus, for instance, the first ECB Regulation ever published by the ECB in the OJ—the Regulation of the European Central Bank of 1 December 1998 on the application of minimum reserves—bears the number "ECB/1998/15"; cf. [1998] OJ L356/1.

[163] On the different forms and effects of ECB law, and on the special case of "ECB Directives", cf. Ch. 3 of this book, *infra*, p. 91 *et seq.* Cf. also Partsch, *supra*, n. 75, Art. 110 CE, para. 3: "*les actes de la BCE sont soumis au même régime que ceux que peuvent adopter les institutions communautaires*".

[164] However, this provision is subject to Art. 43.1 of the Statute and to the Danish and the UK Protocol as regards Sweden, Denmark and the United Kingdom; cf. *infra*, Ch. 4, p. 164 *et seq.*

[165] By Timmermans, *supra*, n. 79, 626.

ECB to adopt decisions, guidelines and instructions to ensure that the national central banks within the ESCB implement monetary policy in a uniform and efficient manner throughout the Member States which participate in the single currency. In addition, the ECB is entitled, like every organisation, to adopt rules governing its internal organisation and that of its decision-making bodies. This follows from the ECB's organisational autonomy which is explicitly recognised in Articles 12.3 and 36.1 of the Statute. To mention an example, the ECB has the normative power to adopt its own language regime[166] for the communication within and between the ECB's decision-making bodies as well as for the legal instruments adopted by the decision-making bodies of the ECB. The Council's "Language Regulation", No 1[167] does not apply to the ECB, as the Council may, under Article 290 EC, merely determine the language regime of "the *institutions* of the Community", to which the ECB does not belong.[168] Of course, the ECB's language regime has to be in line with the general principles of primary Community law and is thus required, as a general rule, to treat all Community languages equally within the exercise of its regulatory power. Therefore, the ECB has decided, in its Rules of Procedure,[169] that the principles of the Council's "Language Regulation"—which are considered as an expression of general principles of primary Community law—shall apply to the legal acts of the ECB foreseen in Article 34 of the Statute.[170] However, it has also established that ECB Guidelines and ECB Instructions which do not need to be published in the Official Journal, shall be adopted in *one* of the official languages of the European Communities,[171] to take into account the specific requirements of speedy action as regards the implementation of monetary policy. Another example is the adoption of Conditions of Employment for staff of the ECB[172]: members of staff are not subject to the Staff Regulations applicable to Community officials and agents,[173] but to this separate set of rules. These

[166] On the language regime of the ECB, cf. Schweitzer in Grabitz and Hilf, *supra*, n. 33, Art. 290, para. 14.

[167] Regulation No 1 of 15 April 1958 determining the languages to be used by the European Economic Community [1958] OJ 17/385, as amended.

[168] Cf. also Art. 21, third subpara. EC, which entitles the citizens of the Union to write in one of the 12 authentic languages of the Community to the Community institutions and bodies referred to in Arts. 7 and 21 EC, and thus not to the ECB, which is listed in Art. 8 EC.

[169] Rules of Procedure of the European Central Bank of 7 July 1998 [1998] OJ L338/28, substituted by Rules of Procedure of the European Central Bank as amended on 22 April 1999 [1999] OJ L125/34, as amended by Decision ECB/1999/6 of 7 October 1999 amending the Rules of Procedure of the European Central Bank [1999] OJ L314/32.

[170] Art. 17.9 of the Rules of Procedure of the ECB, *supra*, n. 169.

[171] Art. 17.2 and 17.6 of the Rules of Procedure of the ECB, *supra*, n. 169.

[172] Decision ECB/1998/4 of 9 June 1998 on the adoption of the Conditions of Employment for Staff of the European Central Bank as amended on 31 March 1999 [1999] OJ L125/32, amended by Decision ECB/2001/6 of 5 July 2001 [2001] OJ L201/25.

[173] Council Regulation (EEC, Euratom, ECSC) No 259/68 of 29 February 1968 laying down the Staff Regulations of Officials and the Conditions of Employment of Other Servants of the European Communities and instituting special measures temporarily applicable to officials of the Commission [1968] OJ L56/1, amended in the last instance by Council Regulation (EC, ECSC, Euratom) No 2594/98 of 28 November 1998[1998] OJ L325/1.

examples show that the regulator of the ESCB is, first of all, the ECB, and not the Council of the European Union.[174]

But the regulatory power of the ECB is not limited to laying down internal rules for its decision-making bodies and for the ESCB as a whole. In addition, the ECB may, through ECB Regulations adopted by its decision-making bodies, directly confer rights and impose obligations on undertakings or other economic agents, or even address ECB Decisions to them. As a matter of substance, the ECB is therefore a regulator whenever regulation is required within its field of competence, in particular within the field of monetary policy, but also in related fields such as statistics (Article 5.1 in conjunction with Article 34.1, first indent of the Statute[175]) or payment systems (Article 22 of the Statute). In addition to being *the regulator of the ESCB*, the ECB is also *the Community regulator in the field of monetary policy*, thus reflecting the exclusivity of the competences transferred to the ECB by the Member States through the EC Treaty and the Statute.

It is only by way of exception to this concept that primary Community law originally allowed (and required) the Community institutions to adopt secondary legislation in the field of competence of the ECB.[176] Article 42 of the Statute imposes a duty on the Council of the European Union to adopt so-called[177] "*complementary* legislation" as regards the ECB in eight cases listed exhaustively in these provisions. To mention an example, the Council had to define the limits and conditions under which the ECB may impose fines or periodic penalty payments on undertakings for failure to comply with

---

[174] This situation can be changed only in accordance with the procedures foreseen for an amendment of the primary Community law on EMU: Art. 48(2) EU, which requires a consultation of the European Parliament, the ECB and the Commission, common accord of all 15 Member States and the completion of 15 national ratification procedures for "institutional changes in the monetary area"; or the simplified amendment procedure under Art. 107(5) EC and Art. 41 of the Statute, under which, in addition to the involvement of the European Parliament and the Commission, unanimity is required either in the Council of the European Union or in the Governing Council of the ECB; or the simplified amendment procedure of Art. 105(6) EC under which specific tasks in the field of prudential supervision may be conferred upon the ECB by a unanimous Council decision on a proposal from the Commission, but only after consulting the ECB and after receiving the assent of the European Parliament. In all these cases, a change of the scope of the tasks of the ECB would result not from secondary Community law, but from (amended) primary Community law.

[175] Under Art. 34.1, first indent of the Statute, the ECB may make regulations to the extent necessary to implement, *inter alia*, the tasks defined in Art. 3.1, first indent of the Statute, i.e. to define and implement monetary policy. Good statistics are an essential precondition for an efficient monetary policy. Therefore, Art. 5.1 of the Statute enables the ECB to collect the necessary statistical information either from the competent national authorities or directly from economic agents "in order to undertake the tasks of the ESCB".

[176] In this respect, the case of the ECB clearly differs from that of the EIB. In view of the fact that the EIB enjoys only a functional autonomy, and of the absence of any regulatory power for the EIB, the EIB is subject to secondary law enacted by the Community institutions whenever the application of such secondary law to the EIB does not "undermine the operational autonomy and reputation of the Bank as an independent institution on the financial markets"; cf. Case 85/86, *supra*, n. 78, and Gulmann AG, *supra*, n. 105, para. 11.

[177] Cf. the title of Art. 42 of the Statute. Cf. Smits, *supra*, n. 126, 167, for whom it is clear that the independence attributed by the Treaty to the ESCB is "circumscribed only—in few instances—by the necessity of working on the basis of additional legislation to be adopted by the political institutions".

obligations under ECB Regulations and Decisions (Article 34.3 of the Statute),[178] while it was for the ECB itself to lay down its sanctioning regime and to exercise its sanctioning power conferred upon it directly by Article 34.3 of the Statute.[179] Article 42 of the Statute foresees a similar division of labour between the regulatory power of the ECB and of the Council of the European Union as regards the obligation for national authorities to consult the ECB on any draft legislative provisions within the ECB's field of competence;[180] the imposition of statistical reporting requirements on natural and legal persons;[181] the minimum reserves required by the ECB;[182] the scope of other operational methods of monetary control not yet foreseen in the Statute, if the Governing Council of the ECB sees fit to use such other methods and if they impose obligations on third parties; the details on the subscription to, the paying-up and the increase of the ECB's capital;[183] the call on foreign reserve assets beyond the amount of 50,000 million euro which had to be transferred to the ECB under Article 30.1 of the Statute, whenever such further calls are effected by the ECB.[184]

In all these cases, the Council of the European Union was not entitled to regulate the ECB, but was rather obliged by Article 42 of the Statute to specify and concretise the powers already given to the ECB by primary Community law. The exceptional nature of such Council legislation within the field of competence of the ECB is underlined by its limitation to activities of the ECB which

[178] Council Regulation 2532/98 of 23 November 1998 concerning the powers of the European Central Bank to impose sanctions [1998] OJ L318/4.

[179] Regulation ECB/1999/4 of 23 September 1999 on the powers of the European Central Bank to impose sanctions [1999] OJ L264/21.

[180] Cf. Council Decision 1998/415/EC of 29 June 1998 on the consultation of the European Central Bank by national authorities regarding draft legislative provisions [1998] OJ L189/42.

[181] Cf. on the one hand Council Regulation 2533/98 of 23 November 1998 concerning the collection of statistical information by the European Central Bank [1998] OJ L318/8; and on the other hand Regulation ECB/1998/16 of 1 December 1998 concerning the consolidated balance sheet of the monetary financial institutions sector [1998] OJ L356/7, as amended by Regulation ECB/2000/8 of 31 August 2000 [2000] OJ L229/34.

[182] Cf. on the one hand Council Regulation 2531/98 of 23 November 1998 concerning the application of minimum reserves by the European Central Bank [1998] OJ L318/1; and on the other hand Regulation ECB/1998/15 of 1 December 1998 on the application of minimum reserves [1998] OJ L356/1, as amended by Regulation ECB/2000/8, *supra*, n. 181.

[183] Cf. on the one hand Council Decision 382/98 of 5 June 1998 on the statistical data to be used for the determination of the key for subscribtion of the capital of the European Central Bank; and Council Regulation 1009/2000 of 8 May 2000 concerning capital increases of the European Central Bank [2000] OJ L115/1, [1998] OJ L171/33. Cf. on the other hand Decision ECB/1998/1 of 9 June 1998 on the method to be applied for determining the national central banks' percentage shares in the key for the capital of the European Central Bank [1999] OJ L8/31; Decision ECB/1998/2 of 9 June 1998 laying down the measures necessary for the paying up of the capital of the European Central Bank [1999] OJ L8/33; Decision ECB/1998/13 of 1 December 1998 on the national central banks' percentage in the key for the capital of the European Central Bank [1999] OJ L125/33; Decision ECB/1998/14 of 1 December 1998 laying down the measures necessary for the paying-up of the capital of the European Central Bank by the non-participating national central banks [1999] OJ L110/33; Decision ECB/2000/14 of 16 November 2000 providing for the paying-up of capital and the contribution to the reserves and provisions of the European Central Bank by the Bank of Greece, and for the initial transfer of foreign-reserve assets to the ECB by the bank of Greece and related matters [2000] OJ L336/10.

[184] Cf. Council Regulation 1010/2000 of 8 May 2000 concerning further calls of foreign reserve assets by the European Central Bank [2000] OJ L115/2.

involve important obligations for the Member States or for economic agents and therefore require the ECB, in accordance with democratic principles, to share its legislative power with the Council of the European Union. Even in such cases, the ECB remains the *primary* regulator (as opposed to a *complementary* regulator) in the field of monetary policy. This is emphasised by the fact that in such cases the Council of the European Union may act only upon a recommendation from, or after consultation of, the ECB (cf. Article 42 of the Statute), while the decision-making bodies of the ECB may always exercise their regulatory power without the need formally to involve the Community institutions. The Council may even renounce its right to adopt complementary legislation and rely instead on the expertise of the ECB in a specific field by passing on its complementary competences to the ECB under Article 34.1, first indent, of the Statute, while neither the EC Treaty nor the Statute foresees a corresponding competence of the ECB to renounce its right and obligation to regulate in a field which has been primarily entrusted to it by the Member States when they ratified the Maastricht Treaty.

Finally, it should not be disregarded that the adoption of complementary legislation to enable the application of a number of Statute provisions is not up to the discretion of the Council; instead, Article 42 of the Statute makes the enactment of such legislation an *obligation* of the Council ("shall")—an obligation under a time-limit, as it has to be fulfilled "immediately after the decision on the date for the beginning of the third stage", this means immediately after the confirmation by the Council of the European Union of 13 December 1996 to start the third stage of EMU not in 1997 or in 1998, but on 1 January 1999.[185] The enactment of the complementary legislation enumerated in Article 42 of the Statute therefore forms part of the duty of all Community institutions under Protocol No 24, annexed to the EC Treaty, on the transition to the third stage of economic and monetary union "to expedite all preparatory work during 1998, in order to enable the Community to enter the third stage irrevocably on 1 January 1999 and to enable the ECB and the ESCB to start their full functioning from this date". Article 42 of the Statute presumes that the complementary legislation which it lists would have been adopted already when the ECB started fully to exercise its powers on 1 January 1999. Since then, legal certainty and the independence of the ECB have required stability of the complementary legal framework as laid down by the Council, so that the possibility of future changes to that framework by the Council must be restrictively construed, in view of the exceptional character of the complementary procedure of Article 42 of the Statute.

In view of the numerous limitations of the power of the Council to enact complementary legislation as regards the ECB, conflicts of competences between the regulatory power of the Community institutions and the ECB are more likely to

---

[185] Council Decision 96/736/EC of 13 December 1996 in accordance with Art. 109j(3) of the Treaty establishing the European Community, on entry into the third stage of economic and monetary union [1996] OJ L335/48.

arise in areas which concern the general policies of the Communities, but at the same time have an impact on the tasks of the ECB or the institutional set-up of EMU. Such areas of mutual concern are in particular the policies concerning the single market and the co-ordination of economic policies of the Community and the Member States, as both in many respect interact closely with the policies concerning the single currency. In these fields, the existence of two different legal persons at the supranational level with law-making powers inevitably leads to *horizontal* conflicts of competence between the regulatory power of the Community institutions and of the ECB, which have to be carefully distinguished from *vertical* conflicts of competence between the Communities and the ECB on the one hand, and the Member States on the other hand.[186] But this new potential for a conflict of competences is less dramatic than it may seem at first glance. Both the EC with its institutions and the ECB are subject to the principle of conferred powers, i.e. each of them may act only within the limits of the powers conferred upon them by primary Community law (cf. Articles 5(1) and 7(1) EC on the one hand, and Articles 8 EC and 1.1 of the Statute on the other hand). This should exclude *a priori* any overlap of competences. In addition, most of the time, the EC Treaty and the Statute are very clear in delimiting the competences of the Community institutions and of the ECB's decision-making bodies. In the field of statistics—to take an example which is relevant for the proper functioning both of the single market or the co-ordination of economic policies and for the monetary policy of the ECB—Article 285(1) EC enables Council and Parliament to adopt measures for the production of statistics only where necessary for the performance of the activities *of the Community*. From the latter, one could already conclude "not for that *of the ECB*", which has its own regulatory power in the field of statistics under Article 5 in conjunction with Article 34.1, first indent of the Statute. The drafters of Article 285(1) EC have been even more explicit and added that the joint legislative competence of Council and Parliament shall be "without prejudice to Article 5 of the Protocol on the Statute of the European System of Central Banks and of the European Central Bank". In addition, the ECB is required, by Article 5.1, second sentence of the Statute, to "co-operate" in the field of statistics with the Community institutions and bodies, while Article 105(4), first indent EC requires all[187] Community institutions to consult the ECB on any draft legislative proposal in the ECB's field of competence.

---

[186] To write about "competences" and "powers" of the legal person ECB which can, both inside the Community legal order and at the international level, come into conflict with the competences conferred on the legal person EC, is thus not an "error" (as claimed by Torrent, *supra*, n. 3, 1234), but a logical consequence of our view of the ECB's legal nature. The existence of such horizontal conflicts of competence between the EC and the ECB is also seen by Cafaro, "I primi accordi della Comunità in materia di politica monetaria e di cambio" [1999] *Il Diritto dell'Unione Europea* 243 (244); and by Weinrichter, "The World Monetary System and External Relations of the EMU—Fasten your Safety Belts!" [2000] *EIoP* No. 10, 15.

[187] This results from a comparison with Art. 5.3 of the Statute of the European Monetary Institute (EMI), the ECB's predecessor, under which the EMI had to be consulted only "by the Council regarding any proposed Community act within its field of competence", while today, Art.

In line with the above analysis, it follows from the legal nature of the ECB as a legal person distinct and on an equal footing with the original European Communities that the relationship between secondary Community law adopted by the Community institutions and ECB law is not one of hierarchy, but that they coexist at the same normative level. This new constitutional balance existing between the Community institutions and the ECB is not merely a theoretical concept. In line with the case law of the ECJ,[188] the authors of the EC Treaty have also given the ECB the power to defend its regulatory prerogatives in the ECJ. If a situation should occur in which the Community institutions legislated in the field of competence of the ECB although neither the EC Treaty nor the Statute provides for a corresponding regulatory power, the ECB could, under Articles 230 and 241 EC, challenge such secondary Community law for two reasons in the ECJ: for lack of competence, and for an infringement of the Treaty, *viz.* of Article 108 EC, the *effet utile* of which does not allow circumvention through legislative means of the prohibition to give instructions to the ECB.

3. The control of the ECB's financial resources

We have seen that the ECB's independence also has an important financial aspect, as the ECB's capital, the foreign reserves transferred to it and the income accruing from its monetary policy functions do not form part of the budget by which EC, ECSC and EAEC are covered.[189] We have also seen that Article 101 EC prohibits any credit facilities of the ECB in favour of the Community institutions and bodies.

Financially, the resources of the ECB are therefore completely separated from the budget of the original three Communities, and its financial interests are far from being identical to those of the Communities.[190] This is also recognised in Article 27.1 of the Statute according to which the accounts of the ECB are not

---

105(4), first indent EC requires general consultation of the ECB "on any proposed Community act in its field of competence".

[188] Cf. Case C–70/88, *European Parliament* v. *Council (Chernobyl)* [1990] ECR I–2041, para. 26 *et seq.*

[189] Cf. *supra*, p. 19.

[190] This is even the case when one applies the very broad interpretation of "financial interests of the European Communities", as laid down in Art. 1(2) of Council Regulation (EC/Euratom) 2988/93 of 18 December 1995 on the protection of the European Communities' financial interests [1995] OJ L312/1 and including "the general budget of the Communities or budgets managed by them". Unlike the budget of, to mention an example, the European Regional Development Fund, through which the EC takes action (cf. Art. 159 EC) and which is administered by the Commission's Directorate-General for Regional Policy, the financial resources of the ECB are managed exclusively by the decision-making bodies of the ECB. The financial independence of the ECB results from a deliberate decision of the intergovermental conference at Maastricht. Early French proposals, under which the Member States and/or the EC would have owned the capital of the ECB, were rejected; cf. Bailleix-Banerjee, *supra*, n. 51, 102, 103, 130 and 311.

audited by the Court of Auditors of the European Communities,[191] but by independent external auditors (for the moment, by Coopers and Lybrand[192]). This absence of a financial or even budgetary link between the three Communities and the ECB may have a bearing on the current dispute between the Commission and the ECB as regards the conflicting competences of the European Anti-Fraud Office (OLAF), established by the Commission to protect the financial interests of the Community,[193] and of the Anti-Fraud Committee of the European Central Bank, established by the ECB to protect the financial interests of the ECB.[194] Being a matter *sub judice*,[195] we abstain here from any comment. It is now for the ECJ to decide how far the financial and institutional independence of the ECB requires protection by the rule of law.[196]

4. The liability question

An understanding of the ECB as an independent specialised organisation of Community law also solves the interpretation problem as regards Article 288(3)

[191] The Court of Auditors may examine only the operational efficiency of the management of the ECB; cf. Art. 27.2 of the Statute. In contrast to this, the EIB is subject to the supervision of the Court of Auditors whenever it manages Community expenditure and revenue, i.e. whenever it acts as a "Community agent"; cf. Art. 248(3) third subpara. EC.

[192] Cf. Recommendation ECB/1998/3 of 19 June 1998 on the external auditor of the European Central Bank [1998] OJ C246/5, and Council Decision 98/481/EC of 20 July 1998 approving the external auditors of the European Central Bank [1998] OJ L216/7. The auditors were thereafter appointed by the ECB. Cf. also Decision ECB/1998/NP1 of 19 June 1998 on the appointment and the duration of the mandate of the external auditor of the European Central Bank [2001] OJ L55/75 (publication *a posteriori*).

[193] Cf. Commission Decision 1999/352/EC, ECSC, Euratom of 28 April 1999 [1999] OJ L136/20, adopted on the basis of Art. 162 of the EC Treaty (now Art. 218 EC). Cf. also Regulation 1073/1999 of the European Parliament and of the Council of 25 May 1999 concerning investigations conducted by the European Anti-Fraud Office (OLAF) [1999] OJ L136/1, and Council Regulation (Euratom) 1074/1999 of 25 May 1999 concerning investigations conducted by the European Anti-Fraud Office (OLAF) [1999] OJ L136/8, by which the competences of OLAF have been extended to all "institutions, bodies, offices and agencies established by, or on the basis of, the Treaties".

[194] Cf. Decision ECB/1999/5 of 7 October 1999 on fraud prevention [1999] OJ L291/36. The legal basis is Art. 12.3 of the Statute.

[195] On 12 January 2000, the Commission began two actions before the ECJ on the basis of Art. 230 EC, one against the ECB and one against the EIB, because they both rely on their own anti-fraud regimes; cf. the Commission's press release IP/00/22 of 12 January 2000 and the summary of its main legal argument in [2000] OJ C122/8–10. The Commission's anti-fraud regime has meanwhile been challenged by a group representing 70 Members of the European Parliament; as a consequence, the CFI has granted an interim measure against OLAF; cf. Case T–17/00R, *Rothley and others* v. *European Parliament*, Order of 2 May 2000 [2000] ECR II-2085.

[196] Cf. the analysis by Selmayr, "Die EZB als Neue Gemeinschaft—ein Fall für den EuGH?", *supra*, n. 2; Lohmann, "Olaf hat keine Zuständigkeit für die Europäische Zentralbank", *Vereinigte Wirtschaftsdienste* of 1 December 1999; Selmayr and Kamann, "Streit um die Unabhängigkeit", *Frankfurter Allgemeine Zeitung* No 86, 11 April 2000, 14, with a reaction by Theato, "Mit Olaf einen Schritt vorwärts", *Frankfurter Allgemeine Zeitung* No 79, 26 April 2000, 12. Cf. also Mager, "Das Europäische Amt für Betrugsbekämpfung (OLAF)—Rechtsgrundlagen seiner Errichtung und Grenzen seiner Befugnisse" [2000] ZEuS 177; and the opposing view presented by Kuhl and Spitzer, "Das Europäische Amt für Betrugsbekämpfung (OLAF)" [2000] *EuR* 671.

EC and Article 35.3 of the Statute already mentioned at the beginning of our analysis. From the wording of these Articles, it is not completely clear *who* would be liable if the conditions for liability were satisified. Some analysts have taken the view that the Community would be liable for damage caused by the ECB, as the Community would also be liable for damage caused by its institutions and servants under Article 288(2) EC, and because Article 288(3) EC would explicitly refer to its preceding paragraph and its conditions.[197] It is submitted that this is a quite formalistic point of view which does not take into account that the ECB, though established by the EC Treaty and contributing to the objectives of the Community, is not only formally separated from the Community through its own legal personality, but also enjoys complete independence towards the Community and its institutions under Article 108 EC. The ECJ has only attributed the responsibility for the activities of separate legal persons to the Community under the condition that they acted "in the name and on behalf of the Community".[198] This cannot be said for the activities of the ECB which, though serving the general purposes of the Community, are conducted solely in the name and under the responsibility of the ECB, following its special and primary objective of price stability. In view of the absence of links between the budget of the European Communities and the financial resources of the ECB, and in view of the fact that the ECB is, as a general rule, legally prohibited from acting as "Community agent" and does not serve as financial instrument of the Community, there is no reason why the Communities should finance reparations for damage caused by the ECB from their own budget. On the contrary, as Article 108 EC excludes the possibility of the Community institutions and bodies to direct the ECB in its activities, it would be quite absurd to hold the Communities liable for injury caused in the course of the performance of the ECB's tasks. Instead, it seems logical that the ECB would have to pay from its own resources for such injury.[199] In case of litigation at the ECJ, individuals will therefore have to seek redress in such cases directly from the ECB by an action for damages under Articles 235, 288(3) EC and Article 35.3, first sentence, of the Statute, since Article 288(3) EC has to be read as follows: "In the case of non-contractual liability, the ECB shall, in accordance with the general principles common to the laws of the Member States, make good any damage caused by its decision-making bodies or by its servants in the performance of their duties".[200]

---

[197] This is in particular the view of M. Weber, "Das Europäische System der Zentralbanken" [1998] *WM* 1465 (1470), who, however, admits that "this is, as a matter of substance, not really justified".

[198] Cf. Case C–370/89, *supra*, n. 105, as regards the EIB.

[199] This view is shared by La Marca, "Il controllo guirisdizionale sulla Banca Centrale Europea e sull'Istituto Monetario Europeo" in *Il diritto dell'Unione europea* (Milan, 1996), 773 (789 *et seq.*); and, concerning the EIB, by Hilf, *Die Organisationstruktur der Europäischen Gemeinschaft* (Berlin, 1982), 40 *et seq.* On the distribution of liability between the ECB and the national central banks inside the ESCB, cf. Ch. 3, *infra*, p. 124 *et seq.*, and p. 129 *et seq.*

[200] This seems to follow from the case law of the ECJ if applied to the ECB, cf. *supra*, n. 72.

5. The ECB in international relations

A final practical consequence of the new constitutional balance inside the EU is the ECB's potential for international legal personality.[201] International practice—which is a constitutive element of international legal personality—is already starting to accept the new actor which has existed since 1 January 1999 inside the European Union's first pillar.[202] In this sense, the ECB, upon an invitation from the Board of Directors of the Bank for International Settlement (BIS), became a member of this international organisation by subscribing for shares of the third tranche of the capital of the BIS;[203] on that occasion, Article 56(d) of the Statutes of the BIS[204] has been amended to include in the definition of "country" "a monetary zone extending over more than one sovereign state". The President of the ECB has also been accepted as a regular participant in G–7 summits[205] where he is the only participant who is able to ground his participation on Community law.[206] Moreover, the ECB has been awarded observer status at the International Monetary Fund in Washington[207] under Article X of the IMF's Articles of Agreement, which is entitled "Relations with Other International Organisations". It is also noteworthy that the ECB is entitled to foreign sovereign immunity under the US Foreign Sovereign Immunities Act

---

[201] On this, cf. Smits, "Positie en bevoegdheden van een Europese Centrale Bank" in *Een Economische en Monataire Unie (EMU) in Europa—Juridische en Institutionele Consequenties*, Asser Instituut Colloquium Europees Recht (1990), 25–33, 26 and 32. See *infra*, Ch. 5, p. 179 *et seq*, for a more detailed analysis of the ECB's international legal personality.

[202] Cf. Padoa-Schioppa, "The External Representation of the Euro Area", published at http://www.ecb.int/key/st990317.htm.[203] Cf. BIS, Press Release No 40/1999E of 8 November 1999. The ECB became a member on 9 December 1999.

[203] CF. BIS, Press Release No 40/19999E of 8 November 1999. The ECB became a member on 9 December 1999.

[204] Cf. Statutes of the Bank for International Settlements of 20 January 1930, as amended on 8 November 1999, published at http://www.bis.org/about/index.htm.

[205] Cf., as an example, the Tokyo Statement of G–7 Finance Ministers and Central Bank Governors of 22 January 2000, published at http://www.library.utoronto.ca/g7/finance/fm002201. htm, which was made by the Finance Ministers of the G–7 countries, the Central Bank Governors of Canada, Japan, the United States, and the United Kingdom, the Euro–11 Presidency, and the President of the ECB.

[206] On Art. 6.1 and 6.2 of the Statute. The participation of the "euro group"-Presidency is not based on Community law, as the "euro group" is a body not foreseen in the EC Treaty; cf. *infra*, Ch. 4, p. 149 *et seq*. The proposal of an additional participation of the Commission in G 7-meetings was rejected by the non-European G 7-members.

[207] Cf. the relevant IMF Executive Board's Decision No 11875-(99/1) of 21 December 1998, published in IMF, *Selected Decisions*, *supra*, n. 145, 551 *et seq*. In this context, we would like to point to those academics and practitioners, but also to the Group of Ten, which share our view—almost ridiculed by Torrent, *supra*, n. 3, 1239—that the IMF is, primarily, an international *monetary* organisation, the participation within which is therefore in the natural interest of every central bank; cf., as an example, Duisenberg and Sasz, "The Monetary Character of the IMF" in Frenkel and Goldstein (eds.), *International Financial Policy: Essays in Honour of Jacques Polack* (Washington, 1991), 254 (where a number of communiqués of the Group of Ten are quoted which stress the "monetary role" or the "monetary character" of the IMF); cf. also Louis, *supra*, n. 100, 406 *et seq*.; and Smits, *supra*, n. 126, 444

1976[208] and has been granted tax exemptions in the United States under section 895 of the Internal Revenue Code.[209] In addition, the Board of Governors of the US Federal Reserve System has formally amended its interpretation of Regulation D to designate the ECB as "supranational entity" eligible to open US international banking facilities,[210] alongside the EC, the ECSC, the EAEC and the EIB.[211] Recently, the United States of America even asked to establish a diplomatic mission at the ECB in Frankfurt.[212] As in the case of the EIB—the international legal personality of which is today widely recognised—international practice seems to be much more pragmatic as regards the ECB's international personality than sometimes is legal doctrine.

V. A DEMOCRATIC DEFICIT?

The idea of the ECB as an independent specialised organisation of Community law or even as a "new Community" might fuel the debate on the so-called "democratic deficit" of the European Central Bank which has already been criticised by a number of authors.[213] In this sense, the situation resembles to some extent the debate led in the United States of America during the 1930s when President Roosevelt's New Deal caused the emergence of hundreds of

---

[208] On the interpretation thereof, cf. Patrikis, "Sovereign Immunity and Central Bank Immunity in the United States" in Current Legal Issues Affecting Central Banks (Washington 1992), 159. Cf. also Krauskopf and Steven, "Immunität ausländischer Zentralbanken im deutschen Recht" [2000] WM 269, who show, in their comparative analysis of different legal systems, that independent central banks with their own legal personality are today widely recognised as independent bearers of foreign sovereign immunity.

[209] Cf. 28 USC § 1603 et seq.

[210] The advantage of such a designation is that it renders the ECB eligible to deposit funds with an international banking facility exempt from the prohibition against the payment of interest on demand deposits established under Fed regulations. In addition, international banking facility time deposits held by the ECB are exempt from the Fed's 10% marginal reserve requirement applicable to specified deposits with US depositary institutions.

[211] Vgl. Federal Register/vol. 65, No 48 of 10 March 2000. Under Regulation D, there are three categories of eligible entities: (1) foreign (commercial) banks, (2) foreign national governments, or agencies or instrumentalities thereof; (3) foreign international or supranational entities specifically designated by the Board of Governors of the Federal Reserve System. It is in line with the view of the ECB's legal nature presented in this Ch. that the ECB was held to fall not under category (2), but under (3) in the Fed's interpretation.

[212] In accordance with Arts. 17 and 23 of the Protocol No 34 on Privileges and Immunities of the European Communities, which applies to the ECB by virtue of Art. 291, second sentence EC. Interestingly, it was also the US Ambassador who became the first diplomat accredited to the EEC in 1958; cf. 1st General Report on the Activities of the European Economic Community, point 168.

[213] Cf. Gormley and De Haan, "The Democracy Deficit of the European Central Bank" (1996) *EL Rev.* 95; cf. also De Witte, *supra*, n. 6, 67 *et seq.*, who takes the chapter on EMU as the EC Treaty's most prominent example of "a lack of democratic control". Torrent's criticism (cf. *supra*, n. 3, 1234) seems in particular to be based on the undemocratic nature of our argument, as he emphasises that central banks, including the ECB, "lie within and not outside the system of democratically organised power". On this topic, cf. also Gormley and De Haan, "Independence and Accountability of the European Central Bank" in Andenas, Gormley, Hadjiemmanuil and Harden (eds.), *European and Monetary Union: The Institutional Framework* (The Hague/London/Boston, 1997); Amtenbrink, *The Democratic Accountability of Central Banks* (Oxford/Portland, 1999); but also the German Federal Constitutional Court's *Maastricht* judgement, *supra*, n. 154, 261 *et seq.*

independent agencies and commissions led by technocrats which were not placed under the control of Congress.[214] In the words of the US Committee on Administrative Procedures, these agencies were:

> in reality miniature governments set up to deal with the railroad problem, the banking problem, or the radio problem. They constitute a headless 'fourth branch' of the government, a haphazard deposit of irresponsible agencies and unco-ordinated powers. They do violate the basis theory of the American Constitution that there should be three branches of government and only three.[215]

When considering the proper place of the ECB within the organisational structure of Community law, a number of traditional Community lawyers will, despite the special characteristics of this "new Community", at first glance certainly insist that "there should be three Communities and only three". However, as already indicated, one should not forget that the balance of powers established by Community law is as *sui generis* as is the entire Community legal order. The existence of several Communities and associated supranational legal persons does not at all reflect the principle of separation of powers known from national legal systems, but has its origin in the history of European integration during which an increasing number of technical, economic and eventually also political functions were pooled by the Member States. To add the ECB as an independent specialised organisation of Community law to this pool of functions is not a deviation from the principle of separation of powers, but reflects the fact that at the Community level there exists today a novel form of governance which follows in many respects new patterns as regards the separation of powers.

One can certainly not deny that the ECB's special status inside the organisational framework of the European Union puts it (on purpose) at a certain distance from the normal process of democratic governance both at the national and at the supranational level.[216] However, to call this "undemocratic" would ignore the fact that this special status has not been created by the ECB itself, but stems from the EC Treaty and the Statute, both documents of constitutional rank which have been duly ratified by all 15 Member States by means of democratic procedures, in Austria, Denmark, France, Ireland, Finland and Sweden even by way of a referendum.[217] One can therefore hardly say that the surrender of monetary sovereignty to the ECB as an independent supranational organisation inside the

---

[214] Cf. Shapiro, *Who Guards the Guardians? Judicial Control of Administration* (Athens, Ga., 1988), 38 *et seq.*

[215] On this statement, and on its meaning within the context of the Communities, cf. Majone, "The European Community—an 'Independent Fourth Branch of Government'?" in Brüggemeier (ed.), *Verfassungen für ein ziviles Europa* (Baden Baden, 1994), 23 (24).

[216] Cf. Smits, *supra*, n. 126, who underlines, at 176, that "it needs to be recognized that the independence has been written in stone, a feature which may be considered at variance with the imperatives of democracy" but also states that "accountable independence" can be achieved. He finally concludes, at 500, that "in a field as sensitive as monetary policy [it] can be considered wise and not at variance with the requirements of democracy" to hive off part of the legislative power and of the executive from the representatives of the people.

[217] Cf. Issing, *supra*, n. 100, 3: "By signing the Maastricht Treaty, in a democratic legitimate act, the 15 EU Member States established a constitution for stable money".

Community legal order has happened unnoticed for the European citizens[218]—at least not more unnoticed than all the other transfers of sovereignty which have taken place as a consequence of the Maastricht and the Amsterdam Treaties.

It is self-evident that the democratic *naissance* of the ECB does not entitle it to conduct its policy behind closed doors or in isolation from both the political Community institutions and the citizens in the Member States. No public organisation, and even less a supranational organisation can fulfil its tasks properly without the general support of the citizens from which, ultimately, it derives all its authority. The ECB therefore pays much attention to promoting transparency and accountability in its daily work,[219] even though it is not directly bound by the transparency requirement of Article 255 EC, which addresses only the European Parliament, the Council and the Commission.[220] In particular, the ECB has made public its detailed strategy for monetary policy and thus guarantees that market participants are not taken by surprise by monetary policy decisions of the ECB.[221] It also publishes monthly bulletins on the major economic factors determining the definition and implementation of monetary policy. Even though Article 15.3 of the Statute requires only an *annual* report on the activities of the ESCB to be addressed to the European Parliament, the President of the ECB visits the European Parliament at least four times a year to give a report on the ECB and its policy. Moreover, though not a Community institution, the ECB has decided[222] to submit itself to the control of the European Ombudsman, which is appointed by the European Parliament in accordance with Article 195 EC, and now also may receive complaints from any natural or legal person in the Union concerning instances of maladministration in the activities of the ECB. Finally, the ECB has decided to publish, for the sake of enhancing the transparency of the regulatory framework of the ESCB, certain ECB legal acts and instruments,[223] even though Community

---

[218] This is suggested by Torrent, *supra*, n. 3, 1241.

[219] On this, cf. Hahn, "Berichtspflichten und Informationsmöglichkeiten der Europäischen Zentralbank" [1999] *JZ* 957. Cf also the opinion of the former Deputy Chairman of the Federal Reserve Board, Blinder in *Kauppalehti*, 8 December 1999, 7 according to whom "the ECB is ahead of the Fed in terms of openness". Cf. also the table in Deutsche Bundesbank, "Transparenz in der Geldpolitik", *Monatsbericht* (March 2000), 15 (20), which shows that the ECB has, as regards transparency, in most fields a better record than the US Federal Reserve, the Bank of Japan, the Bank of England, and also the Bundesbank itself.

[220] Art.110(2), fourth subpara., EC refers only to "Articles 253, 254 and 256", but not to Art. 255 EC. This is, again, an expression of the special legal status of the ECB, which differs from that of the Community institutions. As a central bank, the ECB is—similar to the ECJ—subject to strict rules of confidentiality, which do not always allow for publication or public access to documents. On the controversial question of access to the minutes of meetings of the Governing Council of the ECB under Art. 10.4 of the Statute, cf. the case study by Selmayr, "Die Grenzen der Geldpolitik der Europäischen Zentralbank—eine Fallstudie", in Rohde and Köhler, *Geldpolitik ohne Grenzen* (Berlin, 2001—in press); cf. also Scheller, *Die Europäische Zentralbank* (Frankfurt am Main, 2000), 89.

[221] Cf. ECB, "The Stability-oriented Monetary Policy Strategy of the Eurosystem", *Monthly Bulletin* (Frankfurt am Main, January 1999), 39. For an update cf. ECB, "The Two Pillars of the ECB's Monetary Policy Strategy", *Monthly Bulletin* (Frankfurt am Main, November 2000), 37.

[222] Cf. Press Releases Nos 4/99 and 6/99, http://www.euro-ombudsman.eu.int/DECISION/EN/ecb.htm.

[223] By Decision ECB/2000/12 of 10 November 2000 on the publication of certain legal acts and instruments of the European Central Bank [2001] OJ L55/68. Cf. also Decision ECB/2000/14 of

law provides for only a limited publication obligation in Article 110(4) and (5) EC and Article 34.2, subparagraphs 4 and 5 of the Statute. The ECB thus views itself not only as an independent specialised organisation of Community law, but also as the servant of the citizens which use the euro in their daily life.

VI. CONCLUSION

The above analysis has shown that the ECB is an integral part of the European Union's first and central pillar. Our proposal to view the ECB as an independent specialised organisation of Community law, or even as a "new Community", combines both the new degree of central bank independence, as entrenched in Article 108 EC, and the firm embodiment of this new supranational organisation into the Community legal order by which it has been established. The ECB is thus not an institution, body, department or agency dependent on or subject to the Communities or the Member States, but an independent supranational organisation distinct from and on an equal footing with the original three Communities, to which the ECB has been associated by the EC Treaty. Over the bond of association between the Communities and the ECB, only the ECJ exercises its supervision—both to safeguard the ECB's still young independence and to maintain its link with the "unity of ideals" which the Treaties and the case law of the ECJ have already created between the Communities and the EIB. The complete denationalisation and depoliticisation of monetary policy in the hands of the "new Community" is therefore accompanied and compensated for by an increased *juridification* of a field in which legal control or even court litigation traditionally has been rather the exception than the rule.

We are aware that the legal nature of the ECB will continue to give rise to academic controversy. However, the existence of a "new Community" can only be a sensational revelation for those who are already viewing the European Union as a federal state and thus want to place the ECB inside this Union in a position where central banks traditionally used to be in their respective Member States, where they "were and are simply Central Banks, no more, no less".[224] In contrast to this, the legal analyst has to admit that the ECB represents the exceptional case of a central bank without a state, as for the moment the single currency is not (yet?) paralleled by a United States of Europe.[225] Hitherto, Member States have merely pooled an increasing number of important sovereign rights in a conglomerate of supranational Communities which are all held together not by the power of an omnicompetent supranational legislator or government, but just by a, albeit very intensive, system of law.

16 November 2000 providing for the paying-up of capital and the contribution to the reserves and provisions of the ECB by the Bank of Greece, and for the initial transfer of foreign-reserve assets to the ECB by the Bank of Greece and related matters [2000] OJ L336/110, where Art. 6 provides for the publication of Guideline ECB/2000/15 as Annex to the decision "for reasons of transparency".

[224] Torrent, *supra*, n. 3, 1234.
[225] Cf. Issing, *supra*, n. 100, 2, who speaks of "a unique, historical asymmetry".

The very existence of the ECB may therefore trigger two alternative future developments of the European Union.[226] First, the distance of the independent ECB from the political process may intensify the voices of those who consider this situation to be, in the long run, not viable without the ECB being accompanied by and integrated into a true Federation.[227] Alternatively, it could also serve as an argument supporting a new and *sui generis* form of mixed national, supranational, and intergovernmental governance,[228] which permits functional considerations and which deals with different fields of public activity in pillars, Communities and other flexible forms of integration like those introduced by the Amsterdam Treaty and enhanced by the Nice Treaty. Such a new and truly European model of governance could build on the historical experiences of European integration[229] which has never made much progress through ambitious federalist methods of "constitution-making", but has always advanced through functional, sometimes unusual, steps[230] which, slowly but continuously, have entailed further integration in other fields.

[226] Cf. Snyder, "EMU—Metaphor for European Union? Institutions, Rules and Types of Regulation" in Dehousse (ed.), *Europe after Maastricht. An Ever Closer Union?* (Munich, 1994), 63 and "EMU Revisited: Are We Making a Constitution? What Constitution Are We Making?" in Craig and de Búrca, *supra*, n. 8, 417. Cf. also Dehousse, *supra*, n. 9, who contrasts two visions of the missions and the institutional architecture of the European Union: a parliamentary model and a regulatory model.

[227] On the prospects for a true constitutionalisation of the European Union, cf. Piris, "Does the European Union have a Constitution? Does it Need One?" (1999) *EL Rev.* 557. A comprehensive approach to institutional reform has been proposed by von Weizsäcker, Dehaene and Simon, "The Institutional Implications of Enlargement" (the so-called "Three Wise Men Report") (Brussels, 18 October 1999), published at http://europa.eu.int/igc2000/repoct99_en.htm.

[228] Not a United States of Europe, but promoting new forms of European governance, with a new balance between action by the Commission, the other institutions, the Member States and civil society, is also the aim envisaged by the Prodi-Commission in its Communication of 9 February 2000 to the European Parliament, the Council, the Economic and Social Committee and the Committee of the Regions: Strategic Objectives 2000–2005, "Shaping the New Europe", COM(2000) 154 final, published at http://www.europa.eu.int/comm/off/work/2000–2005/index_en.htm.

[229] Cf. the various contributions on the history and theory of European integration in von Bogdandy (ed.), *Die Europäische Option: Eine interdisziplinäre Analyse über Herkunft, Stand und Perspektiven der Europäischen Union* (Baden Baden, 1993).

[230] In the same sense, see Gustavsson, "Reconciling Suprastatism and Democratic Accountability" in Hoskyns and Newman (eds.), *Democratizing the European Union. Issues for the 21st Century* (Manchester, 2000), pre-published as Jean Monnet Working Paper No 11/99 at http://www.law.harvard.edu/programs/JeanMonnet. He argues that "a *piecemeal* constitutional engineering is preferable to a *utopian* strategy. Provisional suprastatism is the least worst alternative when trying to establish monetary union without fiscal union".

2

Who Governs the European System of Central Banks?

I. INTRODUCTION

NOT ONLY THE organisational structure of the European Union, but also the world of banking and finance entered a new era on 1 January 1999, the starting date for the third stage of EMU. Since then, natural and legal persons operating in the financial markets, have been able to use a new and still unique currency, the euro. They also have had to get used to a new legal framework for their activities, a framework which is determined by the new European System of Central Banks (ESCB).

At first glance, the ESCB seems to be a rather complex system. Since 1 January 1999, credit institutions which are requesting central bank liquidity, and likewise traders in the foreign exchange markets and participants in payment systems, have found themselves often face to face with a number of seemingly different counterparties, including the ECB and the national central bank of their home country (for example, the Bundesbank, Banque de France or Banca d'Italia). Natural and legal persons thus have a legitimate interest in identifying their real counterparty in a specific central banking context in order to understand who sets interest rates and who could intervene in the foreign exchange markets; who has regulatory power, in particular the competence to impose minimum reserves or statistical reporting requirements; who has the competence to sanction non-compliance with such obligations; who is the appropriate addressee of claims regarding contractual and non-contractual liability; whom a credit institution or a trader could, in the last resort, sue in court; and which court would have jurisdiction in such a case. These issues are of crucial importance for all those who want to know whether there is still any difference between accessing central bank facilities in Frankfurt or in Paris, in Rome or in Vienna, in Lisbon or in Helsinki.

This chapter is intended to contribute to a better understanding of the organisational structure of the ESCB. As the law of the ECB, by its very nature, belongs to the first pillar of the European Union (cf. chapter 1), it goes without saying that also the rules governing the ESCB are laid down in primary Community law, i.e. in the EC Treaty and in the Statute of the European System of Central Banks and of the European Central Bank (the Statute).[1] They thus

---

[1] The Statute is contained in a Protocol attached to the EC Treaty. Such Protocols are considered to be an integral part of the EC Treaty by virtue of Art. 311 EC.

form part of those rules which the ECJ considers to be an integral and supreme part of the legal order applicable in the territory of each of the Member States and which are therefore a direct source of rights and duties for all those affected thereby.[2] The starting point of this chapter is the observation that the ESCB has a two-level organisational structure, but is governed exclusively by the ECB (II). In accordance with this observation, the chapter then shows how the EC Treaty and the Statute have centralised decision-making within the ESCB in the hands of the decision-making bodies of the ECB in order to guarantee an efficient conduct of the single monetary policy and thereby to contribute to price stability for the euro (III.).

II. THE ORGANISATIONAL STRUCTURE OF THE ESCB

The establishment of the ESCB and the ECB has provoked a number of quite opposite statements on its organisational structure which is sometimes said to represent "an institutional nicety".[3] While for some authors the new system responsible for the single currency of the Community has made the existing national central banks including the famous Bundesbank "superfluous",[4] other observers note that the ESCB is an extremely decentralised structure in which the ECB is only the "daughter" of the national central banks which use the ECB as a mere co-ordinating secretariat.[5] Both types of statements have to be considered as mere policy views as they in no way provide an exact analysis of the legal relationship between the ECB and the national central banks within the ESCB.

1. The ESCB's two-level organisation

At the beginning of the 1990s, when the drafters of the EC Treaty and of the Statute had to make up their minds about the organisational structure of the new central banking system for the forthcoming single currency, there were

---

[2] Cf. Case 106/77, *Amministrazione delle Finanze dello Stato* v. *Simmenthal SpA* [1978] ECR 629, para. 14 *et seq.*

[3] See Timmermans, "Editorial Comment: Executive Agencies within the EC: The European Central Bank a model?" (1996) *CML Rev.* 623 (625).

[4] Cf. J. Gross, Capital No 5/1998, "Abspecken", Capital No 5/1998, 3, according to whom the Bundesbank has been completely superfluous from 1 January 1999 and who thinks that the only Bundesbank element which will remain is "its ugly building in Frankfurt".

[5] This is the view of Kral and Kurm-Engels, "Die nationalen Zentralbanken haben im EZB-Rat Übergewicht", *Handelsblatt* 10 June 1998; even stronger is D. Gros, "Euro-Zentralbank ist eine Schönwetterkonstruktion", *Frankfurter Rundschau*, 6 October 1998, 13, who in particular points to the striking discrepancy between the number of people employed by the ECB (then 500, today around 960) and the national central banks, taken together (50,000); cf. also Seidel, "Die Euro-Zentralbank ist nicht nach dem Vorbild der Bundesbank gestaltet", *Frankfurter Rundschau*, 8 October 1998, 12.

essentially two alternatives[6]: either to create a unitary structure by dissolving the existing national central banks and replacing them by a new European Central Bank; or to create some type of dualist structure which would be based both on the existing national central banks and the new European Central Bank.

For some, the first alternative might have appeared completely unthinkable in view of the fact that the European Union as such is not a unitary "super-state", but rather a *sui generis* federal system, based on the existence of 15 Member States and three European Communities as separate legal persons. This two-level organisation of the European Union, with a Community level and a national level, could have excluded *a priori* a one-level organisational structure for the Union's central bank. However, it was soon discovered that just to copy the organisational structure of the Union to the new central banking system would not take into account the specific requirements of central banking. Nowhere in the world is the organisational structure of a central bank identical to that of its state, and even states with a remarkable federal tradition have often chosen an extremely unitary structure for their central bank. Thus, we find in federal Switzerland a Swiss National Bank, in federal Austria an Austrian National Bank and in Belgium (a federal state since 1994) a Belgian National Bank, central banks which are all allocated exclusively at the federal level of governance and organised in a centralised manner. Only at first glance does the situation differ in federal Germany. It is true that the Bundesbank structure today comprises nine so-called *Land* Central Banks which seem to represent a kind of organisational federalism. However, a closer look shows that the existence of these *Land* Central Banks is not much more than federal cosmetic:[7] the Bundesbank Act itself states that the Bundesbank was established by a merger of the *Land* Central Banks,[8] which were as such dissolved[9] and are today only main offices[10] of the Bundesbank. Legally, the Bundesbank structure is therefore, in essence, a unitary, and not a federal structure.[11]

---

[6] From a historic perspective, it is interesting to note that a very similar debate took place in the 1950s in Germany when the central bank constitution of the Bundesbank was discussed; cf. Wagenhöfer, "Der Föderalismus und die Notenbankverfassung" in Seidel (ed.), *Festschrift zum 70. Geburtstag von Dr. Hans Ehard* (Munich, 1957), 97. As Wagenhöfer observes at 98, already at that time, "centralists" were opposed to "federalists", and terms like "federalism", "decentralisation" and "subsidiarity" were used more as policy statements than in their precise legal meaning.

[7] The designation of the Bundesbank's sub-entities as *Land* Central Banks is called misleading by Gleske, "Organisation, Status und Aufgaben der zweistufigen Zentralbanksysteme in den Vereinigten Staaten von Amerika, in der Bundesrepublik Deutschland, in der künftigen Europäischen Währungsunion" in A. Weber (ed.), *Währung und Wirtschaft. Das Geld im Recht. Festschrift für Prof. Dr. Hugo J. Hahn zum 70. Geburtstag* (Baden Baden, 1997), 123 (132).

[8] See s. 1 of the Bundesbank Act.

[9] See s. 38(1) of the Bundesbank Act.

[10] See s. 8 of the Bundesbank Act: "Hauptverwaltung mit der Bezeichnung Landeszentralbank". In addition, s. 29(1) of the Bundesbank Act provides that the *Land* Central Banks and their branches are not authorities of the German *Länder*, but federal authorities ("*Bundesbehörden*").

[11] Gramlich, *Bundesbankgesetz Währungsgesetz Münzgesetz. Kommentar* (Cologne/Berlin/Bonn/Munich, 1988), on s. 1(2) of the Bundesbank Act speaks of "centralisation" of the Bundesbank's organisational structure. The centralised structure of the Bundesbank was a reason for the federal states of Bavaria and Rheinland-Pfalz to vote against the Bundesbank Act in the

That even federal states have favoured a unitary central banking structure can be explained by the indivisible character of most of a central bank's tasks. In particular, an efficient monetary policy is possible only if it is determined by a centralised organisation which guarantees a uniform definition and implementation of this policy throughout the currency area for which a central bank is responsible.[12] *Central* banking, by definition, seems to require centralised organisational structures, and thus is entrusted even in federal states to a federal authority.[13]

It would thus not have been inconceivable also to create a completely unitary structure for the management of the single currency of the European Community.[14] The drafters of the EC Treaty and the Statute, however, did in the end decide not to abolish the existing national central banks, but to integrate them, together with the newly established ECB, into a central banking system called ESCB. In line with this intention, Article 107(1) EC provides that "the ESCB shall be composed of the ECB and of the national central banks". The ESCB is thus, from a formal perspective, a two-level organisation which comprises today 16 legal persons: the ECB, which has been endowed with legal personality by Article 107(2) EC[15] and by Article 9(1) of the Statute, and the central banks[16] of the 15 Member States[17] of the European Union, which have kept their legal personality under national law.

Bundesrat, the second (federal) chamber of the German Parliament. Some federalist features may be detected within the organizational structure of the Bundesbank solely at the implementation level: on this see Ch. 3, p. 115, n. 172.

[12] This is stressed by the former president of the Bundesbank Tietmeyer, "Ein dezentrales Umsetzen der gemeinsamen Geldpolitik sichert nahtlosen Übergang auf europäische Ebene", *Frankfurter Rundschau*, 9 October 1998, 13: *"Gemeinsames Geld fordert eine zentrale Verantwortlichkeit für das Festlegen und Durchführen der Geldpolitik"*.

[13] This view is supported by the judgment of the US Supreme Court in *McCulloch* v. *Maryland*, 17 US (4 Wheat) 316, 4 L Ed. 579 (1819). Even though no provision could be found in the US Constitution of 1787 which would have empowered Congress to incorporate a central bank, the Sup. Ct. held that the federal legislature possessed an implied power to establish the Bank of the United States in 1816: "The sword and the purse, all the external relations, and no inconsiderable portion of the industry of the nation, are intrusted to its government. It may, with great reason be contended that a government with such ample powers, on the due execution of which the happiness and prosperity of the nation so vitally depends, must also be intrusted with ample means for their execution".

[14] In this see Friedman, "A Case for Floating Rates", *Financial Times*, 18 December 1989, 21, who then wrote: "A truly unified European currency would make a great deal of sense. But to achieve it requires eliminating all central banks in Europe except one".

[15] This includes the ECB's international legal personality; on this see *infra*, Ch. 5, p. 179 *et seq.*

[16] In the case of Luxembourg which, by virtue of the monetary union with Belgium, did not have its own central bank, the Central Bank of Luxembourg was established in parallel with the establishment of the ECB.

[17] Although only 12 Member States have adopted the single currency, the national central banks of all 15 Member States are integrated into the ESCB; on their differentiated legal status cf. *infra*, Ch. 4, p. 155 *et seq.*

This decision in favour of a two-level organisational structure was certainly influenced by the fact that most of the provisions related to the ESCB were drafted by the Committee of Governors, an advisory body of the Community which was composed of the governors of the national central banks of the Member States.[18] The maintenance of the national central banks inside the ESCB was seen as an opportunity to found the new system on the experience, the traditions and the reputation of the national central banks some of which (like Sveriges Riksbank, founded in 1668, or the Bank of England, founded in 1694) belong to the oldest central banks in the world.[19] In addition, the drafters of the EC Treaty and the Statute could also point to one very successful precedent for a central bank with a two-level organisational structure: to the Federal Reserve System of the United States, the famous Fed, which comprises the Board of Governors in Washington and 12 Federal Reserve Banks.

2. The ECB as governor of the ESCB

Despite the fact that the ESCB is a two-level organisation, with the ECB level and the level of the national central banks, it is somewhat misleading to call it a "federal" system,[20] as this would associate the organisational structure of the

[18] The Committee of Governors was already established in 1964 by Council Decision 64/300/EEC of 8 May 1964 on co-operation between the Central Banks of the Member States of the European Economic Community [1964] OJ 77/1206. Its consultative functions were extended in 1990, in parallel with the start of the first stage of EMU, by Council Decision 90/142/EEC of 12 March 1990 amending Council Decision 64/300/EEC on co-operation between the central banks of the Member States of the European Economic Community [1999] OJ L78/25. On 1 January 1994, the starting date of the second stage, the Committee was dissolved and replaced by the European Monetary Institute, the predecessor of the ECB; cf. Art. 109f(1) EC (as it was prior to the Amsterdam amendments). On the influence of the Committee of Governors on the contents of the Statute of the ESCB, see Sandholtz, "Monetary Bargains: The Treaty on EMU" in Cafruny and Rosenthal (eds.), *The State of the European Community: the Maastricht Debates and Beyond* (Harlow, 1993), 125 (128). A further argument for keeping the national central banks was probably also the cost which their dissolution would have caused; cf., as a parallel, Art. 38(2) of the Bundesbank Act which required the German federation to indemnify the *Länder* when their central banks were merged to become the Bundesbank.

[19] Cf. the Commission's communiqué on EMU of 21 August 1990, SEC(90)1659, para. 2.1 which refers to the nature of the Community and the long experience of the national central banks as justification for a two-level organisation comprising both the ECB and the national central banks.

[20] Cf. Lagayette, "Répartition des rôles au sein du SEBC", *Aujourd'hui l'écu/The ecu today*, special edn., June 1992, 4: "*Pourquoi le traité a-t-il prévu un système et non pas une banque centrale unique? Le principe fédératif sous-tend l'architecture institutionnelle de l'union économique et monétaire*"; D. Gros, "Mehr Gewicht für die Europäische Zentralbank", *Frankfurter Allgemeine Zeitung*, 2 May 1998, 15, even calls the structure of the ECB "extremely federal"; cf. also M. Weber, "Das Europäische System der Zentralbanken" [1998] *WM* 1465 (1472), who calls the inclusion of the national central banks in the ESCB "*bundesstaatsähnlich-föderativ*" and therefore often describes the ESCB's organisational structure by analogy to the German federal system. Similar terminology is used by Gnan in Von der Groeben, Thiesing and Ehlermann (eds.), *Kommentar zum EU-/EG-Vertrag* (5th edn., Baden Baden, 1999), nach Art. 109 m, Satzung ESZB und EZB Artikel 14, para. 9: "*föderalistische Lösung*". The position of Louis is ambivalent; cf. "A Legal and Institutional Approach for Building a Monetary Union" (1998) *CML Rev.* 33, where he writes at 50: "The ESCB has been conceived as a federal and decentralised system", but then states, at 51, that the ECB and the national central banks "effectively appear as levels within a hierarchy".

ESCB with that of federal states. Apart from the fact that it is quite daring to compare a sectoral organisation limited to very special tasks and functions with a state, it has to be taken into account that federalism, despite its many faces in federal states throughout the world,[21] has a very specific legal meaning which cannot simply be transferred one to one to the organisational structure of a central banking system.

2.1. The division of powers in federal States

To call the organisational structure of a state a federal one presupposes not only a two-level organisation, but also a true division of powers between these two levels.[22] From a legal point of view, the federal nature of a state is maintained only if both the federal level and the level of its component entities (be they called provinces, cantons, communities, regions, states, or *Länder*) have substantial powers in the field both of decision-making, in particular legislation, and of the implementation of such decisions. This comes from the fact that component entities in a federal state are also legally seen as states,[23] and thus have their own legislature and administration which very often are even older than the federal state itself.[24]

Therefore, both the federation and the component entities in a federal state perform legislative and executive tasks, not as tasks *delegated* to them by the federal level of governance, but as *autonomous* tasks which belong to them by

---

[21] An extensive analysis, taking into account features of federalism in the United States, Switzerland, Canada, Belgium, Spain, and in the European Community is made by Lenaerts, "Constitutionalism and the Many Faces of Federalism" (1990) *Am. J Comp.L* 204.

[22] Cf. the decision of the Austrian Constitutional Court [1952] ccR 2455. The Constitutional Court, after a comparative review of other federal constitutions, considered that it is a typical characteristic, to be found in all federal constitutions, that the functions of the state are divided between the federal level and the level of the component entities. The same conclusion is reached by Lenaerts, *supra*, n. 21, 206 who states that federalism is characterised by "the respect of the powers of the component entities", even in the case of a "devolutionary federalism" where the component entities receive, in the course of devolution, "an autonomous status within their field of responsibility". Such a federal devolution must, however, be carefully distinguished from (unitary) devolution; cf. *infra*, n. 42.

[23] This is very clearly stated in Art. 3 of the Swiss Federal Constitution of 1999: "The *Cantons* are sovereign insofar as their sovereignty is not limited by the federal Constitution". It is also stressed by the German Federal Constitutional Court in its judgment of 23 October 1951, *Constitutional Court Reports, vol. 1*, 14 (34): "*Die Länder sind als Glieder des Bundes Staaten mit eigener wenn auch gegenständlich beschränkter nicht vom Bund abgeleiteter, sondern von ihm anerkannter staatlicher Hoheitsmacht*". Because of the statehood of the component entities of a federal state, the constitutions of a number of federal states provide that not only the federal state as such, but also the component entities themselves are entitled to conclude international agreements with third countries; cf. Art. 51 of the Swiss Federal Constitution of 1999; Art. 32(3) of the German Basic Law of 1949; Art. 16 of the Austrian Federal Constitutional Act of 1920; Art. 127(1), No 3 and Art. 167(1) of the Belgium Constitution of 1994. Only the US Constitution of 1787 prohibits agreements concluded by the federal states; cf. its Art. I, section 10(1): "No State shall enter into any Treaty, Alliance or Confederation".

[24] Wagenhöfer, *supra*, n. 6, 98 considers therefore as characteristic of federalism that there is a plurality of those institutions which take final decisions.

virtue of their own statehood and of which they cannot be deprived.[25] There is thus *no hierarchy* between the different levels of governance.[26] In the United States this idea of a non-hierarchical balance between the two levels of governance requires that legislation is, as a matter of principle, implemented by the level of government which is responsible for its enactment. A duty of the states to implement federal legislation is seen, under the US Constitution, as being contrary to the states' integrity.[27] Less restrictive in this respect are the German and the Austrian federal systems. They allow for a so-called *"Vollzugsföderalismus"* (federalism in the execution of laws, or implementing federalism)[28] which makes it even a general rule that federal legislation is implemented through the federal state's component entities. To reflect nevertheless the autonomous legal status of the component entities, such implementation of federal legislation is, in German and Austrian constitutional law, always considered to be competence of the component entities for which they alone bear the responsibility and the risk of liability towards third parties, even where such implementation is exceptionally subject to instructions issued by the federal government.[29] Incompatible with the principles of federal organisation would,

[25] Cf. the German Federal Constitutional Court in its judgment of 26 July 1972, *Constitutional Court Reports*, vol. 36, 9 (19 *et seq.*): "*Die 'Länder' sind hier, wie es dem Begriff und der Qualität des Bundestaates entspricht, gegen eine Verfassungsänderung gesichert, durch die sie die Qualität von Staaten oder ein Essentiale der Staatlichkeit einbüßen. Ob die Länder der Bundesrepublik 'Staaten' sind oder von Körperschaften 'am Rande der Staatlichkeit' zu 'höchstpotenzierten Gebietskörperschaften' in einem dezentralisierten Einheitsstaat herabsinken, läßt sich nicht formal danach bestimmen, daß sie eine eigene Verfassung haben und daß sie über irgendein Stück vom Gesamtstaat unabgeleiteter Hoheitsmacht verfügen, also irgendeinen Rest von Gesetzgebungszuständigkeit, Verwaltungszuständigkeit und justizieller Zuständigkeit ihr eigen nennen. Die Länder im Bundesstaat sind nur dann Staaten, wenn ihnen ein Kern eigener Aufgaben als 'Hausgut' unentziehbar verbleibt.*"

[26] Cf. Pernthaler, *Der differenzierte Bundesstaat* (Vienna, 1992), 9 *et seq.* who considers *Bund* and *Länder* in Austria to be equal partners; this view is shared, as regards the relationship between Swiss cantons and the Swiss federation, by Kölz, "Bundestreue als Verfassungsprinzip?" [1980] *Schweizer Zentralblatt für Staats- und Gemeindeverwaltung* 145. As regards Canadian federalism, cf. Lenaerts, *supra*, n. 21, 238, who considers it decisive that customary constitutional law there recognises the provinces as "autonomous political powers, acting besides and not under the central government". Lenaerts, *supra*, n. 21, 241, also notes that in Belgium the legislatures of the Regions and the Communities "are deemed to stand at the same normative level as the national Parliament for those matters belonging to their sphere of competence".

[27] The absence of such an "executive federalism" is explained by Lenaerts, *supra*, n. 21, 231, with reference to the case law of the Supreme Court: "The main reason for these doubts is that both the federal and the State governments should bear themselves the entire political responsibility for their acts, when facing the electorate; it would therefore be unacceptable to oblige a State to pass legislation which they did not freely decide upon, but for which the voters may hold their elected officials politically accountable".

[28] Cf. Frowein, "Integration in the Federal Experience in Germany and in Switzerland" in Cappelletti, Seccombe and Weiler (eds.), *Integration Through Law: Europe and the American Federal Experience* (Berlin, 1986), 586 *et seq.*

[29] Even in this case, there is no hierarchy, but a clear division of powers between the federal level, which enjoys a substantive competence ("*Sachkompetenz*"), and the level of the component entities, which possess an autonomous competence for implementation ("*Wahrnehmungskompetenz*"), of which they cannot be deprived; cf. the German Federal Constitutional Court's judgment of 22 May 1990, *Constitutional Court Reports*, vol. 81, 310 (331). On the *sui generis* nature of the implementation of Community law through the Member States cf. *infra*, Ch. 3, p 113 *et seq.*

however, be a mere implementing federalism, i.e. an organisational structure in which decision-making powers are entrusted exclusively to the federal level, while only implementing powers are left to the component entities.[30] This would neglect the fact that the component entities also possess autonomous legislative competences and would transform them into mere implementing agencies of the federation.

In all federal states, the way autonomous legislative and implementing powers are distributed among the different levels of government is governed by *the principle of subsidiarity*, the constitutional *Leitmotiv* of federalism.[31] This is also true for the Community legal system[32] where Article 5(2) EC makes it a general principle of Community law. Subsidiarity is a hotly disputed concept as it is interpreted by many people very differently depending on their respective backgrounds and origins.[33] It is certainly not a "magic formula", but a rather simple idea which is expressed very well in Encyclical Quadragesimo Anno of 15 May 1931 according to which "it is an injustice, a grave evil and a disturbance of the right order, for a larger and higher association to arrogate itself functions which can be performed more efficiently by smaller and lower societies". This quotation shows that subsidiarity presupposes, in an organisational system, the existence of different organisational levels with own powers, and establishes the rule that tasks should always be dealt with at the lowest possible level which can reach the aim of a measure in an efficient manner. Subsidiarity is thus a concept closely related to the principle of effectiveness and thus can justify both centralised and decentralised action in a federal system. Only where there are several levels of government which are able to achieve the result envisaged *in an equally efficient manner* does subsidiarity contain a presumption in favour of the lowest of these levels. In this sense, the concept of subsidiarity points to the real objective behind federalist structures, which is not so much the maintenance of regional disparities, but rather the introduction of a new degree of vertical division of powers in a state between equally efficient levels of

---

[30] On the debate of the 1970s on introducing such a model into federal Austria, see Novak, "Ist ein 'Vollzugsföderalismus' noch föderalistisch?" in Novak, Sutter and Hasiba (eds.), *Föderalismus-Studien*, vol. 1: *Historische und aktuelle Probleme des Föderalismus in Österreich* (Vienna/Cologne/Graz, 1977), 27.

[31] On this, see S. Cassese, "L'aquila e le mosche. Principio di sussidiarietà e diritti amministrativi nell'area europea" [1995] *Il Foro Italiano* 375; Constantinesco, "Who's Afraid of Subsidiarity?" [1991] *YEL* 33; Peterson,"Subsidiarity: A Definition to Suit Any Vision?" [1994] *Parliamentary Affairs*, 116; Schweitzer and Fixson,"Subsidiarität und Regionalismus in der EG" [1992] *Jura* 579.

[32] On federalism in the EU cf. Lenaerts, "Federalism: Essential Concepts in Evolution—The Case of the European Union"[1998] *Fordham Int. LJ* 747. On subsidiarity in the EC, cf. Lenaerts and van Ypersele, "Le principe de subsidiarité et son contexte: étude de l'art. 3 B du Traité CE" [1994] *CDE* 3; Zilioli, "L'applicazione del principio di sussidiarietà nel diritto comunitario dell'ambient" [1993] *Rivista Giuridica dell'Ambiente* 533.

[33] As the French politician, Jean-Pierre Cot, put it, only subsidiarity could manage to "put Delors perfectly in tune with Mrs Thatcher . . . on a misunderstanding", quoted by Peterson, *supra*, n. 31, 117. Cf. also Cassese, *supra*, n. 31, 375, who notes the remarkably divergent use of the concept of subsidiarity.

governance and thus the protection of the individual against an accumulation of power or even totalitarism by a state organisation.[34]

One should be aware of the fact that subsidiarity, as a general legal principle, operates in various ways in federal organisational structures.[35] First of all, it is the decisive legal criterion for the drafters of a federal constitution when they have to decide to which level to allocate legislative and executive competences. This application of subsidiarity in the making of a constitution ("constitutional subsidiarity") may lead to entrenching a number of competences as exclusive competences of either the federal level or that of the component entities already in the constitutional charter, for example, to entrust defence solely to the federation, while education and environment are reserved to the lower entities.[36] This "constitutional subsidiarity" best protects the autonomous position of all levels of governance within a federal state, as it reserves some competences for each of them in a way which can be modified only through an amendment of the constitution, if such an amendment is not even completely excluded by the constitution itself.[37]

However, it will normally not be possible to distribute all competences once and for all in the constitution. In view of the need to react flexibly to forthcoming events, the constitution will therefore foresee not only exclusive competences of the different levels of governance, but also so-called concurrent competences which belong both to the federal level and to that of the component entities. In this case, the need for a specific measure will determine the level at which such a measure will be decided and implemented; as long as the federal level has not taken a decision, the component entities remain competent to act themselves. In fields of concurrent competence, it will therefore be for the legislator and the executive, at a given moment in time, to justify, again in accordance with the principle of subsidiarity, that there are efficiency reasons which require federal action. To give guidance to such decisions, subsidiarity is,

[34] On this vertical division of powers in a federal state cf. Stein, *Staatsrecht* (14th edn., Tübingen, 1993), 119; cf. also Lenaerts, *supra*, n. 32, 749: "balance of sovereignty between the central authority and the component entities as a way of constituting a system of limited government based on the rule of law".

[35] On the need to distinguish carefully between subsidiarity as a constitutional, a legislative, and an administrative principle cf. Cassese, *supra*, n. 31, 376.

[36] Cf. Art. 30 of the German Basic Law of 1949: "The exercise of governmental power and the discharge of governmental functions shall be incumbent on the *Länder* in so far as this basic law does not otherwise prescribe or permit". The United States constitution's 10th Amendment asserts: "The powers not delegated to the United States by the Constitution, nor prohibited by it to the States, are reserved to the States respectively, or to the people". Art.15(1) of the Austrian Federal Constitutional Act of 1920 reserves all competences which have not been expressly attributed to the federal level to the *Länder*.

[37] In the Federal Republic of Germany and in Austria, the existence of core legislative and executive competences of the component entities is considered to be such a key concept that it forms part of those constitutional principles where the constitution itself rules out an amendment. Cf. Art. 79(3) of the German Basic Law of 1949 and the Federal Constitutional Court's judgment of 26 July 1972, *supra*, n. 25: "*unentziehbares 'Hausgut'*"; a similar interpretation is given to Art. 44(3) of the Austrian Federal Constitutional Act of 1920; cf. Pernthaler, *supra*, n. 26), 5 *et seq.*: "*Länder als 'historische Individualitäten' und 'unzerstörbare Staaten'*".

as a governing principle, written down in the constitution.[38] When this written principle of subsidiarity is applied, it can be distinguished into *"legislative subsidiarity"*, whenever the decision-making process is concerned, and into *"subsidiarity in implementation"*, whenever it relates to the appropriate level of implementation.[39] Of course, there is no room for these dynamic types of subsidiarity in cases where the constitution itself has already established exclusive competences for the federal level of governance or for the component entities. Constitutional subsidiarity thus always takes precedence over, and excludes, legislative subsidiarity or subsidiarity in implementation.[40]

The division of powers in federal states can thus be clearly distinguished from the organisational system of unitary states like France or the United Kingdom. Legislative and executive competences in these countries are governed by the idea of the indivisibility of both legislative and executive power.[41] Even though such unitary states rely often on sub-entities like *départements*, administrative regions, or local government for the execution of public tasks, these sub-entities do not possess competences of which they cannot be deprived. All their competences are only *delegated* to them by the state's central legislature or by central government and therefore may be taken back at any time whenever the centre so wishes.[42] This shows that a two-level organisation does not suffice to make an organisational system a federal one.[43] Academic writers therefore carefully avoid federally inspired terminology when they characterise the relationship

[38] This element of subsidiarity is inherent in Art. 72(2) of the German Basic Law of 1949, which allows the federation to legislate in fields of concurrent competence solely if and in so far it is necessary in the interest of the whole state to guarantee equivalent living conditions or the maintenance of the legal and economic unity. The legal quality of this principle is stressed by the availability of a specific action by which the federal chamber of Parliament, every *Land* Government and every *Land* Parliament could challenge federal legislation for violation of that principle at the Federal Constitutional Court; cf. Art. 93(1), No 2a of the German Basic Law of 1949.

[39] According to Cassese, *supra*, n. 31, 377, subsidiarity in implementation will become in practice the most relevant field of application of the principle of subsidiarity.

[40] This is made crystal clear in Art. 5(2) EC where the principle of subsidiarity law is said to apply, as regards the Community, solely "in areas which do not fall within its exclusive competence". See also Art. 72(2) of the German Basic Law of 1949 which applies only to concurrent competences.

[41] Cf. Art. 2 of the French Constitution of 1958: *"La France est une République indivisible"*. On the limits set by this sentence to all projects of decentralisation cf. Luchaire and Conac, *"La constitution de la république française"* (2nd edn., Paris, 1987), 130 *et seq*.: *"La collectivité inférieure doit tenir ses compétences de l'Etat et celui-ci doit toujours pouvoirs les modifier ou les reprendre"*.

[42] This is particularly true for the model of two-level government used in the UK, which is called (unitary) devolution. See the Report of the Royal Commission on the Constitution 1969–1973 (Kilbrandon Report), which defined "devolution", in para. 543, as "the delegation of government power without relinquishing sovereignty". An example of such devolution was the Government of Ireland Act 1920 under which, in order to solve the Irish question, a number of legislative and executive powers were delegated to Northern Ireland and a Parliament and an executive body were established in Stormont, near Belfast. However, as a reaction to the civil disturbances at the end of the 1960s, Parliament in Westminster demonstrated its omnicompetence by resuming direct rule over Northern Ireland in 1972 and by dissolving the Northern Ireland Parliament and its executive body by a new Act of Parliament; on this, cf. Munro, *Studies in Constitutional Law* (London, 1987), 22 *et seq*. Recent devolution to Scotland and Wales is again a reversible step; cf. section 28(7) of the Scotland Act 1998.

between the centre and the regional or local sub-entities in unitary states, which they describe, not as true federal decentralisation, but as *déconcentration*.[44] The technique of *déconcentration* is today used in most unitary states, but also in large companies, to delegate some tasks from the centre to administrative sub-entities which operate locally and thus help to achieve the efficient implementation of the decisions taken by the centre. But with the exception of the two-level organisational structure thereby established, such organisational systems have nothing in common with the truly decentralised structure of a federal state[45] which is characterised by the existence of autonomous legislative and implementing powers at all levels of government, the attribution of which is entrenched by means of constitutional law and the exercise of which follows the principle of subsidiarity, as regards both decision-making and the implementation of such decisions.

2.2. The model chosen for the division of powers inside the ESCB

Against this background, can one really call the ESCB a "federal" system? It is true that, as in a federal state, there are two organisational levels within the ESCB, that of the ECB and that of the national central banks. But do both levels possess autonomous decision-making and implementing powers?

At a first and very superficial glance, one could be inclined to deduce such a federal structure from Article 105(2) EC and Article 3.1 of the Statute which list the core tasks of the new central banking organisation, in particular the definition and implementation of the monetary policy of the Community (Article 105(2), first indent EC). These tasks are said "to be carried out through the ESCB". Neither Article 105(2) EC nor Article 3(1) of the Statute specifies at which ESCB level decision-making and implementation shall take place. One could be tempted to take this to mean that all these tasks were concurrent competences of the ECB and the national central banks[46] and would have to be allocated inside the ESCB in accordance with the principle of subsidiarity.[47] This

---

[43] Cf. von Bogdandy, "Die Europäische Union als einheitlicher Verband" [1998] *EuR* 165 (177 *et seq.*): "*Eine dezentralisierte Organization liegt bei der organisatorischen Verselbständigung von Entscheidungsbefugnissen vor; verlangt ist die Delegation von Entscheidungsmacht, spricht Kompetenzen, auf Teile des Systems . . . Die schlichte Konzeption unterschiedlicher Rechtspersönlichkeiten allein führt nicht zur Dezentralisierung*".

[44] This is the terminology of French administrative law; see Guillien and Vincent, *Lexique de termes juridiques*, Centralisation (8th edn., Paris, 1990). Some writers also talk in this case of "administrative decentralisation", which they however carefully distinguish from so-called "independent decentralisation", as used in federal systems; cf. Peters, *Lehrbuch der Verwaltung* (Berlin, 1949), 46.

[45] On the necessary legal distinction between "*déconcentration*" and truly federal "decentralisation", cf. Wagenhöfer, *supra*, n. 6, 99.

[46] In this sense see Kral and Kurm-Engels and Gros, *supra*, n. 5.

[47] The application of the principle of subsidiarity to the ESCB is suggested in particular by authors with a national central bank background: cf. Aspetsberger and Schubert, "Möglichkeiten und Grenzen der Subsidiarität in einer Europäischen Währungsunion", *Berichte und Studien der Oesterreichischen Nationalbank* (1993), 110 (113 *et seq.*); Lagayette: "In Maastricht Subsidiarität vereinbart", *Deutsche Bundesbank, Auszüge aus Presseartikeln*, No 22 of 20 March 1992. In the

could mean that all tasks entrusted to the ESCB under Article 105(2) EC should, as a rule, be dealt with at the lowest possible level, thus at the level of the national central banks, and that the ECB would always need to prove efficiency reasons to centralise the decision-making and the implementation process in a specific field. But is this really the organisational structure chosen for the ESCB?

The question of the division of competences inside the ESCB was of course intensively discussed during the negotiations on the EC Treaty and the Statute provisions related to the ESCB. After the decision had been taken not to merge the national central banks into a unitary structure, but to establish a multi-level system, essentially two alternative models for the organisational structure of the ESCB were discussed in the negotiations:

—As *Model 1*, it was suggested to give the ESCB as such legal personality and/or to attribute to it its own decision-making bodies, a Governing Council and an Executive Board.[48] These would thus have been the joint decision-making bodies of the ESCB as a whole. Inside the system, the ECB and the national central banks would have represented two alternative—and hierarchically equal—levels for the fulfilment of the tasks entrusted to the ESCB. Such coexistence of the ECB and the national central banks inside the ESCB would have resembled the division of powers in a federal state.

—*Model 2* intended to establish a hierarchy between the two organisational levels inside the ESCB. Not the ESCB, but only the ECB should be given legal personality and decision-making bodies. Decision-making inside the ESCB should be centralised in the hands of the decision-making bodies of the ECB. In this model, only the implementation of decisions could take place alternatively at the ECB level or at the level of the national central banks.

Both the EC Treaty and the Statute demonstrate that their drafters opted in the end, and without any reservations and compromises, in favour of the second model.[49] This is reflected, first of all, very clearly by Article 107(2) EC and Article 9.1 of the Statute which attribute legal personality to the ECB, but not to the ESCB. The ESCB is thus just the common roof for the joint existence of the ECB and the national central banks in a system with common principles and

---

same direction see Remsperger (now chief economist of the Bundesbank), "Subsidiarität in der Zentralbankpolitik: Erfahrungen und Perspektiven" in Filc and Köhler (eds.), *Integration und Desintegration der Weltwirtschaft?* (Berlin, 1994), 13.

[48] The Delors Report, at para. 31, thus suggested an "ECBS Council" and an "ECBS Executive Board" to reflect the federal structure of the "European Central Banking System (ECBS)" originally envisaged; cf. *Report on Economic and Monetary Union in the European Community* (Office for Official Publications of the European Communities, Luxembourg, 1989). Cf. also Hahn, "Europe: A Single Currency and A Single Central Bank?" [1990] *Michigan J Int. L* 121 (133) who wrote, in parallel to the negotiations in 1990, about the envisaged "ESCB Council" and "ESCB Directorate".

[49] On the debate about a one-, two- or even three-level organisation of the ESCB cf. Stadler, *Der rechtliche Handlungsspielraum des Europäischen Systems der Zentralbanken* (Baden Baden, 1996), 98 *et seq.* who considers it decisive that the ESCB was denied legal personality.

Model 1: The ESCB as governor of the System (not put into practice)

Model 2: The ECB as governor of the System (as provided for by the EC Treaty and the Statute)

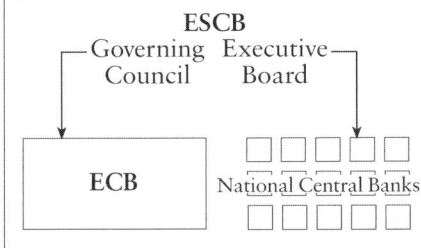
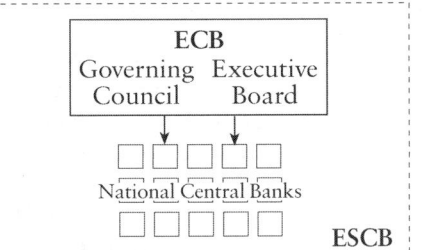

Fig. 2 *The governance of the ESCB—myth and legal reality*

common rules.[50] This resembles to a certain extent the institutional structure of the European Union itself, which has no legal personality, but provides a framework within which the three Communities and the 15 Member States operate, following common principles and objectives.

The choice of the second model is further confirmed by Article 107(3) EC which states that "the ESCB shall be governed by the decision-making bodies of the ECB which shall be the Governing Council and the Executive Board". This rule, which is repeated in Article 8 of the Statute as a "general principle", clarifies that the Governing Council and the Executive Board are decision-making bodies *of the ECB*, and not of the ESCB.[51] Within the two-level organisation of the ESCB, the EC Treaty thus has made the ECB the central organisation of the system and has allocated unequivocally the responsibility for all decision-making to the higher level of governance.[52]

---

[50] The same view is taken by Hahn, *Der Vertrag von Maastricht als völkerrechtliche Übereinkunft und Verfassung* (Baden Baden, 1992), 69; Nicolaysen, *Rechtsfragen der Währungsunion* (Berlin/New York, 1993), 26; Stadler, *supra*, n. 49, 88 *et seq.* Cf. also Louis in *Commentaire Mégret. Le Droit de la CEE* (2nd edn., Brussels, 1998), 56, who refers to the Commentary of the Committee of Governors on the Draft Statute of the European System of Central Banks and of the European Central Bank, which says: "The term 'System' should be understood to describe the existence of the ECB and the national central banks as integral parts of the System, governed by a common set of rules and committed to the objectives and tasks assigned to it". Cf. also ECB, "The institutional framework of the European System of Central Banks", *Monthly Bulletin* (Frankfurt am Main, July 1999), 55.

[51] Cf. also Art. 237(d) EC which speaks of the Governing Council as "Council of the ECB". The German text of the EC Treaty always uses *"EZB-Rat"* for the Governing Council of the ECB. It is thus intentionally misleading when Seidel, "Im Kompetenzkonflikt: Europäisches System der Zentralbanken (ESZB) versus EZB" [2000] *EuZW* 552 (552) still avoids this term and instead speaks of a "Gouverneursrat" or "Rat der Zentralbankpräsidenten", to demonstrate the "dominance" of the national central banks in the ESCB.

[52] It is also the ECB which decides how the ESCB shall be represented in the field of international monetary co-operation; cf. Art. 6.1 of the Statute. National central banks may participate in international monetary institutions only subject to the ECB's approval; cf. Art. 6.2 of the Statute; on this see Ch. 5, *infra*, p. 176 *et seq.*

The legal enforcement of the requirements of the EC Treaty and the Statute and of the ECB's decisions is also centralised in the hands of the ECB. Article 237(d) EC[53] allows the ECB to start infringement proceedings against a national central bank, a procedure paralleling infringement proceedings started by the Commission against Member States under Article 226 EC. However, while the Member States are also entitled to start infringement proceedings against each other under Article 227 EC, proceedings among national central banks are foreseen neither by the EC Treaty nor by the Statute. This shows that the responsibility for enforcing the Community law applicable to the component parts of the ESCB lies solely with the ECB.

The governance by the decision-making bodies of the ECB over the ESCB even extends to the implementation level.[54] This is stressed by Article 9.2 of the Statute which states that it shall be the ECB which ensures that the tasks entrusted to the ESCB are implemented, either by the ECB's own activities or through the national central banks. It is thus exclusively up to the ECB to decide whether to implement its decisions itself or indirectly by having recourse to the national central banks.[55] In this sense, the EC Treaty goes even further than a mere *"Vollzugsföderalismus"* ("implementing federalism"), as even if the ECB decided that implementation always had to take place through the national central banks, such implementation would not be a task of the national central banks, but only a task *delegated* to them by the decision of the ECB under Article 9.2 of the Statute; the power to implement could thus at any time be claimed back by the decision-making bodies of the ECB.[56]

The exercise of delegated tasks implies that inside the ESCB the national central banks are legally subordinated to the ECB and its decision-making bodies. This is confirmed by Article 14.3 of the Statute which provides that the national central banks are "an integral part of the ESCB" and that they "shall act in accordance with the guidelines and instructions of the ECB". Inside the ESCB, the national central banks are thus not partners on an equal footing with the ECB,[57] but they are conceived, by primary Community law itself, to act as the *operating arms* of the ECB[58] and to follow its instructions.[59] Such a hierarchical

---

[53] Cf. also Art. 35.6 of the Statute.

[54] According to the ECJ, the Community law concept of implementation "comprises both the drawing up of implementing rules and the application of rules to specific cases by means of acts of individual application"; cf. Case 16/88, *Commission* v. *Council* [1989] ECR 3457, para. 11.

[55] On the meaning of Arts. 5.2 and 12.1 of the Statute for the implementation of the ESCB's tasks and on the limitations of these provisions, see *infra*, Ch. 3, p. 116 *et seq.*

[56] This is not taken into account by Aspetsberger and Schubert, *supra*, n. 47, 113, according to whom the ESCB resembles the Austrian model of *"Vollzugsföderalismus"*. More cautious is the comparison with the model of *"Vollzugsföderalismus"* made by A. Weber, "Die Wirtschafts- und Währungsunion nach dem Maastricht-Urteil des BVerfG" [1994] *JZ* 53 (59).

[57] This is also the position of Potacs, "Nationale Zentralbanken in der Wirtschafts- und Währungsunion" [1993] *EuR* 31 (40).

[58] Cf. Sauerzopf and Selmayr, "Das Europäische System der Zentralbanken als Hüter eines stabilen Euro" [1998] *Der Wirtschaftstreuhänder* 12 (14); Smits, *The European Central Bank. Institutional Aspects* (The Hague/London/Boston, 1997), 94.

[59] This view is not shared by von Hagen, "Die EZB ist keine Superbundesbank", *Vereinigte*

organisation[60] is not compatible with federal systems. While in federal states decision-making and implementing powers are divided between the two levels of governance by the constitution, the EC Treaty and the Statute prescribe that inside the ESCB there shall be only one decision-making level, that of the ECB. By their integration into the ESCB, the national central banks have been deprived of the very essence of a central bank's task: to take monetary policy decisions and to decide on their implementation.[61] The ESCB's organisational structure is thus one of *decisional centralism*.[62]

It is easy to understand why the drafters of the EC Treaty and of the Statute in the end[63] opted in favour of such a centralised model. Even though the members of the Committee of Governors were certainly keen on reserving some competences to the national central banks within the ESCB, they all knew, as experienced central bankers, about the indivisibility of monetary policy. They were certainly aware of the ultimate goal of Monetary Union which was to establish a *single* currency and a *single* monetary policy, as is stated today explicitly in Article 4(2) EC. They also knew that, historically speaking, decentralised structures for decision-making and implementation had always been

---

Wirtschaftsdienste, 11 August 1998, who considers Art. 14.3 of the Statute to be nothing more than "*bloße Absichtserklärung*". However, he provides no argument why in this particular case primary Community law should be deprived of the legally binding effect it always enjoys.

[60] Louis, *supra*, n. 20, 51 describes ECB and NCB as "levels within a hierarchy". Smits, *supra*, n. 58, 94 speaks of "a clear line of command" within the system. Stadler, *supra*, n. 49, 156, calls the national central banks the recipients of orders ("*Befehlsempfänger*") of the ECB. According to Weinbörner, *Die Stellung der Europäischen Zentralbank (EZB) und der nationalen Zentralbanken in der Wirtschafts- und Währungsunion nach dem Vertrag von Maastricht* (Frankfurt am Main, 1998), 388, the ESCB is a two-level organisation characterised by "hierarchy and subordination". Cf. also Zilioli in Von der Groeben, Thiesing and Ehlermann (eds.), *supra*, n. 20, nach Art. 109 m, Satzung ESZB und EZB Artikel 12, para. 32. Hahn goes even further, *supra*, n. 50, 74, according to whom the national central banks have been "functionally and substantially deprived of their powers" inside the ESCB.

[61] In the terminology of the German Federal Constitutional Court, one could say that the "*Hausgut*" of the national central banks has been transferred irrevocably to the ECB and that they thus have lost their character as central banks. This is not yet always understood at the national level, as Giavazzi observes in "Il banchiere debole di Francoforte", *Corriere della Sera*, 29 October 1998: "*Le banche centrali nazionali, impegnate in una difesa dei loro vecchi privilegi, non hanno mai accettato che la guida della politica monetaria venisse trasferita alla Bce*".

[62] This is acknowledged by the President of the Austrian National Bank Liebscher in his speech, "Die Rolle einer nationalen Zentralbank im ESZB am Beispiel der OeNB" (1998), published on the Internet at http://www.oenb.co.at/tagung/refer17.htm: "*Die grundlegende Philosophie bei der Organization des ESZB ist, daß die Entscheidungen zentral bei der EZB getroffen werden*".

[63] Only few traces of the original controversy surrounding the organisational structure of the ESCB can today still be identified in the Treaty. Art. 8 EC says that both the ESCB *and* the ECB "shall *act* within the limits of the powers conferred upon *them* by the Treaty", and Art. 105(1), third sentence EC provides that "the ESCB shall *act* in accordance with the principle of an open market economy with free competition". It seems that the wording in particular of the first of these provisions has not been harmonised with the decision in favour of Model 2, as in law powers can be conferred only on legal persons or on their institutions, and only these are able to act in a legal sense. However, such traces in the Treaty are only regrettable for purists of legal drafting. In the light of the general scheme of the Treaty, in particular of the clear rules laid down in Art. 107(3) and in Arts. 8, 9.2 and 14.3 of the Statute, there can be no doubt today about the hierarchical structure of the ESCB.

inefficient or at least extremely problematic in a central banking context, as had been demonstrated by the two most known decentralised experiments in this field[64]:

—The first decentralised experiment was undertaken in the early years of the *Federal Reserve System of the United States of America* which originally had left a number of autonomous decision-making and all implementing powers to the Federal reserve banks. At that time, the individual Federal reserve banks controlled their own discount policies,[65] were competent to conduct security sales and purchases and could decline to participate in open market purchases recommended by the Board in Washington, the Fed's central institution.[66] The Federal reserve banks also assumed the competences to conclude international agreements with foreign central banks, as is shown by the agreement concluded in 1930 between the Federal Reserve Bank of New York, the German Reichsbank, Banque de France and the Bank of England on a reduction of the discount rate of the Federal reserve bank of New York, which was signed without even consulting the Board in Washington.[67] This unusual degree of decentralisation was identified by a number of economists as decisive for the failure of the "Fed" to cope with the Great Depression[68]— a negative experience which later led to a complete centralisation of the decision-making process inside the Fed in the hands of the Board of Governors and of what is today the Federal Open Market Committee, a decision-making body located at the central level of the system which now takes all decisions on interest rates.[69]

[64] As a further example of such "decentralised experiments", one could mention the historic case of a newly established state which succeeded to several previous ones, each equipped with a central bank. For practical reasons, these central banks were allowed for a while to maintain their powers, at the time mainly the one of issuing banknotes. However, very soon this "decentralised" approach was terminated for efficiency reasons by the establishment of only one central bank, corresponding to the one unitary state. On the case of Italy, cf. Mazzaferro, "Unity through Diversity. Banknotes and coins in the European Monetary Union", *ECU Newsletter,* June 1992, 29; Vanthoor, *European Monetary Union since 1948—A Political Historical Analysis* (Cheltenham, 1996), 17; Sannucci, "The Establishment of a Central Bank: Italy in the Nineteenth Century" in De Cecco (ed.), *A European Central Bank?* (Cambridge, 1988), 244; Hertner, "Modern Banking in Italy" in Pohl (ed.), *Handbook on the History of European Banks* (Hants, 1994), 561.

[65] The Federal Reserve Act 1913 stated: "Every Federal reserve bank shall have the power to establish from time to time, subject to review and determination of the Federal Reserve Board, rates of discount to be charged by the Federal reserve banks for each class of paper, which shall be fixed with a view of accommodating commerce and business".

[66] This division of decision-making powers inside the early Fed is also noted by Gleske, *supra,* n. 7, 127.

[67] Cf. Eichengreen, "Designing a Central Bank for Europe: A Cautionary Tale from the Early Years of the Federal Reserve System" in Canzoneri (ed.), *Establishing a Central Bank: Issues in Europe and Lessons from the US* (Cambridge, 1992), 13 (26).

[68] Cf. Eichengreen, *supra,* n. 67, 26 *et seq.*

[69] Therefore, Hasse, *Die Europäische Zentralbank. Perspektiven für eine Weiterentwicklung des Europäischen Währungssystems* (Gütersloh, 1989), 163, rightly calls the Federal Reserve System a uniform central banking system with centralised monetary decision-making. The same view is taken by Wagenhöfer, *supra,* n. 6, according to whom the "Fed" is not a truly federal system; he points to a source of terminological misunderstanding that to call an authority "federal" in the United States

—The second example of a decentralised central banking structure was that of the *Bank of German States ("Bank deutscher Länder")*[70] which was responsible for the monetary policy in the west of post-war Germany from 1948 to 1957. It was composed of 11 *Land* Central Banks[71] which had been created between 1946 and 1948 and originally fulfilled the tasks of central banks at the level of the different federal states of what in 1949 became the Federal Republic of Germany. In legal terms, the Bank of German States was only the common "daughter" of these *Land* Central Banks which alone held its capital and appointed its management. The Bank of German States was not a true central bank,[72] but just offered a common framework in which the *Land* Central Banks were able to reflect the needs of the different regions in Germany, for example by varying interest and discount rates.[73] However, this organisational structure of the Bank of German States can be explained only by the specific political circumstances in post-war Germany. Its structure had been decentralised on request of the Allied powers which at that time were occupying Germany and had an understandable interest in achieving an economic decentralisation of the country which had twice brought war over Europe.[74] In practice, however, the Bank of German States always tried to act as if it had been one central bank,[75] and soon after the Federal Republic of Germany regained its sovereignty in 1955, the decentralisation of the German

means that it is an authority which belongs to central government, and not to the federal states. The decisional centralisation inside the Fed is not taken into account by Heun, "Die Zentralbank in den USA—das Federal Reserve System" [1998] *Staatswissenschaft und Staatspraxis* 241, who speaks of the "Fed"'s federalist structure and organisation.

[70] For a comparison between the ESCB and the Bank of German States cf. Gleske, *supra*, n. 7; and Hahn, *supra*, n. 48, 126 *et seq.*

[71] This number comes from the fact that originally, there were 12 federal states in Germany, the Saarland not yet being part of the Federal Republic, while there were three federal states in the place of what is today Baden-Württemberg. Bremen originally was not given its own *Land* Central Bank by the British military government.

[72] Wagenhöfer, *supra*, n. 6, 107 *et seq.*, calls it "an institute of co-ordination with banking functions" and stresses the absence of any hierarchy between the Bank of German States and the *Land* Central Banks. Cf. also Prost, "Zur Rechtsnatur des Zentralbanksystems der Bundesrepublik (Bank deutscher Länder und Landeszentralbanken)" [1952] *DöV* 237; Bickerich, *Die D-Mark. Eine Biographie* (Berlin, 1998), 178: "*Sie war weder eine Zentralbank noch ein Geldinstitut der Länder, sondern eine Art Clearingstelle der einzelnen Landeszentralbanken*"; cf. however also Scheller, *Die Europäische Zentralbank* (Frankfurt am Main, 2000), 38, n. 7 and 148, n.17, who clarifies that the Bank of German States had the monopoly of the issue of the banknotes; a rather important function, indeed.

[73] On this regional flexibility, which was possible by virtue of Art. III, No 10 of the Bank of German States Act 1948, see Hasse, *supra*, n. 69, 165 *et seq.*, and Weinbörner, *supra*, n. 60, 204.

[74] This is stressed by the then Vice-President of the Bundesbank Könneker, "Vom Zentralbanksystem zur Deutschen Bundesbank" [1957] *Zeitschrift für das gesamte Kreditwesen* 796 (796); his view is shared by the first president of the Executive Board of the *Bank deutscher Länder*, Vocke, "Schwieriger Start der neuen Zentralbank" [1973] *Zeitschrift für das gesamte Kreditwesen* 549 (549).

[75] According to Gleske, *supra*, n. 7, 130, this was due to the centralised spirit of the officials working in the *Land* Central Banks, which all were rooted in the tradition of the Reichsbank, Germany's most centralised central bank it ever had. Cf. also *Report of the Deutsche Bundesbank for the year 1957*, "From the Central Banking System to the Deutsche Bundesbank", 3: "People have talked from time to time about the two-level structure of the Central Bank System, and in doing so have chiefly

monetary policy, atypical for a true central bank, was terminated by the merger of the *Land* Central Banks into what then became the Bundesbank.

These historical precedents might in the end have convinced the drafters of the EC Treaty and of the Statute to choose, from the beginning, a centralised structure for the ESCB. For natural and legal persons operating in the financial markets, a first conclusion can therefore be reached: in the performance of its tasks, the ESCB is governed entirely by the decision-making bodies of the ECB, and within the ESCB, no operations can take place without a decision of the ECB in this respect. Legally, the ECB is thus the governor of the ESCB.[76]

2.3. Does subsidiarity apply within the ESCB?

The history of the drafting process of the EC Treaty and the Statute has shown that today's organisational structure of the ESCB is the result of the application of "constitutional subsidiarity": since it was acknowledged as common sense during the negotiations that efficient central banking in a Monetary Union could be conducted only under the governance of a European Central Bank, and not by divergent actions of the national central banks, it was seen as the only efficient solution to allocate decision-making competences within the ESCB exclusively to the ECB level.

In the daily operation of the ESCB, there is thus no longer scope for an application of "legislative subsidiarity" or "subsidiarity in implementation", as foreseen in Article 5(2) EC. This is first of all true because no concurrent competences are assigned to the national central banks, but all tasks entrusted to the ESCB are subject to the decision-making of the ECB, as regards both the definition of policies and their implementation (Article 107(3) EC and Article 9.2 of the Statute). These tasks fall thus, from the beginning of the third stage of Economic and Monetary Union, into the *exclusive competence*[77] of the ECB. Article 5(2) EC therefore cannot apply to them, as it comes into play only in areas where there are *concurrent* legislative or implementing competences. In addition, it is certainly not by chance that there is in Article 8 EC a specific provision on the competences of the ECB and their exercise. This provision contains parallel wording to that in Article 5(1) EC and thus also subjects the ECB to the principle of conferred powers; but strikingly it does not parallel Article

had in mind its legal form. In reality it became clear, soon after the establishment of the System, that the actual work and operation of central banking in a unitary economic area cannot be performed on different levels, but only in a unitary fashion".

[76] Cf. Sauerzopf and Selmayr, *supra*, n. 58, 12: "Leiterin des ESZB"; this view is shared by Scheller, "Das Europäische System der Zentralbanken" in Glomb and Lauk (eds.), *Euro-Guide: Handbuch der Europäischen Wirtschafts- und Währungsunion*, 16.

[77] Cf. also Cassese, *supra*, n. 31, 376, who mentions monetary policy as an example of an exclusive and absolute competence. Along the same line is Zilioli, *supra*, n. 32, in n. 42. The exclusiveness of the ECB's competences relates not only to monetary policy in the narrow sense of Art. 105(2), first indent, EC, but extends to all tasks assigned to the ESCB, i.e. to monetary policy in the encompassing sense of Ch. 2 of Title VII of the Third Part of the EC Treaty. As an example, in the field of payment systems, the ECB has exclusive competence to adopt regulations under Art. 22 of the Statute.

5(2) EC. Therefore, the general scheme of the EC Treaty confirms that Article 5(2) EC does not apply to the ESCB,[78] inside which concurrent competences do not exist.

Finally, the spirit of the principle of subsidiarity also excludes its application to a central bank's organisational structure. While it is the intention of subsidiarity to increase individual freedom by separating powers, the very purpose of an independent central bank is to increase and maintain individual freedom, and in particular the freedom of property and to pursue economic activities, by guaranteeing a stable development of the currency for which it is responsible.[79] This purpose is explicitly recognised by Articles 4(2) and 105(1), first sentence, EC and by Article 2 of the Statute, which make price stability the ESCB's primary objective.[80] Such a stable development of prices, however, is possible only if the central bank in question has the means at its disposal to act speedily and efficiently in order to stabilise the internal value of a currency. For the sake of individual freedom, central banking thus requires not a day-to-day subsidiarity, but a centralisation *ab initio* of the decision-making and implementation process.

The above analysis confirms that the ESCB's two-level organisation is not sufficient to qualify its organisational structure as federal, because federalism is characterised, in addition, by the autonomy of both levels of governance, by the absence of any hierarchy between them and by discrete decision-making and implementing tasks for both the federal level and that of the component entities. As subsidiarity does not apply for decision-making and implementation inside the ESCB, it is therefore preferable not to call it a "federal" system in a legal analysis. Like the US "Fed", the ESCB can at most be defined as *a quasi-federal System*,[81] which appears to be federally structured only at a superficial analysis, but which is, in law, a centralised system. This requires an extremely cautious approach when using analogies with federal states to explain the organisational structure of the ESCB.[82]

---

[78] The same conclusion is drawn by a number of authors; cf. Hahn, *supra*, n. 50, 57; Smits, *supra*, n. 58, 111 *et seq*.; Stadler, *supra*, n. 60, 158 *et seq*.; Weinbörner, *supra*, n. 60, 396; Lenarts and van Ypersele, *supra*, n. 32, 9.

[79] Cf. the German Federal Constitutional Court in its "Euro" judgment of 31 March 1998, Constitutional Court reports, vol. 97, 350 (371), which further elaborates on the intrinsic relation between price stability and individual freedom.

[80] On the definition of price stability in the EC Treaty and in the ECB cf. Selmayr, "Wie unabhängig ist die Europäische Zentralbank? Eine Analyse der ersten geldpolitischen Entscheidungen der EZB" [1999] *WM* 2429.

[81] A similarly cautionary terminology is suggested by Hahn, *supra*, n. 50, 35: "quasi-federal orientation of the ESCB".

[82] A general warning against the use of analogies with federal states in Community law is also expressed by the ECJ in Case C–359/92, *Germany* v. *Council* [1994] ECR I–3681, as a reaction to the argument advanced by the German government that the powers conferred upon the Commission by a directive exceeded those which, in a federal state such as the Federal Republic of Germany, were enjoyed by the *Bund* in relation to the *Länder*, "since, under the German Basic Law, the implementation of federal laws rests with the *Länder*". The ECJ stated, at para. 38: "So far as concerns the

2.4. *The "daughter" argument*

Despite the clear rules in the EC Treaty and in the Statute and their purpose to centralise decision-making inside the ESCB at the ECB level, the argument is sometimes advanced that, in reality, it was the national central banks which governed the ESCB. Economically speaking, the ECB would just be the daughter of the national central banks, as all financial means of the ECB were transferred to it by the national central banks; and as in a corporation, the question of where the money comes from would be conclusive for a decision on the real division of competences.[83]

It is true that Article 28.2 of the Statute states that the national central banks are the sole subscribers to and holders of the capital of the ECB, which is 5,000 million euro. In addition, the national central banks initially provided the ECB with foreign reserve assets up to an amount equivalent to 50,000 million euro under Article 30.1 of the Statute. It is also true that the income accruing in the performance of the ESCB's monetary policy functions is allocated to the national central banks in proportion to their paid-up shares in the capital of the ECB, whether such income accrues to the national central banks (Article 32.5 of the Statute) or to the ECB (Article 33.1(b) of the Statute). However, here the company law analogy reaches its limits. Apart from their share in the ECB's profit, the national central banks do not enjoy the rights and privileges normally enjoyed by shareholders.[84] The ECB's shareholders elect neither the President of the ECB nor its Executive Board,[85] as these are appointed by the Governments of the Member States which have adopted the single currency, in accordance

---

argument that the power thus conferred on the Commission goes beyond that which, in a federal state such as the Federal Republic of Germany, is enjoyed by the Bund in relation to the Länder, it must be borne in mind that the rules governing the relationship between the Community and its Member States are not the same as those which link the Bund with the Länder".

[83]   This seems to be the view of Pipkorn, "Legal Arrangements in the Treaty of Maastricht for the Effectiveness of the Economic and Monetary Union" [1994] *CML Rev.* 263 (282) who notes "an obvious parallel with the legal basic structure of a group of companies"; cf. also Kral and Kurm-Engels, *supra*, n. 5, who call the ECB the daughter of the national central banks; the same view is taken by Seidel, *supra*, n. 5, who speaks of the ECB as the "*Tochterinstitut*" of the national central banks which is "*unter der absoluten Kontrolle des Systems der Zentralbanken. Letzteres beherrscht als Kapitaleigner und durch sein Leitungsorgan (sic!) die EZB in einer Weise, die eine eigene Geldpolitik der Frankfurter Institution ausschließt.*" A more critical approach is chosen by Timmermans, *supra*, n. 3 who explains the limited value of a company law perspective in view of the institutional complexity of the ESCB.

[84]   This is also the view of Smits, *supra*, n. 58, 94; see also M. Weber, "Das Europäische System der Zentralbanken" [1998] *WM* 1465 (1466).

[85]   At first glance, one could be inclined to consider the Governing Council of the ECB as its shareholders' assembly. However, not only the Governors of the ECB's shareholders, but also the six members of the Executive Board are represented there. The only aspect which reminds one of a shareholder structure is the fact that the Governors' votes are weighted in accordance with their share in the ECB's capital, but only when the Governing Council of the ECB takes capital-related decisions. In all policy decisions of the ECB, unlike in a company structure, every Governor has just one vote; on this, see *infra*, Ch. 3, p. 88 *et seq.*

with Article 112(2)(b) EC.[86] Incompatible with the company law analogy is also Article 14.3 of the Statute which requires the shareholders to act in accordance with the guidelines and instructions of their "daughter"—it was once correctly stated that any company law system would consider such a relationship "to be too incestuous to be allowed".[87]

It should further be noted that the decision of the member companies of a corporation to provide the corporation with financial means originally is an entirely voluntary decision, mostly based on economic considerations. In contrast to this, the subscription to the ECB's capital and the transfer of foreign reserve assets to the ECB does not originate in a decision of the national central banks, but is prescribed by Community law. Therefore, the Statute says that the capital of the ECB "*shall* be ECU 5,000 million" (Article 28.1 of the Statute), that the national central banks "*shall* be the sole subscribers to and holders of the capital of the ECB" (Article 28(2) of the Statute), and that the ECB "*shall* be provided by the national central banks with foreign reserve assets" (Article 30.1 of the Statute). The national central banks are thus legally obliged to give the ECB the financial means which it requires to perform its functions. The ECB can even extend these obligations by increasing its capital (Article 28.1 of the Statute) and by effecting further calls of foreign reserve assets (Article 30.4 of the Statute).[88] Even in financial terms, the ECB has thus to be viewed as a quite independent daughter,[89] which does not depend on "pocket-money" from its parents, but which is entitled to a substantial minimum amount which it can even decide to increase on its own motion.

III.   THE LEGAL POSITION OF THE NATIONAL CENTRAL BANKS: NATIONAL AUTHORITIES OR ECB AGENTS?

The question remains what is the role of the national central banks[90] within the ESCB, in view of the dominant position of the ECB. Is the two-level organisation of the ESCB just "federal cosmetic", similar to the existence of the *Land* Central Banks within the Bundesbank structure; or is there room for autonomous functions to be performed at the level of the national central banks?

Some writers take the view that, in spite of their integration into the ESCB, the national central banks remain exclusively national authorities which still

---

[86] In this respect, the ESCB sharply contrasts with the Bank of German States where the *Land* Central Banks appointed the President of the Central Bank Council and of the Executive Board.

[87] Cf. Timmermans, *supra*, n. 3.

[88] Subject to the limits and conditions established by the EU Council on a recommendation from the ECB; cf. Council Regulation 1009/2000 of 8 May 2000 concerning capital increases of the European Central Bank [2000] OJ L115/1; and Council Regulation 1010/2000 of 8 May 2000 concerning further calls of foreign reserve assets by the European Central Bank [2000] OJ L115/2.

[89] Cf. Sauerzopf and Selmayr, *supra*, n. 58, 14.

[90] On the particular position of the Sveriges Riksbank, Danmarks Nationalbank and the Bank of England, cf. *infra*, Ch. 4, p. 155 *et seq*.

exercise national competences.[91] They justify this conclusion by the observation that legal personality is given to the national central banks by national law, and that it essentially remains part of the Member States' *"autonomie organisation-nelle"* to organise the internal structure of their respective national central banks by a national central bank statute. These writers point again to the example of federal systems where the component entities always remain autonomous legal persons which need to be carefully distinguished from the federal level of governance and do not become federal agents even though they may from time to time implement federal legislation under federal instructions. This would be true in particular in Community law where the Member States and their national authorities never became agents of the Community. Even though they sometimes implemented and applied Community law, they would always be doing this on their own behalf, and not on behalf of the Community.[92]

It has already been stated that it is misleading to compare the ESCB with a federal state, as the ESCB is characterised by decisional centralism, which includes the decision on the appropriate level for the implementation of ESCB tasks (Article 9.2 of the Statute). In addition, though it is true that in federal states the implementation of federal tasks by the component entities does not transform them into agents of the higher level, even when they exceptionally have to act upon instructions of the federal government,[93] it is submitted that this general principle of autonomous implementing powers has not been incorporated into Community law. It cannot be disputed that most of the time the implementation and application of Community law are up to the Member States, but it is not only legal doctrine which qualifies national authorities, and even national courts, as "Community authorities"[94] and "Community courts"[95]

---

[91] See in particular Weber, *supra*, n. 20, 1472; cf. also M. Weber, *Die Kompetenzverteilung im Europäischen System der Zentralbanken bei der Festlegung und Durchführung der Geldpolitik* (Munich, 1995), 52 *et seq.*

[92] This is mentioned by Weber, *supra*, n. 91, 1472 as a general principle of Community law which would also apply to the ESCB as there was no indication to the contrary to be found in the Treaty.

[93] Cf. the German Federal Constitutional Court, *supra*, n. 29. This so-called *"Wahrnehmungs-kompetenz"* of the German *Länder* even in the course of the implementation of federal legislation and federal instructions goes back to the *"Rechtsträgerprinzip"*, a general principle of German constitutional law according to which responsibility within the federal state's organisation is—to safeguard the autonomy of the different legal persons involved—attributed to the legal person which acts and not to the legal person the functions of which are fulfilled. However, this principle applies only in the relations between the federal government and the *Länder*. Inside the *Länder*, the *"Landrat"* (a district official) is a legal phenomenon famous for having "a double nature": it depends on the function which he performs whether he acts as a district official or as a *Land* official. On these organisational features of *"Auftragsverwaltung"* and *"Organleihe"* see Maurer, *Allgemeines Verwaltungsrecht* (13 th edn., Munich, 2000), 524 *et seq.*

[94] Cf. Temple Lang, "The Duties of National Authorities under Community Constitutional Law" [1998] *EL Rev.* 109 (109); Cassese, *supra*, n. 31, 376: *"le amministrazioni nazionali agiscono 'in rete' con quelle sovranazionali"*. Cassese calls this phenomenon *"coamministrazione"*.

[95] Cf. Curtin, "The Constitutional Structure of the Union: A Europe of Bits and Pieces" [1993] *CML Rev.* 17 (31); Mancini, "The Making of a Constitution" [1989] *CML Rev.* 595 (597); Temple Lang, "The Duties of National Courts under Community Constitutional Law" [1997] *EL Rev.* 3.

when they implement or apply Community law.[96] Also the ECJ, when attributing legal responsibility, has never regarded the legal personality of an actor to be decisive, but has always adopted a functional approach which allows to look behind the legal form and to understand who really has the say in a particular case.[97]

When the question came up in the *Krohn* case[98] whether injury caused to a trader by a German agricultural authority in the course of the implementation of a Community regulation had to be borne by Germany or by the Community, the ECJ did not simply qualify the act in question as an act of the German state—which it was, as a matter of form—but analysed "whether the unlawful conduct alleged in support of the application for compensation is *in fact* the responsibility of a Community institution and cannot be attributed to the national body".[99] As the regulation in question actually empowered the Commission "to dictate the decisions of the national authorities", and "as it had in fact exercised that power by giving an instruction"[100] to the German authority, the ECJ held that the unlawful conduct alleged was not to be attributed to the German authority, "which was bound to comply with the Commission's instructions, but to the Commission itself". If the applicant had been successful,[101] this would have led to the non-contractual liability of the

---

[96] A different view is taken by some German writers on Community law who, possibly inspired by the federal structure of their state, consider national authorities and courts still as purely national authorities even when they implement or apply Community law; cf. Aubin, *Die Haftung der Europäischen Wirtschaftsgemeinschaft und ihrer Mitgliedstaaten bei gemeinschaftsrechtswidrigen nationalen Verwaltungsakten* (Baden Baden, 1982), 100 *et seq.*; Zuleeg, *Das Recht der Europäischen Gemeinschaften* (Cologne/Berlin/Bonn/Munich, 1969), 221 *et seq.* Against such "federal analogies" cf. Rengeling, *Rechtsgrundsätze beim Verwaltungsvollzug des Europäischen Gemeinschaftsrechts* (Cologne/Berlin/Bonn/Munich, 1977), 29 *et seq.* who recommends an analysis in each individual case whether national authorities are acting on their own behalf or whether their tasks are delegated Community tasks.

[97] Thus, in Case C–370/89, *Société Générale d'Entreprises Electro-Mécaniques SA (SGEEM) and Etroy* v. *EIB* [1992] ECR I–6211, para. 12 *et seq.*, the ECJ held that the Community could be liable for damage caused by the EIB, despite its separate legal personality (cf. Art. 266 EC), as in this case the Community had acted "through a Community body" (the EIB) which was "authorised to act in its name and on its behalf". On this case, cf. *supra*, Ch. 1, p. 24 *et seq.*

[98] Case 175/84, *Krohn & Co. Import–Export GmbH & Co. KG* v. *Commission* [1986] ECR 753, para. 19 *et seq.*

[99] Emphasis added.

[100] It is interesting to note that most German and Austrian writers on Community law deny that the Community institutions have a power to give instructions to national authorities, in view of the "*autonomie organizationnelle*" of the Member States; cf. Hummer in Grabitz and Hilf, *Kommentar zur Europäischen Union*, Art. 155, para. 7; Schiller, "Weisungsrechte der EG nach dem EWG-Vertrag bei nationalem Verwaltungsvollzug von EG-Recht?" [1985] *RIW* 36; Streinz, *Europarecht* (4th edn, Heidelberg, 1999), para. 476; Zuleeg, *supra*, n. 96, 217 *et seq.* (no individual instructions). This view has led the Administrative Court of Frankfurt to declare it illegal for a national authority to follow an instruction given by the Commission; cf. its judgment of 26 May 1983, published in [1984] *RIW* 227. The *Krohn* case however demonstrates that instructions have been—even before the start of the third stage of EMU—a quite common instrument used in particular in the field the common customs and common agricultural policy.

[101] The *Krohn* company in the end lost the case as the ECJ did not identify any unlawful conduct of the Commission; cf. the second part of Case 175/84, *supra*, n. [1987] ECR 97.

Community under Article 288(2) EC, according to which the Community has to "make good any damage caused by its institutions or by its servants in the performance of their duties".[102]

When being prepared to consider national authorities as agents of the Community institutions, provided that they have acted upon instructions of these institutions, the ECJ seems to follow the doctrine of *"dédoublement fonctionnel"*.[103] This doctrine applies to all multi-level organisations, whether they are unitary or federal,[104] and says essentially that within such organisations, officials of the sub-entities may simultaneously become officials of the higher organisational level whenever they act to perform functions of that level.[105] This functional approach of the ECJ seems to be perfectly suitable also to explain the

---

[102] The ECJ had already applied such functional criteria in Case 23/59, *Acciaieria Ferriera di Roma (FERAM)* v. *High Authority of the ECSC* [1959] ECR 245 (251) where it was held that the fraudulent behaviour of a Dutch official who issued certificates on the origin of ferrous scrap, could not be imputed to the High Authority, as this official "was not subject to the control of the High Authority and did not receive orders from it, but acted in his capacity as a national official" and as nothing else indicated that he had acted "on behalf of or in the name of the Community". The ECJ applied the *Krohn* test again in Joined Cases C–104/89 and C–37/90, *Mulder and others* v. *Council and Commission* [1992] ECR I–3601, para. 9, where the Community was held to be liable when national authorities apply EC Regulations. This functional method of reasoning was followed by the German Federal Court in its judgment of 27 January 1994 where it held that the German state was not liable for damage incurred because of the application of an EC Regulation by German authorities; cf. BGHZ 127, 27 (37 *et seq.*)—*Embargo against Iraq*.

[103] This doctrine, which one could translate into English as "functional duplication", was invented by Scelle, "Le phénomène juridique du dédoublement fonctionnel" in Schätzel and Schlochauer (eds.), *Rechtsfragen der Internationalen Organization, Festschrift für Hans Wehberg zu seinem 70. Geburtstag* (Frankfurt am Main, 1956), 324. Its application to the implementation of Community law by national authorities was already favoured by Kovar, *Le pouvoir réglementaire de la Communauté européenne du Charbon et de l'Acier* (Paris, 1964), 55; Reuter, *La Communauté européenne du Charbon et de l'Acier* (Paris, 1953), 105 *et seq.* On the Italian debate on *"dédoublement fonctionnel"* in Community law see Migliazza, *Le Comunità europee in rapporto al diritto internazionale e al diritto degli Stati membri* (Milan, 1964), 27; S. Cassese, "Remarks on Scelle's Theory of 'Role Splitting' *(dédoublement fonctionnel)*" in International Law" [1990] *EJIL* 210 (232 *et seq.*); Weiler, *Il sistema comunitario europeo* (Bologna, 1985), 96.

[104] As an example of *"dédoublement fonctionnel"*, Scelle, *supra*, n. 103, 331, mentions the French Préfet, which is at the same time an agent of central government and a departmental official. However, he stresses, at 332, that *"dédoublement fonctionnel"* is a phenomenon which can be observed both in federal and in unitary states: "*Le phénomène se retrouve constamment, soit que ce dédoublement résulte d'un accord entre gouvernants des divers ordres, soit qu'il soit imposé par les gouvernants d'un ordre hiérarchiquement supérieur à ceux d'un autre.*" As *"dédoublement fonctionnel"* is an entirely functional concept, it is thus the task which is decisive, not the legal order to which the respective agent belongs: "*Qu'on n'objecte pas à ces constatations que les agents appartenant à l'ordre juridique qui les à institués et réglemente leur compétence appartiennent uniquement à cet ordre juridique. Ce serait là une erreur certaine de technique consistant à confondre le critère formel avec le critère matériel. Du point de vue matériel, la fonction doit être rattachée à l'ordre juridique qu'il s'agit de réaliser et non à celui dont le contenu normatif demeure totalement étranger aux actes de réglementation, d'administration ou de juridiction intervenus*".

[105] In the words of Scelle, *supra*, n. 103, 331: "*Ce phénomène pourra se définir ainsi: les agents dotés d'une compétence institutionnelle ou investis par un ordre juridique utilisent leur capacité 'fonctionnelle' telle qu'elle est organisée dans l'ordre juridique qui les a institués, mais pour assurer l'efficacité des normes d'un autre ordre juridique privé des organes nécessaires à cette réalisation, ou n'en possédant que d'insuffisants*".

legal position of the national central banks inside the ESCB. Even though, from a mere formal point of view, national central banks keep in touch with the institutional structure of the Member States by virtue of their legal personality which originates in national law, they are *functionally disconnected* from the institutional framework of the Member States whenever they act to fulfil their tasks within the ESCB.[106] This is, first of all, due to Article 108 EC according to which the national central banks, when carrying out the tasks and duties conferred upon them by the EC Treaty and the Statute, are not allowed to seek or to take instructions from any government of a Member State or from any other body, while at the same time the governments of the Member States are obliged not to seek to influence the members of the decision-making bodies of the national central banks in the performance of their tasks. Since the possibility of giving instructions is considered by the ECJ as a decisive criterion for allocating responsibility to the issuer of such instructions, this prohibition on giving instructions must be interpreted, from a functional perspective, as drawing an insurmountable line between the national central banks and their respective Member State.

Instead of being connected to the institutional framework of a Member State, the national central banks are now "an integral part" of the ESCB (Article 14.3 of the Statute) where they shall act in accordance with the guidelines and instructions of the ECB. In view of the *Krohn* case, this power of the ECB to dictate the activities of the national central banks is a strong indication for allocating responsibility inside the ESCB to the ECB, as it allows the ECB to use the national central banks as its agents. This is further confirmed by the instruments which the EC Treaty and the Statute put at the ECB's disposal to control and supervise the national central banks' activities. Article 14.3, second sentence, of the Statute empowers and requires the Governing Council of the ECB to take the necessary steps to ensure compliance with the ECB's guidelines and instructions. Article 237(d) EC and Article 35.6 of the Statute even give the ECB the possibility of opening infringement proceedings directly against a national central bank which it considers to have acted in breach of the EC Treaty or the Statute: first out of court, by delivering a reasoned opinion and giving the national central bank concerned an opportunity to submit its observations, but then also by bringing the matter before the ECJ.[107] This is the only instance in Community law where a "national" authority can directly be sued before the ECJ, which is normally only competent to settle disputes between the Community institutions and the Member States as such.[108] In addition, if a national central bank has not

---

[106] Cf. Selmayr, "Gefahr für die Europäische Zentralbank?" [1998] *Europablätter* 39 (40); cf. also Seidel, "Probleme der Verfassung der Europäischen Gemeinschaft als Wirtschafts- und Währungsunion" in Baur (ed.), *Europarecht, Energierecht, Wirtschaftsrecht. Festschrift für Bodo Börner*, 417 (425, 427). However, Seidel has not adhered to his original view in his more recent publications; cf. *supra*, n. 5.

[107] Cf. *supra*, Ch. 1, p. 33 *et seq.*

[108] In cases where a national authority has breached Community law, the Commission will normally start infringement proceedings against the respective Member State under Art. 226 EC.

acted in accordance with the guidelines and instructions of the ECB, the ECB may always substitute itself for that national central bank and assume directly the responsibility for carrying out the ESCB's task through its own activities (Article 9.2, first alternative, of the Statute).[109]

The close link between the ECB and the national central banks is finally stressed by the statutes of the national central banks the content of which, though formally having the character of national legislation, is in essential parts determined by Community law. With the entry into the third stage of EMU, the Member States are no longer free to draft their national central bank statutes, but have to ensure that they comply with the requirements of Community law. This obligation, which is set out in Article 109 EC and repeated in Article 14.1 of the Statute,[110] includes the compatibility of the national central bank's objectives with Article 105(1) EC and the primacy of price stability, the compatibility of its monetary policy instruments with those prescribed in the Statute, and finally the compatibility of the institutional structure of the national central bank with the requirements of central bank independence, including the prohibition of instructions and a minimum term of office of five years for the Governor of the national central bank. These compatibility requirements set substantial limits to the *"autonomie organisationnelle"* of the Member States as regards the organisation of "their" national central banks: for the first time, Community law itself prescribes essential organisational features of a "national" authority. Article 14.2, second paragraph, second sentence, of the Statute even gives a central bank's Governor a specific legal remedy by which he or she could bring an action before the ECJ against his or her own Member State if he or she was relieved of his office in breach of the independence requirements. This is the first time ever that a "national" authority has been allowed to challenge its own Member State in a supranational court.[111] All this shows that inside the ESCB, the national central banks no longer act as national authorities, but as *agents of the ECB*,[112] just as, since 1 January 1999, the national banknotes and coins of the participating Member States have no longer represented national currencies, but have been simply denominations of the euro.[113]

---

[109] This corresponds to what in Italy is know as *"intervento sostitutivo"* (cf. Cassese, *supra*, n. 31, at 378).

[110] Slot, "The Institutional Provisions of the EMU" in Curtin and Heukels (eds.) *Institutional Dynamics of European Integration. Essays in Honour of Henry G. Schermers* (Dordrecht/Boston/London, 1994), ii, 229 (233) compares these provisions with a "very far-reaching 'directive'. It is also an open-ended obligation as the tasks of the ECB may be altered".

[111] On this, cf. *supra*, Ch. 1, p. 34, n. 153.

[112] Smits, *supra*, n. 58, 94: "no longer acting as bodies of their own States"; and 252: "the NCBs are held to have emancipated from a status as agencies of their States to that of organs of a Community body". In the same direction is Louis, *supra*, n. 20, 55, according to whom the national central banks "formally remain organs of the Member States although they are agents *of the ESCB* in the realization of the tasks pertaining to it". At 56, he calls the national central banks "the executive branches *of the ESCB*" (emphasis added). It is submitted, however, that the fact that legal personality and the right to give instructions have been attributed to the ECB by the EC Treaty and the Statute makes it more appropriate to call the national central banks agents *of the ECB*.

[113] Cf. Arts. 2 and 6 of Council Regulation 974/98 of 3 May 1998 on the introduction of the euro

Only exceptionally will the national central banks act as true national authorities. This is presupposed by Article 14.4 of the Statute which allows national central banks "to perform other functions than those specified in this Statute". The second sentence of Article 14.4 of the Statute draws the logical conclusion from this as it states that these functions "shall not be regarded as being part of the functions of the ESCB" and that they "shall be performed on the responsibility and liability of national central banks"—this proves again, *a contrario*, that all activities inside the ESCB are to be attributed to the ECB. The possibility for a national central bank to act outside the ESCB is limited both in substantive and in procedural terms. As regards substance, in view of the encompassing character of the ESCB's tasks laid down in the Statute, only in a few cases is there still scope for purely national activities of national central banks; the only relevant field seems to be prudential supervision where the ESCB essentially has mere advisory functions (Article 25 of the Statute). In addition, the Governing Council of the ECB always remains entitled to stop such autonomous activities of national central banks when it considers, by a majority of two thirds of the votes cast, that they interfere with the objectives and tasks of the ESCB (Article 14.4, first sentence of the Statute).

The national central banks will therefore only rarely still be able to activate the other side of their *"dédoublement fonctionnel"*, i.e. their character as national authorities. Their daily function will in any event be that of ECB agents. One could say with some justification that the integration of the national central banks into the ESCB has led to a *"denationalisation"* of most of the national central banks' functions and to a *"communautarisation"*[114] of the national central banks[115]—a development which represents the most far-reaching example of a *"dédoublement fonctionnel"* ever witnessed in Community law[116] and which

---

[1998] OJ L139/1, as amended by Council Regulation 2596/2000 of 27 November 2000 amending Regulation 974/98 on the introduction of the euro [2000] OJ L300/2.

[114] In this sense see Brentford, "Constitutional Aspects of the Independence of the European Central Bank" [1998] *ICLQ* 75 (86).

[115] In view of this new Community character of national central banks it seems questionable whether today it is still permitted to reserve employment (including management positions) in a national central bank to nationals. Art. 39(4) EC allows for such discriminatory restrictions on the free movement of workers only in cases of "employment in the public service"—an exception interpreted very narrowly by the ECJ as referring solely to posts which "involve direct or indirect participation in the exercise of powers conferred by public law and duties designed to safeguard the general interests of the State or of other public authorities. Such posts in fact presume, on the part of those occupying them, the existence of a special relationship of allegiance to the State and reciprocity of rights and duties which form the foundation of the bond of nationality". Cf. Case 149/79, *Commission* v. *Belgium* [1980] ECR 3881, para. 10. As since 1 January 1999, national central banks have no longer been exercising a national, but a supranational authority on behalf of the ECB, Gros, *supra*, n. 5, rightly suggests that the national central banks should start to employ nationals of other Member States. Another example which asks for an adaptation to the new role of national central banks seems to be § 9.1 of the Austrian National Bank Act, as it reserves the shares of 50% of the Austrian National Bank to Austrian nationals and thus restricts the free movement of capital (Art. 56(1) EC; cf. also Art. 294 EC) in a discriminatory manner for which the once national character of the bank's tasks no longer provides a justification.

[116] The same view is taken by Louis, *supra*, n. 20, 56: "The '*dédoublement fonctionnel*'", to

shows again the close link between the ECB and the national central banks inside the organisational structure of the ESCB.

IV. THE PRINCIPLE OF "SYSTEM INTEGRITY"

The transformation of national central banks into ECB agents and their close relationship with the ECB and its decision-making bodies already indicate that it would be a very formalistic attitude still to point to the distinct legal personality of the ECB and the national central banks to create any kind of opposition between the ECB's interest and those of the national central banks. In this sense, the relationship between the ECB and the national central banks has to be distinguished from the relationship between the Community institutions and the Member States. In contrast with the ECB's tasks in the framework of the ESCB, the Community institutions' tasks are not encompassing and therefore leave a number of fields in which the Member States still have autonomous competences and may pursue interests other than those of the Community. To ensure nevertheless a certain coherence, Article 10 EC obliges the Member States always to facilitate the achievement of the Community's tasks and to abstain from any measure which could jeopardise the attainment of the EC Treaty objectives. The ECJ has drawn from this provision quite extensive duties of sincere co-operation to apply in the relationship between the Community institutions and the Member States.[117] Therefore, Article 10 EC is often compared to the principle of *"Bundestreue"* ("federal loyalty"),[118] which is a

---

follow Georges Scelle, has never been pushed so far". The potential for such a development in Community law was already recognised by Rengeling, *supra*, n. 96, p. 42: *"Allerdings kann die hierarchische Zuordnung nationaler Verwaltungsorgane ausschließlich zur nationalen Verwaltungsspitze bei fortschreitender Integration in Frage gestellt werden"*.

[117] Cf. Case 230/81, *Luxembourg* v. *European Parliament* [1983] ECR 255, para. 37: the rule imposing on Member States and the Community institutions mutual duties of sincere co-operation, as embodied in particular in Art. 10 EC, requires that the governments of the Member States, when using their exclusive competence to take decisions on the seat of the European Parliament, ensure that the exercise of this competence does not impede the due functioning of the Parliament; Case C–25/94, *Commission* v. *Council (FAO)* [1996] ECR I–1469, para. 48: the duty to ensure best possible co-operation to guarantee unity of external representation of the Community and the Member States in the case of shared competences; Case C–265/95, *Commission* v. *France* [1997] ECR I–6959, para. 32 *et seq.*: duty for Member States to use their autonomous instruments of police powers and criminal law to prevent that private parties creating obstacles to intra-Community trade of goods, which is guaranteed by Art. 28 EC.

[118] Against this background, a number of authors even speak of *"Gemeinschaftstreue"* (Community loyalty), as noted and criticised by von Bogdandy in Grabitz and Hilf, *Kommentar zur Europäischen Union*, Artikel 5, para. 6, as this has the unfortunate connotation of a federal state's organizational structure. It should be noted that the German Federal Constitutional Court has used this principle to claim the existence of a "relationship of co-operation" between itself and the ECJ— an open effort to question the exclusive jurisdiction of the ECJ on questions of Community law; on this, cf. Selmayr and Prowald, "Abschied von den 'Solange-Vorbehalten'—Die wahre Bedeutung des 'Kooperationsverhältnisses' des BVerfG zum EuGH" [1999] *DVBl* 269.

constitutional principle to co-ordinate the plurality of decision-making levels in federal states and to guarantee respect for the autonomy of all component entities.[119]

It is remarkable that Article 10 EC, unlike other EC Treaty provisions, has not been amended to cover also the new institutional relationship between the ECB and the national central banks. This does of course not mean that in this relationship the duty of sincere co-operation does not apply, *au contraire*: to extend Article 10 EC to the ESCB would have been superfluous in view of the close legal link already established by the EC Treaty and the Statute between the level of the ECB and that of the national central banks, the latter being considered, by Article 14.3 of the Statute, as "an integral part of the ESCB".

From this follows that the loyalty of all component parts of the ESCB to the System and its objectives does not need to be legally prescribed in a separate provision, as it is the very essence on which the existence of the ESCB, a System integrating both the ECB and the national central banks, is based.[120] To distinguish it from the loose obligation of federal loyalty, one could call this the unwritten principle of *"System integrity"*, which goes much further than any duty of co-operation in federal systems as it is not an instrument to co-ordinate potentially divergent action of a plurality of autonomous legal entities. It rather characterises the organisational structure of the ESCB which excludes *a priori* the existence of diverging actions and interests, as both the ECB and the national central banks are committed to the same objective, which is, as prescribed by the EC Treaty and by the Statute, first of all, the maintenance of price stability for the euro, and in the pursuance of which all its component parts are submitted to the governance of the decision-making bodies of the ECB.

---

[119] This principle goes back to Smend, "Ungeschriebenes Verfassungsrecht im monarchischen Bundesstaat" in *Festgabe für Otto Mayer* (1916), 247 (261). It has been inserted into German constitutional law by the judgment of the German Federal Constitutional Court of 21 May 1952, Constitutional Court Reports vol. 1, 299 (315): "*Dem bundesstaatlichen Prinzip entspricht vielmehr die verfassungsrechtliche Pflicht, daß die Glieder des Bundes sowohl einander als auch dem größeren Ganzen und der Bund den Gliedern die Treue halten und sich verständigen. Der im Bundesstaat geltende verfassungsrechtliche Grundsatz des Föderalismus enthält deshalb die Rechtspflicht des Bundes und all seiner Glieder zu 'bundesfreundlichem Verhalten'. d.h. alle an dem verfassungsrechtlichen 'Bündnis' Beteiligten sind gehalten, dem Wesen des Bündnisses entsprechend zusammenzuwirken und zu seiner Festigung und zur Wahrung seiner und der wohlverstandenen Belange seiner Glieder beizutragen*".

[120] In this context, it is interesting to note that the ECJ has held several times that duties of sincere co-operation apply in inter-institutional relationships at Community level, e.g. between the Council and the European Parliament: cf. Case 204/86, *Greece* v. *Council* [1988] ECR 5323, para. 16; Case C–65/93, *European Parliament* v. *Council* [1995] ECR I–643, para. 23 *et seq*. This case law is today acknowledged by Declaration No 3 on Art. 10 of the Treaty establishing the European Community, annexed to the Final Act of the Nice Treaty.

V. CONCLUSION

The above analysis has demonstrated that, since 1 January 1999, a unique central banking organisation has taken over the responsibility for monetary policy of 11—since 1 January 2001: 12—EU Member States. The ESCB represents a completely new model of denationalised central banking in which both the decision-making and the implementation processes follow a supranational pattern.

For the world of banking and finance, this new legal framework for the activities of economic operators will certainly require some adaptation. As the above analysis has shown, the ECB, its system and its law may not be understood properly by simply applying well-known national legal concepts. Like the Community itself, the ECB is now the centre of gravity of a new and autonomous legal order which requires new legal thinking, in particular as regards the effects of legal instruments, questions of liability and legal remedies.

But the Community law framework also represents a challenge for the central banking community itself. The traditional opposition between divergent national and supranational interests in monetary policy—demonstrated so clearly in the history of the Bretton Woods System, but also in the development of the first European Exchange Rate Mechanism created in 1979—came to an end on 1 January 1999. Since then, Community law has allowed solely for a single and thus necessarily European monetary policy. This also means that inside the ESCB, one should now not try artificially to create new oppositions between the ECB's interest and that of the national central banks. The principle of System integrity, which has to be respected by all component parts of the ESCB, rather requires an unequivocal and strong stance of the ESCB as a whole.[121] A nice symbol in this respect was the co-ordinated decision of the national central banks of the Member States which participate in the single currency, to harmonise, on 3 December 1998, their interest rates at 3 per cent—a decision taken at a time when monetary sovereignty had not been fully transferred to the ECB, but when the national central banks were already emphasising that they considered themselves solely committed to the objectives of the single currency. This is proof of a truly historic transformation of the national central banks from national to European authorities.

---

[121] This is also the view of the former president of the Bundesbank Tietmeyer, *supra*, n. 12, who calls for a new self-understanding of national central banks as "European" institutions.

3

The Making and Implementation of ECB Law

I T WAS DEMONSTRATED in chapter 2 that the model chosen for the organisational structure of the ESCB is that of decisional centralism, as the ESCB is governed by the decision-making bodies of the ECB. This leads us now in chapter 3 to a closer analysis of the way in which decisions are taken by the ECB and of the kind of law that results from these decisions (II.). The chapter will then turn to the specific mechanisms used for the implementation of this law within the ESCB (III.).

II. THE MAKING OF ECB LAW

At a first glance on decision-making inside the ECB, "federalist" analysts will certainly concentrate on the question of how far the "national" interests of the ESCB's component entities participate in central decision-making, having in mind the bicameral legislature to be found in all federal states.[1] We recommend, again, the cautionary use of such terminology. A closer look reveals that the centralised organisational structure of the ESCB also finds reflection in the decision-making process inside the ECB.

1. The supranational decision-making bodies of the ECB

Article 107(3) EC mentions two decision-making bodies by which the ESCB shall be governed: the Governing Council and the Executive Board of the ECB. Article 45.1 of the Statute adds the General Council as a third transitory decision-making body, which acts mainly in an advisory capacity. Therefore, without disregarding the importance of the General Council for associating the

---

[1] Cf. M. Weber, *Die Kompetenzverteilung im Europäischen System der Zentralbanken bei der Festlegung und Durchführung der Geldpolitik* (Munich, 1995), 75, who considers the predominance of governors as a result of the ESCB's federal structure; Weinbörner, *Die Stellung der Europäischen Zentralbank (EZB) und der nationalen Zentralbanken in der Wirtschafts- und Währungsunion nach dem Vertrag von Maastricht* (Frankfurt am Main, 1998), 383 talks of "a federal interplay" inside the ECB's decision-making bodies; Stadler, *Der rechtliche Handlungsspielraum des Europäischen Systems der Zentralbanken* (Baden Baden, 1996), 98, considers voting in the Governing Council as an element which characterises the federal structure of the ESCB.

national central banks which do not yet fully participate in the ESCB, the decision-making process within the ECB, in particular as regards monetary policy decisions, takes place in the Governing Council and the Executive Board.[2]

1.1. The Executive Board of the ECB

The Executive Board comprises the President of the ECB, its Vice-President and four other members (Article 112(2)(a) EC).[3] It is a permanent decision-making body which is responsible for the current business of the ECB (Article 11.6 of the Statute). In a central bank, "current business" is of decisive importance, as monetary policy may require decisions to be taken every day, every hour, sometimes every minute, in particular in case of need of emergency measures.[4] The Executive Board is thus responsible for the daily management of the ECB and for the implementation of the ECB's monetary policy, in particular for giving instructions to the national central banks for this purpose (Article 12.1, second subparagraph, of the Statute). These important tasks, which are exclusive competences of the Executive Board, justify calling it *"Europe's monetary executive"*.[5] To enable the Executive Board to fulfil its tasks on a permanent basis, all work units of the ECB are placed under the managing direction of the Executive Board and have to act in accordance with its administrative circulars.[6] In addition, the Executive Board of the ECB has adopted specific Rules of Procedure[7] which allow, *inter alia*, for the adoption of decisions by means of teleconferencing where special circumstances so require.[8]

The Executive Board's importance is stressed by the procedure which is provided for in the EC Treaty for the appointment of its members. It requires a decision taken by *common accord* by the governments of the Member States which have adopted the single currency, meeting at the level of Heads of State or Government. Such a high-profile appointment procedure is foreseen neither for the members of the Commission nor for the Judges and Advocates General at

---

[2] This is also taken into account by Art. 45.1 of the Statute according to which the establishment of the General Council is "without prejudice to Article 107(3) of the Treaty", thus also without prejudice to the decision-making competences of the Governing Council and the Executive Board. On the composition and function of the General Council, cf. *infra*, Ch. 4, p. 158 *et seq.*

[3] Cf. also Art. 11.1 of the Statute.

[4] This is stressed by Slot, *supra*, n. 110, 235, who considers the daily business to be "of decisive importance" and therefore sees also a crucial role attributed to the Executive Board of the ECB. The Executive Board is required to take emergency measures whenever it is not possible to convene the Governing Council of the ECB or at least a teleconfernece meeting in time.

[5] Selmayr, "Die Wirtschafts- und Währungsunion als Rechtsgemeinschaft" [1999] *AöR* 357 (353).

[6] Arts. 10 and 11 of the Rules of Procedure of the European Central Bank of 7 July 1998 [1988] OJ L338/28, substituted by Rules of Procedure of the European Central Bank as amended on 22 April 1999 [1999] OJ L125/34. There is only one exception, the independent Anti-Fraud Committee, cf. Art. 9a of the Rules of Procedure of the ECB, introduced by Decision ECB/1999/6 of 7 October 1999 amending the Rules of Procedure of the European Central Bank [1999] OJ L314/32.

[7] Decision ECB/1999/7 of 12 October 1999 concerning the Rules of Procedure of the Executive Board of the European Central Bank [1999] OJ L314/34.

[8] Art. 4 of the Rules of Procedure of the Executive Board of the ECB, *supra*, n. 7.

the ECJ, where the requirements of the EC Treaty are satisfied by the common accord of national ministers.[9] Also the term of office of the members of the Executive Board exceeds by (non-renewable) eight years the length of all terms of office of the members of the Community institutions,[10] to guarantee the independence of the ECB.

With just six members, the Executive Board of the ECB is the first institution established under the EC Treaty to which not all Member States can send one of their nationals.[11] The only nationality requirement for the Executive Board is that its members shall be nationals of the Member States which have adopted the single currency. For the rest, the sole criterion to be applied in the appointment procedure is that the Board members are "persons of recognised standing and professional experience in monetary or banking matters" (Article 112(2)(b) EC). The Executive Board is thus conceived by the EC Treaty not as a body of national representatives, but as an expert body of *a truly supranational character*, which is allowed to seek or to take instructions neither from Community institutions or bodies nor from the Member States (Article 108 EC). This and the importance of the Executive Board of the ECB help one understand better why the appointment of the first Executive Board originally caused so much controversy between the Member States before the first President of the ECB was appointed, as prescribed by the EC Treaty, for a term of office of eight years.[12]

---

[9] Cf. Arts. 214 (Commission) and 223 (ECJ) EC. Members of the Court of Auditors are appointed not on government level, but by a unanimous Council Decision (Art. 247(3) EC).

[10] Members of the Commission are appointed for five years (Art. 214(1) EC), Judges and Advocates General at the ECJ and Members of the Court of Auditors for six years (Art. 223 and 247(3) EC).

[11] Even for the Commission, which is conceived as "completely independent" by the Treaty and "*le caractère supranational*" of which was originally stressed by Art. 9(5) of the ECSC Treaty, Art. 213(1), fourth subpara., EC prescribes that it "must include at least one national of each of the Member States"; on the impact of the Nice Treaty on this situation cf. *supra*, Ch. 1, n. 131. Only seemingly similar to the Executive Board of the ECB is the case of the Management Committee of the EIB, which consists of eight members (Art. 13.1 of the Statute of the EIB in conjunction with the Decision of the Board of Governors of 3 March 1995). However, unlike the Executive Board of the ECB, the EIB's Management Committee does not have its own law-making competences, but simply prepares the meetings of the EIB's Board of Directors, for which each Member States nominates one to three directors (Art. 11 of the Statute of the EIB). On a detailed comparison of ECB and EIB cf. Selmayr, "Die EZB als Neue Gemeinschaft—ein Fall für den EuGH?" [1999] *Europablätter* 170; cf. also *supra*, Ch. 1, p. 25 *et seq*.

[12] Cf. Art. 1.1 of Decision 98/345/EC of 26 May 1998 taken by common accord of the Governments of the Member States adopting the single currency at the level of Heads of State or Government appointing the President, the Vice-President and the other members of the Executive Board of the European Central Bank [1988] OJ L154/33: "Mr Wim DUISENBERG is hereby appointed President of the European Central Bank for a term of office of eight years". That there are today no legal doubts as regards the length of the President's term of office is demonstrated by Selmayr, *supra*, n. 5, 388 *et seq*; cf. also Zilioli in Von der Groeben, Thiesing and Ehlermann (eds.), *Kommentar zum EU-/EG-Vertrag* (5th edn., Baden Baden, 1999), following Art. 109 m, Satzung ESZB and EZB Art. 11, para 6.

1.2. The Governing Council of the ECB

The Governing Council is the other decision-making body of the ECB. Unlike the Executive Board, it is not available every day in Frankfurt, but meets there on a regular basis, at least 10 times a year (Article 10.5 of the Statute); the current practice is meetings every two weeks. The Governing Council is responsible for adopting the guidelines and taking the decisions necessary to ensure the performance of the tasks entrusted to the ESCB (Article 12.1, first paragraph of the Statute). In particular, it is the Governing Council which formulates the monetary policy for the euro and thus takes decisions on intermediate monetary objectives, key interest rates and the supply of reserves in the ESCB. The Governing Council is thus responsible for laying down the general legislative framework in which the Executive Board and—subject to the Board's instructions—the national central banks operate to implement the ECB's monetary policy. Behind each activity of the Executive Board and the national central banks, there is thus a major policy decision taken by the Governing Council. When traders in the financial markets look every second Thursday to Frankfurt, that is because the Governing Council meets then in the Eurotower and decides whether or not to change the interest rate applicable in particular to the main refinancing operations to be carried out through the ESCB.[13]

The composition of the Governing Council is unique among the institutions created by Community law. This comes from the fact that it comprises both the Governors of the national central banks of the 12 Member States which have adopted the single currency *and* the six members of the Executive Board. The Executive Board is thus not only the ECB's decision-making body for the implementation of the ECB's monetary policy decisions, but is also wholly involved in the making of such decisions. Decisions are taken, as a rule,[14] by a simple majority of the votes cast, while each member of the Governing Council has only one vote (Article 10.2, second paragraph, first and second sentence of the Statute).[15]

Very often, authors point to the numerical dominance of central bank Governors in the Governing Council of the ECB, and therefrom conclude that

---

[13] On 22 December 1998, the ECB's first main refinancing rate was set by the Governing Council of the ECB at a level of 3%; cf. [1999] OJ C2/1. The current rate is always published at http://www.ecb.int.

[14] The exception, as explained below, is capital-related decisions under Art. 10.3 of the Statute.

[15] However, it should be noted that the Nice Treaty will introduce a new Art. 10.6 into the Statute, which enables the Council of the Union, meeting in the composition of the Heads of State or Government, to amend Art. 10.2 by a unanimous decision; in addition, subsequent ratification by all the Member States is required. The ECB, in its opinion (Opinion of the European Central Bank of 5 December 2000 at the request of the Presidency of the Council of the European Union on a proposal to amend Art. 10.2 of the Statute of the European System of Central Banks and of the European Central Bank (CON/00/30) [2000] OJ C362/13 emphasised that "the core constitutional principle of government of the monetary policy of the ECB is 'one member, one vote' and has welcomed the intention not to change this core constitutional principle in the course of future amendments under Art. 10.6 of the Statute.

the ECB is a form of joint venture controlled by the national central banks.[16] Normally, such authors make a comparison with the relationship between the representation of "the centre" and "the periphery" in other so-called federally organised central banks.[17] They point to the fact that in the Federal Open Market Committee of the Federal Reserve System, the Federal Reserve Board has seven votes and thus always a clear majority against the 12 Presidents of the federal reserve banks who may cast only five votes.[18] Less dominant is the "centre" within the Central Bank Council of the Bundesbank, where the Executive Board has up to eight votes against nine votes for the *Land* Central Banks.[19] Against this background,[20] it is often deemed problematic, and proof of the ECB's weakness, that "the centre" has only six votes in the Governing Council of the ECB, as compared to the national central banks' 12 votes.[21]

Such comparisons are flawed as they neglect the decisive position enjoyed by the Executive Board which is, as demonstrated, responsible for the daily management of the ECB and thus may even issue instructions to the national central banks—a competence which is enjoyed neither by the Board of Governors in Washington nor by the Bundesbank's Executive Board in Frankfurt.[22] In addition, the six members of the ECB's Executive Board, by virtue of their six votes, have a substantial say in the Governing Council. This influence is further increased by the fact that the President of the ECB chairs the meetings of the Governing Council (Article 13.1 of the Statute) and has a casting vote in the event of a tie (Article 10.2, second paragraph, third sentence of the Statute).

---

[16]   See Brentford, *supra*, Ch. 2, n. 114, 86. On this "daughter"-argument cf. *supra*, Ch. 2, p. 72 *et seq*.

[17]   This is done by Gros, *supra*, Ch. 2, n. 5 and 20; by and Kral and Kurm-Engels, *supra*, Ch. 2, n. 5.

[18]   These always include the President of the Federal Reserve Bank of New York, because of New York's position as the most important financial market. The Federal Reserve Bank of New York also has a dominant position within the implementation of the Fed's monetary policy. On the decision-making process inside the Fed cf. Eichengreen, *supra*, Ch. 2, n. 67; *Gleske, supra*, Ch. 2, n. 7, 125 *et seq*.; Hasse, *supra*, Ch. 2, n. 69, 161 *et seq*.

[19]   According to Art. 7(2) of the Bundesbank Act, the Executive Board has up to eight members, while Art. 8 provides that there are nine *Land* Central Banks, the governors of which are represented in the Central Bank Council by virtue of Art. 6(2) of the Bundesbank Act.

[20]   Normally not mentioned in this context is the example of the Bank of German States; cf. *supra*, Ch. 2, p. 69 *et seq*, legally a truly federal system in which the Central Bank Council was composed of nine *Land* Central Bank Governors and only one representative of the centre who had the right to vote: the President of the Executive Board. The eleventh member, the President of the Central Bank Council, was elected by the *Land* Central Banks' Governors and therefore had a somewhat neutral position.

[21]   D. Gros, *supra*, Ch. 2, n. 3, even points to the possibility of the Executive Board's position being reduced to insignificance in the course of forthcoming enlargements of the European Union, as then the ratio would change to 26:6. The same problem is seen by the European Parliament's Committee on Institutional Affairs in its Report on the constitutional implications of EMU in the context of enlargement (*Rapporteur*: Mr José Barros Moura), para. 6 of the motion for a resolution, where it is affirmed "that, in view of the prospective enlargement of the EU, a system of rotation must be introduced to maintain the current ratio between the (six) members of the Executive Board of the ECB and the governors of the national central banks (currently eleven), to avoid the twin prospect of the Governing Council being transformed into a chamber of national representatives and the ECB being reduced to a mere secretariat of the ESCB".

[22]   Only the Central Bank Council of the Bundesbank may issue instructions both to the Executive Board and to the Land Central Banks; cf. Art. 6(1), fifth sentence of the Bundesbank Act.

Even more importantly, it is the Executive Board which has the task of preparing the meetings of the Governing Council (Article 12.2 of the Statute). If one really wants to see a natural division between "the centre" and "the periphery" in the Governing Council, it should also be noted that it is much more likely that the six members of the Executive Board will cast their votes in the same direction as the 12 Governors, given the fact that they are working together every day, advised by the ECB's staff in Frankfurt, and that they jointly prepare for the meetings of the Governing Council.

However, it is submitted that it is not even appropriate to view the central bank Governors in the Governing Council of the ECB as representatives of their respective national central banks and thus of a kind of national or peripheral interest within the ECB's decision-making process. Only at first glance might one want to point to the example of the Council of the European Union, the members of which are said to be both members of a Community institution *and* representatives of their respective Member States; membership of the Council of the European Union is thus another example of "*dédoublement fonctionnel*" in Community law, with a certain dominance of the national element, as national governments may sometimes issue quite detailed instructions as regards voting behaviour in the Council.[23] The national element is also stressed by Article 205(2) EC, according to which qualified majority voting in the Council—its normal voting method—is always done with the votes weighted in accordance with a key which gives a more important vote to large than to small countries.[24] The case of the Governing Council of the ECB has to be carefully distinguished from this example. First of all, it should be stressed again that the six members of the Executive Board also participate and vote in the Governing Council. In addition, and in contrast to the Council of the European Union, every member of the Governing Council has only one vote when monetary policy decisions are taken; thus, the Governor of the Bundesbank legally has the same say in the course of the adoption of the ECB's key interest rates as the Governor of the Central Bank of Luxembourg and as every single member of the ECB's Executive Board (Article 10.2, second paragraph, first and second sentence of the Statute).[25]

It is true that, exceptionally, in the case of decisions which directly relate to the ECB's capital or the transfer of foreign reserves to the ECB and to the allocation of profits and losses within the ESCB, the votes of the Governors are also

---

[23] On "dédoublement fonctionnel", cf. *supra*, Ch. 2, p. 76 *et seq*. Austria has a unique right of instruction with a far-reaching binding effect where the *Länder*, by formulating a common position, the Nationalrat—Austria's first chamber of the Parliament—or the Bundesrat—Austria's second chamber of the Parliament—can instruct the Austrian Council representative in such a way that this instruction can be disregarded only in the exceptional case of "overriding interests of foreign or integration policy"; cf. Art. 23d(2), 23e(2) and (6) of the Austrian Federal Constitutional Act of 1920.

[24] Cf. Art. 205(2) EC, according to which the vote of France is weighted with 10 and Luxembourg's vote with 2.

[25] For possible changes in this situation after the entry into force of the Nice Treaty, cf. *supra*, n. 15.

weighted to reflect the capital share of the national central banks (Article 10.3 of the Statute), and the vote of the Executive Board members in the Governing Council is weighted with zero.[26] In this case, one could view the Governors as both members of a decision-making body of the ECB *and* representatives of the interests of their respective national central banks in their capacity as shareholder of the ECB.[27] However, it should not be forgotten that also in this case the Governors are legally completely disconnected from the decision-making bodies of their national central banks when they debate in the Governing Council or cast their votes. In fact, Article 108 EC prohibits not only the Community institutions and Member States governments to instruct the members of the ECB's decision-making bodies, but also "any other body"—a very broad wording which also includes the national central banks. This has first of all the far-reaching consequence that the decision-making bodies of the national central banks have no direct influence on the decision-making process inside the ECB, whether it concerns policy or capital-related decisions; they thus change, within the scope of the ESCB's tasks, their nature from decision-making bodies to deliberating bodies which are not allowed even to seek to influence the ECB's decisions.[28] It also means that as members of the Governing Council of the ECB, central bank Governors are—even in case of capital-related decisons—no longer national officials, but, like the Governing Council members from the Executive Board, solely committed to the supranational objectives of the ECB, in particular to the maintenance of price stability in the "euro area" as a whole. If they vote, they always cast their votes in a personal capacity as Governing Council members,[29] and not in the name or on behalf of their respective national

---

[26] The capital share of each national central bank was laid down by Decision ECB/1998/1 of 9 June 1998 on the method to be applied for determining the national central banks' percentage shares in the key for the capital of the European Central Bank [1999] OJ L8/31. It goes from 0.1469% for the Banque centrale du Luxembourg to 24.4096% for the Deutsche Bundesbank.

[27] In this direction see Zilioli in Von der Groeben, Thiesing and Ehlermann (eds.), *supra*, n. 12, following Art. 109 m, Satzung ESZB and EZB Art. 10, para. 10 *et seq.*, where the "technical" character of capital-related decisions is underlined. The representative character of Governors' decisions should however not be confused with representation in a contractual principal/agent relationship: it rather resembles the representation of the electorate through a Member of Parliament who is, in a representative democracy, not subject to the instructions of his/her electorate.

[28] This is recognised explicitly by the Landeszentralbank Hessen, "The Role of the Land Central Banks within the European System of Central Banks", *Frankfurter Finanzmarkt-Bericht* No 32, November 1998, 1(2): "the role of the central bank council of the *Bundesbank* in the field of monetary policy is changing from a decision-making to a deliberating body". The prohibition on seeking to influence the ECB's decision also extends to the so-called "ESCB Committees" which are composed of representatives of the ECB and of the national central bank of each participant Member State. They are formed to *assist* in the work of the ESCB (cf. Art. 9(1) of the Rules of Procedure of the ECB, *supra*, n. 6), but not to depart from the decision-making process foreseen by the Treaty and the Statute. On the legal limitations of the role to be performed by ESCB Committee cf. Selmayr, *supra*, Ch. 2, n. 81.

[29] Cf. Zilioli in Von der Groeben, Thiesing and Ehlermann (eds.), *supra*, n. 12, following Art. 109 m, Satzung ESZB and EZB, Art. 10, para 5. *et seq.* In case of normal—in particular monetary policy—decisions, this is stressed by Art. 10.2 of the Statute according to which "only members of the Governing Council present in person shall have the right to vote". The fact that in case of capital-related decisions, the Governors may appoint an alternate only serves to ensure that the interests of

central bank.[30] To ensure that they can do this without any pressure from their respective Member States, Article 10.4 of the Statute guarantees in all cases—regarding both policy decisions and capital-related decisions—absolute confidentiality of the minutes of meetings of the Governing Council.[31] Seen from the outside, the Governing Council thus will always take its decisions unequivocally, within the spirit of a true supranational institution.[32]

The *communautarian* position of the central bank Governors within the Governing Council of the ECB is an appropriate reflection of the far-reaching degree of *denationalisation* of the national central banks inside the ESCB. Legally, the Governing Council can therefore not be seen as the national central bank's decision-making body, but represents, as stated in Article 107(3) EC, solely a decision-making body of the ECB. Even enlargement of the European Union would thus not so much create the problem of a "re-nationalisation" of the Governing Council, but rather call into question efficient decision-making in this body. This might indeed require further consideration in the near future.[33]

all shareholders are always duly taken into account, but does not transform the vote cast by the Governor or his/her alternate into the vote of a national official: in fact, the Statute leaves the Governors (and not the national central banks) completely free in their choice of an alternate. Theoretically, they could even appoint an alternate who does not belong to the national central bank in question.

[30] They are thus only *"europäische Geldpolitiker"*, as all 17 [now 18] members of the Governing Council are called by the former President of the Bundesbank Tietmeyer, *supra*, Ch. 2, n. 12. Already the famous Delors committee, which had the task of preparing the decisive report on the move to EMU, was composed of the central bank Governors which were appointed for this task *ad personam*; cf. the conclusions of the European Council of Hannover of 27/28 June 1988, published in Bull.EC 6–1998, 166. The legal situation of central bank governors within the Governing Council of the ECB may be contrasted with their previous position within the Council of the EMI. According to Art. 8 of the EMI Statute, the members of the EMI Council had a double nature: they were "the representatives of their institution", but at the same time had to "act according to their own responsibilities". That there is no similar provision in the ESCB Statute confirms the unequivocally supranational nature of the Governing Council of the ECB.

[31] On this see Zilioli in Von der Groeben, Thiesing and Ehlermann (eds.), *supra*, n. 12, following Art. 109 m, Satzung ESZB and EZB, Art. 10, para. 16 *et seq.*; Selmayr, *supra*, n. 5, 387 *et seq.*

[32] From an economic perspective, it is considered to be advantageous in a monetary union, where there is not yet a strong political centre, to have a decision-making process in which not national representatives, but independent governors are represented; cf. von Hagen and Süppel, "Central Bank Constitutions for Federal Monetary Unions" (1994) 38 *European Economic Review* 774–782 (777 *et seq.*).

[33] This problem not only concerns the decision-making bodies of the ECB, but is also one for the Community institutions. Cf. the Protocol No 7 on the institutions with the prospect of enlargement of the European Union, annexed to the Treaties by the Amsterdam Treaty, and Declaration No 50 relating to the Protocol on the institutions with the prospect of enlargement of the European Union, annexed to the Final Act of the Amsterdam Treaty, now replaced by a more detailed Protocol attached to the Nice Treaty. To reflect on the potential consequences of enlargement, the ECB and Suomen Pankki, the Finnish central bank, jointly organised a high-level "Seminar on the Accession Process" which took place in Helsinki on 11 and 12 November 1999, gathering the Eurosystem and the governors of the central banks of the 12 EU accession countries. On 14 and 15 December 2000, a further such seminar took place in Vienna. It is in this context that the Nice Treaty introduced the possibility of amending Art. 10.2 of the Statute in the future; cf. *supra*, n. 15. To respect the independence of the ECB, the intergovernmental conference at Nice did not itself amend the relevant provisions of the Statute by the new Protocol on the enlargement of the European Union, but rather left the initiative for the adaptation of the ECB's institutional structure for the

2. ECB law and its effects

The decisional centralisation inside the ESCB has the consequence that the EC Treaty and the Statute had to put at the disposal of the ECB's decision-making bodies a wide range of legal instruments which they may use to regulate, organise and steer the activities and operations to be carried out through the ESCB. These legal instruments can be summarised under the notion of *ECB law*. Together with the EC Treaty, the Statute and complementary legislation adopted by the Council of the European Union (cf. Article 42 of the Statute), this ECB law is the sole relevant law for the determination of the activities of the ECB and the national central banks within the ESCB. It comprises two categories: ECB law intended to produce external effects, and ECB law intended to produce legal effects among the component parts of the ESCB.[34]

2.1. ECB law intended to produce external legal effects

Article 110(1) EC and Article 34.1 of the Statute list those legal acts which the ECB's decision-making bodies may adopt and by which they may impose obligations or grant rights to all those who are or may come within the scope of the ESCB's tasks. They include regulations, decisions, recommendations, and opinions and so parallel the legal acts which are listed in Article 249 EC and which the Community institutions may adopt to fulfil their tasks.

2.1.1. ECB Regulations

The most far-reaching legal act of the ECB is the ECB Regulation, which, as stated in the first subparagraph of Article 110(2) EC,[35] shall have general application, be binding in its entirety and directly applicable in all Member States. ECB Regulations, which are normally adopted by the Governing Council of the ECB,[36] are thus comparable to national legislation with the difference that they are, from their entry into force, directly applicable law throughout the

---

ECB. At the same time, Declaration No 19 on Art. 10.6 of the Statute of the European Systems of Central Banks and of the Europan Central Bank was annexed to the Final Act of Nice, which calls upon the ECB to present the recommendation required for such an amendment "as soon as possible". This implies that the ECB as well as the Community institutions involved should endeavour to complete the envisaged amendment of Art. 10.2 at the latest before the next round of accessions to the Union.

[34] On an enumeration and description of the different types of ECB law, cf. ECB, "Legal Instruments of the European Central Bank", *Monthly Bulletin* (Frankfurt am Main, November 1999), 53.

[35] Cf. also Art. 34.2 of the Statute.

[36] Cf. Art. 17(1) of the Rules of Procedure of the ECB, *supra*, n. 6. The Governing Council may also delegate the adoption of regulations to the Executive Board (Art. 12.1, second subpara., third sentence of the Statute). Art. 17(3) of the Rules of Procedure of the ECB specifies that this may happen for the purpose of implementing ECB Regulations and Guidelines.

European Union,[37] and that they enjoy—as integral parts of Community law—supremacy over all kinds of national law, including constitutional law.[38] By virtue of their direct applicability, ECB Regulations not only apply independently of any measure of reception into national law, but a national transposition of ECB Regulations is even prohibited as it might conceal their Community law nature from those subject to them and also the exclusive competence of the ECJ to rule on their validity and their interpretation.[39]

For natural and legal persons operating in the financial markets, there are for the moment three important ECB Regulations of which they should be aware of:

—*Regulation ECB/1998/15 of 1 December 1998 on the application of minimum reserves*[40] requires credit institutions and their branches to hold minimum reserves on reserve accounts of the national central banks of the Member State in which they are established.[41] The reserve ratio is set at 2.0 per cent. The holding of the reserve requirement is remunerated in accordance with the rate of the ECB's main refinancing operations, set by the Governing Council of the ECB.[42] The compliance with the minimum reserve requirement is crucial for credit institutions as it is a precondition for taking part in any refinancing operation of the ECB.[43]

—*Regulation ECB/1998/16 of 1 December 1998 concerning the consolidated balance sheet of the monetary financial institutions sector*[44] imposes statistical reporting obligations on monetary financial institutions resident in participating Member States to enable the ECB to fulfil the ESCB's tasks.[45] The Regulation specifies the data which monetary financial institutions have to report to the ECB or to the national central bank of the Member State where

---

[37] Although they cannot confer rights or impose obligations on Member States with a derogation or special status; cf. Art. 43.1 of the Statute, Art. 8 of the Protocol on the United Kingdom and para. 2 of the Protocol on Denmark. However, such Regulations are still part of Community law for these Member States; cf. *infra*, Ch. 4, p. 164 *et seq.*

[38] Cf. the ECJ's famous rulings in Case 6/64, *Costa* v. *ENEL* [1964] ECR 585; and Case 11/70, *Internationale Handelsgesellschaft* v. *Einfuhr- und Vorratsstelle für Getreide und Futtermittel* [1970] ECR 1125.

[39] Case 39/72, *Commission* v. *Italy* [1973] ECR 101, para. 17 *et seq.*; Case 34/73, *Variola* v. *Amministrazione italiana delle Finance* [1973] ECR 981, para. 10 *et seq.*

[40] [1988] OJ L356/1, amended by Regulation ECB/2000/8 of 31 August 2000 amending Regulation ECB/1998/15 on the application of minimum reserves and amending Regulation ECB/1998/16 concerning the consolidated balance sheet of the monetary financial institutions sector [2000] OJ L229/34. Cf. also Regulation ECB/2000/11 of 2 November 2000 concerning transitional provisions for the application of minimum reserves by the European Central Bank following the introduction of the euro in Greece [2000] OJ L291/28.

[41] In accordance with Art. 19.2 of the Statute, the basis for the minimum reserves, the maximum permissible ratios between those reserves and their basis, and the appropriate sanctions in case of non-compliance are laid down in Council Regulation (EC) No 2531/98 of 23 November 1998 concerning the application of minimum reserves by the European Central Bank [1988] OJ L318/1.

[42] Cf. *supra*, n. 13.

[43] Cf. Guideline ECB/2000/7 of 31 August 2000 on monetary policy instruments and procedures of the Eurosystem [2000] OJ L310/1, Annex I, Chapter 2, 2.1: "Only institutions subject to the ESCB's minimum reserve system are eligible to be counterparties".

[44] [1988] OJ L356/7, as amended by Regulation ECB/2000/8, *supra*, n. 40.

they are established. The monetary financial institutions which are subject to such statistical reporting obligations of the ECB are enumerated in the List of MFIs for statistical purposes which is established and maintained by the Executive Board of the ECB and which can be accessed by the institutions concerned either via the Internet[46] or requested in paper form from the ECB or from the national central banks.[47]

—*Regulation ECB/1999/4 of 23 September 1999 on the powers of the European Central Bank to impose sanctions*[48] by which the ECB uses its regulatory powers to specify the arrangements whereby sanctions may be imposed by the ECB. The Regulation ensures that undertakings failing to comply with obligations under ECB Regulations and ECB Decisions can be investigated and santioned efficiently. At the same time, the Regulation provides for a high level protection of the rights of defence of the undertaking concerned and the confidentiality of the infringement procedure.

Of course, the adoption of ECB Regulations is also subject to the principle of conferred powers, which is a general principle of Community law[49] mentioned in Article 5(1) EC and explicitly extended to the activities of the ECB by Article 8 EC and Article 1.1 of the Statute. However, the limitations stemming from this principle should not be overestimated in view of the fact that the provisions of the EC Treaty and the Statute which confer normative powers to the ECB are, as usual in Community law, very broadly worded. In this sense, Article 110(1), first indent, EC[50] states that the ECB shall make regulations "to the extent *necessary* to implement the tasks defined in Article 3.1, first indent, Articles 19.1, 22 and 25.2 of the Statute of the ESCB and in cases which shall be laid down in the acts of the Council referred to in Article 107(6)".[51] The ECB's regulatory power is thus not limited to cases in which a specific power to adopt regulations is given to it by the Statute[52] or in legal acts adopted by the Council of the European Union,[53] but in

---

[45] In accordance with Art. 5.4 of the Statute, the natural and legal persons subject to statistical reporting obligations, confidentiality requirements and the appropriate provisions for enforcement are defined by Council Regulation 2533/98 of 23 November 1998 concerning the collection of statistical information by the European Central Bank [1988] OJ L318/8.

[46] At http://www.ecb.int. For any queries about this List of MFIs, the ECB can be contacted directly via electronic mail at mfi-assets.hotline@ecb.int.

[47] Art. 3 of Regulation ECB/1998/16, *supra*, n. 44.

[48] [1999] OJ L264/12. On the ECB's sanctioning regime see *infra*, p. 122 *et seq.*

[49] Opinion 2/94, *European Convention on Human Rights* [1998] ECR I–1763, para. 23 *et seq.*

[50] Cf. also Art. 34.1, first indent of the Statute.

[51] Emphasis added. The wording of these provisions shows that they are not restricted to listing the legal acts available to the ECB and to define their effects, but that they provide, in addition, a legal basis. In this sense, they differ from Art. 249 EC, which only lists and defines the legal acts available to the Community institutions, but does not itself contain a legal basis.

[52] As an example, Art. 22 of the Statute confers a specific power to the ECB to "make regulations to ensure efficient and sound clearing and payment systems within the Community and with other countries".

[53] For example, Art. 5 of Council Regulation 2533/98, *supra*, n. 45, which provides for the adoption of ECB Regulations for the definition and imposition of the ECB's reporting obligations on the actual reporting population of participating Member States.

addition extends to all cases in which it is necessary to implement the tasks conferred upon the ESCB, in particular the definition and implementation of the monetary policy of the Community.[54] In the context of monetary policy, the ECB thus has a normative power which is, although limited to this specific area, similar in quality to the one given to the Council of the European Union under Article 308 EC: a fall-back provision which enables the Council to take the appropriate measures whenever it "should prove necessary to attain, in the course of the operation of the common market, one of the objectives of the Community", even though the EC Treaty has not (explicitly or implicitly[55]) provided for the necessary powers.

2.1.2. ECB Decisions

Article 110(1), second indent, EC[56] confers the power on the ECB "to take decisions necessary for carrying out the tasks entrusted to the ESCB under this Treaty and this Statute" . A decision is defined as a legal act which "shall be binding in its entirety upon those to whom it is addressed" (Article 110(2), second subparagraph, EC[57]). ECB Decisions may be adopted by the Governing Council or the Executive Board in their respective domain of competence.[58]

ECB Decisions thus enable the ECB's decision-making bodies, first of all, to address legal acts to natural and legal persons in the Member States. Such a decision would be required, for instance, whenever the ECB wants to request statistical data from an undertaking[59] or when it decides to exempt an individual institution from reserve-requirements.[60] Also a decision would be needed whenever the ECB imposed sanctions on institutions for non-compliance with the minimum reserve requirements or statistical reporting requirements (Article 34.3 of the Statute).[61] Finally, the ECB also may adopt ECB Decisions addressed to the Member States which have adopted the single currency in accordance with the EC Treaty, for example in order to make use of its exclusive right, in existence since 1 January 1999, to approve the volume of coins issued by these Member States.[62]

---

[54] This broad meaning of the regulatory powers of the ECB is also noted by Weinbörner, *supra*, n. 1, 427 and by Louis, "A Legal and Institutional Approach for Building a Monetary Union" (1998) *CML Rev.* 33 (58 *et seq.*).

[55] This priority of implied powers before having recourse to Art. 308 EC is stressed by *Opinion 2/94*, *supra*, n. 49, para. 28.

[56] Cf. also Art. 34.1, second indent of the Statute

[57] Cf. also Art. 34.2, second subpara. of the Statute.

[58] Art. 17(4) of the Rules of Procedure of the ECB, *supra*, n. 6.

[59] This is possible under Art. 5.1 of the Statute.

[60] This can be done under the conditions set out in Art. 2(2) of Regulation ECB/1998/15, *supra*, n. 40; cf. also Art. 5 of this Regulation.

[61] For more details on the ECB's sanctioning competences cf. *infra*, p. 122 *et seq.*

[62] Cf. Decision ECB/1999/11 of 23 December 1999 on the approval of the volume of coin issuance in 2000 [2000] OJ L4/16; and Decision ECB/2000/17 of 14 December 2000 on the approval of the volume of coin issuance in 2001 [2000] OJ L336/118.

However, in Community law, the power *"to take decisions"* has a broad meaning and is not limited to the adoption of decisions with addressees.[63] It further extends to a number of other legal acts which have to be located somewhere in between Regulations and Decisions with addressees, and which are called in legal doctrine "atypical decisions", "decisions without addressees", *"Beschlüsse"*[64] or simply "legal acts *sui generis*".[65] That such atypical decisions are also available to the ECB[66] is, first of all, demonstrated by the broad wording of Article 110(1) EC itself which entitles the ECB to take all *necessary* decisions. This is repeated in Article 12.1, first subparagraph, first sentence of the Statute, according to which the Governing Council is responsible for taking "the decisions necessary to ensure the performance of the tasks entrusted to the ESCB under this Treaty and this Statute". The second sentence of this provision prescribes that such atypical decisions shall be used whenever the Governing Council formulates the monetary policy of the Community, in particular for "decisions on intermediate monetary objectives, key interest rates and the supply of reserves within the ESCB".

The main characteristic of all such atypical decisions is that they are—like regulations—of a normative character, as they produce legal effects for an unlimited number of persons and cases, and therefore—unlike typical decisions—do not have addressees;[67] however, they could be distinguished from regulations because they do not produce their legal effect automatically, but still require to be put into practice by subsequent legal instruments. An example is the setting of the ECB's main refinancing interest rate where fixed rate tenders have been chosen. As soon as it is set by the ECB, it is the rate to be applied to all refinancing operations throughout all Member States participating in the

---

[63] Cf. Art. 87(3)(e) EC which enables the Council to specify "by decision" categories of state aid compatible with the common market. This provision has always been understood in a broad sense and serves as a legal basis for the adoption of decisions, directives and regulations; cf. Mederer in Von der Groeben, Thiesing and Ehlermann (eds.), *supra*, n. 12, Art. 92, para. 212. As an example, cf. Council Directive 90/684/EEC of 21 December 1990 on aid to shipbuilding [1990] OJ L380/27.

[64] This German word, which indicates that the legal act in question does not necessarily have addressees and is thus a sub-group of an *"Entscheidung"*, is sometimes used in the German text of the EC Treaty; cf. Arts. 205(2) and (3), 219, 230(1) EC. A similar linguistic distinction can be observed in secondary Community legislation, in the German, Dutch and Danish versions of Community legislation where the words *"Beschluß"*, *"besluit"* and *"afgørelse"* are used.

[65] Cf. Bleckmann, *Europarecht* (6th edn., Cologne/Berlin/Bonn/Munich, 1997), para. 470 *et seq.*, and Louis, *L'ordre juridique communautaire* (6th edn., Luxembourg, 1993), para. 73 *et seq.*, who both mention a number of examples from Community practice. Cf. also Art. 14 of the ECSC Treaty which simply states that "decisions are binding in their entirety" and thus may either be of general application or only apply to individual cases, in which case they have to be notified to the individual concerned (Art. 15 of the ECSC Treaty).

[66] This is also the view of Louis, *supra*, n. 54, 54, and of Smits, *The European Central Bank. Institutional Aspects* (The Hague/London/Boston, 1997), 105 *et seq.*

[67] Atypical decisions thus resemble the *"Allgemeinverfügung"* known in German administrative law, which is an administrative act without addressees; cf. s. 35, second sentence of the German Administrative Procedure Act. As an example of such an *"Allgemeinverfügung"*, a number of writers pointed at the decision on the discount rate applied by the Bundesbank; cf. Gramlich, *supra*, Ch. 2, n. 11, Introduction, para. 23 *et seq.*; extensively Feldhahn, *Die Rechtsnatur der Diskontsatzfestsetzung der Deutschen Bundesbank und der dagegen gegebene Rechtsschutz* (Munich, 1991).

single currency; however, the legal effect of such a decision will extend to a credit institution only at the moment when this credit institution participates, by the conclusion of a contract with the ECB or a national central bank, in one of the ECB's refinancing operations.

Hitherto, the Governing Council of the ECB has used atypical decisions not only for some of its monetary policy decisions, in accordance with Article 12.1 of the Statute, but, in addition, on matters which concerned the organisational structure of the ECB,[68] its capital,[69] its annual accounts,[70] and the protection of its financial interests.[71] A number of further decisions without addressees were adopted which are interesting for the public at large and were therefore also published in the Official Journal of the European Communities:

—By *Decision ECB/1998/6 of 7 July 1998 on the denominations, specifications, reproduction, exchange and withdrawal of euro banknotes,*[72] the Governing Council of the ECB has, in particular, taken the decision that the euro banknotes—the issue of which falls within the ECB's exclusive competence under Article 106(1) EC—will include seven denominations in the range from 5 to 500 euro.

—By *Decision ECB/1998/12 of 3 November 1998 concerning public access to documentation and archives of the European Central Bank,*[73] a procedure has been established under which an individual may apply for access to administrative documents of the ECB.

—By *Decision ECB/2000/12 of 10 November 2000 on the publication of certain legal acts and instruments of the European Central Bank,*[74] the ECB made use

---

[68] In particular the Rules of Procedure of the ECB, *supra*, n. 6. Cf. also the Rules of Procedure of the General Council of the ECB of 1 September 1998 [1999] OJ L75/36, with Corrigendum [1999] OJ L156/52. Cf. also Decision ECB/1998/NP1 of 19 June 1998 on the appointment and on the duration of the mandate of the external auditor of the European Central Bank [2001] OJ L55/75 (published *a posteriori*).

[69] Cf. Decision ECB/1998/1, *supra*, n. 26; Decision ECB/1998/2 of 9 June 1998 laying down the measures necessary for the paying-up of the capital of the European Central Bank [1999] OJ L8/33; Decision ECB/1998/14 of 1 December 1998 laying down the measures necessary for the paying-up of the capital of the European Central Bank by the non-participating national central banks [1999] OJ L110/33; Decision ECB/2000/14 of 16 November 2000 providing for the paying up of capital and the contribution to the reserves and provisions of the ECB by the Bank of Greece, and for the initial transfer of foreign-reserve assets to the ECB by the Bank of Greece and related matters [2000] OJ L336/110.

[70] Cf. Decision ECB/2000/16 of 1 December 1998 on the annual account of the European Central Bank as amended on 15 December 1999 and on 12 December 1999 [2001] OJ L33/1.

[71] Cf. Decision ECB/1999/5 of 7 October 1999 on fraud prevention [1999] OJ L291/36. By this decision, the ECB established an Anti-Fraud Committee in order to to combat fraud and other illegal activities detrimental to its financial interests. Meanwhile, this decision has become the subject of an action for annulment of the Commission under Art. 230 EC, as the Commission claims the competence to protect the financial interests of the ECB for its Anti-Fraud Office OLAF; on the OLAF controversy, cf. *supra*, Ch. 1, p. 43 *et seq*.

[72] [1999] OJ L8/36, as amended by Decision ECB/1999/2 [1999] OJ L258/29. In its German version, this atypical decision is called a "*Beschluß*".

[73] [1999] OJ L110/30. Also, this decision is called a "*Beschluß*" in its German version.

[74] [2001] OJ L55/68—again a "*Beschluß*" in the German version.

of the possibility Article 110(2), fifth subparagraph EC and Article 34.2, fifth subparagraph of the Statute give them to enhance the transparency of the regulatory framework of the ESCB. Through a publication *a posteriori*, a number of important legal instruments, which were adopted by the EMI Council and the Governing Council of the ECB in 1998 and 1999, thereby were made accessible to the general public.

All these legal acts can be said to be very similar to regulations, and their effects on those to whom they apply are regulation-like, although they do not directly impose obligations on private parties. Therefore, a purist could question the legal form chosen by the ECB for these legal acts.[75] However, it should not be forgotten that the choice of the legal format is handled very flexibly in Community law; even the important legal act according to which initially 11 Member States of the European Union qualified for the adoption of the single currency was taken in the format of a decision addressed to the Member States,[76] although it clearly concerned immediately every individual in the European Union. The ECJ has compensated such flexible practice by its case law according to which, in the case of judicial review, not the format of a legal act is decisive, but the legal effects it intends to produce or in fact produces.[77]

2.1.3. ECB Recommendations

ECB Recommendations may be adopted both by the Governing Council and by the Executive Board of the ECB in their respective domains of competence.[78] Although ECB Recommendations are defined by Article 110(2), second subparagraph, EC[79] as having "no binding force", this does not mean that they are ECB law without any importance.

First of all, ECB Recommendations are an instrument for the ECB to initiate legislative procedures at Community level which lead to the enactment of complementary secondary legislation related to the ECB and its competences (Article 107(6) EC[80]). They thus enable the ECB to assume, within the Community's legislative process, the role of the Commission as initiator of

---

[75] For the denominations and technical specifications of euro coins intended for circulation, the Council—competent by virtue of Art. 106(2) EC—chose the format of a regulation; cf. Council Regulation 975/98 of 3 May 1998 [1998] OJ L139/6.

[76] Council Decision 98/317/EC, *supra*, Ch. 1, n. 93.

[77] Cf. in particular Case 147/83, *Binderer* v. *Commission* [1985] ECR 2572, para. 12, according to which the choice of form cannot alter the nature of a measure. Cf. also Case 22/70, *Commission* v. *Council (ERTA)* [1971] ECR 263, para. 40 *et seq.*: "The objective of this review [under Article 230] is to ensure, as required by Article 164 [now Article 220], the observance of the law in the interpretation and application of the Treaty. It would be inconsistent with this objective to interpret the conditions under which the action is admissible so restrictively as to limit the availability of this procedure merely to the categories of measures referred to by Article 189 [now Article 249]. An action for annulment must therefore be available in the case of all measures adopted by the institutions, *whatever their nature or form*, which are intended to have legal effect" (emphasis added).

[78] Art. 17(4), first sentence of the Rules of Procedure of the ECB, *supra*, n. 6.

[79] Cf. also Art. 34.2, second subpara. of the Statute.

[80] Cf. also Art. 42 of the Statute.

secondary legislation, as the Council can in this case act alternatively upon an ECB Recommendation or on a proposal from the Commission.[81] By virtue of a unanimous ECB Recommendation, the Governing Council could also initiate the simplified procedure for amending the Statute, which is provided for in Article 107(5) EC.[82] The Governing Council of the ECB[83] has used its initiating role several times already to influence the legal framework to be laid down by the Council of the EU as regards the ECB's minimum reserve requirements,[84] its sanctioning regime,[85] its statistical reporting obligations,[86] the external auditors of the ECB and of the national central banks,[87] further calls on foreign reserve assets by the ECB[88] and capital increases of the ECB.[89] It can be observed that the Council of the EU has hitherto relied on the expertise of the ECB as it has taken over the content of ECB Recommendations into its regulations without substantial amendments.[90]

But the ECB's competence to adopt recommendations is not restricted to participation in the Community's legislative process, as it amounts to a general power to formulate recommendations, comparable to that of the Commission under Article 211, second indent, EC. Therefore, the Governing Council of the ECB has also adopted ECB Recommendations on its own motion, for example

---

[81] The voting rules in the Council depend on whether it acts on an ECB Recommendation (qualified majority) or on a proposal from the Commission (unanimity is necessary to deviate from the proposal). Cf. now Art. 4(3) of Council Decision 1999/385/EC, ECSC, Euratom of 31 May 1999 adopting the Council's Rules of Procedure where the ECB's "right of initiative" is explicitly mentioned, thus mirroring the role of the Commission.

[82] Cf. also Art. 41 of the Statute.

[83] According to Art. 17(4), second sentence, of the Rules of Procedure of the ECB, *supra*, n. 6, ECB Recommendation for secondary Community legislation are always adopted by the Governing Council of the ECB.

[84] Recommendation of the European Central Bank of 7 July 1998 for a Council Regulation concerning the application of minimum reserves by the European Central Bank [1988] OJ C246/6; Recommendation ECB/2001/2 of 1 March 2001 for a Council Regulation concerning an amendment to Council Regulation (EC) No 2531/98 of 23 November 1998 concerning the application of minimum reserves by the European Central Bank [2001] OJ L00/00.

[85] Recommendation of the European Central Bank of 7 July 1998 for a Council Regulation concerning the powers of the European Central Bank to impose sanctions [1988] OJ C246/9.

[86] Recommendation of the European Central Bank of 7 July 1998 for a Council Regulation concerning the collection of statistical information by the European Central Bank [1988] OJ C246/12.

[87] Recommendation ECB/1998/3 of 19 June 1998 to the Council of the European Union on the external auditor of the European Central Bank [1988] OJ C246/5; Recommendation ECB/1998/5 of 12 November 1998 on the External Auditors of the national central banks [1988] OJ C411/11; Recommendation ECB/2000/2 of 10 February 2000 on the External Auditors of the national central banks [2000] OJ C62/21; Recommendation ECB/2000/10 of 5 October 2000 on the External Auditors of the national central banks [2000] OJ L259/65.

[88] Recommendation ECB/1999/1 for a Council Regulation concerning further calls of foreign reserve assets by the European Central Bank [1999] OJ C269/9.

[89] Recommendation ECB/1998/11 for a Council Regulation concerning the limits and conditions for capital increases of the European Central Bank [1998] OJ C411/10.

[90] Cf. Council Regulation 2531/98, *supra*, n. 41; Council Regulation 2532/98 concerning the powers of the European Central Bank to impose sanctions [1988] OJ L318/4; Council Regulation 2533/98, *supra*, n. 45; Council Regulation 1009/2000 of 8 May 2000 concerning capital increases of the European Central Bank [2000] OJ L115/1; Council Regulation 1010/2000 of 8 May 2000 concerning further calls of foreign reserve assets by the European Central Bank [2000] OJ L115/2.

Recommendation ECB/1998/7 of 7 July 1998 regarding the adoption of certain measures to enhance the legal protection of euro banknotes and coins,[91] which is addressed to the EU Council, the European Parliament, the Commission and the Member States. This ECB Recommendation provides, *inter alia*, that existing national legislation protecting the exclusive right of national central banks to issue national banknotes should, where necessary, be adapted before 2002 to cover the exclusive right conferred on the ECB by the EC Treaty with regard to banknotes. Moreover, the Recommendation underlines the need for a harmonisation of penal laws in the field of counterfeiting and for co-operation between national police forces through Europol, the Commission and the ECB; several legislative provisions have been adopted or are under discussion which are clearly inspired by this ECB Recommendation.[92]

It should be noted that, in accordance with the case law of the ECJ, an ECB Recommendation cannot be regarded as having no legal effect: the national courts are rather bound to take ECB Recommendations into consideration in order to decide disputes submitted to them, in particular when they cast light on the interpretation of national measures adopted in order to implement them or where they are designed to supplement binding Community provisions.[93] ECB Recommendations, like recommendations in Community law in general, thus can be said to have an *indirect direct effect* within the national legal orders.

2.1.4. ECB Opinions

The last legal act explicitly mentioned in Article 110(1) EC[94] is the ECB Opinion, which has no binding force, but nevertheless plays a significant role within the performance of the ECB's tasks. The power of the ECB to deliver opinions—which normally pertains to the Governing Council of the ECB[95]—is a very general one and includes the delivery of ECB opinions on its own motion and upon consultation.

---

[91] [1999] OJ C11/13.

[92] Cf. Council Framework Decision 2000/383/JHA of 29 May 2000 on increasing protection by criminal penalties and other sanctions against counterfeiting in connection with the introduction of the euro [2000] OJ L140/1, which explicitly notes the preceding ECB Recommendation; Council Regulation 1338/2001 of 28 June 2001 laying down measures necessary for the protection of the euro against counterfeiting [2001] OJ L181/6, based on Art. 123(4) EC; and Council Regulation 1339/2001 of 28 June 2001 extending the effects of Council Regulation 1338/01 laying down measures necessary for the protection of the euro against counterfeiting to those Member States which have not adopted the euro as their single currency [2001] OJ L181/11, based on Art. 308 EC. The influence of the ECB in the field of prevention of euro counterfeiting is also stressed by the joint press release of Commission, Europol and ECB of 7 March 2001, published at http://www.europol.eu.int/content.htm?news/prnew/en.htm;http://www.ecb.int/press/01/pr010307en.pdf;http://europa.eu.int/rapid/start/cgi/guesten.ksh?p_action.gettxt=gt&doc=IP/01/322|0|RAPID&lg=EN.

[93] Case 322/88, *Grimaldi* v. *Fonds des maladies professionnelles* [1989] ECR 4407, para. 18.

[94] Cf. also Art. 34(1) of the Statute.

[95] Art. 17(5) of the Rules of Procedure of the ECB, *supra*, n. 6. ECB Opinions may exceptionally be adopted by the Executive Board unless not fewer than three Governors state their wish to retain the competence of the Governing Council for the adoption of specific opinions. Such ECB Opinions adopted by the Executive Board have to be in line with comments provided by the Governing Council and have to take into account the contribution of the General Council of the ECB.

Consultation of the ECB by the Community institutions is foreseen in Article 105(4), first indent, EC. Under this provision, consultation of the ECB is compulsory for *any* proposed Community act in its field of competence. This is a very broad obligation[96] which extends to all Community institutions and bodies whenever they intend to adopt an act intended to produce legal effects, in particular regulations, directives, decisions, recommendations and opinions. The consultation of the ECB is thus today an integral part of the Community legislative process whenever it relates to legal acts in the field of Economic and Monetary Union or when it has an impact on the institutional structure of the ECB, as this also falls within the competence of the ECB (Articles 12.3 and 36.1 of the Statute). In some cases, the obligation for the Community institutions to consult the ECB is explicitly laid down in the Treaty, for example as regards amendments of the Protocol on the excessive deficit procedure (Article 104(14), second subparagraph EC),[97] the negotiation and conclusion of agreements concerning monetary or foreign exchange regime matters (Article 111(3) EC),[98] the decision to abrogate a derogation of a Member State which has not yet adopted the single currency (Article 123(5) EC) and also amendments of the Treaty as such whenever they include "institutional changes in the monetary area" (Article 48, second subparagraph, of the Treaty on European Union).[99]

Consultation of the ECB is not limited to the Community's legislative process, but has also become an essential part of national legislative procedures by virtue of Article 105(4) EC which requires consultation of the ECB "by national authorities regarding any draft legislative provision in its field of competence".[100] The EU Council set out the limits and the conditions of such consultation in Council Decision 98/415/EC of 29 June 1998 on the consultation of the European Central Bank by national authorities regarding draft legislative provisions.[101] According to this decision, national authorities shall consult the ECB in particular on draft legislative provisions on currency matters, on means of

---

[96] In contrast to this, the EMI, the ECB's predecessor, had only to be consulted by the EU Council on proposed Community acts; cf. Art. 117(6) EC. Cf. also *supra*, Ch. 1, n. 187.

[97] When this provision was used to adopt, in the context of the "Stability and Growth Pact", Council Regulation 1467/97 of 7 July 1997 on speeding up and clarifying the implementation of the excessive deficit procedure [1997] OJ L209/6, the EMI was consulted as the ECB's predecessor, in conformity with Art. 117(8) of the Treaty. Any amendments to this part of the "Pact" would today require an ECB Opinion.

[98] As an example, an ECB Opinion was delivered at the request of the EU Council on three Recommendations of 30 December 1998 for three Council Decisions concerning monetary relations with the Principality of Monaco, the Republic of San Marino and the Vatican City [1999] OJ C127/4.

[99] Under this provision, the ECB was consulted by the French Presidency on the proposal to amend Art. 10.2 of the Statute; cf. Opinion of the European Central Bank of 5 December 2000 at the request of the Presidency of the Council of the European Union on a proposal to amend Art. 10.2 of the Statute of the European System of Central Banks and of the European Central Bank (COM/00/30) [2000] OJ C362/13.

[100] This obligation applies also without limitations to Member States with a derogation by virtue of their participation in the third stage of EMU; cf. *infra*, Ch. 4, p. 135 *et seq*. On the peculiarities of the Danish and UK special status, cf. *infra*, Ch. 4, p. 137 *et seq*.

[101] [1988] OJ L189/42.

payment, on national central banks, on the collection, compilation, and distribution of monetary, financial, banking, payment systems and balance of payments statistics, on payment and settlement systems and on rules applicable to financial institutions in so far as they materially influence the stability of financial institutions and markets. From the purpose of this consultation process and from the way in which it is organised,[102] it becomes apparent that the consulting national authority is required to await the ECB Opinion and to take it duly into consideration *before* its decision on the substance. In the light of the case law of the ECJ on consultation requirements in the course of national legislative procedures which are imposed by Community law, and of the effect of non-compliance with such requirements (inapplicability of the relevant national legislation),[103] the importance of ECB Opinions should therefore not be underestimated. It seems very likely that non-compliance with the requirement to request an ECB Opinion and to take its content into account during the adoption of national legislation could be considered by the ECJ as a procedural defect[104] which would render such legislation inapplicable and which could be invoked by all individuals to which such legislation would apply.

2.1.5. ECB Directives?

A comparison between Articles 110 and 249 EC, which list the legal acts available to the ECB and to the Community institutions respectively, makes apparent the absence of directives in the ECB's catalogue.[105] Only at first glance does this seem to be a surprising *lacuna* in the EC Treaty.

Article 249(3) EC defines a directive as a legal act which "shall be binding, as to the result to be achieved, upon each Member State to which it is addressed, but shall leave to the national authorities the choice of form and methods" . A

---

[102] Art. 4 of *ibid.* requires each Member State to ensure effective compliance with the decision. Art. 3(4) thereof states that only in case of the expiry of a time limit set by the consulting national authority for the submission of the ECB Opinion, "the absence of an opinion shall not prevent further action by the consulting authority". Even in this case, the Member State concerned has to ensure that an ECB Opinion delivered after the expiry of the time limit is brought to the knowledge of its competent authorities. From this, one can conclude that the national authorities are prevented from taking any further action, in particular from taking any decision on the substance as long as they have not received the ECB Opinion and taken its content into consideration.

[103] Cf. in particular Case C–194/94, *CIA Security International SA* v. *Signalson and Securitel* [1996] ECR I–2201, para. 54, where the ECJ concludes that "Directive 83/189, under which Member States are required to notify certain technical reluations to the Commission, is to be interpreted as meaning that breach of the obligation to notify renders the technical regulations concerned inapplicable, so that they are unenforceable against individuals". It is submitted that the transfer of this conclusion to the obligation to consult the ECB on draft national legislation in its field of competence is not affected by the fact that this obligation is—apart from resulting directly from Art. 105(4), second indent, EC—not laid down in a Directive, but in a Decision addressed to the Member States, as the ECJ has taken the view that decisions addressed to the Member States may produce direct effect under the same conditions as directives; cf. Case 9/70, *Grad* v. *Finanzamt Traunstein* [1970] ECR 825, para. 5; Case C–156/91, *Hansa Fleisch Ernst Mundt GmbH & Co. KG* v. *Landrat des Kreises Schleswig-Flensburg* [1992] ECR I–5567, para. 2 *et seq.*

[104] Case C–194/94, *supra*, n. 103, para. 45.

[105] This is also noted by Louis, *supra*, n. 54, 54.

directive is thus the ideal instrument of two-stage legislation: the general rules and objectives are laid down in the directive itself by the Community institutions, while it is for the national authorities, in particular for the national legislature, to implement the directive by means of the national legal order. The instrument of the directive thus requires, by its very nature, legislative powers both at the Community level and at the level of the Member States.

Against this background, it makes perfect sense that no ECB Directives are mentioned in Article 110(1) EC.[106] As demonstrated in chapter 2, there is, within the ESCB, just one decision-making level, namely that of the ECB. The competences of the ECB are thus fields of exclusive competence where all national legislative competences have passed definitely and irrevocably to the Community level. Also in other areas of Community law where there is an exclusive competence—in particular in the field of the Common Agricultural Policy—regulations are used instead of directives. The absence of directives within the catalogue of the ECB's legal acts is thus not a *lacuna*, but again a reflection of the centralisation of decision-making powers within the ESCB.

There is only one case where the EC Treaty leaves some scope for the adoption of ECB directives, i.e. legal acts addressed by the ECB to the Member States which would require implementation by national law. As can be seen from Article 105(3) EC, the exclusive competence of the ECB to hold and manage the official foreign reserves of the Member States is without prejudice to the holding and management by the governments of the Member States of their foreign exchange working balances. There is thus a—though very limited—residual competence of the Member States in this field. As transactions of the Member States with their working balances may have an impact on the monetary policy defined by the ECB, Article 31.2 and 31.3 of the Statute enable the ECB to adopt exceptionally legal acts addressed to the Member States to approve or to facilitate such operations in order to ensure consistency with the monetary and exchange rate policies, in particular with their primary aim of price stability. From their legal nature, such acts could thus be regarded as the exceptional example of ECB Directives—a legal situation which is not recognised by the English version of the Statute, which calls them "guidelines", but by the German text of Article 31.3 of the Statute where these legal acts are referred to as "*Richtlinien*" (directives).[107]

---

[106]   The same is true for Art. 34.1 of the Statute.

[107]   This view is shared by Louis, *supra*, n. 54, 55. Cf. also the Spanish text of Art. 31.3 of the Statute where the word "*directrices*" is used instead of "*orientaciones*" (guidelines); this resembles the "*directivas*" (directive), although the difference in wording suggests that the *sui generis* nature of ECB directives was recognised in the Spanish version. On ECB Directives cf. also Selmayr, *supra*, n. 5, 374. On 3 November 1998, the Governing Council of the ECB adopted a "Guideline", based on Art. 31.3 of the Statute, addressed to the Member States which have adopted the single currency, and therefore to be qualified, from its legal nature, as an ECB Directive. According to this ECB Directive, the participating Member States will have to give advance notice to the ECB of any transactions with their foreign exchange working balances which exceed a certain amount; cf. ECB, *Monthly Bulletin* (Frankfurt am Main, January 1999), 38.

2.2. ECB law intended to produce legal effects inside the ESCB

As the relationship between the ECB and the national central banks is a legal relationship, established by the EC Treaty and the Statute, it is necessary that the ECB also has legal instruments at its disposal which apply in this relationship and thus serve to maintain the integrity of the System. Two types of such legal instruments may be distinguished: ECB law which is, first of all, intended to produce external legal effects, but also applies inside the ESCB; and ECB law which is addressed only to the Executive Board of the ECB and/or to the national central banks, the so-called ECB Guidelines, and ECB Instructions.

2.2.1. The effects of ECB Regulations, ECB Decisions, ECB Recommendations, ECB Opinions and ECB Directives inside the ESCB

It is almost self-evident in a system governed by the rule of law that all legal acts adopted by the ECB—the System's governor—which are intended to produce external legal effects, automatically also bind all component parts of the ESCB. Thus, an ECB Regulation, adopted by the Governing Council of the ECB with the purpose of applying uniformly in all Member States which have adopted the single currency, has to be, from the moment of its entry into force, observed and—if its content so requires—applied also by the ECB itself and the national central banks.

The fact that ECB law intended to produce, first of all, external legal effects also has legal effects within the system can be seen very clearly from the example of Regulation ECB/1998/16 of 1 December 1998 concerning the consolidated balance sheet of the monetary financial institutions sector.[108] This ECB Regulation not only imposes statistical reporting obligations on private individuals, but also requires the ECB and the national central banks to make accessible the List of MFIs to the institutions concerned.[109] In addition, it obliges the national central banks to define the reporting procedures[110] and exercise the right to verify or compulsorily to collect information from the reporting agents.[111]

It is submitted that even if the ECB and the national central banks are not mentioned explicitly in legal acts adopted by the ECB's decision-making bodies, they are bound to observe and—where necessary—to comply with the rules laid down in such legal acts. For the ECB, this results from the general legal principle that by creating a legal act one can only deviate from it by amending this legal act.[112] For the national central banks, this follows from their position as an

---

[108] *Supra*, n. 44.
[109] *Ibid.*, Art. 3.
[110] *Ibid.*, Art. 4.
[111] *Ibid.*, Art. 6.
[112] This principle of *"patere legem"* is also said to apply to the ECB by Louis, *supra*, n. 54, 56. Cf. also Case 68/86, *United Kingdom* v. *Council* [1998] ECR 855, para. 48: "The Council is therefore under a duty to comply with the procedural rule which it itself laid down in Art. 6(1) of its Rules of Procedure. It cannot depart from that rule, unless it formally amends those rules".

integral part of the ESCB (Article 14.3 of the Statute) and from their submission to the governance by the ECB's decision-making bodies (Article 107(3) EC and Article 8 of the Statute). A practical example are ECB Decisions on interest rates: as soon as the Governing Council has decided on the interest rate for the main refinancing operations to be carried out through the ESCB, all component parts of the ESCB have to apply this interest rate. This is an automatic legal consequence of such a decision, which is binding on the system as a whole from the moment of its adoption; it is thus not necessary to address this decision explicitly to the national central banks or even to adopt a new legal act which requires the national central banks to "implement" the decision on the interest rate. The centralised decision-making structure of the ESCB thus necessarily also leads to a monist legal system which consists of only *one* legal order, not of the ECB's legal order and the 15 legal orders of the national central banks, which would require implementation of ECB law.

Accordingly, all legal acts adopted by the ECB's decision-making bodies automatically become law within the whole system from the moment of their adoption. Against this background, the principle of System integrity requires the ECB to ensure that all component parts of the system are notified about the content of ECB law immediately after its adoption,[113] and that the national central banks take such law duly into account or even apply it, if so required by its content.

2.2.2. ECB Guidelines and ECB Instructions

In addition to ECB law which is intended to produce external legal effects, but also automatically binds the ESCB's component entities, the Statute provides for two further legal instruments which can be used to address primarily the legal relationships inside the system.[114] Articles 12.1 and 14.3 of the Statute call such legal instruments "guidelines" and "instructions", and in the Rules of Procedure of the ECB they are referred to as "ECB Guidelines" and "ECB Instructions".[115] They are used as instruments to ensure the implementation of the ESCB tasks either by the ECB's own activities or through the national central banks (Article 9.2 of the Statute).

ECB Guidelines are normally adopted by the Governing Council of the ECB[116] and have two potential addressees: either the Executive Board, which,

---

[113] The notification could be made also electronically; cf. Art. 17(2) and 17(6) of the Rules of Procedure of the ECB, *supra*, n. 6. On the principle of System integrity, cf. *supra*, Ch. 2, p. 80 *et seq.*

[114] Cf. also Louis, *supra*, n. 54, 55, who considers guidelines and instructions as "the typical instruments for the relations between the ECB and the NCBs" and Smits, *supra*, n. 66, 104, according to whom because of this different function "guidelines and instructions are not to be taken in the form provided for in Art. 34.1; they are binding legal acts *sui generis*".

[115] Art. 17(2) and 17(6) thereof, *supra*, n. 6.

[116] This is stated in Art. 17(2) of the Rules of Procedure of the ECB, *supra*, n. 6. However, Art. 17(3) thereof allows for a delegation of this normative power to the Executive Board for the purpose of implementing an ECB Regulation or an ECB Guideline.

by virtue of Article 12.1, second subparagraph, first sentence, of the Statute, shall implement monetary policy in accordance with the guidelines of the Governing Council; or the national central banks, which have to act in accordance with ECB Guidelines because of Article 14.3 of the Statute. At first glance, one could take the name "guideline" to indicate that they are a kind of "soft law" and thus policy orientations rather than legally binding instruments.[117] However, one should remember that in Community law, as already mentioned, it is not the name given to a legal act, but its legal nature which is decisive.[118] For ECB Guidelines, it is particularly important to analyse their legal nature in each individual case, as in Community practice the term "guideline' has been used very flexibly.[119] One finds them in the form of mere guidelines,[120] as a part of communications,[121] resolutions,[122] conclusions,[123] and recommendations,[124]

[117] This is suggested in particular by the name given to guidelines in the French ("*orientations*"), the Italian ("*indirizzi*"), the Spanish ("*orientaciones*") and in the Portuguese ("*orientacões*") versions of the Statute.

[118] *Supra*, p. 97 and n. 77. This can be seen most drastically at the example of EC directives which are only called "Recommendations" by the ECSC Treaty, but nevertheless defined to "be binding as to the result to be achieved" both by Art. 249(3) of the EC Treaty and Art. 14(3) of the ECSC Treaty.

[119] Examples of guidelines which are explicitly mentioned in the EC Treaty are: the broad *guidelines* of the economic policies of the Member States and of the Community (Art. 99(2) EC); the *guidelines* for employment under Art. 128(2)–(5) EC; the *guidelines* covering the objectives, priorities and broad lines of measures envisaged in the sphere of trans-European networks (Art. 155(1), first indent, EC); the *guidelines* prescribed by para. 5 of the Protocol No 30 on the application of the principle of subsidiarity and proportionality, annexed to the EC Treaty, which are thus guidelines established by primary Community law. In secondary Community law, to mention just one example, Art. 6 of Council Decision 83/516/EEC on the tasks of the European Social Fund [1983] OJ L289/38 entitles the Commission to adopt each year and for the three following years "the Fund-management *guidelines* for determining those operations which reflect Community priorities as defined by the Council and in particular the action programmes in the area of employment and vocational training". The Commission shall forward to the European Parliament and the Council these guidelines drawn up in close consultation with the Member States, taking account of any views expressed by the European Parliament, and shall publish them in the OJ.

[120] Cf. the guidelines of 9 March 1998 for strengthening operational co-ordination between the Community and the Member States in the field of development co-operation [1988] OJ C97/1; guidelines of 20 June 1994 for joint reports on third countries [1996] OJ C274/52; Medium-term guidelines for coal 1975 to 1985 [1975] OJ C22/1.

[121] Cf. Communication from the Commission—Community guidelines on state aid for environmental protection [1994] OJ C72/3. On the legal effect of such guidelines cf. Jestaedt and Häsemeyer, "Die Bindungswirkung von Gemeinschaftsrahmen und Leitlinien im EG-Beihilfenrecht" [1995] *EuZW* 787; cf. also Case T–150/95, *UK Steel Association* v. *Commission* [1997] ECR II–1433 where the ECJ refused an automatic application of these EC guidelines within the context of the ECSC Treaty, but did not deny that they had legal effect.

[122] Council Resolution of 13 December 1993 concerning future guidelines for the "Europe against Cancer" programme following evaluation of it for the period 1987 to 1992 [1994] OJ C15/1; Council Resolution of 6 February 1979 concerning the guidelines for Community regional policy [1979] OJ C36/10.

[123] Conclusions of the Ministers of Culture meeting within the Council of 12 November 1992 on guidelines for Community cultural action [1992] OJ C336/1.

[124] Cf. Council Recommendation of 22 April 1996 on guidelines for preventing and restraining disorder connected with football matches [1996] OJ C131/1.

but also clothed in inter-institutional-agreements,[125] decisions,[126] directives,[127] regulations[128] and even primary Community law.[129] From the scheme of the Statute, it can be seen that ECB Guidelines are considered to be separate legal instruments to be used for determining legal relations within the ESCB. However, this certainly does not rule out that sometimes rules which, taken in isolation, would be ECB Guidelines, could be contained in an ECB Decision or an ECB Regulation. This would be the case in particular where the technique of legal drafting, for reasons of consistency and transparency, had to deal with obligations of individuals and of national central banks in a single legal text.[130]

That ECB Guidelines are meant to be legally binding instruments is demonstrated, first of all, by Articles 12.1 and 14.3 of the Statute which require the Executive Board and the national central banks to act in accordance with ECB Guidelines; one can hardly be required to act in accordance with a text if it is not legally binding. The binding nature of ECB Guidelines is further confirmed by a comparison with the guidelines which could be adopted by the European Monetary Institute (EMI), the ECB's predecessor. While Article 15.3 of the EMI Statute explicitly stated that "EMI guidelines shall have no binding force", the striking absence of such a provision for ECB Guidelines shows, *a contrario*, that these are considered to be legally binding.[131] This understanding of ECB Guidelines is stressed by Article 17(3) of the Rules of Procedure of the ECB[132] which circumscribes the competence of the Governing Council of the ECB to adopt regulations and guidelines with "*normative* powers".

From their legal nature, ECB Guidelines can thus be clearly distinguished from the so-called "broad guidelines of the economic policies of the Member States and of the Communities", which are foreseen in Article 99(2) EC as an instrument of economic policy co-ordination. These broad economic policy guidelines are originally contained only in a conclusion adopted by the European Council, which is a political institution and not a body entitled to enact Community law. At a later stage, the broad guidelines are clothed by the

---

[125] Cf. Inter-institutional agreement of 11 December 1997 between the European Parliament, the Council of the European Union and the Commission on Common guidelines for the quality of drafting of Community legislation [1988] OJ C73/1.

[126] Commission Decision 93/326/EEC of 13 May 1993 establishing indicative guidelines for the fixing of costs and fees in connection with the Community eco-label [1993] OJ L129/23.

[127] Cf. Commission Directive 98/88/EC of 13 November 1998 establishing guidelines for the microscopic identification and estimation of constituents of animal origin for the official control of feedingstuffs [1988] OJ L318/45.

[128] Council Regulation 1334/92 of 18 May 1992 fixing the guideline figure for the 1992/93 milk year for the fat content of standardised whole milk imported into Ireland and the United Kingdom [1992] OJ L145/5.

[129] Cf. the guidelines on the application of the principle of subsidiarity and proportionality, *supra*, n. 119.

[130] As an example, one could point to Regulation ECB/1998/16, *supra*, n. 44.

[131] This is also the view of Scheller in Von der Groeben, Thiesing and Ehlermann (eds.), *supra*, n. 12, following Art. 109 f, Satzung EWI Art. 15, para. 3, n. 68.

[132] *Supra*, n. 6.

EU Council in a recommendation[133] (Article 99(2), third subparagraph, EC); this means in a legal act without binding force and therefore of only limited legal effect.[134] In contrast to this, ECB Guidelines are adopted by a decision-making body of the ECB, which is entitled to make law, and the Statute itself attributes legal effect to them by obliging both the Executive Board and the national central banks to act in accordance with them. The normative distinction between these broad guidelines and ECB Guidelines thus reflects the different degree of legal integration in the context of economic union (mere co-ordination of the economic policies of the Member States) and of monetary union (irreversible transfer of the competence for monetary policy to the Community level).

The scheme of the Statute implies that ECB Guidelines are legal instruments which normally only lay down rules of a general and abstract character, but require implementation either by the Executive Board or the national central banks. They have thus a certain similarity with EC directives, which may be adopted by the Community institutions to bind the Member States as to the result to be achieved, but leave to them the choice of form and methods for their implementation.[135] However, there are two main differences between EC directives and ECB Guidelines: from a formal point of view, EC directives are addressed to the Member States, while ECB Guidelines are addressed either to the Executive Board or to the national central banks. From a substantial point, EC directives are, as already mentioned, the typical instrument for a two-stage-legislative process in fields where both the Community institutions and the Member States have the competence to legislate. Within the ESCB, however, all law-making powers have been transferred to the decision-making bodies of the ECB. Therefore, ECB Guidelines, at least when addressed to the national

---

[133] As a first example, cf. Council Recommendation 94/7/EC of 22 December 1993 on the broad guidelines of the economic policies of the Member States and of the Community [1994] OJ L7/9. Cf. also Council Recommendation 2000/517/EC of 19 June 2000 on the broad guidelines of the economic policies of the Member States and of the Community [2000] OJ L210/1.

[134] As seen, *supra*, n. 93, the format of a recommendation does not mean that these broad guidelines cannot produce any effect. The EC Treaty itself prescribes a surveillance procedure under Art. 99(3) and (4) EC under which the Council assesses whether the Member States' economic policies are consistent with the broad guidelines. Inconsistency may be sanctioned by means of a further recommendation addressed to a deviating Member State and of a publication of this recommendation; this happened for the first time with Council Recommendation 2001/191/EC of 12 February 2001 with a view to ending the inconsistency with the broad guidelines of economic policies in Ireland— Application of Art. 99(4) of the Treaty establishing the European Communities [2001] OJ L69/22, where the Council "reprimanded" the Irish government for the adoption of a pro-cyclical and therefore inflationary budget. It should also be noted that the broad economic guidelines form the framework for the new "guidelines for employment", as these have to be consistent with them (Art. 128(2), second sentence EC). The legal status of these guidelines for employment is similar to that of the broad economic policy guidelines, as they are clothed in Council resolutions—cf., as a first example, the Council Resolution of 15 December 1997 on the 1998 Employment Guidelines [1988] OJ C30/1—as Member States are obliged to "take into account" these guidelines in their employment policies and as they have to implement their employment policies "in the light of the guidelines for employment" (Art. 128(3) EC).

[135] The same comparison is made by Louis, *supra*, n. 54, 55 *et seq.*; cf. also Zilioli in Von der Groeben, Thiesing and Ehlermann (eds.), *supra*, n. 12, following Art. 109 m, Satzung ESZB and EZB Art. 12, para. 6.

central banks, cannot require legislative implementation, but only implementation by means of administrative measures or by the conclusion of contracts, either by the Executive Board or the national central banks.

In contrast to the abstract and general nature of ECB Guidelines, *ECB Instructions* allow for a very detailed legal prescription of the addressee's behaviour. Only the Executive Board of the ECB has the power to give ECB Instructions,[136] which are always to be addressed to one or more national central banks. That the competence to give ECB Instructions is entrusted to the Executive Board shows the context in which they shall be used: in the course of the daily management of the ECB and its monetary policy, in particular if a speedy reaction to developments in the financial markets appears necessary. Article 14.3 of the Statute confirms the legally binding character of such instructions, as the national central banks have to act in accordance with them.

2.2.3. External legal effects of ECB Guidelines and ECB Instructions

The fact that both ECB Guidelines and ECB Instructions are, as a rule, legal instruments used only inside the ESCB does not preclude them from producing certain external effects.[137] First of all, it is a common principle of most national legal systems,[138] which is also recognised in Community law, that legal instruments used by the administration internally can have, externally, the legal effect that they set forth a rule of conduct indicating the practice to be followed and from which the administration may not depart without giving reasons, since otherwise the *principle of equality of treatment* would be infringed.[139] Also the ECB and the national central banks will thus have to pay attention to not departing in an arbitrary or capricious manner from the rules of conduct established by ECB Guidelines and ECB Instructions—a behaviour which would in any event be highly unusual for a central banking system committed to price stability and thus keen on promoting also a stable legal environment for its monetary policy operations.

In addition, the ECJ traditionally has shown its readiness to recognise a so-called *direct effect* of all measures of Community law which are legally binding.[140]

---

[136] Of course, the scope of this instructing power depends very much on the legal framework under which it is exercised: the more detailed the obligations already imposed on the national central banks by regulations, decisions and guidelines of the Governing Council of the ECB are, the less is there a need for further prescriptions by the Executive Board.

[137] Louis, *supra*, n. 54, 57 stresses that it would be "misleading to regard guidelines as internal acts for the organisation of the System".

[138] Cf., as an example, the potential external effect of administrative circulars in German administrative law, as mentioned by Maurer, *supra*, Ch. 2, n. 93, 613 *et seq.*

[139] In the case of an "internal directive" of the Commission, such legal effect was confirmed by the ECJ in Case 148/73, *Louwage* v. *Commission* [1974] ECR 81, para. 12.

[140] On primary EC law, cf. Case 26/62, *Van Gend & Loos* [1963] ECR 1 (12). On directives, cf. Case 8/81, *Becker* v. *Finanzamt Münster-Innenstadt* [1982] ECR 53, para. 22: "It would be incompatible with the binding effect which Article 189 [now Article 249 EC] ascribes to directives to exclude in principle the possibility of the obligations imposed by them being relied on by persons concerned"; on decisions, cf. Case 9/70 and Case C–156/91, *supra*, n. 103: "It would be incompatible with the binding effect attributed to decisions by Article 189 [now Article 249 EC] to exclude in principle the possibility that persons affected may invoke the obligations by the decision".

As a consequence, individuals may invoke the provisions of Community law before national authorities against any conflicting provision of national law or rely on them in national courts, independently of any implementation measures and under the sole condition that they are sufficiently precise, i.e. sufficiently clear and unconditional.[141] In this context, it is irrelevant whether or not the individual is an addressee of the Community law provision in question, as the ECJ has always considered it as a means of ensuring the effectiveness of obligations created by Community law for the Member States and their authorities to enable individuals directly to rely on such obligations.[142]

Against this background, and in view of the binding character of ECB Guidelines and ECB Instructions, it seems likely that the ECJ would also attribute to them such direct effect, in any case where individuals attempt to rely on sufficiently precise terms of an ECB Guideline or an ECB Instruction.[143] The fact that ECB Guidelines are addressed to the Executive Board and/or the national central banks and that ECB Instructions are addressed solely to the national central banks would not rule out such direct effect, nor could the ECB or the national central banks by other means exclude such direct effect in favour of individuals concerned.[144]

---

[141] On primary Community law, cf. Case 26/62, *supra*, n. 140, 12: "Independently of the legislation of the Member States, Community law therefore not only imposes obligations on individuals but is also intended to confer upon them rights which become part of their legal heritage. These rights arise not only where they are expressly granted by the Treaty, but also by reasons of obligations which the Treaty imposes in a clearly defined way upon individuals as well as upon the Member States and upon the institutions of the Community". On directives, cf. Case 8/81, *supra*, n. 140, para. 25: "Thus, wherever the provisions of a directive appear, as far as their subject-matter is concerned, to be unconditional and sufficiently precise, those provisions may, in the absence of implementing measures adopted within the prescribed period, be relied upon as against any national provision which is incompatible with the directive or in so far as the provisions define rights which individuals are able to assert against the State".

[142] On primary Community law, cf. Case 26/62, *supra*, n. 140, 13: "The fact that under this Article it is the Member States who are made the subject of the negative obligation does not imply that their nationals cannot benefit from this obligation. The vigilance of individuals concerned to protect their rights amounts to an effective supervision". On directives, cf. Case 8/81, *supra*, n. 140, para. 19: "Particularly in cases in which the Community authorities have, by means of a directive, placed Member States under a duty to adopt a certain course of action, the effectiveness of such a measure would be diminished if persons were prevented from relying upon it in proceedings before a national court and national courts were prevented from taking it into account as an element of Community law".

[143] This view is shared by a number of legal writers; cf. Louis, *supra*, n. 54, 56 *et seq.*: "Third parties can draw rights from the guidelines and instructions"; Selmayr, *supra*, n. 5, 375; Weber, *supra*, n. 1, 160 *et seq.*: "unmittelbare Wirkung der Ausführungsleitlinien" and 213 *et seq.*: "unmittelbare Wirkung der Weisung"; Zilioli in Von der Groeben, Thiesing and Ehlermann (eds.), *supra*, n. 12, following Art. 109 m, Satzung ESZB and EZB Art. 12, para. 13. In view of the case law of the ECJ, the view of Stadler, *supra*, n. 1, 153, n. 155, appears to be too narrow, as he qualifies guidelines as "*systeminternes 'Binnenrecht'*" which, as a matter of principle, may not deploy "*systemexterne Rechtswirkungen*".

[144] In the light of the case law of the ECJ, the following sentence in the Introduction to Guideline ECB/2000/7 on the monetary policy instruments and procedures of the Eurosystem, *supra*, n. 43, has to be interpreted narrowly: "The general documentation does not in itself confer rights on counterparties". It cannot be excluded that counterparties concerned could, in individual cases, rely on the duties imposed on national central banks by this ECB Guideline, e.g. the duty to grant institutions which fulfil the general counterparty eligibility criteria (specified in Section 2.1 of the General documentation, attached as annex to the Guideline) access to the marginal lending facility.

A practical case of such direct effect could arise if a national central bank did not properly implement an ECB Guideline or an ECB Instruction, for example in a contract with a credit institution.

However, as ECB Guidelines and ECB Instructions are not addressed to private individuals, but normally to the national central banks, their binding nature exists—in accordance with the settled case law of the ECJ[145]—only in relation to each national central bank to which they are addressed. It follows that ECB Guidelines and ECB Instructions may not in themselves impose obligations on an individual, and that their provisions may neither be relied upon as such by the ECB nor by the national central banks against such a person.[146]

The ECB has recognised the possibility that its guidelines and instructions may produce legal effects outside the ESCB by publishing the contents of some ECB Guidelines, either in a summarised form[147] or even in the Official Journal of the European Communities; the latter is now increasingly the case, as demonstrated by the following list of published ECB Guidelines:

—*Guideline ECB/1998/NP10[148] of 3 November 1998 on the implementation of Article 52 of the Statute of the European System of Central Banks and of the European Central Bank,[149] now supplemented by Guideline ECB/2000/6 on the implementation of Article 52 of the Statute of the European System of Central Banks and of the European Central Bank after the end of the transitional period[150];*

—*Guideline ECB/1998/17 of 1 December 1998 on the statistical reporting requirements of the European Central Bank in the field of balance of payments and international investment position statistics[151];*

—*Guideline ECB/1998/NP28 of 22 December 1998 concerning the rules and minimum standards to protect the confidentiality of the individual statistical information collected by the European Central Bank assisted by the national central banks[152];*

—*Guideline ECB/1999/3 of 7 July 1998 on certain provisons regarding euro banknotes, as amended on 26 August 1999[153];*

---

[145] Cf. Case 80/86, *Kolpinghuis Nijmegen BV* [1987] ECR 3969, para. 9.

[146] This is already stressed by Zilioli in Von der Groeben, Thiesing and Ehlermann (eds.), *supra*, n. 12, following Art. 109m, Satzung ESZB and EZB Art. 12, para. 13.

[147] Cf. ECB, *The single monetary policy in stage three: General documentation on ESCB monetary policy instruments and procedures* (Frankfurt am Main, September 1998). Today, this general documentation is published as Guideline ECB/2000/7, *supra*, n. 43.

[148] "NP" means "non-published" and indicates that originally this guideline was meant to be a legal instrument for the internal use of the ESCB only.

[149] [2001] OJ L55/69 (published *a posteriori*).

[150] [2001] OJ L55/66.

[151] [1999] OJ L115/47.

[152] [2001] OJ L55/72 (published *a posteriori*).

[153] [1999] OJ L258/29, as amended by Guideline ECB/1999/3 [1999] OJ L258/32, with corrigendum [2000] OJ L287/68.

—*Guideline ECB/1999/NP11 of 22 April 1999 on the authorisation to issue national banknotes during the transitional period*[154];
—*Guideline ECB/2000/1 of 3 February 2000 on the management of the foreign reserve assets of the European Central Bank by the national central banks and the legal documentation for operations involving the foreign reserve assets of the European Central Bank* [155];
—*Guideline ECB/2000/7 of 31 August 2000 on monetary policy instruments and procedures of the Eurosystem*[156];
—*Guideline ECB/2000/15 of 16 November 2000, amending the (unpublished) Guideline of the European Central Bank of 3 November 1998 on the composition, valuation and modalities for the initial transfer of foreign-reserve assets, and the denomination and remuneration of equivalent claims*[157];
—*Guideline ECB/2000/18 of 1 December 1998 on the legal framework for accounting and reporting in the European System of Central Banks as amended on 15 December 1999 and 14 December 2000*[158];
—*Guideline ECB/2001/1 of 10 January 2001 adopting certain provisions on the 2002 cash changeover*[159];
—*Guideline ECB/2001/3 of 26 April 2001 on a Trans-European Automated Real-Time Gross Settlement Express Transfer system (Target).*[159a]

The legally binding nature of these ECB Guidelines is underlined by publication in part L (legislatio) of the Official Journal and by their last recital, which states: "Whereas, in accordance with Articles 12.1 and 14.3 of the Statute, ECB Guidelines form *an integral part of Community law*".[160]

2.3. ECB law with internal and external effects: is there really a difference?

One may finally ask the legitimate question whether it is really necessary to distinguish between those legal acts of the ECB which are intended to produce external legal effects, and ECB Guidelines and ECB Instructions, if the former are always automatically binding on all component parts of the ESCB and also

---

[154] [2001] OJ L44/71 (published *a posteriori*).

[155] [2000] OJ L207/24.

[156] Cf. *supra*, n. 147.

[157] [2000] OJ L336/114.

[158] [2001] OJ L33/21.

[159] [2001] OJ L55/80.

[159a] [2001] OJ L140/72.

[160] This sentence is identical to the famous formula used by the ECJ to show that international agreements concluded by the Community form "an integral part of Community law" from the date they come into force and without the need of further implementing measures"; cf. Case 181/73, *Haegeman* v. *Belgium* [1974] ECR 449, para. 5. The consequence of this is that, first, the ECJ has exclusive jurisdiction on the interpretation of such agreements; secondly, that such agreements are directly applicable both in the Community legal order and in those of the Member States; thirdly, that they enjoy, like all Community law, supremacy over all types of national law; and fourthly, that their provisions may create individual rights under the condition that they are sufficiently precise; cf. Case 104/81, *Hauptzollamt Mainz* v. *Kupferberg* [1982] ECR 3641, para. 9 *et seq*. On this monist incorporation of international agreements into the Community legal order cf. Schroeder and Selmayr, "Der EuGH, das GATT und die Vollzugslehre. Warum der EuGH manchmal das Völkerrecht ignoriert" [1998] *JZ* 344.

the latter may deploy external effects. It is true that against this background, whether or not to choose a legal act under Article 110(1) EC and Article 34.1 of the Statute becomes more a matter of degree than a matter of varying the legal effects of the legal instrument in question. It thus resembles the general problem of the distinction between regulations and directives in Community law which has become more and more irrelevant in view of the jurisprudence of the ECJ which has increasingly assimilated directives and regulations.

However, two fundamental differences justify maintaining a distinction between ECB legal acts under Article 110(1) EC and Article 34.1 of the Statute on the one hand, and ECB Guidelines and ECB Instructions on the other hand: first, publication is prescribed by Article 110(2) EC and Article 34.2 of the Statute only for ECB Regulations and ECB Decisions which, being of general application, have effects similar to those of ECB Regulations. ECB Guidelines and ECB instructions are thus a useful instrument for dealing with legal issues inside the ESCB in a confidential manner, where the tasks of the ESCB so require; they are also not subject to the general language requirements of Community law[161] so that one could very well imagine the ECB adopting ECB Guidelines and ECB Instructions solely in, say, English and notifying them to the national central banks electronically, for the sake of a speedy and efficient implementation of the ECB's monetary policy.[162] The second difference is that the ECB is able to impose obligations on private individuals only through ECB Regulations or ECB Decisions, while ECB Guidelines and ECB Instructions may create obligations exclusively inside the ESCB.

III. THE IMPLEMENTATION OF ECB LAW

While the making of ECB law is done solely by the decision-making bodies of the ECB, its implementation follows a different pattern. It should be noted that for a central bank, the implementation of its policy is not of secondary importance. *Au contraire*, it is only at the level of implementation that banknotes are put into circulation, central bank liquidity is allocated to individual credit institutions, payment systems are operated and statistical data are collected. The implementation of ECB law is thus the decisive point of interaction with credit institutions, traders and other individuals which are operating in the financial markets, and it is in this field that the national central banks, as ECB agents, still fulfil an important role. Because Article 9.2 of the Statute provides for two alternative methods of implementation of ECB law: either by the ECB's own activities (direct implementation) or through the national central banks (indirect implementation).[163]

---

[161] On the language regime of the ECB, cf. *supra*, Ch. 1, p. 37 *et seq.*

[162] This possibility was already seen by Louis, *supra*, n. 54, 58 *et seq.* Today, it is incorporated in Art. 17(2), first sentence, and 17(6), first sentence of the Rules of Procedure of the ECB, *supra*, n. 6.

[163] The distinction between direct and indirect implementation in Community law has been recognised by the ECJ in Case 294/83, *Parti écologiste "Les Verts"* v. *European Parliament* [1986] ECR 1339, para. 23: "where the Community institutions are responsible for the administrative implementation . . . Where implementation is a matter for the national authorities".

1. The decision on direct or indirect implementation

Whether ECB law should be implemented directly or indirectly has been controversially discussed and will certainly continue to keep academic writers busy in the foreseeable future.[164] This comes from the fact that the implementation of ECB law is the only field of the ESCB's tasks where there could still be scope for discrete competences for the national central banks. Against this background, some authors argue that both the scheme and the general spirit of the EC Treaty would establish, as regards implementing powers, a strong presumption in favour of indirect implementation which would go so far as to exclude centralisation in the implementation of ECB law, since this would not respect the autonomy of the national central banks.[165] Some stress this by referring again, now in the context of the implementation of ECB law, to the principle of subsidiarity or by even talking of a *"Wahrnehmungskompetenz"* (autonomous competence to implement) of the national central banks,[166] thus assimilating again the national central banks to the legal position of autonomous sub-entities in federal systems.

1.1. The presumption in favour of indirect implementation in Community law

At first glance, the position of these authors seems to be justified by general principles of Community law. It is true that the distinction between direct and indirect implementation inside the ESCB resembles the methods used by the Community institutions for the implementation of Community law. Direct implementation means implementation through the Community institutions themselves and is foreseen in Article 202, third indent, and Article 211, third indent, EC (implementation by the Council or, upon delegation, by the Commission); a rare example of such direct implementation is the competition procedure under Council Regulation No 17[167] which allows Commission officials themselves to conduct investigations directly at the premises of undertakings concerned in the case of alleged breaches of the Community's competition rules.[168] Indirect implementation, i.e. implementation through the Member

---

[164] A good overview of this controversy is given by Stadler, *supra*, n. 1, 156 *et seq.*

[165] Cf. Lagayette, *supra*, Ch. 2, n. 20.

[166] This is done by Weber, *supra*, n. 1, 52 *et seq.*, 125 *et seq.*, who distinguishes this from the ECB's *"Sachkompetenz"*; he thus uses exactly the same legal concepts used by the German Federal Constitutional Court to delimitate the competences of the federal government and the *Länder*; cf. *supra*, Ch. 2, n. 29.

[167] First Regulation of 6 February 1962 implementing Art. 85 and 86 of the Treaty [1962] OJ 13/204.

[168] The reason for the choice of direct implementation in this case is given in recitals 7 and 8 of *ibid.*: "Whereas, in order to secure uniform application of Articles 85 and 86 [now Articles 81 and 82 EC] in the common market, rules must be made under which the Commission, acting in close and constant liaison with the competent authorities of the Member States, may take the requisite measures for applying those Articles; whereas for this purpose the Commission must have the

States and their authorities, is seen by the ECJ, "far from presenting an anomaly", as no more than the implementation of the general obligation expressed in Article 10 EC, whereby the Member States are required to take all appropriate measures to ensure the fulfilment of the obligations resulting from action taken by the institutions of the Community and, in general, to facilitate the achievement of the Community's tasks.[169]

In view of the limited number of Community officials, indirect implementation has meanwhile become the rule in Community practice.[170] This is confirmed in Declaration No 43, attached to the EC Treaty by the Treaty of Amsterdam as guidance for the application of the principles of subsidiarity and proportionality. In this Declaration, the Member States stress "that the administrative implementation of Community law shall in principle be the responsibility of the Member States in accordance with their constitutional arrangements". One can take this as an express confirmation of a presumption that, in the field of implementation of Community law, normally the Member States remain competent, if Community law does not exceptionally prescribe direct implementation.

1.2. The ECB's discretion under Article 9.2 of the Statute

Can one transfer this presumption to the ESCB and thus assume that, in principle, the implementation of ECB law is for the national central banks, and not for the ECB itself? We suggest that the answer is no. It has already been demonstrated that the principle of subsidiarity does not apply inside the ESCB, in view of the exclusivity of the ECB's competence as regards the decision on the definition of the monetary policy of the Community and on its implementation. In addition, Article 9.2 of the Statute shows that even in the context of the implementation of ECB law, there is no room for a presumption ruling in favour of indirect implementation through national central banks, as this provision explicitly attributes the competence to decide between direct and indirect implementation to the ECB. The allocation of implementing powers is thus not

co-operation of the competent authorities of the Member States and be empowered, throughout the common market, to require such information to be supplied and to undertake such investigations as are necessary to bring to light any agreement, decision or concerted practice prohibited by Article 85(1) or any abuse of a dominant position prohibited by Article 86". On the way in which the Commission has to conduct such investigations, cf. Joined Cases 46/87 and 227/88, *Hoechst AG v. Commission* [1989] ECR 2859.

[169] Case 30/70, *Otto Scheer v. Einfuhr- und Vorratsstelle für Getreide und Futtermittel* [1970] ECR 1197, para. 8. It should be noted that in this case, the ECJ made clear that its conclusions were valid only at "the present stage of Community law".

[170] This has led the Commission to propose indirect implementation instead of direct implementation also in the field of competition law; cf. the Commission's White Paper on modernisation of the rules implementing Arts. 85 and 86 of the EC Treaty [1999] OJ C132/1 and Commission Proposal of 27 September 2000 for a Council Regulation on the implementation of the rules on competition laid down in Articles 81 and 82 of the Treaty amending Regulations 1017/68, 2988/74, 4056/86 and 3975/87 ("Regulation implementing Articles 81 and 82 of the Treaty") [2000] OJ C365/284.

decided by general principles or by presumptions, but is in each individual case up to the discretion of the ECB's decision-making bodies.[171] In an extreme case, it would thus be legally possible to imagine that all ECB law is implemented exclusively by the ECB's own activities.[172]

1.3. Unfettered discretion

In most cases, the Statute does not contain rules which would direct the exercise of the ECB's discretion on how to implement its law, but allows the ECB to choose between direct and indirect implementation:

—According to Article 16 of the Statute,[173] both the ECB and the national central banks can issue euro banknotes once they have been authorised by the Governing Council of the ECB.

—According to Article 17 of the Statute, both the ECB and the national central banks may open accounts for market participants and accept assets as collateral.

—Article 18.1 of the Statute entitles both the ECB and the national central banks to operate in the financial markets and to conduct credit operations, in accordance with the monetary policy laid down in the decisions and guidelines of the Governing Council of the ECB.

—Under Article 19.1 of the Statute, the minimum reserves required from credit institutions by the ECB could be held on accounts both with the ECB and with the national central banks.

—Article 22 of the Statute allows both the ECB and national central banks to provide facilities to ensure efficient and sound clearing and payment systems within the Community and with other countries, in accordance with the Regulations which the ECB may adopt in this context.

—Finally, Article 23 of the Statute provides that both the ECB and the national central banks may conduct operations with central banks and financial institutions in other countries and, where appropriate, with international organisations. This includes in particular the conduct of foreign exchange operations under the authority of the ECB.

---

[171] This is stressed by Zilioli in Von der Groeben, Thiesing and Ehlermann (eds.), *supra*, n. 12, following Art. 109 m, Satzung ESZB and EZB Art. 12, para. 31.

[172] This contrasts with the implementation of decisions inside the Bundesbank. Even though the Bundesbank structure is organised in a unitary way, s. 8(2) of the Bundesbank Act has entrusted implementing powers to the *Land* Central Banks, of which they cannot be deprived by the decision-making bodies of the Bundesbank. As a matter of legal technique, this was achieved by elevating the management of the *Land* Central Banks to the third decision-making body inside the Bundesbank; cf. s. 5 of the Bundesbank Act. One could therefore talk of a "*Wahrnehmungskompetenz*" of the *Land* Central Banks and of a limited form of "*Vollzugsföderalismus*" inside the Bundesbank. This feature of the Bundesbank's organisational structure is stressed by Wagenhöfer, *supra*, Ch. 2, n. 6, 110 and by Weber, *supra*, n. 1, 84 *et seq*.

[173] Cf. also Art. 106(1) EC.

In all these cases, the Statute thus gives the ECB a wide margin of discretion which allows it to adopt the method of implementation to the specific requirements of its policy.

1.4. Article 12.1 of the Statute

In some cases, the discretion of the ECB as regards its choice between direct and indirect implementation receives legal guidance from the provisions of the Statute. The most important provision in this respect is to be found in Article 12.1 of the Statute. This provision not only attributes the competence to take monetary policy decisions to the Governing Council of the ECB, and the competence to implement them to the Executive Board, but also states in its third subparagraph[174]:

> To the extent deemed possible and appropriate and without prejudice to the provisions of this Article, the ECB shall have recourse to the national central banks to carry out operations which form part of the tasks of the ESCB.

By this, the discretion enjoyed by the ECB under Article 9.2 of the Statute is directed in such a way that it makes it a legal requirement ("shall") to choose indirect implementation of the ECB's monetary policy decisions. However, this legal requirement is made subject to two cumulative conditions. The first condition is that indirect implementation must be *"deemed possible and appropriate"*. By whom?, may one legitimately ask, as the word "deemed" indicates that this is a subjective decision to be taken in each individual case, not an objective condition prescribed by law. In view of the decisional centralism inside the ESCB, where exclusively the decision-making bodies of the ECB may take decisions also as regards implementation, it is submitted that it is necessarily the ECB which must deem it possible and appropriate in an individual case to choose indirect implementation and the extent to which it is used.

The second condition for indirect implementation is that the delegation of implementing powers to the national central banks in the context of monetary policy must be *"without prejudice to the provisions of this Article"*. This has a double meaning:

—First of all, as Article 12.1, first subparagraph, attributes the power to adopt guidelines and to take decisions on monetary policy to the Governing Council of the ECB, the delegation of implementing powers to the national central banks may not reverse this centralisation of the formulation of the monetary policy of the Community. It would thus be unlawful to delegate, under Article 12.1, third subparagraph, of the Statute, competence to the national central banks to adopt varying regional interest rates or to entitle them to provide more liquidity if they wished to compensate for an economic recession in their

---

[174] On this provision, cf. Zilioli in Von der Groeben, Thiesing and Ehlermann (eds.), *supra*, n. 12, following Art. 109 m, Satzung ESZB and EZB Art. 12, para. 31.

Member State.[175] This prohibition of a delegation of the ECB's exclusive decisional competences is not only made express in the wording of Article 12.1, third subparagraph, of the Statute, but is also in line with the spirit of the EC Treaty. The ECJ has always considered the transfer of exclusive competences to the Community level to be *"permanent"*,[176] *"total and definitive"*[177] and *"irreversible"*[178] and in particular incompatible with a re-delegation of discretionary powers to other levels of governance.[179]

—Secondly, the delegation of implementing competences to the national central banks must also respect Article 12.1, second paragraph, of the Statute, according to which it is, first of all, a competence of the Executive Board of the ECB to "implement monetary policy" and which also requires that "in doing so, the Executive Board shall give the necessary instructions to the national central banks". That indirect implementation shall be without prejudice also to these core implementing competences of the Executive Board confirms that indirect implementation is not meant to take place by autonomous actions of the national central banks, but is allowed solely under the control and surveillance of the Executive Board and in accordance with its instructions. This shows again that the national central banks are not independent implementing agencies, but that they are implementing ECB law in their capacity as a wholly integrated part of the ESCB and that also the implementation of ECB law is entirely governed by the decision-making bodies of the ECB. The wording of Articles 9.2 and 12.1, third subparagraph, of the Statute reflects appropriately the role of the national central banks as operating arms of the ECB also in the

---

[175] This is very vehemently stressed by the former president of the Bundesbank Tietmeyer, *supra*, Ch. 2, n. 12: *"Da der Euro aber eine supranationale Währung ist, kann es künftig nur eine einheitliche Geldpolitik mit einem einheitlichen Notenbankzins im gesamten Euroraum geben. Regional unterschiedliche Notenbanksätze oder spezielle Refinanzierungslinien einzelner nationaler Zentralbanken sind damit unvereinbar"*.

[176] Cf. Case 6/64, *Costa* v. *ENEL* [1964] ECR 1251, para. 1270, where the ECJ characterised the transfer of competences by the Member States to the Community as a *permanent* limitation of their sovereign rights (emphasis added).

[177] Cf. Case 804/79, *Commission* v. *United Kingdom* [1981] ECR 1045, para. 17: "since the expiration on 1 January 1979 of the transitional period, powers to adopt, as part of the common fisheries policy, measures relating to the conservation of the resources of the sea has belonged *fully and definitely* to the Community". Even a failure of the Community institutions to take such measures could not restore the Member States' power and freedom to act unilaterally in this field, "the transfer to the Community of powers in this matter being *total and definitive*" (para. 20, emphasis added).

[178] Cf. Case 43/75, *Defrenne* v. *Sabena* [1976] ECR 455, para. 56/58. The "irreversible character" of the transfer of monetary policy to the Community level and the "irrevocable" entry into the third stage of EMU are stressed explicitly by Protocol No 24 on the transition to the third stage of EMU, attached to the EC Treaty by the Maastricht Treaty.

[179] Cf. Case 9/56, *Meroni & Co., Industrie Metallurgiche, società in accomandita semplice* v. *High Authority of the ECSC* [1958] ECR 133 (152) where the ECJ held that a delegation of powers of the High Authority to the Brussels agencies "can only involve clearly defined executive powers, the use of which must be entirely subject to the supervision of the High Authority. To delegate a discretionary power, by entrusting it to bodies other than those which the Treaty has established to effect and supervise the exercise of such powers each within the limits of its own authority, would render that guarantee [of balance of power] ineffective".

context of indirect implementation of ECB law, as these provisions state that the ECB carries out the ESCB's tasks *"through* the national central banks", and shall "have *recourse"* to their implementing capacities.

In view of these preconditions, Article 12.1, third subparagraph, of the Statute certainly does not represent an application of the principle of subsidiarity, but establishes a rather tight regime of indirect implementation, as it always means implementation by the Executive Board of the ECB which has recourse to the national central banks to carry out operations and for this purpose gives the necessary instructions to them.[180] It is therefore somewhat misleading or, at least, legally imprecise, to say that the implementation of ECB law through the national central banks is done in a *"decentralised"* manner.[181] When national authorities implement Community law, the ECJ speaks of *"decentralised management"* only in cases where the national authorities have their own implementing powers and where the Community institutions are neither empowered to check the correctness of their exercise nor able to correct wrong decisions taken in specific cases, but can secure the uniform application of Community law solely by infringement proceedings under Article 226 EC.[182] From such a system of decentralised management, the ECJ distinguishes clearly, in its case law, the *"centralised management"* of the implementation of Community law through national authorities which is sometimes used to ensure the proper functioning of common market organisations and the equal treatment for all economic operators in the Member States, for example, in the case of the common organisation of the market in bananas.[183] Such centralised management of the indirect implementation of Community law is characterised by the fact that the Community institutions are entitled to lay down detailed implementing rules and that the Member States have no decisional powers, but are required to assume a number of technical functions on behalf and subject to the control of the Community institutions which are entitled to check and even to revise national implementing measures.[184]

---

[180] Cf. also Smits, *supra,* n. 66, 111, who notes: "Although this provision was related by the Committee of Governors, in the introductory report to its Draft Statute, to the subsidiarity principle, it is in effect not an application thereof". Cf. also the distinction between Art. 12.1 of the Statute and the principle of subsidiarity made by Zilioli in Von der Groeben, Thiesing and Ehlermann (eds.), *supra,* n. 12, following Art. 109m, Satzung ESZB and EZB Art. 12, para. 31. This is unfortunately not taken into account by Smulders in the same publication, Satzung ESZB and EZB Art. 9.

[181] This is, however, done by Weber, *supra,* n. 1, 133, who considers Art. 12.1, third subpara., of the Statute as laying down *"den Grundsatz der dezentralen Umsetzung und Durchführung (Vollzug) der einheitlich festgelegten Geldpolitik als spezieller Ausformung des Subsidiaritätsgrundsatzes".* More flexible is the position of Louis, *supra,* n. 54, 50 *et seq.,* where he states that "hierarchy and decentralisation are complementary"; this view is however not in line with the terminology of the ECJ which considers "hierarchy" as a characteristics of "centralised management".

[182] Joined Cases C–106/90, C–317/90 and C–129/91, *Emerald Meats Ltd* v. *Commission* [1993] ECR I–209, para. 39 *et seq.*

[183] Cf. Council Regulation 404/93 of 13 February 1993 on the common organisation of the market in bananas [1993] OJ L47/1.

[184] Cf. Case C–478/93, *Netherlands* v. *Commission* [1995] ECR I–3081, para. 32 *et seq.*

In the light of this jurisprudence of the ECJ, the indirect implementation of ECB law thus rather resembles the model of centralised indirect implementation.[185] To ensure the uniform implementation of its monetary policy decision, the ECB is in no way restricted to starting infringement proceedings under Article 237(d) EC[186] against national central banks in cases of incorrect implementation of ECB law, but is entitled[187] to steer every single stage of the implementation process by means of instructions issued by the Executive Board with which national central banks have to comply in each individual case (Article 14.3 of the Statute). In the event that indirect implementation of ECB law through the national central banks would prove inefficient or result in a divergent application of ECB law, the decision-making bodies of the ECB would even be free to deem that indirect application is no longer "possible and appropriate" and to reverse their decision under Article 9.2 of the Statute and to assume the full responsibility to carry out the ECB's policy by the ECB's own activities.

The background to this is of course not that excessive centralist tendencies prevailed in the negotiations on the EC Treaty and Statute provisions on the implementation of ECB law—this would be quite surprising in view of the fact that the whole process was almost entirely in the hands of central bank governors and representatives of the Member States. The centralised model chosen for indirect implementation of ECB law rather reflects, again, the common ground that a *single* currency can work only if monetary policy is not just formulated centrally, but also implemented uniformly throughout the currency area in question. In view of the fact that in Community law even the common market organisations in the field of the Community's agricultural policy and the application of the common customs tariff sometimes require the Community institutions to choose centralised models of indirect implementation, it is quite obvious that it cannot be compatible with Community law and the legal requirement of a *single* currency and a *single* monetary policy (Article 4(2) EC) to allow for a truly decentralised implementation of ECB law, as this could endanger the uniform and efficient application of the ECB's policy.

1.5. Article 5.2 of the Statute

The exercise of the ECB's discretion to choose between direct and indirect implementation receives also legal guidance when the collection of statistical

---

[185] This seems also to be the view of Smits, *supra*, n. 66, 112, where he qualifies implementation through the national central banks merely as "a working arrangement which puts emphasis on local, instead of central, performance of Community tasks". This definition shows that implementation of ECB law has much more in common with the model of *déconcentration* in unitary states, cf. *supra*, Ch. 2, p. 63 and n. 44 than with a true *décentralisation* of implementation, as known in federal systems.

[186] Cf. also Art. 35.6 of the Statute.

[187] Of course, the extent to which the ECB makes use of this power depends on the policy choices within the general legal framework for the ECB's monetary policy. For the moment, this framework is structured in such a manner that the need for giving punctual instructions to the national central banks is reduced: for instance, the choice of imposing minimum reserve requirements limits the need for fine-tuning measures to exceptional circumstances. Cf. *infra*, p. 122.

data, either from the competent national authorities or directly from economic agents, is required by the ECB to undertake the tasks of the ESCB, for example in case of balance of payments statistics. Here, Article 5.1 of the Statute attributes the power to collect statistical information from the competent national authorities or directly from economic agents to "the ECB, *assisted* by the national central banks". In addition, Article 5.2 of the Statute states:

> The national central banks shall carry out, to the extent possible, the tasks described in Article 5.1.

Throughout the Statute, this wording comes closest to an autonomous implementing competence of the national central banks, although it is limited to the field of statistics. However, it is submitted that also in this case the ECB still can choose whether or not to collect information directly or indirectly through the national central banks, as Article 9.2 of the Statute does not contain any limitations as regards the application of Article 5 of the Statute. This is further stressed by Article 5.1 of the Statute itself, according to which it is first of all the ECB which shall collect statistical information, while the role of the national central banks is circumscribed as mere assistance. This also means that Article 5.2 of the Statute does not include an irrebutable presumption ruling in favour of indirect implementation, but leaves unaffected the appreciation by the ECB whether such indirect implementation is "possible". The margin of discretion of the ECB is, however, narrower than under Article 12.1 of the Statute, as it can choose direct implementation only where indirect implementation appears "impossible", not in cases where it is simply deemed "inappropriate" by the ECB.

1.6. The exclusion of the ECB's discretion

Only exceptionally does the Statute expressly exclude, by means of special provisions, the discretion of the ECB under Article 9.2 of the Statute to choose between direct and indirect implementation. In accordance with the general observation that there exist, within the scope of the ESCB's tasks, no autonomous competences of the national central banks, the Statute contains no special provision which would reserve implementing powers to them and thus exclude the ECB's discretion always to choose implementation by its own activities. However, in some cases the Statute does allow exclusively for direct implementation by the ECB.

Implementing powers are reserved to the ECB first of all in fields which, by their very nature, can only be implemented centrally. An example is Article 32.6 of the Statute which states explicitly that the clearing and settlement of the balances arising from the allocation of monetary income "shall be carried out *by the ECB* in accordance with guidelines established by the Governing Council". This requirement of direct implementation ensures that there will be in the end a uniform ESCB balance as regards monetary income which allows the ECB to allocate that income to the national central banks in proportion to their paid-up shares in the capital of the ECB. The very nature of the matter also requires that it is the ECB, more specifically its Executive Board, which shall draw up the consolidated balance sheet of the ESCB, comprising those assets and liabilities of the national central banks that fall within the ESCB (Article 26.3 of the Statute).

In other cases, the drafters of the Statute seem to have felt that implementation through the national central banks would endanger the objectives of the ESCB and thus have excluded the possibility of choosing such indirect implementation where they identified a particular need for uniformity and effectiveness. An example is the exercise of the ECB's sanctioning powers. According to Article 34.1 of the Statute, only the ECB is entitled to impose fines or periodic penalty payments on undertakings for failure to comply with obligations under ECB Regulations and ECB Decisions. This complete centralisation of the ECB's sanctioning regime conforms to the idea that one cannot delegate essential powers,[188] and also guarantees a uniform application of such sanctions, as required by the rule of law.

2. Direct implementation of ECB law

Direct implementation of ECB law means that the Executive Board, as the ECB's decision-making body responsible for implementation, directly enters into contact with the world of banking and finance. This could be done both by means of ECB Decisions, addressed to individuals, or through the conclusion of contracts on behalf of the ECB. The latter is possible by virtue of the ECB's legal personality in the Member States, which results from Article 9.1 of the Statute and which enables the ECB, represented by the President, or by two members of the Executive Board, or by two members of its staff duly authorised (Article 39 of the Statue), in particular to acquire and dispose of movable and immovable property, whenever the implementation of ECB law so requires.[189]

2.1. Fields in which the ECB has chosen direct implementation of ECB law

Direct implementation of ECB law is, at the present stage, still the exception. This is not due to legal restraints, but merely a factual situation. The ECB is a rather young organisation which started with the full exercise of its powers only on 1 January 1999, as foreseen in Article 123(1), second subparagraph EC, and currently has only around 960 employees. It seems therefore appropriate to rely, for the moment, on the implementing capacities of the national central banks with their 50,000 employees, if taken together. Indirect instead of direct implementation seems also appropriate to ensure a smooth transition into the new

---

[188] Cf. Case 9/56, *supra*, n. 179.

[189] An example of such an ECB contract is the case of the acquisition of the intellectual property rights concerning the euro banknotes, cf. Art. 2.1 of Decision ECB/1998/6, *supra*, n. 72.

operational framework set by the single currency. However, one should not take this *factual* situation as an irreversible decision against direct implementation, as, *legally*, it always remains open to the ECB to choose direct implementation. In this case, the proper functioning of such direct implementation would automatically require an increase of the ECB's personnel[190] and simultaneously allow for a reduction of staff at the level of the national central banks, although the political sensitivity of such a step should not be underestimated.

2.1.1. The exceptional case of a direct implementation of monetary policy

In the context of open market operations which are used in order to implement the monetary policy defined by the ECB, the Governing Council of the ECB envisages direct implementation in particular in the case of fine-tuning operations, although for the moment this possibility of direct monetary policy implementation is reserved for cases of exceptional circumstances.[191] These fine-tuning operations may be conducted by the ECB on an *ad hoc* basis with the aim of managing the liquidity situation in the market and of steering interest rates, in particular in order to smooth the effect on interest rates caused by unexpected liquidity fluctuations in the market. They could be executed in the form of

—*reverse transactions*, i.e. operations whereby the ECB would buy or sell eligible assets under repurchase agreements or conduct credit operations against eligible assets as collateral; these operations aim at providing or absorbing liquidity in the market;
—*outright transactions* whereby the ECB would buy or sell eligible assets outright on the market;
—*foreign exchange swaps* which could consist of simultaneous spot and forward transactions of the euro against foreign currency;
—*collection of fixed-term deposits*, which is an instrument whereby the ECB would, as a measure in order to absorb liquidity in the market, invite counterparties to place remunerated fixed term deposits.

2.1.2. The imposition of sanctions by the ECB

As already mentioned, Article 34.3 of the Statute reserves the right to impose sanctions on undertakings for non-compliance with ECB Regulations and ECB Decisions to the ECB. It is in line with this provision that Council Regulation 2532/98 concerning the powers of the European Central Bank to impose sanc-

---

[190] This is suggested now by ECB President Duisenberg who intends to follow the example of the US "Fed" which employs a staff of around 1,700 in Washington; cf. *Handelsblatt*, 27 May 1999. The relationship between the staff of the Board of Governors and the staff of the Federal Reserve Banks is also seen as a model by the new president of the Deutsche Bundesbank Welteke, "Die Rolle der nationalen Zentralbanken im Europäischen System der Zentralbanken", speech of 10 September 1998, 12, published at http://www.bundesbank.de/lzb-h/index.htm.
[191] Cf. Guideline ECB/2000/7, *supra*, n. 43.

tions[192] and Regulation ECB/1999/4 on the powers of the European Central Bank to impose sanctions[193] establish a regime of direct implementation of such sanctions by the ECB's own activities.

The procedure for the imposition of sanctions resembles the procedure for sanctioning breaches of the Community's competition law, as foreseen in Council Regulation 17,[194] the most prominent example of direct implementation in Community law. The ECB's infringement procedure, as laid down in Article 3 of Council Regulation 2532/98, allows for a participation of the national central banks in its preliminary stage, while the final decision on the imposition of sanctions always lays with the ECB. The procedure for infringements of ECB Regulations and ECB Decisions essentially has the following three stages.

—*Stage 1: Initiation of the procedure and investigations.* The infringement procedure is initiated either by a decision of the Executive Board of the ECB, addressed to the undertaking concerned, or by such a decision[195] taken by the national central bank of the Member State in whose jurisdiction the alleged infringement has occurred. This decision shall disclose to the undertaking concerned the details of the allegations and, where appropriate, require the termination of the alleged infringement, combined with a notice that periodic penalty payments may be imposed. In addition, it may require the undertaking concerned to submit to an infringement procedure during which both the ECB and the national central bank in question have the right to carry out investigations, including to request the submission of documents, to copy books and records of the undertaking, to take copies from such books and records and to obtain written and oral explanations.[196] In case of obstructive behaviour of the undertaking concerned, the ECB and the national central bank in question may even conduct searches at the premises of the undertaking concerned to exercise their rights. However, they can do this only with the assistance of the competent national authorities, which shall be afforded under the Council Regulation,[197] and by respecting the requirements of national

---

[192] *Supra*, n. 90.

[193] *Supra*, n. 48. On this, cf. the analysis by Fernández Martín and Texeira, "The imposition of sanctions by the European Central Bank" (2000) *EL Rev.* 391.

[194] Cf. *supra*, n. 167.

[195] This is the first time that Community law explicitly entitles a "national" authority to take a Community law decision. It is thus again proof of the denationalisation of national central banks; cf. *supra*, Ch. 2, p. 73 *et seq.*

[196] It is submitted that at this stage, unlike Commission officials under Council Regulation 17, neither the ECB nor the national central bank in question is entitled, unless with the assistance of the competent national authorities, to enter the premises of the undertaking and to conduct searches. The reason is that the powers of investigation are defined in a more restrictive manner in Council Regulation 2532/98 which—in contrast to Council Regulation 17—allows neither to ask for oral explanations "on the spot" nor "to enter any premises, land and means of transport of undertakings".

[197] Art. 3(2), subpara. 2, thereof.

procedural law.[198] The ECB or the national central bank in question have, in addition, to ensure that the undertaking's right to be heard is guaranteed.

—*Stage 2: Reasoned decision.* From the second stage, the infringement procedure is centralised in the hands of the Executive Board of the ECB. On the basis of the results of the procedure's Stage 1, the Executive Board has to adopt an ECB Decision which states whether and why the undertaking has committed an infringement, and which also includes the sanctions, if any, to be imposed. The undertaking concerned has the right, first, to request an internal review of this decision by the Governing Council of the ECB, and secondly, to request judicial review by the ECJ under Article 230 EC.

—*Stage 3: Enforcement.* ECB Decisions, and thus also a reasoned decision by which the ECB imposes pecuniary obligations, are enforceable under Article 256, first subparagraph, EC, which is referred to in Article 110(2), fourth subparagraph, as being applicable also to ECB Decisions. This means that where an undertaking refuses to pay the penalty, the ECB can require that the competent national authorities append an order for enforcement to the ECB Decision in question, "without other formality than verification of the authenticity of the decision". The ECB, through its Executive Board, may then proceed to enforcement in accordance with national law. Only the ECJ may suspend such enforcement.

The characteristic of the ECB's sanctioning regime as a case of direct implementation is further demonstrated by Article 3(9) of Council Regulation 2532/98 according to which the proceeds from sanctions imposed by the ECB "shall belong to the ECB". In addition, Article 3(10) of Council Regulation 2532/98 stresses that the procedure just described is the sole procedure which could lead to sanctions for breaches of ECB Regulations and ECB Decisions, as "if an infringement relates exclusively to a task entrusted to the ESCB under the Treaty and the Statute, an infringement procedure may be initiated only on the basis of this Regulation, irrespective of the existence of any national law or regulation which may provide for a separate procedure".

2.2. Liability in the context of direct implementation of ECB law

The determination of liability is quite straightforward in the context of direct implementation of ECB law. As regards contractual liability, it is always the ECB which becomes a party to contracts in these cases, for example, of a repur-

---

[198] Cf. Joined Cases 46/87 and 227/88, *supra*, n. 168, para. 33 *et seq.*, which concerns the parallel procedure under Council Regulation 17 and where the ECJ held "that it is for each Member State to determine the conditions under which the national authorities will afford assistance to the Commission's officials. In that regard, Member States are required to ensure that the Commission's action is effective. It follows that within those limits, the appropriate procedural rules are those laid down by national law. Consequently, if the Commission intends, with the assistance of the national authorities, to carry out an investigation other than with the co-operation of the undertakings concerned, it is required to respect the relevant procedural guarantees laid down by national law".

chase agreement used for a fine-tuning operation carried out exceptionally by the ECB itself. It is thus also the ECB which must perform its obligations under this contract.

Non-contractual liability, i.e. the obligation to make good damage caused by illegal action in the course of the implementation of ECB law, follows the rules laid down in Article 35.3 of the Statute and in Article 288(3) EC. According to these provisions, the liability regime of the ECB is governed by "the general principles common to the laws of the Member States". According to the case law of the ECJ, this means that non-contractual liability is incurred only for damage suffered by individuals as a consequence of action whereby "a sufficiently flagrant violation of a superior rule of law for the protection of the individual" has occurred.[199]

From the wording of Articles 35.3 of the Statute and Article 288(3) EC, it is not completely clear *who* would be liable in case these conditions are satisfied. For the reasons already developed,[200] and in line with the functional approach always chosen by the ECJ for determining non-contractual liability, we suggest that it is the ECB, being an independent specialised organisation of Community law, which would be liable to make good damage caused in the course of direct implementation of ECB law.[201]

2.3. Legal remedies in the context of direct implementation of ECB law

In spite of the normally harmonious relationship between central banks and the world of banking and finance, which is less than litigation-prone, it cannot be ruled out that individuals will want to seek redress in the courts where they feel themselves to be adversely affected by a legal act of the ECB.[202] Judicial control of the ECB's activities is dealt with by Article 35 of the Statute. According to the scheme of this provision, either the ECJ or the national courts have jurisdiction in such disputes.

The ECJ is competent in all cases where jurisdiction is conferred upon it by the EC Treaty or the Statute. This enables individuals to challenge legal acts of the ECB, in particular ECB Decisions addressed to them, by an action for annulment under Article 230 EC. Redress against omissions of the ECB can be sought through an action for failure to act under Article 232 EC.[203]

---

[199] This is settled case law; cf. Case 5/71, *Schöppenstedt* v. *Council* [1971] ECR 975, para. 11.

[200] Cf. *supra*, Ch. 1, p. 44 *et seq.*

[201] For such approach cf. La Marca, "Il controllo guirisdizionale sulla Banca Centrale Europea e sull'Istituto Monetario Europeo" [1996] *Il diritto dell'Unione europea* 773 (789 *et seq.*); Hilf, *Die Organisationstruktur der Europäischen Gemeinschaft* (Berlin, 1982) 40 *et seq.* (as regards the EIB), and Selmayr, *supra*, n. 5, 371.

[202] This is stressed by the CFI in Case T–460/93, *Tête and others* v. *EIB* [1993] ECR II–1257, para. 19: "In that context, it should be noted that the future European Central Bank will be considerably different from the EIB. Article 108a [now Article 110] of the EC Treaty provides for it to adopt regulations and decisions (which will be binding on the addressees), hence the necessity to allow for the possibility of natural and legal persons' bringing actions for annulment".

[203] This is in line with Case 294/83, *supra*, n. 163, para. 23, where the ECJ stressed: "Where the Community institutions are responsible for the administrative implementation of such measures,

The national courts remain competent in all disputes of a contractual nature,[204] i.e. in all disputes between the ECB, on the one hand, and its creditors, debtors or any other person, on the other hand (Article 35.2 of the Statute). However, in such cases the national courts do not exercise a purely national jurisdiction, but have to act as "Community courts"[205] whenever they apply or interpret ECB law in the context of contractual litigation, for example, an ECB Decision or an ECB Guideline which has led the ECB to conclude a certain contract in a specific manner. This is why Article 234 EC enables a national court to refer the matter to the ECJ to decide on the appropriate interpretation of the instrument of ECB law in question; the national court is even obliged to use this procedure of preliminary reference in case where there is no judicial remedy against its decisions (Article 234, third subparagraph, EC) or whenever it intends to question the legality of a legal instrument of the ECB on the application or interpretation of which the outcome of a pending dispute depends.[206] In addition, the contract itself might contain an arbitration clause which explicitly confers jurisdiction upon the ECJ for the whole dispute (Article 35(4) of the Statute).

3. Indirect implementation of ECB law

For the moment, indirect implementation, i.e. implementation of ECB law through the national central banks, represents—for practical reasons—the rule within the ESCB. As mentioned above, this indirect implementation differs considerably from the normal decentralised method of indirect implementation used in Community law as, during the whole implementation process, the national central banks are subject to the guidelines and instructions of the ECB which ensures at all stages of implementation that ECB law is implemented on uniform terms and conditions throughout the Member States participating in the single currency. Even indirect implementation is therefore always centralised implementation under the control of the ECB, in particular of its Executive Board.

3.1. Fields in which the ECB has chosen indirect implementation of ECB law

The ECB has chosen indirect implementation first of all for its *monetary policy operations* where it considers implementation through the national central banks as possible and appropriate, in accordance with Article 12.1, third sub-

---

natural and legal persons may bring a direct action before the Court against implementing measures which are addressed to them or which are of direct or individual concern to them and, in support of such action, may plead the illegality of the general measure on which they are based".

[204] An exception is disputes between the ECB and its servants which fall into the exclusive jurisdiction of the ECJ by virtue of Art. 36.2 of the Statute.

[205] Cf. Temple Lang, *supra*, Ch. 2, n. 94.

[206] Cf. Case 314/85, *Foto-Frost* v. *Hauptzollamt Lübeck-Ost* [1987] ECR 4199, para. 13 *et seq.*

paragraph, of the Statute. This means that, for the moment, all open market operations of the ECB are conducted through the national central banks, including the ECB's main refinancing operations, longer-term refinancing operations, structural reverse operations, the tender of ECB debt certificates, and normally also fine-tuning reverse operations, outright transactions, foreign exchange swaps and the collection of fixed-term deposits.[207] Also the ECB's standing facilities, i.e. its marginal lending facility and its deposit facility, can be accessed exclusively through the national central banks.[208]

It is in accordance with this approach that the ECB's minimum reserve requirements are, for the moment, implemented solely through the national central banks, as the credit institutions concerned have to hold the minimum reserves, at the ratio prescribed by the ECB, on reserve accounts with the national central banks in each Member State in which they have an establishment.[209] For the moment, the ECB has thus not made use of the possibility, provided for in Article 19.2 of the Statute, of requiring such minimum reserves to be held on accounts with the ECB.

Indirect implementation is also the method used by the ECB in the field of *payments systems*. Instead of using its regulatory power under Article 22 of the Statute to set up a new "European Payment System", the ECB has decided rather to rely on the existing national Real-Time Gross Settlement (RTGS) Systems for the implementation of its monetary policy. By means of an ECB Guideline and an Agreement with the national central banks of the Member States which have not yet adopted the euro, the ECB has established an Interlinking System which connects these national RTGS Systems and the ECB Payment Mechanism (EPM), and has thus created the Trans-European Automated Real-time Gross-settlement Express Transfer system, TARGET, a uniform platform for the processing of cross-border payments. As TARGET is based on the existence of the national RTGS Systems, it is very easy to use: to initiate a cross-border payment via TARGET, participants simply have to send their payment orders to the euro RTGS system in which they participate using the domestic message format with which they are familiar. TARGET then takes care of the rest.[210]

The ECB currently also makes use of the experience of the national central banks as regards *the production of euro banknotes*. The exclusive right to authorise the issue of banknotes within the Community, attributed to the ECB by Article 106(1) EC, comprises the competence to define the design, denominations and technical specifications of the euro banknotes as well as the rules on their reproduction, exchange and withdrawal, and the general conditions of issue of such banknotes.[211] The issue of the euro banknotes necessarily

---

[207] Cf. Guideline ECB/2000/7, *supra*, n. 43, ch. 3.

[208] Cf. *ibid.*, ch. 4.

[209] Cf. Art. 6 of Regulation ECB/1998/15, *supra*, n. 40.

[210] For more details, cf. Guideline ECB/2001/3, *supra*, n. 159a; cf. also ECB, *The TARGET Service Level* (Frankfurt am Main, July 1998) and *TARGET, update 2000* (Frankfurt am Main, August 2000). Further information is also available from target.hotline@ecb.int.

[211] Cf. *supra*, n. 72.

encompasses their production which could be carried out both by the ECB itself and through the national central banks. In both cases, in order to guarantee that the euro banknotes will have, say, identical watermarks in all Member States which participate in the single currency, the production of euro banknotes has to be undertaken in accordance with the technical specifications decided in detail by the ECB,[212] with Decision ECB/1998/6 on the denominations, specifications, reproduction, exchange and withdrawal of euro banknotes[213] and with Guideline ECB/1999/3 on certain provisions regarding euro banknotes[214]; however, the production can be carried out in different places, subject to the constant supervision and control of the ECB and its banknote experts.[215]

A final example where the ECB has exercised its discretion in favour of indirect implementation is the field of *statistics*. Guided by the rules in Article 5.1 and 5.2 of the Statute, the ECB's reporting obligations as regards the consolidated balance sheet of the monetary and financial institutions sector are laid down in an ECB Regulation, but have to be fulfilled by reporting agents exclusively by reporting to the national central banks in the Member State[216] in which they are established. The ECB relies even more on the traditional reporting lines established by law and practice in the Member States in the field of balance of payment and international investment position statistics where only an ECB Guideline ensures that such collection takes place in a uniform manner and that the data received are communicated timely and accurately to the ECB.[217]

All these examples show that the ECB has, by using its discretion under Article 9.2 of the Statute, delegated substantial implementing powers to the national central banks. The national central banks thus have, for the moment, the important role of ascertaining that ECB law is implemented in accordance with the uniform terms and conditions set by the ECB, and efficiently in their respective Member States. As the national central banks know best the peculiarities of the national legal systems in which they operate, they are also best qualified to take these peculiarities into account and to bring to the ECB's attention potential problems which the existing differences of national legal systems could create for the uniformity and efficiency of ECB law. This continuous monitoring task of the national central banks serves the objective of enabling the ECB to take, by the means attributed to it under the Treaty and the Statute, rapid action to overcome such difficulties.

For the moment, the implementation of ECB law through the national central banks thus seems to be an appropriate instrument for guaranteeing a smooth transition to the single monetary policy. It also allows natural and legal persons

---

[212] Obviously, to prevent counterfeiting, the technical specifications are strictly confidential.

[213] Cf. *supra*, n. 72.

[214] Cf. *supra*, n. 153.

[215] In addition, by the establishment of a Counterfeit Analysis Centre and a Counterfeit Currency Database (Art. 3 of Guideline ECB/1999/3, cf. *supra*, n. 153), the ECB keeps control of what could be the "weak points" of the production and of the technical specifications of euro banknotes.

[216] Cf. Art. 4 of Regulation ECB/1998/16, *supra*, n. 44.

[217] Cf. Guideline ECB/1998/17, *supra*, n. 151.

operating in the financial markets to continue to use known channels for accessing central bank liquidity or payment facilities at *their* national central bank, although this central bank is today neither a national nor a true central bank any longer, but rather an integral part of the ESCB and therein an operating arm of the ECB.

3.2. Liability in the context of indirect implementation of ECB law

The system of indirect implementation of ECB law requires a differentiated approach as regards contractual and non-contractual liability. As regards contracts, both the national central banks and the ECB could be liable to perform contractual obligations, as contracts may be concluded in two different forms in the field of indirect implementation: either by a national central bank in the name and on behalf of the ECB—in this case, the ECB has to perform the contract—or by a national central bank in its own name; in this case, this national central bank itself bears contractual liability, although, in cases of specific losses arising from monetary policy operations, the ECB may exceptionally decide on an appropriate indemnification of the national central bank in question. (Article 32.4, second subparagraph, of the Statute).

There are also two alternatives in the context of non-contractual liability. They are already indicated by Article 35.3 of the Statute which provides for liability of the ECB in its first sentence and for liability of the national central banks according to their respective national laws in its second sentence. As already mentioned,[218] the ECB—having legal personality (Article 107(2) EC) like the Community itself—is liable for damage caused by its institutions and servants (Article 288(3) EC), and thus also for damage incurred as a consequence of indirect implementation of ECB law through the national central banks in their capacity as ECB agents, in which they are subject to the supervision and to the instructions of the Executive Board of the ECB.[219] It is submitted that this liability extends also to cases where the national central bank in

---

[218] Cf. *supra*, Ch. 1, p. 44 *et seq.*

[219] Cf. Case 175/84, *supra*, Ch. 2, n. 98. This view is favoured by Smits, *supra*, n. 66, 107 *et seq.*: "NCBs may point to the ECB when held liable for actions done or omitted to be done on instruction of the latter". An alternative view is presented by M. Weber, "Das Europäische System der Zentralbanken" [1998] *WM* 1465 (1473), according to whom the national central banks would be liable themselves even when they implement ESCB tasks under the instructions of the ECB, as this would be done in exercise of the national banks' "*Wahrnehmungskompetenz*". M. Weber thus follows also in this sense the analogy with the German federal state's structure. In addition, he wants to give the national central banks in cases in which they have acted upon ECB Instructions a claim for indemnification against the Community—this conforms with his view, presented in [1998] *WM* 1465 (1470) that the Community is liable for injury caused by the ECB. This interesting idea is again inspired by the German federal system where Art. 104a(5) of the Basic Law of 23 May 1998 enables the *Länder* to request indemnification if they have incurred liability in the course of the implementation of the federal government's instructions. However, it has to be noted that a parallel provision exists neither in the EC Treaty nor in the Statute; Art. 32.4 of the Statute endows the ECB with discretion to indemnify, in exceptional circumstances, a national central bank for damage incurred in the context of monetary policy operations, but does not establish a general liability regime between the ECB and the national central banks.

question would incorrectly implement ECB law, as the ECB, in particular its Executive Board, has the obligation and the legal means to supervise and to control the implementation process; at any time, it could revise its decision under Article 9.2 of the Statute and correct, "by its own activities", mistakes or improper implementation.[220] Only in cases where the national central banks perform functions other than those specified in the Statute, i.e. outside the scope of the ESCB's tasks, they are themselves liable (Article 14.4 of the Statute), in accordance with their national law.

3.3. Legal remedies in the context of indirect implementation of ECB law

The method of indirect implementation of ECB law has the consequence that individuals, in their dealings with a national central bank, will not always be able to ascertain whether alleged illegal action is to be attributed to the national central bank or to the ECB on behalf of which the national central bank is acting within the scope of the ESCB's tasks. This complexity can of course not, in a Community based on the rule of law, enable the ECB or the national central bank in question to avoid a review of the question whether the measures adopted by them are in conformity with the Statute and the EC Treaty. As stated by the ECJ, Community law provides for "a complete system of legal remedies and procedures".[221]

This system of legal remedies can be said to represent a two-tier system designed to permit the ECJ always to control the legality of actions undertaken to implement Community law, and which, without any doubt, also applies to the implementation of ECB law[222] through the national central banks. It allows individuals to challenge ECB law directly at the ECJ whenever it is addressed to them or is of identifiable direct and individual concern. In all other cases, they may challenge the implementing measures of the national central bank at the national courts. These have the task of analysing whether the illegality alleged results from the national central bank's actions or is not in truth the responsibility of the ECB—a case which is more likely in view of the ECB's far-reaching powers of control, supervision and instruction as regards national central banks' activities. In the latter case, the national court may—or if it decides a case in the last instance,[223] must—refer questions of Community law, in particular

---

[220] Only theoretically, one could think of the case that the ECB delegates to a national central bank discretionary powers the illegal exercise of which would solely be attributable to the national central bank in question. However, it is suggested that, as a rule, and in view of the exclusivity of the ECB's decision-making competences, it would not be compatible with Community law to delegate to the national central banks more than mere implementing powers; cf. Case 9/56, *supra*, n. 179, where the ECJ has established a general prohibition on delegating discretionary powers. In any event, it is submitted that the ECB could not escape its own liability by means of such a delegation.

[221] Case 294/83, *supra*, n. 163.

[222] The submission, without reservations, of the ECB to the rule of law is stressed by Case T–460/93, *supra*, n. 202.

[223] Cf. *supra*, n. 206.

the legality and interpretation of the ECB law in dispute to the ECJ for a preliminary ruling under Article 234 EC.

IV. CONCLUSION

This chapter has shown that since the establishment of the ECB, there has been a new type of secondary Community law which needs to be taken into account by Community lawyers: Community law which is not enacted by the Community institutions but by the ECB in its capacity as independent supranational organisation of Community law. The way this ECB law comes into being and is implemented in the Member States reflects the specific needs of a supranational central bank: a centralised decision-making process and a centralised management of the implementation of ECB law are efficient legal tools to enable the ECB to fulfil its mandate of price stability for the single currency of currently 12 EU Member States.

4

The European Central Bank and Differentiated Integration

E MU IS THE first comprehensive[1] experiment on differentiated integration in the history of Community law.[2] On 1 January 1999, only 11 EU Member States transferred their monetary sovereignty to the ECB, followed by Greece on 1 January 2001. The remaining three Member States and their central banks are in a quite peculiar relationship as regards the single currency: while still being full EU members, they do not participate in a key area of EC policy.

For Community law, this situation represents a challenge. It is required to reconcile its claim to uniform, non-discriminatory application throughout the EU with the fact that not all Member States are willing or able to take part in the single currency. It goes without saying that this challenge is particularly felt in the daily activities of the ECB, which, as a supranational organisation, is responsible for the definition and implementation of the monetary policy *of the Community* (Article 105(2) second indent, EC), not of a particular group of EU Member States.

---

[1] The attempt of differentiated integration under the Protocol on Social Policy, agreed at the intergovernmental conference at Maastricht, was limited to giving one Member State—the United Kingdom—a special status in this field. Formally, the Protocol allowed all other Member States to proceed further in social policy matters, and for this purpose to make use of the existing institutional framework of the Community. However, altogether only four legal acts were based on the Protocol on Social Policy until the United Kingdom agreed, at the intergovernmental conference of Amsterdam, to integrate the provisions of this Protocol into Arts. 136–145 EC. On this, cf. Schuster, "Rechtsfragen der Maastrichter Vereinbarung zur Sozialpolitik" [1992] *EuZW* 178; and Falkner, "Das Maastrichter Sozialprotokoll: Differenzierte Integration wider Willen" in Breuss and Griller, *Flexible Integration in Europa. Einheit oder Europa "à la carte"?* (Vienna, 1998), 79.

[2] On the history and general theory of differentiated integration cf. Arndt, "Engere Zusammenarbeit und Flexibilität im Vertrag von Amsterdam—Eine neue Entwicklungsstrategie im Hinblick auf die Vertiefung und Erweiterung der Europäischen Union?" in Scholz (ed.), *Europa als Union des Rechts—eine notwendige Zwischenbilanz im Prozeß der Vertiefung und Erweiterung* (Cologne, 1999), 179; Gaja, "How Flexible is Flexibility under the Amsterdam Treaty?" [1998] *CML Rev.* 855; Kortenberg, "Closer Cooperation in the Treaty of Amsterdam" [1998] *CML Rev.* 833; Koenig, "Die Europäische Union als bloßer materiellrechtlicher Verbundrahmen" [1998] *EuR* 139; and Tuytschaever, *Differentiation in European Union Law* (Oxford, 1999). On differentiated integration and EMU cf. the overview given by Häde, "Währungsintegration mit abgestufter Geschwindigkeit" in A. Weber (ed.), *Währung und Wirtschaft. Das Geld im Recht. Festschrift für Hugo J. Hahn zum 70. Geburtstag* (Baden Baden, 1997), 123 (132); see also Smits, *The European Central Bank. Institutional Aspects* (The Hague/London/Boston, 1997), 134 *et seq.*; Louis, "Differentiation and the EMU" in *The Many Faces of Differentiation in EU Law* (Antwerp, 2000); and Vigneron and Mollica, "La différenciation dans l'Union Economique et Monétaire" [2000] *Euredia* 197.

To explain the manifold aspects of differentiated integration, this chapter will first give an overview of the different legal position of the 15 EU Member States *vis-à-vis* the single currency (II.) and illustrate the consequences thereof on the system of Community law (III.). It will then analyse the impact of differentiated integration on the law of the ECB (IV.).

II.   MEMBER STATES IN DIFFERENT LEGAL POSITIONS *VIS-À-VIS* THE SINGLE CURRENCY

Since 1 January 1999, the 15 Member States of the EU have to be subdivided into three groups in so far as their legal relationship with the single currency is concerned: in participating Member States ("ins"), Member States with a derogation ("pre-ins"), and Member States with a special status ("outs").

1. Member States participating in the single currency ("ins")

The first group of Member States consists of the *participants* in the single currency. This group came into being on 3 May 1998 when the Council, meeting in the composition of the Heads of State or Government, confirmed that Belgium, Germany, Spain, France, Ireland, Italy, Luxembourg, the Netherlands, Austria, Portugal and Finland fulfilled the necessary conditions for the adoption of the single currency.[3] On 19 June 2000, a similar confirmation was given to Greece.[4]

As a result of this confirmation, these Member States participate in Stage Three of EMU with all rights and obligations foreseen in the EC Treaty. The group of participating Member States is therefore characterised by the fact that they have transferred irrevocably their monetary sovereignty to the ECB, and that the euro has legally replaced their national currencies. In particular, all provisions which are listed in Article 116(3), second subparagraph, EC and said to apply "from the beginning of the third stage", are applicable to the participating Member States without reservation. This Stage Three Community law[5] requires these Member States, *inter alia*, to avoid excessive government deficits (Articles 104(1) EC) in order not to activate the sanctioning mechanism provided for in Article 104(7)-(11) EC and further specified in the context of the "Stability and Growth Pact".[6] Under Article 105(4) EC, which also applies from the beginning of the third stage, the national authorities of the participating

---

[3] Art. 1 of Council Decision 98/317/EC of 3 May 1998 in accordance with Art. 109j(4) of the Treaty [1998] OJ L139/30.

[4] Council Decision 2000/427/EC of 19 June 2000 in accordance with Art. 122(2) of the Treaty on the adoption by Greece of the single currency on 1 January 2001 [2000] OJ L167/20.

[5] On the application of Stage Three Community law to Member States with a derogation, cf. *infra*, p. 136 *et seq.*

[6] Cf. Council Regulation 1467/97 of 7 July 1997 on speeding up and clarifying the implementation of the excessive deficit procedure [1997] OJ L209/6.

Member States have to consult the ECB on any draft legislative provision in the field of monetary law and central banking legislation.[7] Finally, Stage Three Community law imposes a legal duty on Member States to give full independence to their respective national central banks (Articles 108, 109, 116(3) and (5) EC)—a requirement which led to a remarkably high degree of legal convergence of national central banking legislation in parallel to the establishment of the ECB and the ESCB.

2. Member States with a derogation in Stage Three of EMU ("pre-ins")

The second group consists of those EU Member States which also moved automatically to the third stage of EMU on 1 January 1999, in accordance with Article 121(4), first sentence EC,[8] but which, as a result of the convergence test applied by the Council, did not (yet) fulfil the necessary conditions for the adoption of the single currency. As a consequence, these Member States automatically became so-called "*Member States with a derogation*", as provided for in Article 122(1), second paragraph, EC.

Originally, both Greece and Sweden became subject to such a derogation within Stage Three on 1 January 1999, as neither fulfilled the necessary conditions for the adoption of the single currency.[9] In the case of Greece, national legislation, including the statute of the national central bank, was considered to be compatible with the EC Treaty and the Statute; however, Greece did not fulfil any of the four economic convergence criteria mentioned in Article 121(1), third sentence, EC.[10] In Sweden, national legislation, in particular the statute of Sveriges Riksbank, was not compatible with the independence requirements of Community law. In addition, Sweden did not fulfil the convergence criterion mentioned in the third indent of Article 121(1) EC, as it did not participate in the exchange-rate mechanism of the European Monetary System.[11] From a legal point of view, it was thus not decisive that Sweden chiefly had political reasons for not adopting the single currency, as Sweden—unlike the United Kingdom

---

[7] On this duty to consult the ECB and its legal effect cf. *supra*, Ch. 3, p. 100 *et seq.*

[8] Legally, Art. 109j(4) (now Art. 121(4) first sentence, EC) provided for the automatic start of the third stage of EMU on 1 January 1999; cf. Selmayr, "Die Europäische Währungsunion zwischen Politik und Recht" [1998] *EuZW* 101 with further references to the political and academic controversy surrounding this question.

[9] Recital 4 of Council Decision 98/317/EC, *supra*, n. 3.

[10] Cf. the Commission's Convergence Report, COM(98)1999, 20; and the EMI's Convergence Report (March 1998), 14 *et seq.*, 49 *et seq.* This view was followed in the second recital of Council Decision 98/317/EC, *supra*, n. 3. On the details of the legal situation of Greece, cf. Nicolaysen, "Der rechtliche Status Griechenlands als Mitgliedstaat mit einer Ausnahmeregelung" in Papaschinopoulou (ed.), *Greece on Course Toward the European Economic and Monetary Union. Lessons to be Learnt from the German Experience* (Athens/Baden Baden, 1999), 39.

[11] Cf. the Commission's Convergence Report, COM(98)1999, 30 *et seq.*, 57 *et seq.*; and the EMI's Convergence Report (March 1998), 24 *et seq.*, 97 *et seq.*, 181 *et seq.* This view was shared by the Council of the European Union; cf. Arts. 3 and 13 of Council Recommendation 98/316/EC of 1 May 1998 in accordance with Art. 109j(2) [1998] OJ L139/21; and recital 4 of Council Decision 98/317/EC, *supra*, n. 3.

and Denmark, as will be explained below—does not, under the EC Treaty, enjoy the right of an "opt out" from the third stage of EMU.[12]

A derogation within Stage Three of EMU implies that a number—but not all—of the provisions which normally apply to the Member States as from the beginning of the third stage, do not apply to such a Member State. The provisions from which there is a derogation are listed in Article 122(3) and (4) EC[13] and in Article 43 of the Statute. In addition, some provisions explicitly refer only to "a Member State" which "has a derogation", like Article 124(2) EC, or to "the Member States without a derogation", for example Article 123(4) first sentence EC. All these provisions concern the transfer of monetary sovereignty to the Community level. This transfer does not yet affect Member States with a derogation because these temporarily keep their national currencies, which continue to be steered and managed by their national central banks.

It should be noted however that Member States with a derogation have moved to the Third Stage of EMU.[14] This follows from Article 121(4), first sentence, EC in conjunction with Protocol No 24 on the transition to the third stage of economic and monetary union, where it is laid down that on 1 January 1999 "the Community" moved to Stage Three of EMU; thus all Member States, except where Community law states otherwise, as is the case in the Danish and UK Protocols. As a consequence, all provisions which are applicable as from 1 January by virtue of Article 116(3), second subparagraph, EC, and not explicitly excluded by the derogations under Article 122(3) and (4) EC, or by other provisions, also apply to Member States with a derogation.

In particular, Member States with a derogation are, just like participating Member States, obliged to avoid excessive government deficits in accordance with Article 104(1) EC—which is applicable from the beginning of the third stage of EMU—even though the sanctions of Article 104(9) and (11) EC are excluded by Article 122(3) EC. These Member States are also required to con-

---

[12] This is also stressed by the European Parliament in its Resolution of 30 April 1998 on the Convergence Report of the European Monetary Institute (C4–0201/98) and the document from the Commission entitled "EURO 1999—25 March 1998—Report on progress towards convergence and its recommendation with a view to the transition to the third stage of Economic and Monetary Union" (COM(98)1999 C4–0200/98) [1998] OJ C152/33, where indent 7 before the recitals states "that Sweden does not presently meet all conditions for participation in monetary union; whereas, in particular, there continue to be shortcomings concerning the independence of the central bank; whereas the Swedish Government has stated that it will not be participating in monetary union on 1 January 1999 *in spite of the fact that it did not negotiate an opt-out*" (emphasis added). The "voluntary opt-out" of Sweden is generally considered to be in violation of the EC Treaty; cf. Sideek, "A Critical Interpretation of the EMU Convergence Rules" [1997] *LIEI* 1 (12 *et seq.*); and Selmayr, "Die Wirtschafts- und Währungsunion als Rechtsgemeinschaft" [1999] *AöR* 357 (363 *et seq.*).

[13] Cf. the table with the relevant provisions from Von Estorff and Molitor in Von der Groeben, Thiesing and Ehlermann, *Kommentar zum EU-/EG-Vertrag* (5th edn., Baden Baden, 1999), Art. 109 k, para. 1. A more detailed table is presented by Smits, *supra*, n. 2, 140 *et seq.*

[14] This is very often not seen; cf. Vigneron and Mollica, *supra*, n. 112, 200, who qualifiy a derogation as follows: "*il maintient en quelque sorte l'Etat member en question dans le régime qui prévalait au cours de la deuxième phase de l'UEM pour tous les Etats membres*".

sult the ECB on all national legislation in its field of competence, as there is no derogation from Article 105(4) EC, which thus applies both to participating Member States and to Member States with a derogation. Finally, Member States with a derogation are also subject to the requirement of central bank independence under Article 108 EC. By virtue of this, albeit limited, participation of Member States with a derogation in the third stage, they may be qualified as "pre-ins" in relation to the single currency.

The derogations granted under Article 122(1), second subparagraph, EC are of only a temporary nature. This is underlined by Article 4(2) EC, according to which the objective of introducing a single currency extends to the whole Community and thus to participating Member States and Member States with a derogation alike. It is further emphasised by Article 122(2) EC, which specifies that "at least once every two years or at the request of a Member State with a derogation", the Council shall decide again, on the basis of reports from the Commission and the ECB, whether these Member States fulfil the necessary conditions for the introduction of the single currency. In fact, the Commission and the ECB each presented a new convergence report[15] on Greece[16] and Sweden in spring 2000 which encouraged the Council to abrogate the derogation for Greece with effect from 1 January 2001.[17] Since this date, the euro has therefore been the single currency of 12 Member States, leaving for the moment[18] Sweden as the only Member State with a derogation in the sense of Article 122(1), second paragraph, EC. By virtue of Article 122(2) EC, a new assessment of the Swedish convergence will automatically follow in spring 2002. Until then, Sweden will continue to be required to observe the objectives of the Community, in particular Article 4(2) EC. It thus will have to make all necessary efforts to satisfy the convergence test as soon as possible.

3. Member States with a special status ("outs")

The legal position of the United Kingdom and Denmark *vis-à-vis* the single currency may best be summed up as that of *"Member States with a special status"*. In the Maastricht Treaty, both countries were granted, in two special Protocols (Protocols No 25 and No 26), the right to choose whether or not to participate in the third stage of EMU.[19] Denmark notified the Council its decision not to

---

[15] Commission, *Convergence Report 2000* (Brussels, 2000), COM(2000)277.final; ECB, *Convergence Report 2000* (Frankfurt am Main, 2000), 2, http://www.ecb.int/pub/pdf/cr2000en.pdf.

[16] On 9 March 2000, Greece had explicitly requested such a report by a letter of its Minister of National Economy and Finance; cf. ECB, *supra,* n. 15, 2.

[17] Council Decision 2000/427/EC, *supra,* n. 4.

[18] This is likely to change after enlargement of the EU; cf. *infra,* p. 143 *et seq.*

[19] Cf. Art. 1 of Protocol No 25 on certain provisions relating to the United Kingdom of Great Britain and Northern Ireland (the UK Protocol): "The United Kingdom shall notify the Council whether it intends to move to the third stage before the Council makes its assessment under Art. 109j(2) of this Treaty. Unless the United Kingdom notifies the Council that it intends to move to the third stage, it shall be under not obligation to do so". Cf. Arts. 1 and 2 of Protocol No 26 on certain

join the third stage at the Edinburgh European Council on 11–12th December 1992,[20] while the United Kingdom gave notice on 30 October 1997 that it did not intend to move to Stage Three.[21]

As a first consequence, the Council, on 3 May 1998, did not assess the legal and economic convergence of these two countries.[22] The Council also refrained from doing so on 19 June 2000, when it had to decide on the derogations previously granted to Greece and Sweden,[23] as Article 122(2) EC provides only for the abrogation of a derogation, but not the termination of the special status enjoyed by the United Kingdom and Denmark. This shows that, under Community law, there is no automatic and no timetable for the participation of these two countries in the third stage. Only if they give notice that they intend to abandon their special status will an assessment procedure similar to that under Article 122(2) EC be initiated.[24]

In spite of this parallelism with the legal position of the United Kingdom, the Danish exemption has given rise to considerable controversy in academic doctrine. According to a number of authors Denmark is in the same situation as a Member State with a derogation;[25] some others[26] assimilate the Danish position

provisions relating to Denmark (the Danish Protocol): "The Danish Government shall notify the Council of its position concerning participation in the third stage before the Council makes its assessment under Art. 109j(2) of this Treaty. In the event of a notification that Denmark will not participate in the third stage, Denmark shall have an exemption".

[20] Cf. Decision of 11 December 1992 of the Heads of State and Government, meeting within the European Council, concerning certain problems raised by Denmark on the Treaty on European Union [1992] OJ C348/1, section B(1): "Denmark has given notification that it will not participate in the third stage. This notification will take effect upon the coming into effect of this decision".

[21] This is recorded in recital 5 of Council Decision 98/317/EC, *supra*, n. 3. Strictly legally speaking, such a notification was not required as, under Art. 1 of the UK Protocol, the United Kingdom must notify the Council only if it intends to move to the third stage, not if it wants to maintain its present "opt out".

[22] Cf. recital 7 of Council Decision 98/317/EC, *supra*, n. 3.

[23] Cf. recital 2 of Council Decision 2000/427/EC, *supra*, n. 4.

[24] Cf. Art. 4 of the Danish Protocol, and Art. 10 of the UK Protocol, *supra*, n. 19.

[25] Cf. Louis, "A Legal and Institutional Approach for Building a Monetary Union" (1998) *CML Rev.* 33 (64): "under the Protocol on Denmark, the situation in this country . . . was to be assimilated to that of a Member State with a derogation."; cf. also Schuster, "Der Sonderstatus Dänemarks im Vertrag über die Europäische Union" [1993] *EuZW* 177 (178); Smits, *supra*, n. 2, 137: "When Denmark states that it will remain outside full currency union, it will have an *exemption*. The effect of this status is that Denmark is treated as a Member State with a *derogation*"; Tuytschaever, *supra*, n. 2, 27: "In other words, as a consequence of its notification not to participate, Denmark is put on the same footing as a Member State with a derogation". Cf. also Vigneron and Mollica, *supra*, n. 2, 203: "*Le protocole fixe le régime applicable au Denmark tant que celui-ci ne participe pas à la troisième phase de l'UEM. Ce régime est assimilé à celui d'un Etat membre bénéficiant d'une dérogation (paragraphe 2 du protocole)*". A modified version of this view is taken by Flores in Von der Groeben, Thiesing and Ehlermann, *supra*, n. 13, following Art. 109 m, Protocol (Nr. 11) and (Nr. 12), para. 10 *et seq.*, according to whom Denmark would be in an identical legal situation to Member States with a derogation, with the sole exception that it could by its own motion start the procedure for accessing the single currency.

[26] A rare example is Howarth, "The Compromise on Denmark and the Treaty on European Union: A Legal and Political Analysis" (1994) *CML Rev.* 765 (773). We have already indicated that we, in principle, share this view; cf. Zilioli and Selmayr, "The European Central Bank, its System and its Law" [1999] *Euredia* 187 (225 *et seq.*); and [1999–2000] *YEL*, 347 (376 *et seq.*).

to that enjoyed by the United Kingdom.[27] The compromise on Denmark, adopted by the Heads of State and Government, meeting within the European Council in Edinburgh on 11–12 December 1992[28] after the negative outcome of the Danish referendum (rejection of the Maastrict Treaty by 50.7 to 49.3 per cent of the vote on 2 June 1992), could not shed more light on the Danish position. From a Community law perspective, this *novum* of an "atypical decision of the European Council" certainly cannot amend[29] or interpret[30] the EC Treaty in spite of its high political value.[31] At best, the European Council decision may be qualified as a declaratory "restatement" of a situation that Denmark already enjoys under the EC Treaty and the Danish Protocol.[32]

In Community law, the Danish situation is, however, far from being crystal clear. There is even a striking linguistic discrepancy in paragraph 2, first sentence, of the Danish Protocol as regards the notion used to describe the Danish position. While the English version of paragraph 2 of the Danish Protocol

---

[27] Quite understandably, the legal debate seems to be influenced either by the desire to see the Danish position as a temporary situation and to encourage Denmark to adopt the euro as soon as possible or by the wish to move ahead to further steps of integration without having to wait for "the slowest sloop in the fleet". Cf. also Curtin and Van Oik, "Denmark and the Edinburgh Summit: Maastricht without Tears" in O'Keefe and Twomey (eds.), *Legal Issues of the Maastricht Treaty* (London, 1994), 349 *et seq.*

[28] *Supra*, n. 20, where sections (2) and (3) explain the consequences of the Danish notification not to move to Stage Three: "As a consequence, Denmark will not participate in the single currency, will not be bound by the rules concerning economic policy which apply only to Member States participating in the third stage of Economic and Monetary Union, and will retain its existing powers in the field of monetary policy according to its national laws and regulations, including powers of the National Central Bank of Denmark in the field of monetary policy. Denmark will participate fully in the second stage of Economic and Monetary Union".

[29] The case law of the ECJ on this issue is abundant; cf. only Case 43/75, *Defrenne* v. *Sabena* [1976] ECR 455, paras. 56–58; and Case 59/75, *Manghera* [1976] ECR 91, para. 21.

[30] The ECJ has confirmed the exclusivity of its jurisdiction on many occasions; as an example, cf. Case 314/85, *Foto-Frost* v. *Hauptzollamt Lübeck-Ost* [1987] ECR 4199, para 15 *et seq.* The ECJ has also ruled that so-called "interpretation declarations", which are sometimes attached to legal acts by the Community institutions and/or by the Member States, do not have any legal value of their own; cf. Case 237/84, *Commission* v. *Belgium* [1986] ECR 1247, para. 17; and Case C–292/89, *The Queen* v. *Immigration Appeal Tribunal, ex parte: Antonissen* [1991] ECR I–745, para. 18.

[31] As a matter of principle, Community law doctrine does not regard attempts of the European Council to interpret the EC Treaty as legally binding or even authoritative. This is very clearly stated by Smits, *supra*, n. 2, 491, where he considers the legality of the change of the name of the single currency from ECU to euro through an "interpretation" of the European Council meeting in Madrid on 15–16 December 1995: "On the basis of these constitutional principles, a 'definitive' interpretation is not for the Member States' Governments to make"; cf. also Louis, "L'évolution du Conseil européen à la lumière de la réalisation de l'Union économique et monétaire", in Starace (ed.), *Divenire sociale e adeguamento del diritto. Studi in onore di Francesco Capotorti* (Milan, 1999), ii, 253, who strongly argues against any authoritative role of the European Council within the system of Community law. The same view is taken, as regards the Edinburgh compromise on Denmark, by Howarth, *supra*, n. 26, 774.

[32] This view is shared by Curtin and Van Oik, *supra*, n. 27, 361: "Section B of the Danish decision, therefore, in fact has an entirely declaratory character". The Edinburgh summit therefore did nothing more than to put political emphasis on the Danish situation which already existed, as a matter of law, under the Maastricht Treaty. This is again very clearly stated by Curtin and Van Oik, *supra*, n. 27, 364: "The reason why the Maastricht Treaty did not need to be adapted is that it was not amended at the Edinburgh summit. The texts presented to the Danish population on 18 May 1993 were exactly the same the electorate had already rejected on 2 June 1992".

clearly states that the result of the Danish notification of non-participation in the third stage of EMU is that "Denmark shall have an *exemption*"—thereby indicating that Denmark was given more than just a derogation under Article 122(1) EC—the French version of this paragraph uses the word "*dérogation*", i.e. the same notion which describes the position of Member States under Article 122(1) EC. Neither the English nor the French version may be qualified as a drafting error. One finds the linguistic assimilation of the Danish position with that of a Member State with a derogation not only in the French text, but also in the Finnish, Portuguese, Swedish and Spanish versions of paragraph 2, first sentence of the Danish Protocol; on the other hand, the clear distinction between "exemption" and "derogation" made by the English text is also observed by the German, Danish, Italian, Dutch, Greek and Gaelic versions[33] of the Danish Protocol.

In view of the equal validity of all 12 authentic language versions of the Treaties and the Protocols, prescribed by Article 314 EC, a legal clarification of the Danish position requires resort to the spirit of the Danish Protocol and to the general scheme of the provisions on EMU in the EC Treaty.[34] For this purpose, one has to note that, first, both sentences of the Danish Protocol talk of "participation in the third stage" and, secondly, that recital 2 of the Danish Protocol explicitly provides the following: "the Danish constitution contains provisions which may imply a referendum in Denmark *prior to Danish participation in the third stage of economic and monetary union*".[35] The purpose of the Protocol therefore is clearly not to submit Denmark to the automatic process of the start of Stage Three, but to make Danish participation in the final stage of EMU dependent on the will of the Danish population. In view of the negative outcome of the Danish referendum of 2 June 1992,[36] and in view of the subsequent notification by Denmark "*that it will not participate in the third stage*",[37] one can hardly maintain that Denmark participates in the third stage of EMU like a Member State with a derogation. The key element of the Danish special status is rather that Denmark did not take part in the automatic move to Stage Three of EMU, thereby following the will of its people and making use of an "opt out" given to it by the EC Treaty and the Danish Protocol.[38]

We therefore suggest that, as a matter of principle, the Danish special status is characterised by non-participation in the third stage, just like that of the

---

[33] The Gaelic version of the Protocol makes a clear distinction between "derogation" and "temporary derogation", the latter obviously referring to the status under Art. 122(1) EC.

[34] Cf. Case C–327/91, *France* v. *Commission* [1994] ECR I–3641, para. 35; Case C–84/95, *Bosphorus Hava Yollari Turizm ve Ticaret AS* v. *Minister for Transport, Energy and Communication* [1996] ECR I–3953, para. 16.

[35] Emphasis added.

[36] On 28 September 2000, a new referendum took place in Denmark in which the Danish population, with 53.2 to 46.8 per cent of the vote, rejected the proposal of the Danish government to move from Stage Two to Stage Three of EMU.

[37] Cf. *supra*, n. 20.

[38] Cf. Howarth, *supra*, n. 26, 774: "The notification was in effect the expression of the opt-out that Debmark already possessed according to the Treaty".

United Kingdom. Both Member States are thus "outs" as regards Stage Three of EMU. As a consequence, all Stage Three provisions listed in Article 116(3), second subparagraph, EC do not automatically apply to Denmark, as Denmark, like the United Kingdom, decided to remain in Stage Two and will remain there until further notice. From this it follows that the obligation to avoid excessive government deficits in Article 104(1) EC is not applicable to Denmark, as it applies only "from the beginning of the third stage" (Article 116(3), second subparagraph, EC), to which Denmark does not belong; as Member States in the second stage, Denmark and the United Kingdom are under a duty only to "endeavour to avoid excessive government deficits", as provided for in Article 116(4) EC.[39] The same is true for the Stage Three-requirement of central bank independence in Article 108 EC; both Denmark and the United Kingdom only have "to start the process leading to independence of its central bank" (Article 116(5) EC), without a duty to complete this process as long as their respective special status outside Stage Three continues to be in force.[40]

Whereas the rule is therefore that the Danish and the British special status is comparable because of their joint non-participation in Stage Three of EMU, it should nevertheless be noted that the status of Denmark and the United Kingdom varies in two aspects. The first aspect concerns only the legal technique by which, exceptionally, some selected Stage Three provisions of the EC Treaty and of the Statute are made applicable to these Stage Two Member

---

[39] We must admit that Community practice is not always in line with this legal reasoning; cf. Council Regulation 1467/97 of 7 July 1997 on speeding up and clarifying the implementation of the excessive deficit procedure [1997] OJ L209/6, where recital 5 reads as follows: "Whereas Denmark, referring to paragraph 1 of Protocol (No 12 [now No 26]) to the Treaty has notified, in the context of the Edinburgh decision of 12 December 1992, that it will not participate in the third stage; whereas, therefore, in accordance with paragraph 2 of the said Protocol, paragraphs 9 and 11 of Article 104c [now Article 104 EC] shall not apply to Denmark". In our view, also the obligation under Article 104(1) EC—a Stage Three provision by virtue of Article 116(3) second subparagraph EC—should have been mentioned as not applying to Denmark as a Stage Two Member State.

[40] Different is the case of the obligation to consult the ECB. Even though in our opinion Art. 105(4) EC, as a Stage Three provision, does not apply to Denmark and the United Kingdom, it should not be forgotten that both Member States are subject to the Stage Two obligation of Art. 117(6), second subpara., EC, to consult the EMI on draft legislative provision within its field of competence. Under Art. 123(2), first sentence, EC, the ECB "shall, if necessary, take over tasks of the ECB"; and Art. 44 of the Statute provides that "the ECB shall take over those tasks of the EMI which, because of the derogations of one or more Member States, still have to be performed in the third stage". In our view, the Danish and British obligation of consultation—which is a crucial instrument to guarantee legal convergence within the EU—continues since the EMI was substituted in this task by the ECB. We must admit, however, that Community secondary law seems not to follow this line of reasoning, but differentiates between Denmark and the United Kingdom: cf. Council Decision 98/415/EC of 29 June 1998 on the consultation of the European Central Bank by national authorities regarding draft legislative provisions [1998] OJ L189/42, which refers, in recital 7, to the British special status: "Whereas, in accordance with paragraphs 5 and 8 of Protocol No 11 [now No 25] annexed to the Treaty, this Decision shall not apply to the United Kingdom of Great Britain and Northern Ireland if and so long as that Member State does not move to the third stage of EMU". But one should note that this Council Decision repealed Council Decision 93/717/EC of 22 November 1993 on the consultation of the EMI by the authorities of the Member States [1993] OJ L332/14, which applied to all Member States; and that secondary Community law cannot derogate from obligations already arising directly from the EC Treaty.

States. The Danish Protocol establishes, in its paragraph 2, second sentence, "that all Articles and provisions of this Treaty and the Statute of the ESCB *referring to a derogation* shall be applicable to Denmark". This means that whenever provisions explicitly"[41] contain the word "derogation" or "Member State with a derogation", Denmark also is covered. The UK Protocol uses a slightly different technique, namely to exempt the United Kingdom from *all* Stage Three provisions[42] by listing all such provisions in the UK Protocol itself. The result, however, is the same, as may be demonstrated by the example of Article 124(2) EC. According to this provision, there is a duty for Member States with a derogation to treat the national exchange-rate policy as "a matter of common interest". In spite of its non-participation in the third stage, Denmark is covered by this duty, since Article 124(2) EC explicitly refers to a derogation. For the United Kingdom, the same follows from paragraph 6, second sentence of its Protocol, which states that Article 124 "shall apply to the United Kingdom *as if it had a derogation*".

More important is a second distinction between the British and the Danish special status. The UK Protocol not only states that Stage Three provisions do not apply to the United Kingdom and to the Bank of England, but in addition excludes, in its paragraph 5, further provisions of the *acquis communautaire*. Most important, the UK Protocol excludes the application of Article 4(2) EC, according to which both the Community and the Member States remain committed to the objective of the introduction of a single currency with a single monetary and exchange-rate policy. There is no such exclusion in the Danish Protocol. Even though it is a Member State which does not participate in the third stage of EMU, Denmark is therefore closer to the core group of 12 participating Member States than is the United Kingdom, as Denmark remains committed to the goal of a single currency.

In summary, the Danish special status thus can be said to be a mixture between a "pre-in" and an "out" situation, even though recent political developments—in particular the negative outcome of the Danish referendum of 28 September 2000[43]—have put further emphasis on the latter aspect.

4. Further differentiation in the context of enlargement?

At the moment, it seems guaranteed that the present degree of differentiation within EMU will not be further intensified in the context of the forthcoming process of EU enlargement. The creation of the UK Protocol and the Danish Protocol probably was the only solution to achieve an agreement in principle on the establishment of EMU within the framework of the EU. The Danish and

---

[41] That such a reference must be explicit is particularly clear in the Danish, English, Spanish, French and Portuguese texts of the Danish Protocol.

[42] Cf. Art. 116 (3) EC and *supra*, p. 134 *et seq.*

[43] Cf. *supra*, n. 36.

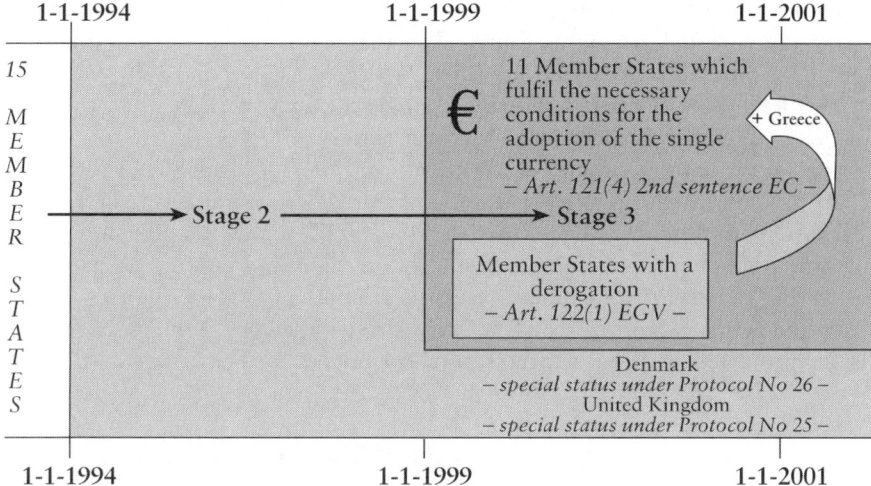

Fig. 3 *The differentiation of the European Union due to EMU*

the British special status therefore appears as the result of very specific political circumstances at the time of the Maastricht intergovernmental conference and during the subsequent ratification process. Against this background, both Protocols leave no room for being applied "by analogy" to new Member States; in addition, both Protocols clearly state[44] that they will cease to apply if and when Denmark and the United Kingdom have notified their intention to move to the third stage of EMU.

Today, there is neither a factual need nor the political will to repeat this experiment—with all the intricate legal questions which inevitably result therefrom—now that the single currency has come into being and that the law of the third stage of EMU has irrevocably become part of the *acquis communautaire*.[45] Thus, it has to be welcomed that in the ongoing accession negotiations with candidate countries in the East and in the South East of Europe, the Community side has made it very clear that there will be no further "opt-outs" from EMU.[46]

---

[44] Cf. para. 5 of the Danish Protocol and para. 10, second subpara., of the UK Protocol.

[45] Cf. Noyer, "Some ECB Views on the Accession Process" (Vienna, 17 January 2001), published at http://www.ecb.int/key/01/sp010117.htm, 2, for whom the proper adoption of the *acquis communautaire* "naturally also includes the provisions relating to Economic and Monetary Union".

[46] CF. ECB, "The Eurosystem and EU Enlargement" in *Monthly Bulletin* (Frankfurt am Main, February 2000), 41 (47): "In the monetary field, it has already been decided that no 'opt-out' clauses, such as those negotiated by the United Kingdom and Denmark, shall be granted to new Member States, thus implying that, when joining the EU, new Member States will be committed to finally adopting the euro". Cf. also Noyer, *supra*, n. 45, 4: "the new entrants will, as far as EMU is concerned, have the status of 'Member States with a derogation'. No 'opt-out' clauses will be available for the future new members".

A new Member State therefore will accede automatically to the third stage of EMU; therein, such a new entrant will in the beginning have the status of a Member State with a derogation under Article 122(1), second subparagraph, EC, while the date of participation in the single currency will depend on the legal and economic convergence of this Member State.[47]

The provisions on enhanced co-operation, introduced by the Amsterdam Treaty and meanwhile refined by the Nice Treaty, also are unlikely to create further differentiation inside EMU. Article 11(1) (a) EC makes it a precondition of any initiative of enhanced co-operation that it "does not concern areas which fall within the exclusive competence of the Community". The single currency, being the prime example of such an exclusive competence,[48] will therefore be legally protected against potential future attempts of further differentiation.

III. THE IMPACT OF DIFFERENTIATED INTEGRATION ON THE SYSTEM OF COMMUNITY LAW

One might have expected that the differentiation of the EU to three groups of Member States, with varying rights and obligations inside the third stage of EMU would have led to a complete re-design of the system of Community law. However, this is not the case. Instead, the provisions of the EC Treaty on EMU are coined by the clear will to leave the institutional set-up of the EC as intact as possible, thereby demonstrating that differentiation in this key area of Community policies shall be only of a temporary nature. Member States with a derogation or with special status have kept, without reservation, their status as full EU members. It is therefore rather the exception than the rule that the EC Treaty provides for a modification of the traditional system of Community law in the field of EMU.

As a consequence, the approach chosen for (temporary) differentiation within EMU must be clearly distinguished from the new method of enhanced co-operation in other fields, as introduced by the Treaty of Amsterdam with the general provisions of Article 11 EC and Articles 43–45 EU, as well as with the special provisions in the field of the free movement of persons in Article 61 *et seq.* EC. In contrast to EMU, these new provisions—in particular Protocol No 4 on the position of the United Kingdom and Ireland and Protocol No 5 on the position of Denmark—provide for a complete non-participation of the United Kingdom, Ireland and Denmark in a new Community policy.

---

[47] Cf. also Noyer, *supra*, n. 45, 2, who distinguishes three phases with different sets of criteria before the accession countries will be able to become participating Member States: EU membership, preceded by compliance with the Copenhagen criteria; participation in ERM II; and the eventual adoption of the euro, based on the fulfilment of the Maastricht criteria".

[48] Cf. *supra*, Ch. 2, p. 70 *et seq.*

1. Differentiated decision-making?

A first demonstration of the maintained coherence of the Community law system in spite of EMU differentiation is that the institutional law governing the Community institutions continues to apply, as a matter of principle, also in EMU matters.

1.1. No differentiation of supranational Community institutions

The provisions on the composition and decision-making process of the European Parliament, the Commission, the ECJ and the Court of Auditors have been left untouched by the advent of EMU, and this for a good reason: these institutions are clearly *supranational* institutions the mandate of which is in no way dependent on the participation of a specific Member State in a Community policy.

Hence, there can be no debate about excluding the "British" or "Swedish" Commissioner from a vote on a Commission decision in EMU matters. These Commissioners only have the nationality of a particular Member State, but are obliged, by Article 213(2) EC, to discuss and act within the Commission with sole regard to the supranational interests of the Community as a whole. Legally, there is thus no French, German or Italian Commissioner, even though this is often suggested in political statements.

The same is true for the members of the European Parliament (MEPs), who, though being directly elected *in* the Member States, neither represent a particular Member State nor need to be nationals of the Member State in which they are elected.[49] Instead, they "are representatives of the peoples of the States brought together in the Community" (Article 189(1) EC)[50]; they therefore sit, in the plenary sessions of the European Parliament, not according to their nationality, but in trans-national political groups like the European People's Party or the Party of European Socialists. As a consequence, nobody has ever questioned the right of MEPs from Sweden, Denmark and the United Kingdom fully to take part in committee meetings and plenary sessions in which EMU matters are on the agenda.[51]

---

[49] This results from Art. 19(2) EC, according to which nationals of the EU Member States have the right, in European Parliament elections, to vote and to be elected in their respective Member States of residence. This would enable, for example, an Italian national to represent the constituency of Munich in the European Parliament.

[50] This supranational status has recently been reaffirmed in Case T–353/00 R, *Le Pen v. European Parliament*, Order of 26 January 2001 (not yet published), where the president of the CFI saw a discretionary power of Parliament to lift the immunity of one of its members even after a national court had decided in favour of such a lifting of the immunity. On this, cf. Rivais, "Le Parlement européen et la jurisprudence Le Pen", *Le Monde*, 13 February 2001, 23, who quotes the ironic statement of the President of the Parliament, Nicole Fontaine, that *"une jurisprudence Le Pen pourrait faire prévaloir la compétence des institutions européennes sur celles des gouvernements nationaux"*.

[51] Only once, in the context of the Maastricht Protocol on Social Policy, did the Liberals ask for the exclusion of MEPs from a non-participating Member State (here, the United Kingdom) from voting in the supranational assembly of the European people; the Parliament, however, rejected this motion by 211 votes to 33 with 6 abstentions. On this incident, cf. Falkner, *supra*, n. 1, 90 *et seq.*

The same principle applies *mutatis mutandis* to judges at the ECJ and auditors at the Court of Auditors, in view of the clearly supranational character of these institutions, and because of the absence of any rules to the contrary.

1.2. Differentiation within the Council

As a consequence of EMU, a certain modification of the Community's decision-making process may be observed only for the Council of the European Union. This may be explained by the double nature of the Council, which is, on the one hand, a Community institution and therefore bound by supranational objectives, but on the other hand also allows, in contrast to the other Community institutions, for a representation of national interests.[52] It therefore has a certain logic that the representation of the interests of Member States which do not participate in the single currency may be reduced in the context of Council decisions on EMU matters.

In spite of this logic, it needs to be stressed that the provisions on EMU have left unchanged Article 203 EC, the provision dealing with the composition of the Council. This means that also in EMU matters, *each* of the 15 Member States continues to have a representative, at ministerial level, in the Council; and that it is only this "Council of the Fifteen" which is entitled to meet and to deliberate in cases where the single currency is concerned. Therefore, Sweden, Denmark and the United Kingdom keep their right to send a representative to Council meetings and to speak on and discuss all EMU matters.

In addition, there is no general rule in the EC Treaty according to which non-participation in the single currency would have as an automatic consequence non-participation in voting whenever EMU is concerned. It is true that such a rule may be found in the provisions on enhanced co-operation, where Article 44(1), second sentence, EU states that "while all members of the Council shall be able to take part in the deliberations, only those representing participating Member States shall take part in the adoption of decisions". However, in EMU law, a different approach has been chosen with the rule in Article 122(5) EC. Under this provision, "the voting right of Member States with a derogation shall be suspended for Council decisions referred to in Articles of this Treaty mentioned in paragraph 3". This provision differs from Article 44(1), second sentence, EU in three respects. First, it talks only about a *suspension* of voting rights, thereby stressing the temporary nature of differentiated decision-making within EMU. Secondly, while Article 44(1) EU forms part of the general provisions on enhanced co-operation in Title VII of the EU Treaty, which is referred to in Article 11 EC and thus in Part I ("Principles") of the EC Treaty, the temporary nature of Article 122 EC is further underlined by its location not in Chapter 3 of Title VII of the EC Treaty, entitled "Institutional provisions", but in Chapter 4 under the heading "Transitional provisions".

---

[52] On this double nature of the Council cf. *supra*, Ch. 3, p. 88.

Thirdly, and most importantly, Article 122(5) EC does not suspend voting rights in *all* EMU matters, but only in those cases where the Council takes decisions under provisions explicitly listed in Article 122(3) EC; and in two further cases—Article 123(4) and (5) EC—where the EC Treaty explicitly reserves voting in the Council to "Member States without a derogation". This situation of Member States with a derogation is mirrored by Denmark by virtue of paragraph 2, second sentence, of the Danish Protocol, while the UK Protocol uses the same method of explicit enumeration as Article 122(5) EC in its paragraphs 5 and 7. Legally, this means that in EMU matters, all Council representatives of the Member States take part in the vote except where the EC Treaty explicitly states otherwise.

This scheme of the EMU provisions has triggered some controversy regarding adoption, by the Council, of legal acts under Article 107(6) EC and Article 42 of the Statute. It has already been explained[53] that these provisions allow the Council to adopt so-called "complementary legislation" which complete the provisions of the Statute. It goes without saying that this complementary legislation is of a highly political nature. This is why the question has arisen whether the representatives of *all* Member States should be allowed to take part in the adoption of complementary legislation.

Some have argued[54] that non-participating Member States should not be allowed to take part in a vote under Article 107(6) EC and Article 42 of the Statute as this would enable non-participating Member States to impede the adoption of a legal framework which is required for the proper functioning of the single currency; in particular after the enlargement of the EU, the involvement of all Member States in such decision-making could even put the participating Member States in a minority situation. Against this background, the spirit of the EC Treaty would not allow Member States with a derogation or a special status to vote on these crucial issues.

In our view, this line of reasoning clearly conflicts with the wording and the scheme of the EC Treaty. Article 107(6) EC and Article 42 of the Statute are

---

[53] *Supra*, Ch. 1, p. 39 *et seq.*

[54] Cf. Vigneron and Mollica, *supra*, n. 2, 219 *et seq.*; cf. also Nicolaysen, *supra*, n. 10. Nine of the participating Member States have even adopted a "declaration of interpretation", which is now attached to the protocol of the Council meeting during which Council Regulation 2531/98 of 23 November 1998 concerning the application of minimum reserves by the European Central Bank [1998] OJ L318/1, was adopted. In this declaration, these Member States reaffirm the restriction of voting rights to the exclusive circle of the "ins"; cf. Vigneron and Mollica, *supra*, n. 2, 225, who quote the French wording of this declaration as follows: "*Les delegations belge, allemande, espagnole, française, irlandaise, italienne, luxembourgeoise, autrichienne et portugaise considèrent que, en application des dispositions prévues à l'article 43 du 18e protocole [ex protocole n° 3 au traité de Maastricht], aux articles 122–3 et 122–5 du Traité instituant la Communauté européenne et des dispositions prévues aux protocoles 25 et 26 du Traité instituant la Communauté européenne, seuls les Etats membres ayant adopté l'euro disposent du droit de vote sur ces règlements. Selon ces délégations, cela signifie que l'adoption de ces règlements et toute éventuelle modification les affectant font l'objet d'un vote réservé aux Etats membres ayant adopté l'euro*". It should be noted, however, that such declarations of interpretation are not recognised, by the ECJ, to have a legal authority of their own; cf. Cases 237/84 and C–292/89, *supra*, n. 30.

listed neither in Article 122(3) EC nor in paragraph 5 of the UK Protocol. Theoretically, this might still leave some scope for a different teleological interpretation, in view of the well-known dominance of this method of interpretation in Community law. However, we suggest that, as far as EMU is concerned, the spirit of the EC Treaty is *not* to differentiate in an extensive manner between the Member States,[55] but to keep the Community legal order as intact as possible to integrate, sooner or later, *all* Member States into full EMU. It is thus on purpose that in the case of all decisions of principle, which have an impact on the shape of EMU as such, the EC Treaty does not suspend the voting rights of Member States which currently do not participate in the single currency. As a consequence, *all* Member States—those which already participate in the single currency and those which are expected to do so in the future—have a right to vote in the Council on the following matters: on a possible transfer of new competences to the ECB in the field of banking supervision under Article 105(6) EC; on an amendment of the Statute by Council decision, as foreseen in Article 107(5) EC and Article 41 of the Statute; on the adoption of complementary legislation in accordance with Article 107(6) EC and Article 42 of the Statute; and on the participation of a new Member State in the single currency, as provided for in Article 122(2), second sentence, EC. Even though these issues are without any doubt of particular interest to those Member States which already participate in the single currency, their quasi-constitutional importance for EMU requires full involvement and equal say also of the non-participating Member States.[56]

We cannot deny that this will sometimes make the decision-making process more difficult and burdensome than in cases where Article 122(3) EC and the UK Protocol provide for a suspension of the voting rights of the non-participating Member States. However, it should also be noted that all the provisions mentioned above allow for qualified majority voting in the Council. In addition, Member States which do not yet participate in the single currency are prevented, by their duty of loyalty under Article 10 EC, to block the adoption of legislation

---

[55] However, cf. Vigneron and Mollica, *supra*, n. 2, 221, according to whom the conclusion that all Member States are allowed to vote under Art. 107(6) EC could only be the result of "*une lecture hâtive et strictement liée à la lettre*" and would also be "*en contradiction flagrante avec la logique de la différenciation—qui est appelée à se perpétuer avec les futures élargissements*".

[56] This view is shared by Louis, "A Legal and Institutional Approach for Building a Monetary Union" (1998) *CML Rev.* 33 (65). Cf. also the "declaration of interpretation", which was attached by the British delegation to the protocol of the Council meeting, mentioned *supra*, n. 54, which is quoted, in French, by Vigneron and Mollica, *supra*, n. 2, 225: "*Le Royaume-Uni estime que, conformément à la procédure prévue à l'article 107, paragraphe 6, du traité CE et à l'article 42 des statuts du SEBC, tous les Etats membres, y compris le Royaume-Uni et les Etats membres faisant objet d'une dérogation, conservent leur droit de voter sur les règlements considérés. Ni l'article 122, paragraphe 3, qui concerne la dérogation, ni le protocole n° 11 [maintenant protocole n° 25] ne citent l'article 107, paragraphe 6, au nombre des dispositions qui ne s'appliquent qu'aux Etats membres participants. Selon le Royaume-Uni, cela signifie que tous les Etats membres devraient participer à l'adoption de la législation en question, et de toute modfication qui pourrait y être apportée à l'avenir*".

that EMU needs for its proper functioning; this is reaffirmed by the spirit of Protocol No 24 on the transition to the third stage of economic and monetary union.[57] Finally, one should also not forget that an early involvement in the shaping of EMU will make the adoption of the single currency a more legitimate undertaking in these Member States. It is therefore within the spirit of Community law not to suspend voting rights of Member States except where the EC Treaty explicitly states otherwise.

1.3. The informal "euro group"

Summarising the law on differentiated decision-making inside the Community institutions, one can state that among the Community institution only the Council has been institutionally affected by EMU differentiation. However, in all EMU decisions the Council is still composed of its 15 members, which take part, with equal rights, in all deliberations, while the voting rights of three of them—of the Swedish, the Danish and the British representatives—are suspended whenever decisions are taken under provisions where application to the participating Member States only is explicitly stated.

Against this background, the creation of the "Euro 11", which today is called the "euro group", requires legal examination. This gathering was created on 13 December 1997 in Luxembourg by the "Resolution of the European Council on economic policy co-ordination in stage 3 of EMU and on Treaty Articles 109 and 109b of the EC Treaty [now Articles 111 and 113 EC]".[58] According to part I.6 of this Luxembourg Resolution, it serves the following purpose:

> The Ministers of the States participating in the euro-area may meet informally among themselves to discuss issues connected with their shared specific responsibilities for the single currency. The Commission, and the European Central Bank (ECB) when appropriate will be invited to take part in the meetings.

The establishment of the "euro group" has been inspired by practical considerations, in particular by the absence of an institutionalised forum for a closer coordination of the economic and fiscal policies of the "ins". The legal question is, however, whether—despite the practical need for such a coordination—the very idea of excluding thereby the "pre-ins" and "outs" (and possibly even the Commission and the ECB) from important political meetings is in line with the spirit of the EC Treaty.[59] The EC Treaty always ascertains the continued participation of all Member States in Council meetings, at least for the deliberations (even though not always for the voting rights); this applies both in EMU matters and in areas of enhanced co-operation. Therefore, to establish a

---

[57] This Protocol lays down, *inter alia*, the obligation of all Member States not to prevent the commencement of the third stage of EMU and to enable the ECB and the ESCB to start their full functioning from 1 January 1999.

[58] [1998] OJ C35/1.

[59] Cf. also Selmayr, "Die Wirtschafts- und Währungsunion als Rechtsgemeinschaft" [1999] *AöR* 357 (384 *et seq*).

parallel informal structure, which is reserved for the participating Member States alone, in our opinion creates an exclusivity that is not intended by the EC Treaty. One should also not ignore that the informal "euro group" operates in a legal vacuum: its activities are subject neither to the supervision of the ECJ nor to the transparency requirements of all Community institutions. Hence, even though the "euro group" will, according to the Luxembourg Resolution of the European Council, refrain from taking formal decisions,[59a] there is no guarantee that inside the "euro group", the principles of Community law—in particular the primacy of price stability and the independence of the ECB—are always properly respected.

One can hardly ignore that the practical rule under which the informal "euro group" always meets in advance of formal Ecofin meetings is modyfying *de facto* the decision-making process in the Council. Therefore it should be emphasised that *de iure*, only the "Council of the Fifteen" remains the competent Community institution for expressing the common political interest of the Member States.

2. Differentiated financing in EMU matters?

Financing is an area that is particular sensitive to a differentiation between rights and obligations of the Member States. A possible legal principle could be: "Those who do not participate should neither pay nor profit" as regards the financial burdens and benefits of EMU politics. As regards new fields of enhanced co-operation, such a rule is in fact laid down in Article 44(2) EU which states that:

> Expenditure resulting from implementation of the co-operation, other than administrative costs for the institutions, shall be borne by the participating Member States, unless the Council, acting unanimously, decides otherwise.[60]

Again, however, there is no such rule in the provisions on EMU where the integrity of the budget of the European Communities has been kept intact. This means that, to mention an example, a public relations campaign of the Commission's Directorate General of Economic and Financial Affairs to make the euro banknotes and coins better known to the public at large will, like all other Commission activities, be financed from the Community budget to which all 15 Member States contribute. Within the Community budget, there is thus no differentiated treatment of EMU-related income and expenditure.[61] It will be

---

[59a] When the Luxembourg Resolution states that "Decisions will in all cases be taken by the Ecofin Council in accordance with the procedures determined by the Treaty", it does nothing but to simply recall the law. It is self-evident that under the EC Treaty, only the competent Community institutions are allowed to enact secondary Community law.

[60] The same principle was already stated in para. 2(3) of the Protocol on Social Policy, agreed at the intergovernmental conference of Maastricht.

[61] In contrast to this was the budgetary practice under the Maastricht Protocol on Social Policy, where the attempt was made to establish a separate budgetary position for Social Policy expenditure in the Community budget; cf. Falkner, *supra*, n. 1, 79 (60).

explained below that financial differentiation in EMU takes place only as regards the financial resources of the ECB,[62] which, however, do not form part of the Community budget, as already mentioned.[63]

3. Differentiated application of Community law?

It is one of the main constitutional principles of the Community legal order that Community law must apply uniformly throughout the EU in order to avoid any discrimination of market participants and any distortions of competition, which could result therefrom. On this principle of uniform application, the ECJ has based the direct applicability of Community law in the Member States,[64] the supremacy of Community law over national law,[65] its own monopoly of jurisdiction[66] as well as important legal principles such as State liability for non-compliance with Community law.[67]

In view of the distinction between participating Member States, Member States with a derogation and Member States with special status, the question has arisen whether the provisions of EMU law for which there is a derogation or an exemption, as well as the legal acts adopted thereunder, are still part of Community law and therefore subject to the principle of uniform application. In Community practice, this issue became relevant on a rather formal occasion, namely the question of the appropriate final sentence of Council regulations adopted under EMU provisions. This comes from the fact that Article 249(2) EC provides that a regulation "shall be directly applicable in all Member States". Is this also true for regulations adopted under Article 106(2) and 123(4) and (5) EC, this means under provisions which apply only to participating Member States?

---

[62] Cf. *infra*, p. 161 *et seq.*

[63] Cf. *supra*, Ch. 1, p. 19 and p. 43 *et seq.*

[64] Cf. Case 106/77, *Amministrazione delle Finanze dello Stato* v. *Simmenthal SpA* [1978] ECR 629, para. 14: "Direct applicability in such circumstances means that rules of Community law must be fully applied in all Member States from the date of their entry into force and for so long as they continue in force".

[65] Cf. Case 6/64, *Costa* v. *ENEL* [1964] ECR 585 (594): "The executive force of Community law cannot vary from one state to another in deference to subsequent domestic laws, without jeopardising the attainment of the objectives of the Treaty set out in Article 5(2) and giving rise to the discrimination prohibited by Article 7".

[66] Case 314/85, *Foto-Frost* v. *Hauptzollamt Lübeck-Ost* [1987] ECR 4199, para. 15: "the main purpose of the powers accorded to the Court by Article 177 is to ensure that Community law is applied uniformly by national courts. That requirement of uniformity is particularly imperative when the validity of a Community act is in question. Divergences between courts in the Member States as to the validity of Community acts would be liable to place in jeopardy the very unity of the Communuty legal order and detract from the fundamental requirement of legal certainty".

[67] Joined Cases C–46/93 and C–48/93, *Brasserie du Pêcheur SA* v. *Germany and The Queen* v. *Secretary of State for Transport, ex parte: Factortame Ltd and others* [1996] ECR I–1029, para. 33: "In addition, in view of the fundamental requirement of the Community legal order that Community law be uniformly applied . . . the obligation to make good damage caused to individuals by breaches of Community law cannot depend on domestic rules as to the division of powers between constitutional authorities".

In the beginning, Community practice seems to have followed a method of "trial and error" to answer this question. The result is that, today, one finds three different variations of final sentences used in Council regulations adopted in the context of EMU:

—*Variation 1:* "This Regulation shall be binding in its entirety and directly applicable in all Member States, in accordance with the Treaty, subject to Protocols 11 and 12 [now 25 and 26] and Article 109k(1) [now Article 122(1) EC]". The Council made use of this extremely complicated wording in Council Regulation 974/98 of 3 May 1998 on the introduction of the euro,[68] which is based on Article 123(4), third sentence EC; and in the final provision of Council Regulation 975/98 of 3 May 1998 on denominations and technical specifications of euro coins intended for circulation,[69] based on Article 106(2) EC.

—*Variation 2:* "This Regulation shall be binding in its entirety and directly applicable in all Member States". This sentence is the one foreseen in Article 249(2) EC. It has been used in Council Regulation 2866/98 of 31 December 1998 on the conversion rates between the euro and the currencies of the Member States adopting the euro,[70] which is based on Article 123(4), first sentence, EC and, thus was adopted with the votes of the participating Member States only. The Council also used the Article 249(2) wording in some of its regulations adopted under Article 107(6) EC and Article 42 of the Statute, for example in Council Regulation 2531/98 of 23 November 1998 concerning the application of minimum reserves by the European Central Bank[71] and in Council Regulation 2533/98 of 23 November 1998 concerning the collection of statistical information by the European Central Bank.[72]

—*Variation 3:* "This Regulation shall be binding in its entirety and directly applicable in the Member States in accordance with the Treaty establishing the European Community". This formula is now prescribed by Part A., paragraph 4, of Annex II to the Rules of Procedures of the Council[73] for all cases "in which a legal act is not applicable to, and in, all Member States". The Council applied this formula in the final provisions of Council Regulation 2596/2000 of 27 November 2000 amending Regulation 974/98 on the introduction of the euro,[74] based on Article 123(5) EC, but also in some more recent regulations adopted under Article 107(6) EC, for example in the case of Council Regulation 1009/2000 of 8 May 2000 concerning capital increases of the European Central Bank[75] and Council Regulation 1010/2000 of 8 May

[68] [1998] OJ L139/1.
[69] [1998] OJ L139/6.
[70] [1998] OJ L359/1.
[71] [1998] OJ L318/1.
[72] [1998] OJ L318/8.
[73] Council Decision 1999/385/EC, ECSC, Euratom of 31 May 1999 adopting the Council's Rules of Procedure, [1999] OJ L147/13.
[74] [2000] OJ L300/2.
[75] [2000] OJ L115/1.

2000 concerning further calls of foreign reserve assets by the European Central Bank.[76]

It is unfortunate that this surprising inconsistency within Community practice has created a lot of uncertainty about the nature of regulations adopted under the EMU chapter. To start with, there can be no question at all about the scope of application of legal acts adopted under Article 107(6) EC and Article 42 of the Statute, as these, as already explained,[77] are not subject to any derogations or exemptions, but involve all Member States and, as a consequence, also apply throughout the EU. But we would go even further: in our view, the EMU provisions in the EC Treaty and in the Statute, as well as all secondary law adopted thereunder, continue to be an integral part of Community law, to have uniform application *in* all Member States of the European Union and, as a consequence, to be an integral and supreme part of the legal orders of all Member States. This comes, first of all, from the fact that there is no provision in the EMU chapter that would provide for a derogation from Article 249(2) EC or otherwise attribute a different normative value to primary or secondary EMU law. In addition, it should be noted that Article 122(3) EC states only that the provisions listed do not apply *to* Member States with a derogation, without depriving such provisions of their uniform application *in* all Member States, which stems from their very nature as Community law.

Finally, we suggest, again, a comparison with the specific provisions on enhanced co-operation, introduced by the Treaty of Amsterdam, this time with the special provisions under Title IV of the EC Treaty on visa, asylum, immigration and other policies related to free movement of persons. Here, Article 2 of Protocol No 4 on the position of the United Kingdom and Ireland, and Article 2 of Protocol No 5 on the position of Denmark provide that measures adopted under that Title do not "form part of Community law as they apply to the United Kingdom or Ireland" or "Denmark". In the case of Denmark, even if it decided to participate in such measures, this only "will create an obligation under international law between Denmark and the other Member States" which Denmark will first have to implement into national law; like an agreement under public international law, such measures would, in the beginning, only be applicable *to* Denmark, but not *in* Denmark, unless the Danish authorities transformed such measures into national law. In our view, the situation in EMU can be clearly distinguished from this new form of differentiation under the EC Treaty. In the absence of any rules to the contrary, EMU law continues to apply uniformly throughout the EU and thus in all Member States, even though three Member States are currently not covered by the substantive effect of these provisions.

EMU law therefore may be compared to a Council regulation that prescribes a particular method for harvesting wild growing citrus fruits. Being an integral

---

[76] [2000] OJ L115/2.
[77] *Supra*, p. 147 *et seq.*

part of Community law, such a regulation would without any doubt be considered to be directly applicable in all Member States, even though, as a matter of substance, it would have no effect in Denmark, Finland and Sweden where wild citrus fruits normally avoid to grow. This distinction between *direct applicability* of EMU law throughout the Union and *substantive effect* only in the participating Member States is not just of academic value. In practice, it enables also judges in non-participating Member States to draw on EMU law provisions when they are to interpret national law and, where necessary, also to refer such matters to the ECJ under Article 234 EC. In addition, the direct applicability of EMU law also in Member States with a derogation and with special status creates, in conjunction with Article 10 EC, an obligation for them not to act in clear contravention of such law, to protect, where necessary, the legal effect of such law also within their jurisdiction, and finally to prepare their national legal systems for the moment when also the substantive effect of such law will extend to them.[78] In this respect, one may compare the effect of EMU law in Member States with a derogation or special status to that of directives before the expiry of the implementation period:[79] as the objective of such directives is already legally binding from the moment of their entry into force, Member States are under a duty to refrain from taking any measures liable seriously to compromise the result prescribed even before the directive becomes directly effective.

4. The "euro area"—a political notion

In the present analysis of EMU differentiation and its impact on the system of Community law, a word needs to be dedicated to the notion of "euro area", which increasingly has found its way into the political language of EMU to indicate the territory of the twelve EU Member States where the euro has been introduced. We understand that the differentiated situation of the EU due to EMU has led to a certain linguistic difficulty for those who have to talk about

---

[78] This idea is stressed in recital 17 of Council Regulation 2533/98 of 23 November 1998 concerning the collection of statistical information by the European Central Bank [1998] OJ L318/8: "Whereas, while it is recognised that the statistical information needed to fulfil the ECB's statistical reporting requirements is not the same for the participating as for the non-participating Member States, Article 5 of the Statute applies to both participating and non-participating Member States; whereas this fact, together with Article 5 [now Article 10] EC, implies an obligation to design and implement at the national level all the measures that Member States consider appropriate in order to carry out the collection of the statistical information needed to fulfil the ECB's statistical reporting requirements and the timely preparations in the field of statistics in order for them to become participating Member States". Cf. also recital 8 of Regulation ECB 1998/16 of 1 December 1998 concerning the consolidated balance sheet of the monetary financial institutions sector [1998] OJ L356/7.

[79] Cf. Case C–129/96, *Inter-Environnement Wallonie ASBL* v. *Région wallonne* [1997] ECR I–71411, para. 45 : "it follows from the second paragraph of Art. 5 in conjunction with the third paragraph of Article 189 of the Treaty and from the directive itself that during that period they must refrain from taking any measures liable seriously to compromise the result prescribed".

the group of the "ins"; from a presentational point of view, the term "partici-pating Member States" (which is also used in secondary Community law)[79a] is neither self-explanatory nor clear for an audience without a sound legal background.

We would nevertheless like to underline that, in Community law, there is no such entity as a "euro area" (or even "euro zone"). The word "euro area" is not used in the EC Treaty, which only recognises legal persons such as the European Community and the ECB, with their respective institutions and decision-making bodies, and in addition notions like EU and ESCB to describe the coherent operational framework and the common set of principles surrounding and comprising these different legal persons. In contrast to this unifying approach of Community law, the term "euro area" emphasises the differenti-ation inside the European Union created by EMU even though such differenti-ation is only a temporary situation and does not call into question the institutional framework of the Community, its financial integrity or the uniformity of Community law. We would therefore view a development in which people talk more about the "euro area" and the "euro group" than about the Community and its Council as not to be welcomed from a Community law perspective, in particular not in a legal context.[80]

IV. THE IMPACT OF DIFFERENTIATED INTEGRATION ON THE LAW OF THE ECB

At first glance, the law of the ECB has chosen a similar approach to differenti-ated integration as the general system of Community law, i.e. emphasis on the unifying elements and coherence rather than on the difference of rights and duties. Hence, the ESCB, through which the ECB implements its policies, is composed of the ECB and the national central banks of *all* 15 Member States,[81] as there is no derogation or exemption in the EC Treaty from the rule in Article 107(1) EC. Herein, one could see a reflection of the *communitarian* nature of the ECB and the ESCB, to which, after all, the task is entrusted to define and imple-ment the monetary policy *of the Community* (Article 105(2), first indent EC).[82]

[79a] Cf. for example Council Regulation 1103/97 of 17 June 1997 on certain provisions relating to the introduction of the euro [1997] OJ L162/1; Council Regulation 974/98 of 3 May 1998 on the introduction of the euro [1998] OJ L139/1; and Council Regulation 2532/98 of 23 November 1998 concerning the powers of the European Central Bank to impose sanctions [1998] OJ L318/4.

[80] However, the term "euro area" has been used both in the title and in the recitals of the "Agreement between the European Central Bank and the national central banks outside the euro area laying down the operating procedures for an exchange rate mechanism in Stage Three of Economic and Monetary Union" (the "ERM 2 Agreement") [1998] OJ C345/6. Now, also Declaration No 7 on Art. 111 of the Treaty establishing the European Community, attached to the Final Act of the Treaty of Nice, refers to "all the Member States in the euro area".

[81] This is ignored by Seidel, "Im Kompetenzkonflikt: Europäisches System der Zentralbanken (ESZB) versus EZB" [2000] *EuZW* 552 (552), who talks only of (then) "11" national central banks inside the ESCB.

[82] Cf., however, para. 5, second sentence of the UK Protocol, according to which the reference to the Community in Art. 105(1) to (5) EC "shall not include the United Kingdom".

However, a closer look reveals that, within the ECB, legal differentiation is much more common than in the Community institutions. The law of the ECB cannot disregard the fact that three Member States have not (yet) transferred their monetary sovereignty to the ECB. The ECB is therefore much more subject to differentiation than are the Community and its institutions, as is demonstrated by the fact that within the Statute, altogether eight provisions (Articles 43 to 49 and Article 53) deal with the details of this differentiation, in addition to Article 122 EC. Such differentiation concerns in particular the decision-making process inside the ECB and its financial structure.

Even though the supranational character of the ECB is particularly clear in the EC Treaty and the Statute and emphasised further by the special degree of central bank independence enjoyed by the ECB under Article 108 EC, this supranationality therefore relates only to those 12 Member States that have transferred their monetary sovereignty to the ECB. As a consequence, the starting point for understanding differentiation inside the ECB must be Article 43.2 of the Statute. According to this provision, "[t]he central banks of Member States with a derogation as specified in Article 122(1) of this Treaty shall retain their powers in the field of monetary policy according to national law". This provision today applies directly only to Sveriges Riksbank, the only central bank of a Member State with a derogation. However, as it refers explicitly to the situation of a derogation, it also applies, albeit indirectly, to Danmarks Nationalbank, by virtue of paragraph 2, second sentence, of the Danish Protocol; and the UK Protocol restates this rule in paragraph 4: "The United Kingdom[83] shall retain its powers in the field of monetary policy according to national law".

1. Differentiated decision-making inside the ECB

The rule on differentiated decision-making inside the ECB is simple: those national central banks the monetary sovereignty of which has not been transferred to the ECB, neither vote nor participate in the making and implementation of monetary policy decisions of the ECB. Membership of the two principal decision-making bodies of the ECB, the Executive Board and the Governing Council of the ECB, is therefore reserved to the nationals and central bank governors from the participating Member States.

---

[83] As the United Kingdom is exempt from the requirement of central bank independence in Art. 108 EC, it has a certain logic that it does, unlike Art. 43.2 of the Statute, link monetary powers not to the central bank, but to the state itself. The UK Protocol thereby explicitly excludes the new degree of central bank independence in Community law, which distinguishes between the central bank and the state/the Community; cf. *supra*, Ch. 1, p. 32 *et seq*.

1.1. Differentiation in the Executive Board of the ECB

For the Executive Board of the ECB, this results from Article 112(2) (b) in conjunction with Article 122(4) EC and with the Danish and the UK Protocols. According to Article 112(2)(b) EC, members of the Executive Board are appointed by common accord of the governments of the Member States at the level of Heads of State or Government, and in addition have to be nationals of Member States. However, "Member States" in this provision must be read as "Member States without a derogation or a special status", as is prescribed by Article 122(4) EC, by paragraph 2, second sentence, of the Danish Protocol and by paragraph 5 and 7, second subparagraph, of the UK Protocol.

As a consequence, the first Executive Board of the ECB was appointed, on 26 May 1998, by common accord of the participating Member States only.[84] Due to the British special status, this decision could not be signed by the British Prime Minister, Tony Blair, who at that time held the EU Presidency, but by Viktor Klima, then Chancellor of Austria and successor of Blair in the EU Presidency. Moreover, the appointment of a Swedish, Danish or British member of the Executive Board of the ECB is, at present, excluded by Community law.

1.2. Differentiation in the Governing Council of the ECB

Regarding the Governing Council of the ECB, Article 10.1 of the Statute provides that it shall comprise the members of the Executive Board of the ECB and the governors of the national central banks. However, by virtue of Article 43.4 of the Statute, "national central banks" has to be read as "central banks of Member States without a derogation" in these provisions.[85] This means that the "pre-ins" and "outs" are not at all integrated into the work of the Governing Council of the ECB, neither via its six members from the Executive Board nor

---

[84] Cf. Decision 1998/345/EC of 26 May 1998 taken by common accord of the Governments of the Member States adopting the single currency at the level of Heads of State or Government appointing the President, the Vice-President and the other members of the Executive Board of the European Central Bank [1998] OJ L154/33. Both Art. 123(1), subpara. 1, first indent EC and Art. 50 of the Statute, the special provisions on the initial appointment of the Executive Board, only apply to participating Member States; cf. Art. 123(1), subpara. 1, first indent EC itself, Art. 43.1 of the Statute and para. 8 of the UK Protocol.

[85] Remarkably, there is no such derogation from Art. 112(1) EC, the provision paralleling Art. 10.1 of the Statute in the EC Treaty. Art. 122(3) and (4) EC only lists Art. 112(2)(b) EC among the provisions to which a derogation applies, but not Art. 112(1) EC. As regards the composition of the Governing Council of the ECB, there is thus a clear conflict between two rules which stand on the same level in the normative hierarchy: on the one hand, Art. 112(1) EC, according to which the Governors of all central banks are members of the Governing Council; on the other hand, Arts. 10.1 and 43.4 of the Statute—itself a source of primary EC law (cf. Art. 311 EC)—which only provides for membership of central bank governors from Member States without a derogation. More precise is the UK Protocol which, in its para. 5, explicitly excludes the application of Art. 112(1) EC to the United Kingdom and the Bank of England. For us, the latter indicates that the omission of a derogation in the EC Treaty is a drafting error; therefore, the rule in Arts. 10.1 and 43.4 of the Statute must prevail.

via the governors from the national central banks.[86] One can clearly see that differentiated decision-making within the ECB goes much further than in the Council of the European Union, where non-participating Member States at least keep their right to take part in the meetings. Whenever the ECB takes decisions, only nationals and central bank governors from participating Member States sit, deliberate and vote in the decision-making bodies of the ECB.

1.3. The General Council of the ECB

In spite of the legal restriction of decision-making inside the ECB to the exclusive circle of the "ins", the law of the ECB also pays tribute to its mandate to define the monetary policy *of the Community* and thus also to take into account that one day, current "pre-ins" or even "outs" may become participants in the single currency. Therefore, the EC Treaty and the Statute provide for a minimum degree of involvement of Sveriges Riksbank, Danmarks Nationalbank and the Bank of England in the institutional process of the ECB. For this purpose, the constitution of a third decision-making body of the ECB, the so-called General Council of the ECB, is foreseen in Article 123(3) EC and Article 45.1 of the Statute.

The General Council of the ECB comprises 17 members: the governors of all 15 national central banks of which the ESCB is composed, and the President and the Vice-President of the ECB (Article 45.2, first sentence of the Statute). In addition, the four other members of the Executive Board may take part in the meetings of the General Council of the ECB, even though without having the right to vote (Article 45.2, second sentence of the Statute). The General Council has adopted its own Rules of Procedure,[87] in accordance with Article 46.4 of the Statute. These provide, *inter alia*, that decisions of the General Council are always taken by simple majority, except where the Statute states otherwise, as in the case of Article 48 of the Statute.

However, voting in the General Council takes place only exceptionally. The Statute clearly makes the General Council an advisory organ of the ECB, which contributes to the work of the Governing Council and of the Executive Board of the ECB, but which itself does not adopt legal instruments addressed to the national central banks, to the Member States or even natural and legal persons in the Member States. The General Council is not even obliged to arrive at a unanimous opinion on a particular issue. In case of comments of the General

---

[86] This exclusion is also reflected at the working level inside the ECB. As a rule, the so-called "ESCB committees" (cf. *supra*, Ch. 3, n. 28) include only experts from central banks of participating Member States; cf. Art. 9.1 of the Rules of Procedure of the European Central Bank of 7 July 1998 [1998] OJ L338/28, substituted by Rules of Procedure of the European Central Bank as amended on 22 April 1999 [1999] OJ L125/34, as amended by Decision ECB/1999/6 of 7 October 1999 amending the Rules of Procedure of the European Central Bank [1999] OJ L314/32.

[87] Art. 4.2 of the Rules of Procedure of the General Council of the ECB of 1 September 1998 [1999] OJ L75/36, with Corrigendum [1999] OJ L156/52.

Council on legal acts to be adopted by the ECB, the Rules of Procedure[88] of the General Council even allow for forwarding the view of a dissenting minority within the General Council to the Governing Council or the Executive Board of the ECB.

The responsibilities of the General Council of the ECB are limited. They are enumerated "in full" in Article 47,[89] as it is stressed in Article 45.3 of the Statute, and include four fields: first, the continuation of tasks which the ECB took over from the EMI (Article 44(1) and Article 47.1, first indent of the Statute), for example the monitoring of the functioning of the European Monetary System (Article 4.1, third indent, of the EMI Statute), which, on 1 January 1999, was replaced by the ERM 2-central bank agreement.[90] Secondly, the General Council of the ECB is involved whenever a derogation or a special status of a Member State is abrogated and this Member State adopts the euro; this follows from Article 44(2) and Article 47.1, first indent, of the Statute, according to which the General Council gives advice in the preparation of the convergence reports, to be compiled by the ECB under Article 122(2), first sentence EC and the Danish[91] or UK Protocol.[92] In addition, Article 47.3 of the Statute requires the General Council to contribute to the tasks of the ECB as regards the necessary preparations for the irrevocable fixing of exchange rates as regards the currencies of new participating Member States.[93] Thirdly, the General Council contributes to the advisory functions of the ECB (Article 47.1, second indent, of the Statute), i.e. it may communicate its views to the Governing Council of the ECB whenever the latter adopts an ECB Opinion upon consultation of the ECB by national or Community authorities under Article 105(4), first subparagraph, EC, or whenever it issues an ECB Recommendation on the ECB's own initiative under Article 105(4), second subparagraph, EC. Finally, Article 47.2 of the Statute gives the General Council the task of contributing to ECB activities in areas that are of concern to the ESCB as a whole. An example is the field of statistics where Article 5 of the Statute obliges *all* national central banks, including those of the "pre-ins" and "outs", to assist the ECB in the collection of statistical information either from the competent national authorities or directly

---

[88] Art. 4.4 of the Rules of Procedure of the General Council of the ECB, *supra*, n. 87.

[89] Para. 9(a) and (b) of the UK Protocol extends the responsibilities under Arts. 44 and 47.3 of the Statute also to the special status of the United Kingdom. For Denmark, such an explicit enactment is not necessary as these provisions of the Statute explicitly refer to a derogation and therefore apply to Denmark by virtue of para. 2, second sentence of the Danish Protocol. Cf. *supra*, p. 142.

[90] Agreement of 1 September 1998 between the European Central Bank and the national central banks outside the euro area laying down the operating procedures for an exchange rate mechanism in Stage Three of Economic and Monetary Union [1998] OJ C345/6. On the nature of this agreement and its legal basis cf. *infra*, Ch. 5, p. 206 *et seq.*

[91] Cf. para. 4 of the Danish Protocol.

[92] Cf. para. 10, second sentence, lit. (a), second sentence of the UK Protocol.

[93] As an example, Regulation ECB/2000/11 of 2 November 2000 concerning transitional provisions for the application of minimum reserves by the European Central Bank following the introduction of the euro in Greece [2000] OJ L291/28, explicitly refers to the contribution of the General Council of the ECB in its recital 7.

from economic agents. Article 47.2, first indent, of the Statute therefore requires the General Council of the ECB to contribute to this task.

In spite of its limited mandate, the General Council of the ECB is a quite remarkable institution. Even though the ECB controls the monetary policy of only 12 Member States, the General Council guarantees a minimum degree of involvement of all central banks in the ESCB;[94] Article 47.4 even states an explicit right of the General Council to be informed by the President about all decisions[95] of the Governing Council of the ECB. The General Council of the ECB is obviously meant as a forum to keep the central bank governors of the "pre-ins" and "outs" on board, and thus to serve as a counter-weight to potential centrifugal forces resulting from the differentiated rights and duties of central banks within the ESCB. One may therefore describe the General Council of the ECB as a centripetal decision-making body inside ESCB differentiation.

The General Council is also a remarkable institution because the EC Treaty and the Statute have made it a decision-making body *of the ECB*, as is clearly stated in Article 123(3) EC and Article 45.1 of the Statute. One could certainly have thought to establish the General Council as mere co-ordinating forum of the ESCB, thereby institutionalising the participation of all national central banks in the ESCB. However, primary Community law has gone one step further and integrated the General Council into the institutional structure of the ECB itself. The involvement of the central banks of the "pre-ins" and "outs" thus takes place at the central level of the ECB; hierarchically, the General Council of the ECB therefore finds itself at the same level as the Executive Board and the Governing Council of the ECB, even though Article 123(3) EC and Article 45.1 of the Statute clearly state that the establishment of the General Council shall be "without prejudice to Article 107(3) of the Treaty"—the provision according to which the ESCB is governed by the Executive Board and the Governing Council of the ECB. To guarantee observance of this rule, the General Council is always chaired by the President or, in his absence, by the Vice-President of the ECB (Article 46.1 of the Statute); the President has also the responsibility to prepare for the meetings of the General Council (Article 46.3 of the Statute). All in all, one can say that even the institutional framework set up to cope with differentiation inside the ECB confirms the centralised organisational structure of the ESCB already described at length in chapter 2.[96]

---

[94] This is also reflected at the working level inside the ECB. By virtue of Art. 9.4, first sentence of the Rules of Procedure of the ECB (*supra*, n. 86), Sveriges Riksbank, Danmarks Nationalbank or the Bank of England "may also appoint a representative to take part in meetings of an ESCB committees whenever it deals with matters which fall within the field of competence of the General Council". In addition, representatives of non-participating national central banks may participate in ESCB committees upon special invitation by the chairperson of the committee and the Executive Board of the ECB; cf. Art. 9.1, second sentence, of the Rules of Procedure of the ECB.

[95] Understood in a broad sense, as in Art. 12.1 of the Statute (cf. *supra*, Ch. 3, p. 95 *et seq.*), and therefore including the adoption of any type of legal instrument by the Governing Council of the ECB.

[96] Cf. *supra*, Ch. 2, p. 63 *et seq.*

In view of the ambition of the EC Treaty to create, one day, full EMU with the participation of all EU Member States, the General Council is of course not designed to be a permanent institution. The General Council is, by definition, a temporary decision-making body of the ECB, as it is established only "if and as long as there are Member States with a derogation" (Article 123(3) EC) or for as long as the Danish or UK special status remains in force. It is within this perspective that the General Council included a provision in its Rules of Procedure[97] providing for its own dissolution, namely Article 9 thereof:

> When, in accordance with Article 109k(2) [now Article 122(2)] EC, all derogations are abrogated by the Council of the European Union and when the decisions provided for in Protocol No 11 [now No 25] are taken, the General Council shall be dissolved and these Rules of Procedure will no longer apply.

2. The differentiated financial structure of the ECB

Unlike the Community budget, which has kept its integrity in spite of EMU differentiation, the financial resources of the ECB are subject, in the Statute, to detailed rules on differentiated financial rights and duties of participating and non-participating national central banks.

2.1. Differentiation of the capital of the ECB

The first set of such rules concerns the capital of the ECB which, according to Article 28.1 of the Statute, is 5,000 million euro since the moment of the establishment of the ECB. The sole subscribers to and holders of this capital are the 15 national central banks, whether they already participate in the single currency or whether they are still subject to a derogation or a special status; this results from Article 28.2 of the Statute, to which there is a derogating provision neither in Articles 43 *et seq.* of the Statute nor in the Danish or the UK Protocol.

However, even though the Governing Council of the ECB decided, on the basis of Article 28.3 of the Statute, that the subscribed capital of the ECB shall be paid up in full,[98] this obligation concerns only the participating national central banks; because there is a special rule on this matter in Article 48, second sentence, of the Statute, repeated in paragraph 9(c) of the UK Protocol, which takes precedence over Article 28.3 of the Statute. This special rule exempts non-participating national central banks from the duty to pay up their capital subscription; however, the General Council of the ECB may decide, by a majority representing at last two thirds of the subscribed capital of the ECB and at least half of the shareholders, that non-participating national central banks pay up a minimum percentage to contribute to the operational costs of the ECB.

---

[97] Cf. *supra*, n. 87.

[98] Art. 1.1 of Decision ECB/1998/2 of 9 June 1998 laying down the measures necessary for the paying up of the capital of the European Central Bank [1999] OJ L8/33.

On 1 December 1998, the General Council of the ECB made use of this provision and decided that non-participating national central banks shall pay up 5 per cent of their respective subscription.[99] This financial contribution of the "pre-ins" and "outs" among ESCB central banks to the ECB budget represents a certain compensation for their integration into the ESCB and their participation in the decision-making process of the ECB through the General Council, in spite of their present legal distance to the single currency itself.

2.2. Differentiation of the foreign reserve assets of the ECB

Financial differentiation within the ECB also extends to the transfer of foreign reserves to the ECB. Article 30.1 of the Statute, which requires national central banks to provide the ECB with foreign reserve assets up to an amount equivalent to 50,000 million euro, does not impose obligations on Member States with a derogation or with special status or on their central banks. This is clearly stated in Article 43.1 and 43.4 of the Statute as well as in paragraph 8 of the UK Protocol.

The consequence of this was that the Governing Council of the ECB decided, by means of an ECB Guideline,[100] that only the participating national central banks had to transfer foreign reserve assets to the ECB, and this is equivalent to the amount of 39,468,960,000 euro, in return for a claim equivalent to this contribution credited by the ECB to these central banks under Article 30.3 of the Statute. This reduced amount—as compared to the maximum amount of 50,000 million euro referred to in Article 30.1 of the Statute—may be explained by the rule in Article 30.2 of the Statute. Thereunder, each national central bank contributes foreign reserve assets "in proportion to its share in the subscribed capital of the ECB". However, according to Article 43.6 of the Statute "subscribed capital of the ECB" in Article 30.2 shall be read as "capital of the ECB subscribed by the central banks of Member States without a derogation"; the same applies, *mutatis mutandis*, to Denmark under paragraph 2, second sentence of the Danish Protocol and to the United Kingdom by virtue of paragraph 8, second and third subparagraphs, of the UK Protocol. Also future transfers of foreign reserve assets, as made possible under Article 30.4 of the Statute,[101] would take place in accordance with the capital proportions of the participating national central banks only.

---

[99] Art. 1.1. of Decision ECB/1998/14 of 1 December 1998 laying down the measures necessary for the paying-up of the capital of the European Central Bank by the non- participating national central banks [1999] OJ L110/33. As the General Council is a decision-making body of the ECB, the decision is as much an ECB Decision as are decisions of the Governing Council or the Executive Board of the ECB.

[100] Cf. the Guideline of the European Central Bank of 3 November 1998 on the composition, valuation and modalities for the initial transfer of foreign-reserve assets, and the denomination and remuneration of equivalent claims, amended by Guideline ECB/2000/15 of 16 November 2000 [2000] OJ L336/114 (published *a posteriori*).

[101] Cf. also Council Regulation 1010/2000 of 8 May 2000 concerning further calls of foreign reserve assets by the European Central Bank [2000] OJ L115/2.

2.3. *Differentiation of the monetary income of the ECB*

The final set of rules which relates to differentiation in the financial resources of the ECB concerns not financial duties, but the income side: the income accruing to national central banks from the monetary policy functions of the ESCB under Article 32 of the Statute. Article 32.4 of the Statute provides for the allocation of the total of this monetary income to the national central banks in proportion to their paid up shares of the capital of the ECB.[102] However, it follows from Article 43.1 of the Statute that this provision shall not confer any rights on Member States with a derogation, and from Article 43.4 that "national central banks" shall be read as "central banks of Member States without a derogation" in Article 30. Paragraph 2, second sentence, of the Danish Protocol extends this rule to Denmark, as does paragraph 8, second subparagraph, of the UK Protocol.

Therefore, in parallel to their exclusion from financial duties within the ECB, non-participating national central banks also do not participate in the profit stemming from the monetary policy operations conducted under the authority of the ECB.

2.4. *How financial differentiation may be terminated*

Upon abrogation of a derogation or of a special status, all financial rights and duties resume by virtue of Article 49 of the Statute and paragraph 10, first sub-paragraph (b) of the UK Protocol.

These provisions were for the first time used when the Council abrogated the derogation of Greece with effect from 1 January 2001.[103] Thereafter, the ECB required the Bank of Greece in a decision of its Governing Council of 16 November 2000:[104]

(1) fully to pay up the remaining 95 per cent of its capital subscription (namely 97,679,000 euro),[105] in accordance with Article 49.1 of the Statute;

---

[102] For the transitional method applied to the allocation of monetary income as long as no euro banknotes circulate, cf. Decision ECB/2000/19 of 3 November 1998 as amended by Decision of 14 December 2000 on the allocation of monetary income of the national central banks of participating Member States and losses of the ECB for the financial years 1999 to 2001 [2000] OJ L336/119.

[103] Council Decision 2000/427/EC, *supra*, n. 4.

[104] Decision ECB/2000/14 of 16 November 2000 providing for the paying-up of capital and the contribution to the reserves and provisions of the European Central Bank by the Bank of Greece, and for the initial transfer of foreign-reserve assets to the ECB by the bank of Greece and related matters [2000] OJ L336/10. For practical reasons, this decision of the Governing Council of the ECB had to be taken before the abrogation of the Greek derogation became effective. As a consequence, the governor of the Bank of Greece did not yet have a formal right to participate and to vote on the adoption of this decision, but was still excluded by virtue of Arts. 10.1 and 43.4 of the Statute. Recital 13 of Decision ECB/2000/14 records that this problem was solved by inviting the Greek governor to attend the Governing Council meeting in accordance with Art. 3.4 of the Rules of Procedure of the ECB (*supra*, n. 86).

[105] Art. 2 of Decision ECB/2000/14, *supra*, n. 104.

(2) to transfer, as foreseen in Article 49.1 of the Statute, foreign reserve assets to the ECB in the same proportion as previously done by the other participating national central banks, thus as if it had been a participating Member State already on 1 January 1999,[106] in return for a claim equivalent to this contribution credited by the ECB to the Bank of Greece under Article 30.3 of the Statute;

(3) and to contribute, as stated in Article 49.2 of the Statute, to the reserves and provisions of the ECB,[107] which serve, in accordance with Article 33.1 (a) of the Statute to cover potential net losses of the ECB.

As some of these transactions resulted in a claim of the ECB against the central bank of Greece, and others in a claim of the Bank of Greece against the ECB, it was agreed, in a special agreement between the ECB and the Bank of Greece,[108] to offset the respective amounts in order to simplify the financial integration of the Bank of Greece into the financial structure of the ECB.

3. Differentiated application of ECB law?

In view of the institutional and financial differentiation inside the ECB, one would not be surprised if there were a similar differentiation as regards the application of ECB law. The question seems justified whether the legal instruments of the Governing Council of the ECB and the Executive Board of the ECB, which are enacted without any involvement from the non-participating Member States, may still claim to be uniformly applicable throughout the EU. Is ECB law still Community law for Sweden, Denmark and the United Kingdom?

The rules laid down in the EC Treaty and in the Statute do not give a clear answer to this, as may be demonstrated by the example of ECB Regulations[109] and ECB Guidelines.[110] ECB Regulations, like Community regulations under Article 249(2) EC, are said to be "directly applicable in all Member States" in Article 110(2), first subparagraph, second sentence, EC and in Article 34.2, first subparagraph, second sentence, of the Statute. However, Article 122(3) EC states that the whole of Article 110 EC does not apply to Member States with a

---

[106] Art. 3 of Decision ECB/2000/14, *supra*, n. 104.

[107] Art. 5 of *ibid.*

[108] Agreement of 16 November 2000 between the European Central Bank and the Bank of Greece regarding the claim credited to the Bank of Greece by the European Central Bank under Art. 30.3 of the Statute of the ESCB and related matters [2000] OJ L336/122. In the absence of any statement to the contrary, this agreement forms, in our view, an integral part of Community law. It was concluded in the context of the financial integration of Greece into the ECB after the decision to abrogate the Greek derogation, and therefore is a legal arrangement by which the ECB and the Bank of Greece meet the requirements under Arts. 30.3 and 49.2 of the Statute. Publication in part L of the OJ confirms this interpretation.

[109] On ECB Regulations, cf. *supra*, Ch. 3, 00 *et seq.*

[110] On ECB Guidelines, cf. *supra*, Ch. 3, 00 *et seq.*

derogation; according to Article 43.1 of the Statute, Article 34 of the Statute shall not confer any rights or impose any obligations on a Member State with a derogation; and Article 43.3 of the Statute requires that "Member States" in Article 34.2 be read as "Member States without a derogation". This ambiguous legal situation is mirrored by paragraph 2, second sentence, of the Danish Protocol. The UK Protocol even goes one step further. As regards Article 110 EC, paragraph 5 of the UK Protocol provides not only that this provision does not apply to the United Kingdom; it also says that therein "references to the Community or to the Member States shall not include the United Kingdom, and references to national central banks shall not include the Bank of England". Paragraph 8 provides for a parallel exemption from the effects of Article 34 of the Statute.

Similarly ambiguous is the case of ECB Guidelines. On the one hand, Article 12.1, second subparagraph, of the Statute requires the Executive Board of the ECB to implement monetary policy "in accordance with the guidelines" laid down by the Governing Council of the ECB; and Article 14.3 of the Statute makes it a legal duty for national central banks that they "shall act in accordance with the guidelines and instructions of the ECB". On the other hand, Article 43.1 of the Statute lists both Article 12.1 and Article 14.3 among the provisions that shall not confer any rights or impose any obligations on Member States with a derogation. The same applies to Denmark by virtue of paragraph 2, second sentence, of the Danish Protocol. The UK Protocol, again, excludes the United Kingdom and the Bank of England from the effects of Articles 12.1 and 14 of the Statute.

We take the view that all these provisions, even those in the UK Protocol, come in no way close to Article 2 of Protocol No 4 on the position of the United Kingdom and Ireland, and Article 2 of Protocol No 5 on the position of Denmark. These provisions, as already explained,[111] exclude the Community law character of legal provisions adopted under Title IV of the EC Treaty for the three Member States concerned. There is no such rule as regards ECB law. In our view, the legal effect of ECB legal instruments therefore may be compared to that of Community law adopted under EMU provisions which apply only to participating Member States:[112] as ECB law, they are and remain an integral part of Community law for all Member States and as such are applicable *in* all Member States; their *substantive effect*, however, is limited to the participating Member States and the participating national central banks.

This view seems to be confirmed by ECB legal practice. As far as ECB Regulations are concerned, it is noteworthy that the ECB avoided following the precedent set by the Community institutions as regards the controversy on the final sentence.[113] Instead, ECB Regulations omit a final sentence on their legal effects. Thereby, the ECB seems to indicate that the legal effect of ECB

---

[111] *Supra*, p. 153.
[112] *Supra*, p. 154.
[113] *Supra*, p. 152 *et seq.*

Regulations is already clear from primary Community law, namely from Articles 110(2), 122(3) EC and Articles 34.2, 43.1 of the Statute: they are directly applicable *in* all Member States, even though they do not confer any rights or impose any obligations *on* non-participating Member States or their central banks. ECB practice is even clearer in the case of ECB Guidelines, which, as already mentioned,[114] provide in their final recital: "Whereas in accordance with Articles 12.1 and 14.3 of the Statute, ECB Guidelines form an integral part of Community law". This not only emphasises the binding legal effect of ECB Guidelines, but also demonstrates that in spite of EMU differentiation, the law enacted by the ECB and its decision-making bodies is as much Community law throughout the EU as all other secondary Community law.

4. The "Eurosystem"—a trade name for the operational ESCB

In practical terms, the most important consequence of "differentiated integration" within the ESCB is that the Executive Board of the ECB may not have recourse to the Sveriges Riksbank, Danmarks Nationalbank and the Bank of England for the implementation of the monetary policy decisions taken by the Governing Council of the ECB (Articles 12.1 and 43.4 of the Statute). Monetary policy operations are thus carried out by the ECB and/or the 12 participating national central banks. In order to make this situation more transparent for counterparties in the financial markets and to enable the public to grasp more easily the complex structure of European central banking, the Governing Council of the ECB decided[115] to give the operational part of the ESCB the trade name "*Eurosystem*".[116]

Of course, "Eurosystem" is nothing but an informal expression that—similar to the political notion "euro area"—wants to make transparent who in fact takes part in the implementation of the monetary policy defined by the ECB. One may therefore call it a trade name. From a legal perspective, however, it goes without saying that the use of the term "Eurosystem" has no implications. The "Eurosystem" is not a new legal entity inside the ESCB; it neither has its

---

[114] Cf. *supra*, Ch. 3, p. 111.

[115] Cf. ECB, "The Eurosystem and the European System of Central Banks", *Monthly Bulletin* (Frankfurt am Main, January 1999), 7.

[116] The competence to adopt a trade name for the ESCB follows from the organisational autonomy of the ECB. By this, the ECB has followed the precedent set by some Community institutions which have chosen, for reasons of transparency, to adapt their names to the new framework created by the Treaty of Maastricht in 1992. Thus, the Council decided to call itself "Council of the European Union", instead of "Council of the European Communities"; cf. Council Decision 93/591/EU, Euratom, ECSC, EC of 8 November 1993 concerning the name to be given to the Council following the entry into force of the Treaty on European Union [1993] OJ L281/18, with corrigendum in [1993] OJ L285/41. The Commission of the European Communities adopted a Resolution on 17 November 1993 according to which it calls itself "European Commission" in all non-legal texts.

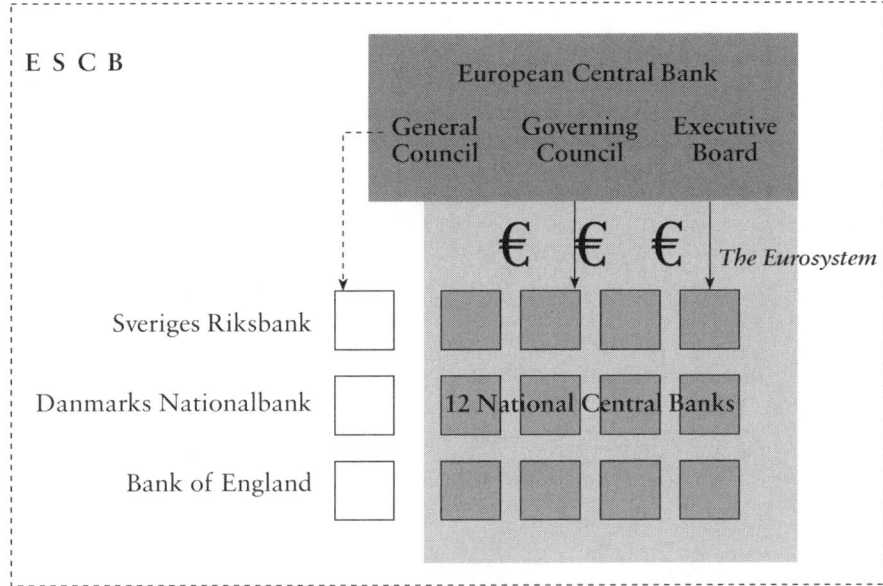

Fig. 4 *Differentiation within the ESCB*

own decision-making bodies nor can it take decisions[117] or become a party to a contract. The introduction of the trade name "Eurosystem" therefore does not change the legal situation according to which all 15 national central banks are a component part of the ESCB, which continues to be governed exclusively by the decision-making bodies of the ECB.

5. Special duties of national central banks with a derogation or a special status

The legal differentiation between the 15 national central banks inside the ESCB leads to a further question: How can one qualify the legal situation of non-participating national central banks inside the ESCB?

We have already seen[118] that the participating national central banks are subject to a unique "*dédoublement fonctionnel*" which transforms them into "ECB agents" whenever they act in a field covered by the tasks of the ESCB, and which only exceptionally allows them to act as national authorities outside the ESCB. We suggest that today also the Sveriges Riksbank, Danmarks Nationalbank and

---

[117] In this respect, there is a certain similarity between the Eurosystem and the informal "euro group"; cf. *supra*, p. 149 *et seq.*

[118] Cf. *supra*, Ch. 2, p. 73 *et seq.*

the Bank of England are subject to this "*dédoublement fonctionnel*", even though in a reversed version.

As a rule, these non-participating national central banks will keep, in their daily operations, their character as *national* central banks, as they are still the sole holders of monetary sovereignty in their respective Member States. However, at the same time they are also integrated into the ESCB, thus in an organisational system governed by supranational legal principles and supranational decision-making bodies, one of which—the General Council of the ECB—even with the participation of the national central banks with a derogation or special status. As a result, these non-participating national central banks are no longer able to act exclusively with regard to national law and national policy objectives, but will at the same time have to observe the framework set by Community law in general, and by ECB law in particular.

In particular, national central banks with a derogation or special status will have to take into account that Article 124 EC obliges them to treat their exchange rate policy towards the euro as "a matter of common interest". In addition, non-participating Member States will have to pursue their monetary policies in accordance with the primary objective of price stability, which applies without differentiation to all central banks within the ESCB by virtue of Article 2 of the Statute—from which neither Article 43 of the Statute nor the Danish or UK Protocols derogate. Most important, the non-participating national central banks, as parts of the ESCB, will have to observe the principle of System integrity.[119] They thus will not only have to refrain from any activities which might prejudice the operations undertaken by the ECB or through the 12 participating central banks; they also will have to co-operate with the ECB and the other central banks to achieve an efficient conduct of monetary policy throughout the European Union.

First steps in that direction have already been undertaken by the conclusion of a number of agreements between the ECB and some or all of the non-participating national central banks. The most famous of these agreements certainly is the so-called "ERM 2 Agreement",[120] concluded between the ECB and the non-participating national central banks. This agreement already guaranteed a smooth transition of the Greek currency to the final stage of EMU. Today it still serves as a close link between the development of the exchange rate of the euro and of the Danish crown; it also remains open for a full participation of Sveriges Riksbank and the Bank of England. A similar purpose is behind the central bank agreement on a Trans-European Automated Real Time Gross-Settlement Express Transfer System (the so-called "TARGET Agreement").[121]

---

[119] Cf. *supra*, Ch. 2, p. 80 *et seq.*

[120] Agreement of 1 September 1998 between the European Central Bank and the national central banks outside the euro area laying down the operating procedures for an exchange rate mechanism in Stage Three of Economic and Monetary Union [1998] OJ C345/6. On this agreement, cf. *infra*, Ch. 5, p. 206 *et seq.*

[121] On the "TARGET Agreement", cf. *infra*, Ch. 5, p. 209 *et seq.*

The TARGET System[122] was established by the ECB and the participating national central banks in order to promote the smooth operation of payment systems throughout the participating Member States.[123] Today, the TARGET Agreement also grants access to this system to non-participating national central banks, thereby allowing for EU-wide settlement of payments among central banks. Both the "ERM 2 Agreement" and the "TARGET Agreement" may be considered as bridges, which should facilitate the full integration of all national central banks in the final stage of EMU in the foreseeable future.[124]

V. CONCLUSION

The above analysis of differentiated integration due to EMU confirms that the ECB is, within the EU, in a special position. It has been shown that this independent specialised organisation of Community law is much more subject to differentiation than the general system of Community law. However, it should at the same time be noted that the EC Treaty and the Statute indicate clearly the Community tension in respect of the introduction of the single currency in all Member States at the next possible date; and that the mechanisms of ECB law today involve non-participating national central banks in ECB policies—in particular the centripetal General Council of the ECB and the unifying principle of System integrity. Hence, there seem to be good reasons to expect that differentiation inside the ECB will be only a temporary phenomenon. This temporary differentiation therefore in no way prejudices the supranational nature of the ECB, on the contrary: it rather emphasises the legal quality of the irreversible transfer of monetary sovereignty to the ECB, even though such transfer was impossible for some Member States, unwanted for others in the beginning.

---

[122] Cf. *supra,* Ch. 3, p. 127.

[123] On the impact of the TARGET system on the financial markets, cf. Sáinz de Vicuña, "Legal Consequences of the Single Currency", in Giovanoli (ed.), *International Monetary Law* (Oxford, 2000), 161 (164): "With regard to the money market, the TARGET system put together by the ESCB has achieved total integration, as is shown by the European-wide benchmark reference rates, the Euribor and EONIA, and the disappearance of local rates".

[124] Cf. also the statement of ECB-President Duisenberg after the negative outcome of the Danish referendum on 28 September 2000, published at http://www.ecb.int, under Press Releases: "I wish to emphasise that this will not in any way affect the co-operation between Danmarks Nationalbank and the European Central Bank."

5

The European Central Bank in International Relations

I. INTRODUCTION

THE ADOPTION OF the euro as the single currency by originally 11, now 12, Member States of the European Union has a considerable impact on the world of international monetary and economic co-operation. Even though the question whether the euro would become a new world currency closely rivalling the dollar is still more a matter of speculation than of scientific analysis,[1] it cannot be denied that, economically, the "euro area" has the potential to become a major player together with the United States and Japan and at the same time an important negotiating partner in international organisations and fora like the International Monetary Fund (IMF), the Organisation for Economic Co-operation and Development (OECD), the G–7 and the G–10.[2] It is not unrealistic to assume that the time when the Americans used to say, "The dollar is our currency, but your problem" might be brought to an end by the advent of the single European currency.[3]

However, to activate its economic potential at the international level will require that the "euro area" speak with one voice. At the moment, this seems to be far from being guaranteed. One may even observe a certain competition between the Community institutions, the Member States, the ECB and some national central banks to assume the role of "spokesman" for the euro.[4] The danger involved in such a competition is that a situation could arise which is only too familiar from the field of the common foreign and security policy: a

---

[1] "The euro will turn Europe into a superpower" is the prediction of Garten, dean of the Yale school of management, *Business Week*, 27 April 1998. The first data confirm this prediction: euro-denominated gross international issues of money market instruments, bonds and notes increased in 1999 to 38% of the total issue (the US dollar was then 41% of total issue) from the 24% of the combined share of the former euro area national currencies and the ECU in 1998. On this, cf. Noyer, "The International Impact of the Euro", (United States, January 2000), published at http://www. ecb.int/key/sp000113.htm.

[2] The economic preconditions for such a potential are analysed by Collignon and Mundschenk, "Die internationale Bedeutung der Währungsunion" [1998] *Integration* 77.

[3] This view is expressed by the chief economist of Deutsche Bank Walter, *The European* (5 May 1998).

[4] Cf. the criticism by Klau, "Heißes Eisen Außenvertretung", *Börsenzeitung*, 26 July 1998, 4.

situation in which our American counterparts would still be asking whom they should call in Europe.[5]

The final part of this book is intended to contribute, from a legal point of view, to the debate on the appropriate way to conduct the external relations for the single currency. It suggests that the EC Treaty, the Statute of the European System of Central Banks and of the European Central Bank (the Statute), and the existing *acquis* of Community law on external relations provide for sufficiently clear guidelines to give the euro a strong and unequivocal voice at the international level. Despite the fact that there are four types of actors within the "euro area" which have the legal personality required to be able to enter into public international law relations—the Community, the ECB, the Member States, and the national central banks (II.)—the EC Treaty and the Statute establish a clear division of competence between these actors (III.). This is also true for the external representation in international organisations and fora where Community law, regardless of the internal structure and the membership requirements of such international organisations, foresees efficient co-ordinating procedures which ascertain that there will be one voice for the euro at the international level (IV.). Finally, there are under the EC Treaty efficient legal remedies to protect, in the case of conflict, the prerogatives of all actors involved (V.).

II. THE ACTORS IN THE EXTERNAL RELATIONS OF THE "EURO AREA"

To be an actor in international relations with its own rights and obligations under public international law presupposes international legal personality. Only entities with international legal personality may enter into public international law agreements or may become members of international organisations.[6]

The "euro area" as such certainly has no international legal personality. As already explained,[7] "euro area" is not even a true legal term, but just a popular description of the territory of the originally 11, now 12 Member States of the European Union which have adopted the single currency in accordance with the EC Treaty. This description seeks to show the difference between these 12 Member States and the remaining Member States which have not fulfilled the necessary conditions for the third stage of economic and monetary union (Sweden[8]) or earlier have opted against the adoption of the single currency on 1 January 1999 (Denmark and the United Kingdom[9]). However, the "euro area"

---

[5] This is a dictum from the former US Secretary of State Kissinger, quoted by Schroeder, "Die Rechtsnatur der Europäischen Union und verwandte Probleme" in Hummer and Schweitzer (eds.), *Österreich und das Recht der Europäischen Union* (Vienna, 1996), 12.

[6] Cf. Brownlie, *Principles of Public International Law* (4th edn., Oxford, 1990), 58.

[7] Cf. *supra*, Ch. 4, p. 155.

[8] Cf. *supra*, Ch. 4, p. 135 *et seq.*

[9] Cf. *supra*, Ch. 4, p. 137 *et seq.*

neither is a legal entity nor has its own decision-making bodies. The so-called "euro group" is no more than an informal gathering to co-ordinate the policies in the "euro area", but has no competence to adopt legal acts or to commit the "euro area"—or even the Community—at the international level.[10]

Also the ESCB, composed of the ECB and the national central banks of all 15 Member States,[11] does not have legal personality.[12] Neither has the "Euro-system", a user-friendly expression by which the ECB and the national central banks of the 12 participating Member States define themselves when performing monetary policy operations,[13] and which simply is a kind of trade name that indicates the "operating arms" performing the monetary policy under the authority of the ECB, but without identifying a legal personality.

It is therefore necessary to look for the appropriate legal persons which have both the competence and the required decision-making bodies and instruments at their disposal to give the euro a strong voice at the international level. Speaking in purely abstract terms, there are four types of actors which would fulfil these conditions: the Member States, the national central banks, the Community and the ECB.

1. The Member States

Historically speaking, the normal actor on the international level is the state.[14] Public international law is still chiefly state-made and governed by the interests of sovereign states. States are born international legal personalities.

However, in the framework of the Community, this international legal personality has been substituted increasingly by that of the Community—and meanwhile also by that of the ECB. This comes from the fact that "the Community constitutes a new legal order of international law for the benefit of which the States have limited their sovereign right, albeit within limited fields".[15] Therefore, the more sovereign rights have been transferred to the Community level, the less likely it is that the Member States themselves will still appear as actors in the international area.

In the field here under analysis, monetary competence was transferred by the participating Member States to the Community level at the beginning of the third stage of monetary union on 1 January 1999 or, as in the case of Greece, at the moment in which the euro became the currency of that Member State, i.e. 1 January 2001. The same is true, though to a more limited extent, for economic policy. Given this transfer of sovereign rights, the legal capacity of the Member

---

[10] Cf. *supra*, Ch. 4, p 149 *et seq.*

[11] Cf. Art. 107(1) EC.

[12] On the historical background of this absence of legal personality, cf. *supra*, Ch. 2, p. 64 *et seq.*

[13] Cf. *supra*, Ch. 4, p. 166 *et seq.*

[14] Ipsen, *Völkerrecht* (Munich, 1990), § 5 speaks of the State as "die Normalperson des Völkerrechts".

[15] Case 26/62, *van Gend en Loos* [1963] ECR 1(12).

States to act on the international plane has been limited accordingly.[16] This is reflected in Article 111(5) EC which, while providing that Member States may still negotiate in international bodies and conclude international agreements, specifies that this shall be "without prejudice to Community competence and Community agreements as regards economic and monetary union". As monetary policy, from 1 January 1999, has become an exclusive competence exercised solely at the Community level,[17] there is in principle[18] no scope for independent external action by the Member States. As long as membership of the Community endures—and the EC Treaty itself presumes that this will be forever, as the Community's movement to the third stage of economic and monetary union is stated to be "irreversible" in Protocol No 24—the scope of the Member States' international legal personality is thus restricted to those subjects that have not been transferred to the Community level.[19]

2. The national central banks

Public banks—i.e. banks entrusted by the State with specific public functions—and in particular central banks today often assume an important role in public international law relations. It is even possible that public banks, under exceptional circumstances, may enjoy international legal personality. This is confirmed by the existence of "international banks", entrusted with specific public functions by states or by central banks themselves: for example, the World Bank, the EBRD and the Bank for International Settlements (BIS),[20] which all are recognised as enjoying international legal personality and thus have their own rights and obligations under public international law. Certainly, public banks—unlike states, but similar to international organisations[21]—never have an *original*, but only a *derivative* international legal personality, the existence of which always depends on the intention of their respective states and on the recognition by third countries. One may therefore circumscribe such legal personality as both *limited* in substance—as it exists only to the extent that exter-

---

[16] Cf. Ruling 1/78, *Draft Convention of the International Atomic Energy Agency on the Physical Protection of Nuclear Materials, Facilities and Transports* [1978] ECR 2151, para. 32.

[17] This can be drawn from Art. 4(2) EC which speaks of "a *single* monetary policy and exchange rate policy". Cf. *supra*, Ch. 2, p. 70 *et seq.*

[18] Some exceptions stemming essentially from the rule in Art. 307 EC are mentioned *infra* p. 213 *et seq.*

[19] This is also the view of Martha, "The Fund Agreement and the Surrender of Monetary Sovereignty to the European Community" (1993) *CML Rev.* 749.

[20] On the international legal personality of the BIS, cf. Giovanoli, "The Role of the BIS in International Monetary Cooperation and its Tasks Relating to the ECU" in Effros (ed.), *Current Legal Issues Affecting Central Banks* (Washington, 1992), i, 39 (*et seq.*).

[21] On the limited and relative legal personality of international organisations cf. Bernhardt (ed.), *Encyclopedia of Public International Law*, 130; Seidl-Hohenveldern and Loibl, *Das Recht der Internationalen Organisationen einschließlich der Supranationalen Gemeinschaften* (7th edn., Cologne/Munich, 2000), 45 *et seq.*

nal competence have been attributed to a public bank by its respective state—and *relative* as regards its addressees, as only those international legal persons are bound to accept that public bank's international legal personality which have (at least implicitly) recognised it.

The fact that public banks normally form part of the institutional framework of a state or an international organisation does not prevent them from having a separate legal personality. On the contrary: the more independent a public bank is conceived to be for the fulfilment of its tasks,[22] the more likely it is also to be awarded the capacity to act autonomously at the international level.[23] Behind this is a development, which has started in the 1930s,[24] according to which the state is increasingly recognised not as an impermeable monolith, but as a conglomerate of different functions which may require differentiated action both internally and externally.[25] The best example is that of federal states which sometimes attribute a limited international personality to their sub-entities.[26] The limited international legal personality of such sub-entities reflects their internal autonomy granted by the respective constitution.

Similar functional considerations sometimes lead states to endow their central banks with a (limited) international legal personality. In this case, central banks may not only have the power to commit, as representatives, their state of

---

[22] At least in developed countries, a clear trend can be detected to grant independence from the government to central banks, since this is considered better to ensure the achievement of long-term economic objectives and in particular price stability. This development reinforces, as a consequence, the position of national central banks as actors in the international sphere.

[23] On the controversy whether central banks are to be considered as organs of the state or as institutions, of private or public law, acting or not on their own behalf, see Radicati Di Bròzolo, "Some Legal Aspects of the European Monetary System" [1980] *Rivista di Diritto Internazionale* 330 (340) who observes that the problem of the nature of central banks is highlighted by the many judicial decisions in cases in which they have claimed sovereign immunity. Further practical examples of independent international action of central banks have arisen in the context of the IMF where the parties to the General Arrangements to Borrow are 8 countries and 2 independent central banks; on this cf. *supra*, Ch. 1, n. 145.

[24] With the advent of the New Deal in the USA where the new independent regulatory commissions (IRCs) were considered to become miniature independent governments, or a "fourth branch of government"; see Shapiro, *Who Guards the Guardians? Judicial Control of Administration* (Athens/London, 1988), 107 *et seq.*; Majone, "The European Community: An Independent Fourth Branch of Government?" in Brüggemeier (ed.), *Verfassungen für ein ziviles Europa* (Baden Baden, 1994), 23. On this, cf. also *supra*, Ch. 1, p. 47 *et seq.*

[25] This functionalist view, according to which "form follows function" was established by Mitrany in *The Progress of International Government* (New Haven, Conn., 1933), and in *A Working Peace System* (London, 1943). On the autonomous role of central banks in external relations cf. Zehetner, "Völkerrechtliche Außenvertretungsbefugnisse der Oesterreichischen Nationalbank?" in *Festschrift für F.A. Mann* (1977), 470, who discovers a need for an "institutional decentralisation" of external competence to reflect the internal need to entrust public tasks to highly specialised agencies.

[26] According to Art. 32(3) of the German Basic Law, the German *Länder* may, in their field of competence, conclude public international law agreements with third countries, subject to the approval of the Federal government. Therefore, the German *Länder* are said to enjoy a *partial international legal personality* ("partielle Völkerrechtssubjektivität"); cf. Schweitzer, *Staatsrecht III* (6th edn., Heidelberg, 1997), para. 112 and 536. The same applies to the *Bundesländer* in Austria (Art. 16 of the Federal Constitutional Act) and the cantons in Switzerland (Art. 9 of the Federal Constitution). Cf. also *supra*, Ch. 2, p. 58, n. 23.

origin,[27] but are sometimes themselves members of sectoral international organisations—the best example is the BIS[28]—and may, in their fields of competence, even enter into public international law agreements[29]—the most outstanding example being the central bank agreement under the European Exchange Rate Mechanism[30] which laid down the operating procedures of the European Monetary System.

Since 1 June 1998,[31] the national central banks in the European Union have become "an integral part"[32] of the ESCB. In cases in which national law attributed to its national central bank the capacity to be an actor in its own right under public international law, such legal personality is formally not affected by the establishment of the ESCB. Thus, national central banks may, in principle, continue to participate in international organisations or to conclude public international law agreements. However, from the integration into the ESCB results a clear subordination of national central banks to the ECB, as it is the ECB which, through its decision-making bodies, governs the ESCB (Article 107(3) EC). In particular, the decision on external representation of the ESCB is centralised in the hands of the Governing Council of the ECB in accordance with Articles 6.1, 6.2 and 12.5 of the Statute.[33]

The sole exception to this subordination of national central banks to the decision-making bodies of the ECB[34] are the three national central banks of the Member States which do not yet participate in the single currency. According to Article 43.2 of the Statute, these central banks shall retain their powers in the

---

[27] Cf. Zehetner, *supra*, n. 24. See also Hahn, *Währungsrecht* (Munich, 1990), § 15 on the interinstitutional arrangements between the Deutsche Bundesbank and the German government as regards participation of the Bundesbank in the decision-making process at the IMF.

[28] According to its Constituent Charter of 30 January 1930, the BIS was founded by the central banks of Belgium, France, Germany, Great Britain, Italy and Japan and by a US banking group; Zehetner, *supra*, n. 24, 488, sees the BIS case as the starting point for the development of a new rule of customary public international law according to which central banks become generally recognised international legal personalities.

[29] See Burdeau, "Indépendance des banques centrales et droit international" in A. Weber (ed.), *Währung und Wirtschaft. Das Geld im Recht. Festschrift für Hahn* (1997), 17 (23): "*Sur le plan conventionnel, la Banque s'engage en principe indépendamment de l'Etat*".

[30] Agreement of 13 March 1979 between the central banks of the Member States of the European Economic Community laying down the operational procedures for the European Monetary System, which is published, as amended, in Monetary Committee, *Compendium of Community Monetary Texts* (Office for Official Publications of the European Communities, Luxembourg, 1995), 62. On the legal nature of the ERM as public international law agreement, see Radicati Di Bròzolo, *supra*, n. 23, at 440.

[31] This the date of the establishment of the ESCB and the ECB.

[32] In accordance with Art. 14.3 of the Statute.

[33] Only Art. 31.1 of the Statute gives a limited autonomous competence to national central banks to perform transactions for the fulfilment of their (existing) obligations towards international organisations, see *infra*, p. 229. However, even in this case the Governing Council of the ECB shall issue guidelines to facilitate such operations and thus to avoid them conflicting with the external policy of the ESCB as defined by the ECB.

[34] Of course, when national central banks are performing functions which are outside the ESCB tasks, they are not subordinated to the ECB decision-making bodies, subject however to Art. 14.4 of the Statute. Cf. *supra*, Ch. 2, p. 79.

field of monetary policy according to national law, despite their participation in the ESCB. This includes also their competence, if acknowledged under national law, to act autonomously at the international level.

3. The European Community

In the past decades a new type of actor, the international organisation, has appeared at the international level. International organisations may be bearers of rights and duties under public international law when endowed by their members with international legal personality, either explicitly or implicitly.[35] This presupposes discrete tasks and decision-making bodies which have the legal power to represent and commit these international organisations under public international law.[36]

The European Community has been awarded international legal personality directly by the Treaty, Article 281 of which states:

> The Community shall have legal personality.

As Article 282 EC confers legal personality on the Community *in* the Member States, i.e. the right to acquire or dispose of movable or immovable property or to be a party to legal proceedings, Article 281 EC can only refer to a legal personality at the international level—a view which is shared by the ECJ[37] and legal doctrine,[38] in particular as is confirmed by other Treaty provisions.[39] An

---

[35] Cf. the Advisory Opinion of the ICJ in *Reparation for Injuries Suffered in the Service of the United Nations* [1949] ICJ Rep. 174 where the UN were said to enjoy international legal personality although the Charter of the UN is silent in this respect.

[36] Cf. Brownlie, *supra*, n. 6, 681; Meng, *Das Recht der Internationalen Organisationen—eine Entwicklungsstufe des Völkerrechts* (Baden Baden, 1979), 41 *et seq.*

[37] This view has been endorsed by the ECJ, which has drawn from Art. 281 EC the Community's treaty-making power. Already in Case 6/64, *Costa v. ENEL* [1964] ECR 585(593), the ECJ defines the Community as "a Community of unlimited duration, having its own institutions, its own personality, its own legal capacity and capacity of representation on the international plane"; as regards Art. 281 EC, see Case 22/70, *Commission v. Council (ERTA)* [1971] ECR 263, paras. 13–14: "This provision, placed at the head of Part Six EC, devoted to 'General and Final Provisions', means that in its external relations the Community enjoys the capacity to establish contractual links with third countries over the whole field of objectives defined in Part One EC, which Part Six supplements"; see also Case C–327/91, *France v. Commission* [1994] ECR I–3641, para. 24 *et seq.*, where the ECJ recognises explicitly that the Community is an international organisation within the meaning of Art. 2(1)(a)(i) of the Vienna Convention of 21 March 1986 on the Law of the Treaties between States and International Organisations or between International Organisations.

[38] Brückner and Louis in *Commentaire Mégret, Le Droit de la CEE* (Brussels, 1980), xii, 1; Schweitzer and Hummer, *Europarecht* (5th edn., Neuwied/Kriftel/Berlin, 1996), 191; Simma and Vedder in Grabitz and Hilf, *Das Recht der Europäischen Union* (14th supplement, Munich, October 1999), Art. 281, para. 2 *et seq.*; Tomuschat in Von der Groeben, Thiesing and Ehlermann (eds.), *Kommentar zum EU-/EG-Vertrag* (5th edn., Baden Baden, 1997), Art. 210, para. 1.

[39] Art. 300 EC contains a procedure for "the conclusion of agreements between the Community and one or more States or international organisations". Arts. 302–304 EC confer the task on the Community to establish co-operation with the United Nations, the Council of Europe, the OECD and other international organisations.

impressive number of third countries and international organisations have recognised the international legal personality of the Community.[40] This recognition is essential for the exercise of the international legal personality of the Community, because, under public international law, the (relative) international legal personality of international organisations is effective only in respect of third countries when those have recognised it.[41]

It has already been mentioned that only states have an original and thus encompassing international legal personality, while the scope of the international legal personality of international organisations always depends on the intention of its founding members, and more specifically on the tasks entrusted to them. This means that the international legal personality of the Community extends also to the field of economic and monetary union. In fact, Article 111(3) EC is based on the assumption that in specific cases "agreements on monetary or foreign exchange regime matters need to be negotiated *by the Community* with one or more States or international organisations", Article 111(1) EC foresees the conclusion of "agreements on an exchange rate system" for the euro in relation to non-Community currencies; Article 111(4) EC presumes that the Community may wish to define its "position at the international level as regards issues of particular relevance to economic and monetary union".

To fulfil its tasks at the international level, the Community there is normally represented by its institutions, which by themselves have no legal personality,[42] but the legal capacity to act on behalf of the Community.[43] Articles 300 to 304 EC normally entrust this representative function to the Commission and to the

---

[40] In 1995, 163 third countries were accredited to the Community; around 130 representation or liaison offices of the Community were established in third countries. Today, the Community is, *inter alia*, a member of the World Trade Organisation and thus also of the General Agreement on Tariffs and Trade (GATT), the General Agreement on Trade in Services (GATS) and the Trade Related Intellectual Property Rights (TRIPs) agreement; of the Food and Agriculture Organisation (FAO); cf. Frid, "The European Economic Community. A Member of a Specialized Agency of the United Nations" [1993] *EJIL* 239; of the EBRD [1990] OJ L372/4; of the North-West Atlantic Fisheries Organisation (NAFO) [1978] OJ L378/2; of the North-East Atlantic Fisheries Convention (NEAFC) [1981] OJ L227/22; and of the North Atlantic Salmon Conservation Organisation (NASCO) [1982] OJ L378/25. Cf. Schermers, "International Organisations as Members of Other International Organisations" in *Festschrift für Mosler* (Berlin etc., 1983), 823; Sack, "Die Europäische Gemeinschaft als Mitglied internationaler Organisationen" in *Gedächtnisschrift für Grabitz* (Munich, 1995), 631.

[41] The reason behind this is the rule that an international treaty must not impose obligations on third parties; this applies also to the founding statute of an international organisation. Brownlie, *supra*, n. 6, 694; cf. Schweitzer, *Staatsrecht III* (6th edn., Heidelberg, 1997), 213; Bognar, *Europäische Währungsintegration und Außenwirtschaftsbeziehungen* (Baden Baden, 1997), 114.

[42] Joined Cases 7/56 and 3/57 to 7/57, *Algera* v. *Common Assembly of the European Coal and Steel Community* [1957] ECR 81 (57): "only the Community has legal personality, and its institutions do not".

[43] This was confirmed by Case C–327/91, *France* v. *Commission* [1994] ECR I–3641, para. 24, where the ECJ held that the "Agreement between the Commission and the United States regarding the application of their competition laws" was an agreement binding on the European Communities: "it is the Community alone, having legal personality pursuant to Art. 210 EC, which has the capacity to bind itself by concluding agreements with a non-member country or an international organisation".

Council. However, in the field of economic and monetary union, Article 111 EC prescribes a different form of external representation. Here, it is the Council that decides, acting unanimously, on the Community's representation at international level (Article 111(4) EC). Also, whenever the Community needs to enter into an agreement concerning monetary or foreign exchange regime matters, it is always the Council that decides in each individual case the arrangements for the negotiation and the conclusion of such agreements (Article 111(3) EC). This is also true for the specific case of formal agreements on an exchange rate system for the euro as regards non-Community currencies, dealt with in Article 111(1) EC. The Commission will only be fully associated to the negotiations, but not necessarily conduct the negotiations itself, as was the case under Article 300(1) EC.

4. The European Central Bank

To some, it may seem surprising to mention also the ECB as a an actor in the external relations of the "euro area", separate from the Community. At first glance, one could think of the ECB as an institution of the Community which, just like the Commission[44] or the Council, might be entitled to *represent* the Community at the international level, but which would never be in a position to act at the international level on the basis of a legal capacity in its own right. However, this understanding is not compatible with the role assigned to the ECB by the EC Treaty.

As shown above, it is not unthinkable that a public bank, and in particular a central bank, may enjoy international legal personality. In the same way as states have sometimes, for functional reasons, endowed public banks, and in particular central banks, with a (limited) international legal personality, Community law is open for an international legal personality of public banks established under the Treaty.

The European Investment Bank (EIB) already enjoys an international legal personality separate from that of the Community. This international legal personality results directly from the wording of Article 265 EC,[45] and has been confirmed by the conclusion of a number of international agreements by the EIB.[46]

---

[44] The Commission itself recognised that it has no international legal personality in Case C–327/91, *France* v. *Commission* [1994] ECR I–3641, reported in the opinion of Tesauro AG, para. 19.

[45] "The European Investment Bank shall have legal personality." In view of the parallel wording of Art. 281 EC, and as Art. 28 of the Statute of the EIB already covers the legal personality of the EIB in the Member States, Art. 266 EC could only be meant to confer international legal personality on the EIB. On this, cf. Hilf, *Die Organisationsstruktur der Europäischen Gemeinschaften* (Berlin, 1982), p. 42 *et seq.*

[46] In particular by the agreement between the EIB and Switzerland, dated 24 March 1972, in which Switzerland recognises explicitly "the international legal personality and capacity to act of the EIB", cf. [1972] Sammlung der Eidgenössischen Gesetze 2765 ff. On the agreements of the EIB, see Henrion, "La banque européenne d'investissement" in Ganshof van der Meersch (ed.), *Droit des communautés européennes* (1969), No 2425 *et seq.*, 967 *et seq.*

Particularly striking is the Agreement establishing the EBRD[47] which provides, in Article 3, for membership of countries, of the European Community *and* the EIB in parallel, and which both the Community[48] and the EIB[49] joined as full members. Behind this legal separation between the Community and EIB is a purely functional consideration: a public bank like the EIB which is meant to be the Community's credit institution[50] requires a certain degree of autonomy to be a reliable partner in financing operations. The ECJ has put this in the following terms:

> the Bank has legal personality distinct from that of the Community . . . In order to perform the tasks assigned to it by . . . the Treaty the Bank must be able to act in complete independence on the financial markets like any other bank.[51]

This reasoning should be born in mind when analysing the legal position of the ECB. Article 105(1), first sentence, EC establishes price stability as a primary objective for the tasks which are entrusted to the European System of Central Banks (ESCB), which is governed by the ECB.[52] Also, to guarantee that the monetary policy for the euro will in future be "de-politicised", as already explained,[53] Article 108 EC constitutionally entrenches a far-reaching independence of the ECB by prohibiting both the Community institutions and bodies and the Member States from giving instructions to the ECB. Against this background, and in view of the international legal personality of the EIB, it is only logical that Article 107(2) EC provides:

> The European Central Bank shall have legal personality.

Since Article 9.1 of the Statute already deals with the legal personality of the ECB *in* the Member States, this provision, in parallel to Articles 281 and 266 EC, can only refer to the ECB's international legal personality. This interpretation is supported by Article 105(2), second and third indents EC, which enables the ECB to conduct foreign exchange operations, and to hold and manage the foreign reserves of the Member States—all these are tasks which may involve legal contacts with other subjects of international law. Moreover, Article 23 of the Statute gives the ECB more specific external competences, for example to establish relations with central banks and financial institutions in other countries and

---

[47] [1990] OJ L372/4.

[48] Cf. Council Decision 90/674/EEC of 19 November 1990 on the conclusion of the Agreement establishing the European Bank for Reconstruction and Development [1990] OJ L372/1.

[49] Cf. Decision of the Board of Governors of 11 June 1990 on the membership of the European Investment Bank in the European Bank for Reconstruction and Development [1990] OJ *L377/3*.

[50] Dunnett, "The European Investment Bank: Autonomous Instrument of Common Policy?" (1994) *CML Rev.* 721.

[51] Case 85/86, *Commission* v. *Board of Governors of the EIB* [1988] ECR 1281, para. 28. On this aspect of the ambivalent legal nature of the EIB cf. *supra*, Ch. 1, p. 21 *et seq.*

[52] As the ESCB is governed by the decision-making bodies of the ECB (Art. 107(3) EC; cf. *supra*, Ch. 2, p. 57 *et seq.*), it is appropriate to say that all tasks entrusted to the ESCB are ECB tasks. In the field of external relations, this is confirmed by Art. 6.1 of the Statute according to which it is the ECB which decides how the ESCB is represented at the international level.

[53] Cf. *supra*, Ch. 1, p. 31 *et seq.*

with international organisations, and to conduct banking transactions in relations with third countries and international organisations. Finally, Articles 6.1 and 6.2 of the Statute explicitly provides for the possibility of the ECB to act at the international level whenever the tasks entrusted to the ESCB are involved. All these provisions show that the ECB has the competence to act independently at the international level, what may also involve the negotiation and conclusion of public international law agreements.[54]

However, the international legal personality of the ECB, granted by Article 107(1) EC, is only a *derivative* one, just like that of international organisations, of national central banks or of the sub-entities of a federal state. Therefore, it is first of all *limited* to the specific fields of tasks which are entrusted to the ECB by the EC Treaty, which are essentially confined to monetary policy and related matters. Secondly, the ECB's international legal personality is only *relative* in nature and thus, in the beginning, only relevant in the legal relationship between the ECB and the parties to the EC Treaty, i.e. the 15 Member States. In this respect, it should be mentioned that the international legal personality of the ECB has already been confirmed:

—by the Agreement between the ECB and the national central banks of the Member States outside the euro area laying down the operating procedures for an exchange rate mechanism in stage three of economic and monetary union, dated 1 September 1998 (the "ERM 2 Agreement");[55]
—by the conclusion, on 18 September 1998, of a Headquarters Agreement between the ECB and the Government of the Federal Republic of Germany which aims at implementing the Protocol on Privileges and Immunities of the European Communities and thus facilitating the full operation of the ECB at its seat in Frankfurt.[56]

---

[54] This view is shared by legal doctrine; cf. Bognar, *supra*, n. 41, 100, who discusses at some length the international legal personality of the ECB's predecessor, the European Monetary Institute; Hahn, *Der Vertrag von Maastricht als völkerrechtliche Übereinkunft und Verfassung* (Baden Baden, 1992), 58 (international legal personality of the European Monetary Institute) and 66 (international legal personality of the ECB); Pernice in Grabitz and Hilf, *supra*, n. 38, Art. 4 a, para. 11; Stadler, *Der rechtliche Handlungsspielraum des Europäischen Systems der Zentralbanken* (Baden Baden, 1996), 92; see also Selmayr, "Gefahr für die Europäische Zentralbank?" [1998] *Europablätter* 39 (40), and "Die Wirtschafts- und Währungsunion als Rechtsgemeinschaft" [1999] *AöR* 357 (369 *et seq*). The opposing view from Weber, "Das Europäische System der Zentralbanken" [1998] *WM* 1465 (1471) is based on the assumption that the ECB externally has only a "communication function", similar to that of the Commission under Art. 302 EC; however, the heading of Art. 23 of the Statute ("External operations") proves that there is a lot more at stake.

[55] [1998] OJ C345/6.

[56] See the German [1998] *Bundesgesetzblatt II* 2995. The autonomy of the ECB towards the Community was confirmed by the fact that this agreement was not concluded by the Commission under Art. 19 of the Protocol No 34 on the Privileges and Immunities of the European Communities, but by the ECB itself (as has happened also in the case of the EIB, which concluded a Headquarters agreement with Luxembourg on 24 February 1986). This comes from the fact that the ECB itself, like an international organisation or the Community itself, has been given privileges and immunities under Art. 291, second sentence EC and Art. 23 of Protocol No 34 on the Privileges and Immunities of the European Communities; see *infra*, p. 210.

More important is that third countries recognise the ECB's international legal personality, as such recognition is, from a public international law perspective, the constitutive element of international legal personality in such relations. The practice of the ECB and third countries will show in the next few years to what extent the ECB will make use of its capacity, conferred on it by the EC Treaty, to act under public international law. For this purpose, there will be a need to explain to third countries and international organisations that the ECB—in contrast with the Commission or the Council—is not a Community institution,[57] but a separate and independent entity which, though linked to the Community by its task to define the monetary policy of the Community (Article 105(2), first indent, EC) and a number of co-operating procedures (Article 113 EC), rather constitutes a "Community of its own"[58] having legal personality both in the Member States and externally.[59] As such an autonomous specialised organisation of Community law, the ECB has the potential to be, within its field of competence, an independent actor at the international level.

When acting at the international level, in particular when it negotiates or concludes international agreements, the ECB needs to be represented. Article 6 of the Statute provides for several possibilities of such international representation: either by the ECB[60] itself, or by (one or more) national central banks, or by the ECB and (one or more) national central banks, acting jointly on behalf of the ESCB. However, the two latter cases are not to be understood as including a concurrent external competence of the national central banks. The wording of Article 6.1 implies that both the ECB and the national central banks always represent the ESCB and thus have to take into account that their international actions relate to a larger framework. Even more importantly, the decisions on external representation are up to the Governing Council of the ECB, as stated in Article 12.5 of the Statute. This means that national central banks could take over the task of speaking externally on behalf of the whole of the ESCB only if

---

[57] Cf. *supra*, Ch. 1, p. 15 *et seq*. This interpretation is now practically undisputed in legal doctrine; cf. Cloos, Reinesch, Vignes and Weyland, *Le Traité de Maastricht. Genèse, Analyse, Commentaires* (Brussels, 1994), 236 ("*la BCE n'est pas une institution communautaire, mais une quasi institution ou une institution communautaire sui generis*"); Häde, "Die Europäische Wirtschafts- und Währungsunion" [1992] *EuZW* 171 (174); Hahn, "The European Central Bank: Key to Monetary Union or Target" [1991] *CML Rev*. 783 (796): Louis, "L'Union économique et monétaire" [1992] *CDE* 251 (280); Potacs, "Nationale Zentralbanken in der Wirtschafts- und Währungsunion" [1993] *EuR* 31, n. 51; Selmayr, "Gefahr für die Europäische Zentralbank?" [1998] *Europablätter* 39 (40); Stadler, *Der rechtliche Handlungsspielraum des Europäischen Systems der Zentralbanken* (Baden Baden, 1996), 93; Weber, "Das Europäische System der Zentralbanken" [1998] *WM* 1465. On recent international recognition of the ECB cf. *supra*, Ch. 1, p. 46 *et seq*.

[58] For more details on the classification of the ECB as an autonomous specialised organisation of the Community cf. *supra*, Ch. 1, p. 29 *et seq*.

[59] The fact that the "members" of the ECB are not states, but central banks, is no obstacle to such a qualification, as is shown by the example of the BIS, which is an international organisation; cf. *supra*, n. 20, and Bognar, *supra*, n. 41, 102 *et seq*.

[60] The ECB would be represented by its President in accordance with Arts. 13.2 and 39 of the Statute.

authorised to do so by the ECB. This corresponds to the institutional structure of the ESCB in which the decision-making process is centralised in the hands of the decision-making bodies of the ECB.[61]

III. THE DIVISION OF EXTERNAL COMPETENCES IN ECONOMIC AND
MONETARY UNION

The fact that there are four potential legal persons which could act at the international level on behalf of the euro shows that economic and monetary union has led to "a new Community of almost bewildering variety" which involves "a new division of labour between the Community, the Member States, other levels of government and other organisations".[62] This institutional variety entails the need clearly to define and delimit the respective fields of competence to avoid confusion. This is in particular necessary as regards the capacity to enter into international agreements, the so-called treaty-making power.

Before the entry into force of the Maastricht Treaty, and thus of the provisions on economic and monetary union, there was a longstanding jurisprudence of the ECJ on the issue of external competence in Community law, the main features of which will be presented in the following section. The analysis will then focus on the two fields of economic and monetary union which follow different rules and are therefore distinguished by the EC Treaty itself:

—*economic policy* on the one hand (Chapter 1 of Title VII of Part Three of the EC Treaty),
—*monetary policy* on the other hand (Chapter 2 thereof).

1. The jurisprudence of the ECJ on external competences: the doctrine of parallelism

External competences represent an issue only marginally dealt with by the EC Treaty. There have always been only a few provisions providing explicitly for the competence to negotiate or to conclude public international law agreements or to participate in international fora.[63] These few provisions did not offer sufficient legal ground for the need of the Community to act at the international level, resulting from the increase of its internal competences following the

---

[61] Cf. *supra*, n. 52.

[62] Snyder, "EMU—Metaphor for European Union? Institutions, Rules and Types of Regulation" in Dehousse (ed.), *Europe After Maastricht. An Ever Closer Union?* (Munich, 1994), 63 (98). Dehousse and Ghemar, "Le traité de Maastricht et les relations extérieures de la Communauté européenne" [1994] *EJIL* 151 (157) fear "*une fragmentation dans les relations extérieures de la Communauté*".

[63] Examples for such explicit external competences are Arts. 133(3), 174(4) and 310 EC.

completion of the common market at the end of the 1960s.[64] This need was soon recognised by the ECJ, which, relying on the doctrine of implied powers,[65] developed what is known today as the *doctrine of parallelism between internal and external competences*. In the leading *ERTA* case,[66] the ECJ stated that the Community's authority to conclude international agreements:

> arises not only from an express conferment by the Treaty, but may equally flow from other provisions of the Treaty and from measures adopted, within the framework of those provisions, by the Community institutions. . . . With regard to the implementation of the provisions of the Treaty the system of internal Community measures may not therefore be separated from that of external relations.

On the basis of this doctrine,[67] the ECJ has recognised so-called *implied external competences* of the Community,[68] in particular when the parallel internal competence had already been used for the adoption of secondary legislation, but also when such an external competence was *necessary* for the attainment of one of the objectives of the EC Treaty.[69] In its more recent jurisprudence, the ECJ makes the existence of a parallel external competence dependent on the question whether such an external competence is *"inseparably linked"* with the exercise of its parallel internal competence.[70]

The ECJ distinguishes two types of external competence of the Community: *exclusive external competences*, which exclude the Member States from any action in this field as this would prejudice the efficiency of the existing Community law[71] and *shared external competences*, when the Member States have not completely lost their power as the (internal or external) competence conferred on the Community by the EC Treaty is limited. In this latter case it is

---

[64]   See Dehousse and Gehmar, *supra*, n. 62, 152 *et seq.*

[65]   This doctrine has its origin in the law of international organisations. Cf. the Advisory Opinion of the International Court of Justice, *supra*, n. 35.

[66]   Case 22/70, *Commission v. Council (ERTA)* [1971] ECR 263, paras. 16 and 19.

[67]   On the doctrine of parallelism see Brückner and Louis in *Commentaire Mégret, Le Droit de la CEE* (Brussels, 1980), xii, Art. 210, 94 *et seq.*; Groux, "Le parallelisme des compétences internes et externes de la CEE" [1978] *CDE* 3; Schweitzer and Hummer, *supra*, n. 38, 198 *et seq.*; Tomuschat in Von der Groeben, Thiesing and Ehlermann (eds.), *supra*, n. 38, Art. 210, para. 5. Since Maastricht, the doctrine of parallelism has been recognised in Art. 300(2) and (3) EC where the voting rules in the Council and the participation of the European Parliament in the conclusion of such agreements are made dependent on the rules and the degree of involvement as regards the adoption of internal rules.

[68]   *Inter alia*, to conclude international agreements on road transport (Case 22/70, *Commission v. Council (ERTA)* [1971] ECR 263, para. 27); and to conclude a convention within the framework of the International Labour Organisation, paralleling the Community's internal competence under Art. 138 EC in the field of social policy (*Opinion 2/91, Convention No 170 of the International Labour Organization concerning safety in the use of chemicals at work* [1993] ECR I–1061).

[69]   *Opinion 1/76, Draft Agreement establishing a European laying-up fund for inland waterway vessels* [1977] ECR 741, para. 4.

[70]   *Opinion 1/94, WTO* [1994] ECR I–5267, para. 100; *Opinion 2/92, OECD* [1995] ECR I–525.

[71]   This is the case where the EC Treaty provides for a common policy or where there is exhaustive or at least extensive Community legislation in the respective field. An example of such an exclusive external competence is the Community's authority to enter into international agreements in the field of commercial policy. Cf. *Opinion 1/75, Local Cost Standard* [1975] ECR 1355.

necessary that both the Community and the Member States become contracting partners of an international agreement with third countries or international organisations (so-called *mixed agreements*[72]).[73]

The logic behind the doctrine of parallelism is easy to understand: if and in so far the EC Treaty confers certain internal powers on the Community, both the internal and the external competences of the Member States are limited accordingly to prevent the efficient exercise of the internal competence of the Community being prejudiced by conflicting action of the Member States at the international level. In other words, Community law recognises a necessity to protect the *effet utile* of internal competences.[74] This logic must be borne in mind when analysing the new and more complex fields of competence inserted into the Treaty by the provisions on economic and monetary union.

2. External competences in economic policy

The EC Treaty does not provide for an explicit external competence of the Community in the field of economic policy. Therefore, and in view of the doctrine of parallelism, it is necessary to analyse the extent of internal Community competences which would be mirrored by a parallel external competence.

In the field of economic policy, Articles 98 *et seq.* EC provide only for a very loose form of co-operation between the Member States. It is true that they shall regard their economic policies as a matter of common concern (Article 99(1) EC), but the internal Community competences are rather limited. On the one hand, there is the competence of the Council to adopt a recommendation setting out the broad guidelines of the economic policies of the Member States and of the Community (Article 99(2) EC), and a multilateral surveillance mechanism, co-ordinated by the Council and supported by the Commission (Article 99(3) and (4) EC). On the other hand, the provisions on economic policy do not foresee an active Community competence, but rather consist of a number of prohibitions for the economic policies of the Member States and of the Community: prohibition on overdraft facilities or any other type of credit facilities (Article 101(1) EC), prohibition on privileged access to financial institutions (Article 102(1) EC), prohibition on bail outs (Article 103 EC) and finally the prohibition on excessive government deficits (Article 104(1) EC).

It would be difficult to imagine a case in which the objectives of such a loosely co-ordinated economic policy would make it *necessary* for the Community to enter into international agreements. The assumption of the whole Chapter on

[72] Cf. Tomuschat in Von der Groeben, Thiesing and Ehlermann (eds.), *supra*, n. 38, Art. 228, para. 9 *et seq*; Schermers and O'Keeffe (eds.), *Mixed Agreements* (Deventer, 1983).

[73] An example is, as recently confirmed by the ECJ the GATS and the TRIPs agreement, cf. *Opinion 1/94, WTO* [1994] ECR I–5267, para. 98.

[74] Cf. Smits, *The European Central Bank, Institutional Aspects* (The Hague/London/Boston, 1997), 369.

economic policy is that economic policy remains a national competence, with only a certain framework being given by the EC Treaty.[75] Even in the exceptional cases in which it would prove necessary for the Community itself to enter into international economic policy agreements, these could not go further as is possible in the internal system of Community powers. This means that such an agreement could establish only broad guidelines, but not lay down precise requirements for the economic policies of the Member States. The procedure for negotiating and concluding such agreements would have to follow the procedure foreseen in Article 300 EC, as the specific provision of Article 111 EC applies only in the field of monetary policy.[76]

Even though Member States remain, as a rule, externally competent in the field of economic policy, they have to observe essentially two restrictions. First, they are free to enter into any agreement they wish only as long as this does not prejudice the idea of the Member State's economic policies as a matter of common concern.[77] The latter restriction results from Article 99(1) EC and the general obligation of loyalty of the Member States under Article 10 EC. Secondly, they must not enter[78] into international agreements which would circumvent the internal prohibitions laid down in Articles 101–104 EC. From the logic of the doctrine of parallelism it follows that it is not only able to give the Community positive external competences where such competences exist internally, but that it also extends limitations of competences to external relations—one might call this *"negative parallelism"*. Member States must therefore not conclude international agreements which would, say, require excessive government deficits, which are prohibited by Article 104 EC.

3. External competences in monetary policy

The definition of external competences in the field of monetary policy is more complex than in that of economic policy. Three factors must be taken into consideration. First, monetary policy became, on 1 January 1999, an *exclusive competence* to be exercised at Community level; this necessarily implies that whenever this single monetary and exchange rate policy is at stake, the potential actors of the "euro area" must speak with only one voice (unless, from the

---

[75] Cf. Smits, *supra*, n. 74, p. 378.

[76] This can be drawn from the position of Art. 111 in Ch. 2 of Title VII of Part Three of the EC Treaty. In this respect, Art. 111(5) EC is purely declaratory when it also mentions "agreements as regards *economic* and monetary union". The reference to economic union may be explained by the fact that sometimes it will be a quite difficult exercise to establish whether a specific agreement falls under "economic" or "monetary union", e.g. an agreement negotiated in the context of the OECD.

[77] This is also the view of the European Council in its Luxembourg Resolution of 13 December 1997 [1998] OJ C35/1, II., para. 10: "On elements of economic policy other than monetary or exchange-rate policy, the Member States should continue to present their policies outside the Community framework while taking full account of the Community interest".

[78] A special case is agreements which have been concluded prior to the entry into force EC; they fall within the scope of Art. 307 EC; see *infra*, p. 215 *et seq*.

beginning, only one of them is allowed to speak at all). Secondly, there are, at Community level, *two actors* which could exercise these external competences, the Community itself and the ECB, both having international legal personality. Thirdly, *Article 111* EC deviates to a certain extent from the classical division of external competences in Community law.

3.1. *The doctrine of parallelism applied to horizontal conflicts*

If one were to apply the ECJ's doctrine of parallelism to monetary policy, one would need to take as a point of departure the exclusive competence in the field of monetary policy, exercised at Community level. This entails a parallel exclusive competence in external relations. There is in principle no scope for any concurrent action by the Member States in this field.

But which would be the entity entitled to act under this exclusive external competence, in view of the two supranational entities with international legal personality, the Community and the ECB? The ECJ never had to deal with such a problem as in all disputes of external relations it had to settle, the conflict was always a *vertical conflict* between the Member States and the Community, but never a *horizontal conflict* between the Community and a separate supranational entity with international legal personality under Community law.[79] Only once, such a horizontal conflict seemed to arise when the Commission concluded an agreement bearing the title "Agreement between the Commission and the United States of America regarding the application of their competition laws". Here, the Commission claimed to be entitled to conclude such an agreement on its own behalf, outside the scope of Article 300 EC, as the Commission would be internally exclusively competent in the field of competition law. This was the first and only occasion where an attempt was made to apply the doctrine of parallelism to a (seemingly) horizontal conflict. However, the Commission itself had to admit that it possessed no international legal personality and therefore could not act at the international level on its own, but only on behalf of the Community—a view which was endorsed by the ECJ in its ruling on the matter.[80]

The case of the ECB has to be distinguished from this precedent. As already stated, the ECB is, unlike the Commission, not a Community institution, but has international legal personality distinct from that of the Community by virtue of Article 107(2) EC; it can therefore act on the international level on its own behalf. There is thus a true horizontal conflict between the Community and

---

[79] On horizontal conflicts of competence between the ECB and the Community institutions, cf. *supra*, Ch. 1, p. 41 *et seq.*

[80] The ECJ was unequivocal in this respect: "It is the Community alone, having legal personality under Art. 281 EC, which has the capacity to bind itself by concluding agreements with a non-member country or an international organisation": Case C–327/91, *France* v. *Commission* [1994] ECR I–3641, para. 24. The Commission's view is reported in the opinion of Tesauro AG, para. 19.

the ECB in the field of external competence,[81] and therefore the question becomes relevant whether it is permissible to apply the doctrine of parallelism not only to vertical, but also to horizontal conflicts.

The logic behind the doctrine of parallelism is to avoid internal competences being circumvented by the conflicting exercise of external competences. As stated in the *ERTA* case, "the system of internal Community measures may not therefore be separated from that of external relations".[82] The jurisprudence of the ECJ thus implies that there should always be identity between the bearer of internal and external competences, as only this makes an efficient and coherent exercise of such competences possible. Following this logic, *the ECB is the natural bearer of external competences in the field of monetary policy*—this includes external representation and the conclusion of agreements in areas paralleling the ECB's internal competences—because:

—it is the ECB, which is internally exclusively competent to define and implement, within the framework of the ESCB, the monetary policy of the Community (Article 105(2), first indent EC); it is thus the specialised organisation which is, at Community level, responsible for the single currency;[83]

—the ECB is not dependent on the Community institutions to exercise its external competences, as it has a separate international legal personality and its own decision-making bodies;

—the conduct of external monetary policy is "inseparably linked" to the efficient exercise of the task of the decision-making bodies of the ECB to define and implement the monetary policy of the Community and to achieve the primary objective of price stability (Article 105(1) EC). A target for (external) exchange rate stability set in an international agreement could seriously prejudice the achievement of (internal) price stability; in particular, international intervention commitments could increase the amount of money in circulation and thus seriously affect the efficiency of the internal monetary policy of the ECB;[84]

---

[81] A similar horizontal conflict of competence may arise between the Community and the EIB, which also enjoys international legal personality, as stated *supra*, at p. 179 *et seq.* However, such a conflict appears to be less problematic than in the case of the ECB. The EIB's members are the Member States of the Community (see Art. 266 EC), and it is committed to the same objectives as is the Community (see Art. 267 EC; cf. *supra*, Ch. 1, p. 22 *et seq*), while the ECB has both its special members—the national central banks—and with price stability a special primary objective which has to prevail on the general objectives of the Community as listed in Art. 2 EC; on this, cf. *supra*, Ch. 1, p. 35 *et seq.*

[82] Case 22/70, *Commission v. Council (ERTA)* [1971] ECR 263, paras. 16 and 19.

[83] This is also stressed by the Commission in its working paper "External aspects of economic and monetary union", SEC (97) 803 of 23 April 1997, point 19.

[84] This is the reason the central banks of Austria and Sweden had themselves the legal authority for the exchange rate regime; cf. *Annual Report 1992 of the Committee of Governors*, 44 *et seq.*, and the *Annual Report 1994 of the EMI*, 103 *et seq.* The Bundesbank, on the other hand, originally had more difficulties in combining its aim to secure the (internal) value of the currency with the competence of the Federal Government to decide on the exchange rate regime and in fixing the parity of the Deutschmark; but in 1978, during the ERM negotiations, the Bundesbank obtained in the course of an exchange of letters what it considers a guarantee from the Federal government that it would be released from the obligations of unlimited interventions should these undermine the monetary policy of the Bundesbank. This arrangement is called an "Emminger clause", after the then President of the Bundesbank, Otmar Emminger; cf. Emminger, *D-Mark, Dollar, Währungskrisen. Erinnerungen*

—the independence of the ECB, in particular the prohibition on giving instructions to the ECB (Article 108 EC), would make it very difficult, if not legally impossible, to bind the ECB, in a detailed instruction-like manner, by an external monetary policy defined by Community institutions.

This logic is also supported by Article 111(4) EC according to which:

> the Council shall, on a proposal from the Commission and after consulting the ECB, acting by a qualified majority decide on the position of the Community at international level as regards issues of particular relevance to economic and monetary union and, acting unanimously, decide its representation *in compliance with the allocation of powers laid down in Articles 99 and 105.*[85]

There are two general conclusions to be drawn from this provision in the present context. First, the relevant question both for determining the position of the Community at international level and its representation is *the allocation of powers laid down in Articles 99 and 105 EC.*[86] This refers not only to the *vertical* division of powers between Member States and the Community, which is especially relevant in the field of economic union, but also includes an important *horizontal* aspect. The reference to Article 105 EC may only be understood as stressing the competence of the ECB against that of the Community, as Article 105 EC exclusively deals with the objectives and tasks of the ESCB. In this sense, Article 111(4) EC must be interpreted as meaning that the Council, when deciding on the position and representation of the Community at international level, will have to take into account that there is a second actor at Community level, distinct from the Community and with its own field of competence, as defined in Article 105 EC. In this field, it is the ECB, and not the Community, which is externally competent.[87]

---

eines ehemaligen Bundesbankpräsidenten (Stuttgart, 1986), 361 *et seq.* Still, in July 1993 the EMS crisis forced the Bundesbank to intervene with 60 Billion Deutschmark before it suspended interventions; cf. Deutsche Bundesbank, *Monthly Bulletin* (Frankfurt am Main, August 1993), 24 *et seq.*

[85] Emphasis added.

[86] Whether the last part of Art. 111(4) EC refers both to the decision on the position of the Community and on its representation is left open by the English, German, Italian, Portuguese, Spanish and Danish versions of the EC, but may be seen clearly in the French text of this para. by a comma: "*Sous réserve du paragraphe 1, le Conseil, sur proposition de la Commission et après consultation de la BCE, statuant à la majorité qualifiée, décide de la position qu'occupe la Communauté au niveau international en ce qui concerne des questions qui revêtent un intérêt particulier pour l'Union économique et monétaire et, statuant à l'unanimité, décide de sa représentation, (sic!) dans le respect de la répartition des compétences prévue aux articles 99 et 105*". In the Swedish and in the Greek texts, this provision is similarly worded. Only the Dutch version may be interpreted differently; however, in view of the other linguistic versions, this appears to be an improper translation.

[87] This is not taken into consideration by Smits, *supra*, n. 74, 172, who interprets "Community" in Art. 111(4) EC as including the ESCB. This view neglects both the ECB's autonomous international legal personality and the fact that Art. 105 EC lists ESCB, and not Community competences. Smits himself has to admit that his view is difficult to reconcile with the letter of Art. 6.3 of the Statute and does not find favour among learned writers (414). Therefore, we consider Art. 111(4) EC to be best understood as a supplementary provision, which parallels the competence of the ECB to decide on the external representation of the ECB under Art. 6.1 of the Statute. As indicated by Smits himself (at 414), this was also the preferred view of the smaller Member States which proposed the insertion of Art. 111(4) EC at a late stage of the negotiations.

A second general statement to be drawn from Article 111(4) EC is that the Council may only decide on a position *of the Community* at the international level, and this only as regards *issues of particular relevance to economic and monetary union*. This stresses that a position of the Community (and thus not of the ECB) will only be required whenever there is a matter of particular *political* importance at stake. In all other cases, in particular as regards the operational aspects of foreign exchange policy, it is not up to the Community to take a position, but this is a competence of the ECB, which may act at the international level in accordance with Article 6 of the Statute.

The authors of the Maastricht Treaty, although in principle loyal to the doctrine of parallelism,[88] did not rely entirely on implied external competences in the field of monetary policy. In addition, they created with Article 105(2), second and third indents, Article 111(1) and (3) EC, and Article 23 of the Statute specific provisions dealing expressly with both the vertical and the horizontal distribution of competence as regards the external aspects of monetary policy, in particular foreign exchange policy. But these provisions are far from being all-encompassing; they do not answer all potential questions on external competences. Therefore, even in respect of these provisions, the doctrine of parallelism offers a useful tool for solving such questions, to cover the *lacunae* left by the EC Treaty and the Statute, and at the same time for creating the legal preconditions for an efficient and coherent exercise of competences in the field of monetary policy.

From this it follows that there are essentially three types of external competences which need to be distinguished in the field of monetary policy:

—*explicit external competences of the Community* laid down in Article 111(1), (3) and (4) EC;
—*explicit external competences of the ECB* laid down in Article 105(2), second and third indents EC and Article 23 of the Statute;
—*implicit external competences of the ECB* which parallel the internal tasks of ESCB.

3.2. *Explicit external competences of the Community under Article 111(1), (3) and (4) EC*

Article 111(1), (3) and (4) EC is a prime example of an explicit external competence in the Treaty.[89] However, its wording was very controversial during the negotiations of the Maastricht Treaty[90] which have led in the end to a quite

---

[88] See Declaration No 10 attached to the EC Treaty stating that the insertion of new provisions such as Art. 111(5) EC does "not affect the principles resulting from the judgement handed down by the Court of Justice in the AETR case". This is a reference to the *ERTA* case and thus to the doctrine of parallelism.

[89] See also Smits, *supra*, n. 74, 369.

[90] See Louis in *Commentaire Mégret, Le Droit de la CEE* (Brussels, 1998), vi, 82 *et seq.*; Schönfelder and Thiel, *Ein Markt Eine Währung. Die Verhandlungen zur Europäischen Wirtschafts- und Währungsunion* (Baden Baden, 1994), 72, 79, 84, 88 *et seq.*, 100, 101, 106, 109, 123 *et seq.*, 128 *et seq.*, 142, 144, 149; Dehousse and Ghemar, *supra*, n. 62, 154.

complicated provision. It may very well be read differently, depending on the respective backgrounds of its readers. For transparency reasons this has to be regretted, but it should encourage legal doctrine to develop a coherent interpretation of Article 111 EC. This is exactly the objective of the following paragraphs.

3.2.1. Article 111(3) EC as explicit external competence of the Community

The main paragraph enabling the Community to conclude agreements in the field of monetary policy is Article 111(3) EC,[91] which reads as follows:

> By way of derogation from Article 300, *where agreements concerning monetary or foreign exchange regime matters need to be negotiated by the Community with one or more States or international organisations*, the Council, acting by a qualified majority on a recommendation from the Commission and after consulting the ECB, shall decide the arrangements for the negotiation and for the conclusion of such agreements. These agreements shall ensure that the Community expresses a single position. The Commission shall be fully associated with the negotiations.
>
> Agreements concluded in accordance with this paragraph shall be binding on the institutions of the Community, on the ECB and on the Member States.[92]

At first glance, one might want to question whether this provision really refers to an external competence. It could very well be said that, first of all, it deals only with the procedure93 for entering into public international law agreements. However, if one compares the wording of Article 111(3) EC to that of Article 300(1) EC on the one hand, and to Treaty provisions which contain, in the view of the ECJ, explicit external competences, on the other hand, the true meaning of Article 111(3) EC becomes apparent:

—Article 300(1) EC says expressly that the procedure foreseen in Article 300 EC applies where "this Treaty provides for the conclusion of agreements between the Community and one or more States or international organisations". Therefore, it comes into play only when a substantive (explicit or implied) external competence to conclude such agreements may be found elsewhere in the EC Treaty. Article 300(1) EC is thus just a procedural provision.[94]

—In contrast to this, the wording of Article 133(3) EC—which in the words of the ECJ[95] and according to the unequivocal opinion of legal doctrine[96] contains an explicit external competence in the field of commercial policy—is almost identical to that of Article 111(3) EC:

---

[91] The Commission also takes Art. 111(3) EC as point of departure for a treaty-making power of the Community; cf. *supra*, n. 83, point 30.

[92] Emphasis added.

[93] This is the view of Smits, *supra*, n. 74, 402: "Paragraph 3 being a procedural provision . . .".

[94] Cf. Tomuschat in Von der Groeben, Thiesing and Ehlermann (eds.), *supra*, n. 38, Art. 228, para. 5; Brückner and Louis, *supra*, n. 38, 21.

[95] *Opinion 1/75, Local Cost Standard* [1975] ECR 1355.

[96] See only Brückner and Louis, *Commentaire Mégret, Le Droit de la CEE* (Brussels 1980), xii, 94, 104 *et seq.*; Schweitzer and Hummer, *supra*, n. 38, 198; Streinz, *Europarecht* (3rd edn., Heidelberg 1996), 198.

Where agreements with one or more States or international organisations need to be negotiated, the Commission shall make recommendations to the Council which shall authorise the Commission to open the necessary negotiations.[97]

The conclusion of such agreements is thus not dependent on a substantive external competence elsewhere in the EC Treaty, but may be justified simply by the *need* to enter into such an agreement.[98]

From this comparison it follows that Article 111(3) EC gives the Community an explicit external competence to enter into public international law agreements on monetary and foreign exchange regime matters whenever there is a need for such agreements to be concluded by the Community.[99] Authors[100] which suggest that only Article 111(1) EC—which deals with the special case of a formal agreement on a foreign exchange system for the euro—would contain an explicit external competence, while Article 111(3) simply deals with procedural aspects, will have to explain, first, why Article 111(1) EC provides for some specific elements of procedure—for example, the possibility of a recommendation from the ECB and the requirement to consult the European Parliament—if Article 111(3) is "the procedural paragraph"; secondly, why does the third paragraph not follow immediately after the first paragraph if it only deals with its procedural aspects; and, thirdly, why do both Article 111(1) and (3) EC start with the words "By way of derogation from Article 300", if only the latter paragraph deals with the procedure? All these questions may easily be answered based on the understanding that Article 111(3) EC includes not only procedural aspects, but also the Community's treaty-making power for monetary and foreign exchange regime matters.[101]

3.2.2. The limited scope of Article 111(3) EC

The scope of the external competence given to the Community under Article 111(3) EC is limited as regards the nature of this competence, its substantive extent and the potential contracting partners with which agreements could be entered into under this provision.

---

[97] Emphasis added.

[98] One should admit that to call such a competence an explicit competence is slightly misleading: even though it explicitly mentions the possibility of concluding agreements, the wording is less a real legal basis for an external competence, but more a presumption that such a competence exists. This shows that, in the EC Treaty, even explicit external competences are never as explicit as one might expect.

[99] This is also the Commission's view; cf. *supra*, n. 83, point 30.

[100] See *supra*, n. 93.

[101] This view is followed by Cafaro, "I primi accordi della Comunità in materia di politica monetaria e di cambio" [1999] *Il Diritto dell'Unione Europea* 243 (251 and n. 22); and by Weinrichter, "The World Monetary System and External Relations of the EMU—Fasten your Safety Belts!" [2000] *EIoP* No. 10, 14.

3.2.2.1. Only a concurrent external competence

The wording of Article 111(3) EC requires the Community always to justify *a need* for the conclusion by it of agreements under this provision. To justify such a need is an important legal exercise which serves to take into account:

—first of all, the residual competence of the *Member States* which, under Article 111(5) EC, still may negotiate and conclude international agreements "as regards economic and *monetary* union", if these do not prejudice the competence of the Community.[102]

—secondly, the external competence of the *ECB* which is internally exclusively competent to define and implement, within the framework of the ESCB, the monetary policy of the Community according to Article 105(2), first indent, EC; the ECB is thus by its very nature the most appropriate entity to represent externally the monetary policy which it is required to lay down independently of the Member States and the Community institutions.

Therefore, the external competence given to the Community by Article 111(3) EC is, unlike the competence under Article 133 EC, not an exclusive external competence, but only a concurrent external competence, paralleled by the remaining external competence of the Member States and, most important, by the competence of the ECB. The Community will thus have to fulfil a *double test* before it is legally permitted to enter into agreements under Article 111(3) EC:

First test: Community level instead of national level   In respect of the Member States' competence, the Community will have to satisfy the subsidiarity test[103] of Article 5(2) EC: whenever there is a concurrent competence,[104] the Community may act only "if and in so far as the objectives of the proposed action cannot be sufficiently achieved by the Member States and can therefore, by reason of the scale or effects of the proposed action, be better achieved by the Community". It is suggested that it will not be too difficult to prove, in the field of monetary policy, a need for external action at Community, and not at national level, and this for two reasons: first, the euro is the single currency of all participating Member States as from 1 January 1999, a fact that cannot be ignored in external monetary and foreign exchange relations and thus is, by its very nature, a strong argument for action only at Community level, if at all. Secondly, the ECB will be the only central bank in the Community which has

---

[102] Obviously, one has to understand here the term "monetary" in the wide sense of the heading of Ch. 2 of Title VI of Part Three of the EC Treaty, i.e. also including prudential supervision and exchange rate policy. As the monetary competences *stricto sensu* listed in Art. 105(2) EC belongs exclusively to the ECB (internally and, by parallelism, externally), there is room here for residual competences of the Member States. On residual competences of the Member States cf. *infra*, p. 213 *et seq*.

[103] On subsidiarity see Lenaerts and Van Ypersele, "Le principe de subsidiarité et son contexte: étude de l'art. 3 B du Traité CE" [1994] *CDE* 3; Zilioli, "L'applicazione del principio di sussidiarietà nel diritto comunitario dell'ambiente" [1995] *Rivista Giuridica dell'Ambiente* 533.

[104] It should be clarified, once more that the subsidiarity test, and the concurrent competence concern only the "residual competences" of the Member States, while in the field of the exclusive competence of the ECB in the monetary field (Art. 105(2) EC) subsidiarity cannot come into play.

the instruments at its disposal to conduct an external monetary policy for the "euro area" as a whole, in particular to conduct foreign exchange operations with respect to the euro. However, it cannot be denied that there is still a (albeit very limited) field of competence for the Member States which could become activated in special cases. Member States retain some competences in the field of foreign exchange working balances, banking supervision, coins, for agreements which predate the entry into force of the Maastricht Treaty and in the case of special external monetary regimes expressly mentioned in the Protocols or Declarations attached to the EC Treaty.[105]

Second test: Community instead of ECB   In respect of the ECB's competence, the Community will have to show a need that not the ECB—as the specialised organisation responsible for the monetary policy of the Community—but the Community itself has to conclude a public international law agreement.[106] This second limb of the test results not only from the separation of internal competence in monetary policy, but also from the wording of Article 111(3) EC: in contrast to Article 133(3) EC, where the Community must prove only a need for negotiating an agreement, Article 111(3) EC requires that such agreements "need to be negotiated *by the Community*"—and not by the ECB, as one might want to add. Such a need could be demonstrated only when it is required to make the agreement at the same time binding on the Community institutions, the ECB, and the Member States. Only agreements concluded by the Community itself will have this effect by virtue of Article 111(3), second subparagraph, EC, while agreements concluded by the ECB would be directly binding only on the ECB.[107] The prime example of an agreement which would involve obligations of the Community institutions, the ECB and the Member States would be that of a formal agreement on an exchange rate system for the euro in relation to non-Community currencies; this is explicitly stated in Article 111(1) EC, which itself refers to Article 111(3) EC and thus confirms that such agreements always need to be concluded by the Community.

3.2.2.2. *Limitation to "agreements concerning monetary or foreign exchange regime matters"*

The scope of Article 111(3) EC is further limited in substance. It is far from covering all external aspects of monetary policy, as laid down in Article 105 *et seq.* EC, to the contrary; the scope of this external competence is restricted to "*agreements concerning monetary or foreign exchange regime matters*".

At first glance, the meaning of this wording is, in the English version of Article 111(3) EC, open to two different interpretations.[108]

---

[105] The residual competence of the Member States is dealt with *infra*, at p. 213 *et seq.*
[106] One might want to call this "horizontal subsidiarity".
[107] On the effect of ECB agreements see *infra*, p 211 *et seq.*
[108] According to the Commission's working paper, *supra*, n. 83, this provision's "scope is not entirely clear".

—A broad definition would extend the Community's competence to (i) agreements concerning *monetary matters*, and (ii) agreements concerning *foreign exchange regime matters*.

—A more restrictive interpretation would include only (ii) agreements concerning *monetary **regime** matters*, and (ii) agreements concerning *foreign exchange **regime** matters*.

The first definition suggests an overall external competence of the Community in all matters where there is an internal competence in monetary matters under Chapter 2 of Title VII of Part Three of the EC Treaty. It would be compatible with the German,[109] the Portuguese,[110] the Finnish,[111] the Greek, the Irish[112] and the Swedish[113] texts of Article 111(3) EC which cover in a more or less broad sense "agreements related to monetary questions or to foreign exchange matters".

However, in the context of such a broad interpretation it appears strange that Article 111(3) EC bothers also to mention "foreign exchange regime matters", as they would already fall under the encompassing term "monetary matters". The reference to foreign exchange regime matters thus appears to be superfluous. In addition, other linguistic versions of Article 111(3) EC clearly support a more restrictive interpretation. According to the French,[114] Italian[115] and Dutch[116] versions, and even more clearly in the Spanish[117] and Danish[118] texts of Article 111(3) EC, the Community's competence extends to "agreements concerning monetary regimes or foreign exchange regimes".

The point of departure of all Community law interpretation must be the equal validity of all 12 authentic linguistic versions of the EC Treaty. In cases in which these diverge, the ECJ has always favoured an interpretation which is coherent with the spirit and the context of the Treaty provision in question.[119] In the present case, a broad interpretation of Article 111(3) EC would mean that the Community was externally competent whenever monetary matters are involved. However, this would contrast with the doctrine of the ECJ that external competences always mirror internal competences. It would prejudice the exclusive internal competence of the ECB under Article 105(2), first indent, EC and endanger the independence of the ECB which is entrenched in Article 108 EC.

[109] *"Vereinbarungen im Zusammenhang mit Währungsfragen oder Devisenregelungen"*.
[110] *"Acordos relativos a questões monetárias ou ao regime cambial"*.
[111] *"Raha- ja valuuttaoloja koskevista sopimuksista"*.
[112] *"Le cúrsaí airgeadaíochta nó cursaí córas malairte eachtraí"*.
[113] *"Avtal angående monetära frågor eller växelkursfrågor"*.
[114] *"Accords sur des questions se rapportant au régime monétaire ou de change"*.
[115] *"Accordi in materia di regime monetario o valutario"*.
[116] *"Moet voeren over aangelegenheden betreffende het monetaire of wisselkoersregime"*.
[117] *"Acuerdos en materia de régimen monetario o de régimen cambiario"*.
[118] *"Aftaler om monetære sprøgsmál eller sprøgsmál verdrørende valutakursordninger"*.
[119] Cf. Case C–327/91, *France v. Commission* [1994] ECR I–3641, para. 35; Case C–84/95, *Bosphorus Hava Yollari Turizm ve Ticaret AS v. Minister for Transport, Energy and Communication* [1996] ECR I–3953, para. 16.

Article 111(3) EC represents an exception both to the principle of parallel competences and to the independence of the ECB. It endows the Community with the competence to enter, in the external relations of monetary policy, into agreements which are binding on the ECB (Article 111(3), second subparagraph, EC). To respect the field of competence of the ECB, the spirit of the EC Treaty requires these exceptions to be interpreted narrowly. Only where there is, also as regards substance, *a need to conclude agreements which require to be binding on the Community institutions, the ECB and the Member States*, the Community is justified in making use of its competence in Article 111(3) EC. In addition, the use of the word "regime" indicates that such agreements will have to represent a quite formalised way of organising external aspects of monetary policy. It also implies that only the regime itself, i.e. the general principles, but not the operating procedures under such a regime, would be the subject of an agreement to be concluded by the Community.

Therefore, Article 111(3) EC must be read as providing the Community with an external competence only in monetary regime matters and foreign exchange regime matters[120]:

—*Monetary regime matters* concern, in the field of external relations, situations in which the monetary regime of the euro is, with the agreement of the Community, extended to a third country, i.e. if a third country wants to use the euro as its currency or as parallel legal tender on its territory, and is allowed to do so by the Community, without any intervention obligations on behalf of the Community or the ECB.

—*Foreign exchange regime matters* cover formal public international law agreements establishing an exchange rate system—this is specifically dealt with in Article 111(1) EC—but also less formal agreements with third countries that seek to influence the exchange rate of the euro but do not amount to a parity grid with intervention obligations of the ECB to upheld the currency levels agreed to;[121] they may involve a (limited) obligation, on the part of the Community and the ECB, to engage in foreign exchange operations or to conduct multilateral surveillance.[122]

---

[120] In this sense cf. also the Commission in its working paper, *supra*, n. 83, point 30.

[121] Such agreements are mentioned by Smits, *supra*, n. 74, 387, and by Louis, *Commentaire Mégret, Le Droit de la CEE* (2ⁿᵈ edn., Brussels, 1998), vi, 83 as falling under Art. 111(2) EC; however, it is difficult to imagine how such agreements could become the subject of general orientations of the Council only; in addition, Smits' position is necessary only if one interprets Art. 111(3) EC as a purely procedural provision, what is not the position of the authors of this book, as shown above.

[122] Such agreements could include obligations of surveillance and co-operation on the foreign exchange regime matters. It should be noted that, under public international law, agreements do not need to be designated as "agreements", but could be contained in protocols, covenants, declarations, exchanges of notes, agreed minutes, memoranda of understanding etc.; it suffices that they were entered into by international legal persons with the intention to produce certain legal effects under public international law; cf. Brownlie, *supra*, n. 6, 605.

3.2.2.3. Limitation to agreements with third countries
A final limitation of the scope of Article 111(3) EC concerns the potential contracting partners with whom the Community could enter into agreements under this provision. Article 111(3), first sentence, EC speaks of agreements "with one or more States or international organisations". The wording and the context imply that this relates only to third countries, i.e. countries outside the European Community, because:

—throughout the EC Treaty, Member States are never referred to as "states", but always as Member States; "states" thus necessarily means "third countries", as it is the case in Articles 133(3) and 300(1) EC, for example;
—Article 111(1) EC, being the prime example of an agreement to be concluded in accordance with Article 111(3) EC, mentions only agreements "in relation to non-Community currencies";
—moreover, it would be difficult to explain why Member States with a derogation are explicitly excluded from the binding effect of such agreements by virtue of Article 122(4) EC if they were envisaged as partners to such agreements.

Therefore, the Community may conclude agreements only with third countries under Article 111(3) EC, but not with those Member States which for the moment do not participate in the single currency.[123]

3.2.3. Procedure for negotiating and concluding Community agreements
under Article 111(3) EC

The arrangements for negotiating and concluding Community agreements under Article 111(3) EC are laid down in a three-step-procedure: recommendation of the Commission; consultation of the ECB; decision of the Council, acting by a qualified majority. The final decision is thus in the hands of the Council which has the task of ensuring, by the arrangements decided, that the Community expresses a single position. The Council has essentially four alternatives in its decision:

—First, *the Council itself* could take over both the negotiation and the conclusion of international agreements. In practice, this could be done by the Presidency of the Council (cf. Article 203(2) EC), supported by the General Secretariat of the Council (cf. Article 207(2) EC). In this context, it is important to note that Article 207(2) EC, as amended and renumbered by the Amsterdam Treaty, provides that the Secretary General of the Council is at the same time the High Representative of the Common Foreign and Security

---

[123] See also Smits, *supra*, n. 74, 377. This does not exclude the possibility of the Community concluding agreements with participating Member States where these do not act on their own behalf, but as representative of its territorial collectivities which are not included in the field of territorial application of the EC Treaty and therefore, in law, have a status similar to that of third states; for the case of Mayotte and St. Pierre et Miquelon cf. *infra*, p. 224 *et seq.*

Policy. The Secretary General therefore will already be familiar with representing the Community in international fora.

—Secondly, the Council could entrust the *Commission* with the negotiations, and theoretically even with both the negotiations and the conclusion of the agreement on behalf of the Community. As far as negotiations are concerned, this would resemble the normal procedure under Article 300 EC. However, it should be noted that the authors of the EC Treaty did not consider negotiations (and certainly not conclusion) by the Commission as the regular case in the field of external monetary policy; this is shown by the introductory words of Article 111(1) and (3) EC which show the clear intention of the authors of the Treaty to derogate from the normal procedure under Article 300 EC; this is further confirmed by Article 111(3), first paragraph, third sentence EC: here, only the full association of the Commission with the negotiations is legally required—a superfluous requirement if the Commission normally were in charge of the negotiations.

—Thirdly, the negotiations, and also the conclusion, of such agreements could be entrusted to the *ECB*.[124] This is excluded neither by the independence nor by the separate international legal personality of the ECB. However, as demonstrated in chapter 1 of this book, given the difference in objectives between the Communities and the ECB,[125] the latter can act as Community agent only in very technical activities, the so-called "fiscal agent functions". Therefore, the Council may delegate to the ECB the power to negotiate and conclude agreements only in limited cases, for instance to implement technically a general political agreement concluded by the Council. It can thus be concluded that it will be the exception rather than the rule that the ECB, as independent specialised organisation of Community law,[126] will ever be entrusted with the negotiations and the conclusion of such agreements on behalf of the Community.

—Finally, one could also think of delegating the task to represent the Community to *one of the Member States*. However, this would be a very exceptional situation which could be justified only where there are specific monetary links between a Member State and a third country or an international organisation. The Member State in question would be in the difficult, if not impossible, situation of representing the Community and thus, in the case of a conflict between its individual national interests and the objectives of the Community, be obliged to deviate from the former for the benefit

---

[124] This possibility is mentioned by Stadler, *Der rechtliche Handlungsspielraum des Europäischen Systems der Zentralbanken* (Baden Baden, 1996), 174; see also Usher, *The Law of Money and Financial Services in the European Community* (Oxford, 1994), 190.

[125] After our position in Zilioli and Selmayr, "The External Relations of the Euro Area: Legal Aspects" (1999) *CML Rev.* 273 (302), we have come to believe that the position of the EIB is different, as it is one of the core functions of the EIB to act in the name and on behalf of the Community; cf. *supra*, Ch. 1, p. 25 *et seq.*

[126] Cf. *supra*, Ch. 1, p. 29 *et seq.*

of the latter. Exactly to avoid such conflicts, there are, at the Community level supranational institutions like the Commission or supranational specialised organisations like the ECB which are committed solely to the objectives laid down in the EC Treaty.[127]

3.2.4. Effects of Community agreements under Article 111(3) EC

By virtue of Article 111(3), second subparagraph, EC, agreements concluded by the Community on monetary regime matters or foreign exchange regime matters become binding on the Community institutions, the ECB and the participating Member States, and are thus considered by the ECJ as "an integral part of Community law".[128] Even though the agreements may involve operations conducted by the ECB or the national central banks, such agreements are to be qualified as Community agreements to which the Community alone is a party under public international law. From this follows that whenever the ECB or a national central bank does not fulfil the obligations arising from the agreement, it is the Community—and not the ECB or a Member State which may have concluded the agreement on behalf of the Community—which is liable for such default under public international law.

3.2.5. The first special case: formal agreements on an exchange rate system for the euro under Article 111(1) and (3) EC

The first paragraph of Article 111 singles out one special type of agreement on foreign exchange regime matters, namely formal agreements on an exchange rate system for the euro. The reason for the predominant position attributed to this provision seems to be history: traditionally, exchange-rate agreements have been for governments the strongest means of determining their exchange rate policy as regards competing nations, and, at the same time, influencing their national economic and monetary policies, including the politics of their respective central bank. In a traditional vision, therefore, this could be defined as the "king provision" of exchange rate policy. It is in line with this political importance of exchange-rate agreements that decision-making under Article 111(1) EC requires unanimity in the Council.

The unanimity requirement, however, has at the same time limited considerably the practical importance of Article 111(1) EC. This is even more the case as in recent decades, the idea of a revival of the historic "Bretton Woods Agreement" has lost almost all its supporters. Hence, the conclusion of a "Bretton Wood No 2" agreement seems to be very unlikely today.[129] This

---

[127] Despite these counter-arguments, the Council used the possibility of delegating both the negotiations and the conclusion to a Member State in the case of agreements with the Principality of Monaco (delegation to France), and with San Marino and the Vatican City (delegation to Italy); on this, cf. *infra*, p. 218 *et seq*. The decisions on the CFA Franc and the Comorian Franc and on Cape Verde are a different case, as shown *infra*, p. 225 *et seq* and p. 227 *et seq*.

[128] Case 181/73, *Haegeman* v. *Belgium* [1974] ECR 449, para. 1.

[129] On the legal and practical limitations for the use of Art. 111(1) EC, cf. *infra*, p. 203 *et seq*.

confirms that, in spite of its prominent place within the context of Article 111 EC, its first paragraph will play only a minor role in practice.[130]

When Article 111(1) EC provides for a special procedure for the conclusion of formal agreements establishing exchange rate systems for the euro in relation to non-Community currencies, this does not constitute a new type of agreement— this is pointed out clearly in Declaration No 8 on Article 111 EC,[131] attached to the Maastricht Treaty—but is just a special type of agreement on foreign exchange regime matters as provided for in the general provision of Article 111(3) EC. It provides for a specialised procedure which, while being centralised in the hands of the Community institutions, in particular of the Council, also takes into account the interest of the ECB in maintaining, as its primary objective, price stability. It is therefore based on the assumption that the Community institutions and the ECB endeavour to reach "a consensus"[132] consistent with the objective of price stability before the Community enters into a formal exchange rate agreement which would be binding also on the ECB under Article 111(3), second subparagraph, EC.

The competence given to the Community under Article 111(1) EC includes the competence to adopt, adjust and abandon the central rates of the euro within such an exchange rate system. Procedurally, the Council may take these decision by qualified majority, but again in an endeavour to reach a consensus with the ECB consistent with the objective of price stability.

3.2.6. The second special case: definition of the position of the Community as regards issues of particular relevance to economic and monetary union under Article 111(4) EC

Very often, international co-operation in economic and monetary matters will not require the conclusion of an international agreement. In these cases, it may suffice that the Community defines a position for a certain course of action in a specific issue. Article 111(4) EC gives a competence to do exactly this to the Community "as regards issues of particular relevance to economic and monetary union". An example of a case in which such a stance would be required is negotiations with Central and Eastern European countries on membership of the European Union if the question is raised during such negotiations whether

---

[130] Recently, some Member States seem to have become more inclined to go back to the "old days of Bretton Woods" or at least to establish a system of transatlantic "target zones" for exchange rates. During the Nice intergovernmental conference, this new tendency became evident when France initiated, via the Economic and Financial Committee, a proposal to shift Art. 111(1) EC from unanimity to majority voting. This attempt—which would have considerably facilitated recurrence to this provisions—failed because of the joint opposition of Germany, the United Kingdom, the Netherlands, Belgium, Greece, Ireland, Luxembourg, Finland, as well as of the ECB and the Commission; cf. *European Voice*, No. 43 of 23 November 2000, 1.

[131] "The Conference emphasises that use of the term 'formal agreement' in Art. 111(1) is not intended to create a new category of international agreement within the meaning of Community law".

[132] This is more than a mere consultation, but less than a requirement of approval, since lack of opposition suffices; see also Dehousse and Ghemar, *supra*, n. 62, 156.

and when such countries would be permitted to join the single currency.[133] Another example is a debate in the framework of the IMF on the benefits of monetary unions. In such cases, Article 111(4) EC provides for the following procedural steps: proposal from the Commission, consultation of the ECB, decision by the Council on the position of the Community by qualified majority. However, such a decision of the Council would have to take into account, as already stated, the distribution of competences under Article 99—i.e. the competences of the Member States as regards economic policy—and Article 105 EC—i.e. the competences reserved to the ECB which, according to Article 6.1 of the Statute, may participate in international monetary co-operation in all fields involving the tasks entrusted to the ESCB.

3.3. *Explicit external competences of the ECB under Article 105(2), second and third indents EC in conjunction with Article 23 of the Statute*

In the field of monetary policy, the EC Treaty and the Statute assign explicit external competences not only to the Community, but also to the ECB itself. This is nothing extraordinary in view of the exclusive competence of the ECB to define and implement the monetary policy of the Community. Explicit external competences of the ECB are to be found in Article 105(2) EC and in Article 23 of the Statute.

According to Article 105(2), second and third indents EC, the ESCB, and thus the ECB, has the task:

— to conduct foreign exchange operations consistent with the provisions of Article 111;
— to hold and manage the official foreign reserves of the Member States;

What does the competence to conduct foreign exchange operations and to hold and manage the official foreign reserves of the Member States mean? There are essentially two possible interpretations:

— First, it could relate only to private law transactions concerning foreign exchange assets which become necessary in the framework of an exchange rate agreement entered into by or with authorisation of the Council under Article 111(1) and (3) EC. The competence conferred by Article 105(2), second and third indents, EC would thus be *a mere implementing power* which could hardly be called a true external competence of the ECB.
— Secondly, it could relate to all kinds of operations concerning foreign exchange, including private law transactions meant to implement exchange rate agreements entered into by the Community (*implementing power*), but also other operations and transactions entered into autonomously by the

---

[133] Of course, Community representatives could not answer this question except in a political manner. Legally, the date of participation in the single currency depends on the fulfilment of the convergence criteria listed in Art. 121(1) EC, which need to be confirmed by the Council under Art. 122(2) EC; cf. *supra*, Ch. 4, p. 143 *et seq.*

ECB, both under private law agreements with private financial institutions and under public international law agreements—concluded by the ECB to fulfil its tasks under the EC Treaty and the Statute[134]—with central banks in third countries, third countries themselves or international organisations. This second possibility may be called *autonomous conduct of foreign exchange operations.*

The first interpretation would be compatible only with an understanding of the role of a central bank as an institution which is subordinate to the political institutions, as was the case with a number of central banks in the European Union in the past and is still the case in some European countries today.[135] However, the position of the ECB is fundamentally different. As already shown, it is not a Community institution and subject to instructions neither from the Community institutions or bodies nor from the Member States. The ECB has its own legal personality, both internally and internationally, its own tasks and its own decision-making bodies. Already this legal position of the ECB within the institutional framework created by the EC Treaty indicates that the second interpretation is the correct one.

More importantly, the second interpretation is supported by Article 23 of the Statute, this means by primary Community law itself.[136] Article 23 of the Statute lists the external operations which the ECB—and also the national central banks, if authorised to do so by the ECB[137]—may conduct. They include:

—the establishment of relations with central banks and financial institutions in other countries and, where appropriate, with international organisations;
—acquisition and sale (spot and forward) of all types of foreign exchange assets and precious metals;
—the holding and management of such assets;

---

[134] Even though such agreements may often involve operations which could also be undertaken by private banks, the very fact that the ECB may conclude such agreements only with the purpose of fulfilling its tasks under the EC Treaty and the Statute attributes a public nature to them. The consequence of this is that the ECB will, unlike private banks, always need to justify why and how it undertakes such operations, in particular in the light of its primary objective, which is price stability. Sometimes this might oblige the ECB to enter into operations which clearly involve an economic loss, something a commercial bank would never do (interventions to stabilise the exchange rate); sometimes on the contrary this might prevent the ECB from becoming involved in a somewhat risky operation in the financial markets although such an operation would be part of the daily business of many private banks. Additionally, the ECB could become a member, in the future, of an international organisation similar to the IMF: clearly here operations will be entered into on the basis of a public international law agreement.

[135] An example is Norges Bank, the central bank of Norway which, since the new Central Bank Act 1985, has been subject to the instructions of the government; cf. Smith, "On Central Bank Independence" in A. Weber (ed.), *Währung und Wirtschaft. Das Geld im Recht. Festschrift für Udo J. Hahn* (Baden Baden, 1997), 93.

[136] Cf. Art. 311 EC.

[137] This follows again from Art. 9.2 of the Statute according to which it is the ECB which is responsible for ensuring that, and by whom, the tasks of the ESCB under, *inter alia*, Art. 105(2) EC are implemented.

—the conducting of all types of banking transactions in relation to third counties and international organisations, including lending and borrowing operations.

This impressive list goes far beyond pure implementing powers and encompasses the whole range of possible foreign exchange operations, both implementing and autonomous ones, both transactions under private law agreements and operations in the context of public international law agreements concluded by the ECB to fulfil its tasks under the EC Treaty and the Statute. The ECB also has the means at its disposal to conduct such operations autonomously as, since 1 January 1999, the foreign exchange reserves of the Member States have been held and managed exclusively by the ESCB in accordance with guidelines, instructions and approvals of the ECB (Articles 105(2), third indent, EC, and 30, 31 of the Statute), with the sole exception of the Member States' foreign exchange working balances (Article 105(3) EC). Therefore, Article 105(2), second and third indents EC in conjunction with Article 23 of the Statute, confer a considerable external competence on the ECB in the field of foreign exchange operations.[138]

However, Article 105(2), second indent, EC provides that these foreign exchange operations shall be consistent with Article 111 EC. This implies that the extent of the ECB's external competence is dynamic and may vary in the following four situations which Article 111 EC would permit:

—*Situation 1:* if the Community entered into a *formal agreement on an exchange rate system* under Article 111(1) and (3) EC ("Bretton Woods No 2"), there would be little scope for an autonomous exchange rate policy of the ECB within the context of such an agreement. The ECB would have to implement the intervention obligations stemming from such an agreement; this would amount to not being responsible for the "if" of such interventions, but still to be able to decide about the modalities ("how") of such interventions. Only in case of an agreement which fails to take into account that the primary objective of both the ECB and the exchange rate policy of the Community is (internal) price stability (Articles 4(2) and 105(1) EC) might the ECB conduct an autonomous exchange rate policy to compensate for this failure.

—*Situation 2:* the case of an *agreement concerning monetary or foreign exchange regime matters* under Article 111(3) EC would have similar consequences, but its impact would necessarily be more limited, as such agreements would not lead to intervention obligations to maintain a specific parity grid. There would be thus more room for manœuvre for the ECB's own policy decisions.

---

[138] This view is shared by Smits, supra n. 74, 377 *et seq.*, where he refers to the ECB's "full competences for the external aspect of the Community's monetary affairs". However, in his view, the ECB's "freedom of manœuvre" could be influenced only by the general orientations of the Council in the absence of a formal agreement under Art. 111(1) EC. Our view is that there is also the possibility of agreements under Art. 111(3) EC.

—*Situation 3:* in the absence of an exchange rate system, the Council could decide to formulate *general orientations for exchange rate policy* in relation to non-Community currencies under Article 111(2) EC.[139] However, as the designation "general orientations" already indicates, these would as such not be binding on the ECB[140]; this comes from the fact that the ECB is independent and may not take any instructions from Community institutions (Article 108 EC) and that a clause similar to Article 111(3), second subparagraph, EC, which deviates from that principle, is missing in Article 111(2) EC. Moreover, Article 111(2), second sentence, EC states that these general orientations shall be without prejudice to the primary objective of the ESCB to maintain price stability. This means that the ECB is still free to conduct autonomously its foreign exchange policy if this is necessary to maintain price stability or to secure the efficiency of the ECB's internal monetary policy.

—*Situation 4:* the full extent of the ECB's external competences comes into play when there are *no specific foreign exchange policy decisions of the Community* under Article 111 EC. In this case, it is the ECB alone which is competent to conduct foreign exchange operations, including entering into public international law agreements with central banks in third countries, with third countries or with international organisations.[141]

During its Luxembourg summit on 12 and 13 December 1997, the European Council adopted a Resolution[142] which concerns, in its part II, the implementation of the Treaty provisions on the exchange-rate policy, external position and

---

[139] A practical example which would give rise to the adoption of such orientations by the Council could be non-binding political agreements like the *Plaza* and *Louvre* accords. In the *Plaza* accord, the Ministers of Finance and Central Bank Governors of the G 5—France, Germany, Japan, the United Kingdom and the United States—meeting on 22 September 1985 in the Plaza Hotel in New York City, stated quite specific policy intentions on multilateral surveillance, recorded their view that "exchange rates should better reflect fundamental economic conditions than has been the case", and considered desirable "some further orderly appreciation of the main non-dollar currencies against the dollar". Cf. Deutsche Bundesbank, *Auszüge aus Presseartikeln No 62* (Frankfurt am Main, 23 September 1985). In the *Louvre* accord, the Ministers of Finance and Central Bank Governors of Canada, France, Germany, Japan, the United Kingdom and the United States referred on 22 February 1987 at a meeting in the Louvre in Paris again to "multilateral surveillance" in their statement, and each participant undertook specific policy undertakings. They agreed that substantial shifts in the exchange rates were no longer warranted and that they would co-operate to keep exchange rates at the levels which then were current; cf. Deutsche Bundesbank, *Auszüge aus Presseartikeln No 15* (Frankfurt am Main, 23 February 1987). Both accords were not meant to produce legally binding effects and therefore do not fulfil the criteria of an agreement on foreign exchange regime matters under Art. 111(3) EC. See Smits, *supra*, n. 74, 380 *et seq.*; Louis, in *Commentaire Mégret, Le Droit de la CEE* (2nd edn., Brussels, 1998), vi, 83.

[140] It could be argued however that they would specify secondary objectives, which the ECB would have to achieve without prejudice to the primary objective of price stability (Art.105(1) EC).

[141] According to Tomuschat in Von der Groeben, Thiesing and Ehlermann (eds.), *supra*, n. 38, Art. 228, para. 41, the limitation of Art. 111(1) EC to formal agreements indicates that less formal agreements between central banks, as have been used traditionally in the context of intervention policy, continue to be legally allowed.

[142] *Supra*, n. 77.

representation of the Community according to Article 111 EC. There, the European Council states that:

—"In general, exchange rates should be seen as the outcome of all other economic policies"; this seems to be a clear indication that there is no intention at the moment to create a "Bretton Woods No 2" under Article 111(1) and (3) EC or even an agreement concerning foreign exchange regime matters under Article 111 (3) EC;

—General orientations may be adopted by the Council only "in exceptional circumstances, for example in the case of a clear misalignment". Even in this case, "such general orientations should always respect the independence of the ECB and be consistent with the primary objective of the ESCB to maintain price stability".

The European Council Resolution thus confirms that, as a rule, it will fall to the competence of the ECB to conduct foreign exchange operations autonomously. Only under exceptional circumstances will the Council of Ministers adopt general orientations which, however, must not prejudice the complete autonomy of the ECB to pursue its primary objective of price stability. A "Bretton Woods No 2", in the framework of which the ECB could become a mere implementing organisation, seems to be practically excluded at the moment, in view of the reality of word economy.[143]

On 22 September 2000, the first intervention of the ECB on the exchange markets confirmed the broad scope of the ECB's external powers under Article 105(2), second and third indents, EC, and Article 23 of the Statute.[144] The purpose of this intervention was to strengthen the external value of the euro and thus to prevent a spill-over of inflationary developments to the "euro area". To this end, the ECB[145] co-ordinated its intervention with the US Federal Reserve and the Bank of Japan and was supported by the Bank of Canada and the Bank of England, thereby using its external powers under Article 23, first indent, of the Statute. The ECB's intervention was preceded neither by general orientations of the Council under Article 111(2) EC[146] nor by an informal "Prague

---

[143] See also Louis, *Commentaire Mégret, Le Droit de la CEE* (2nd edn., Brussels, 1998) vi. The preference for an exchange rate system between Euro, Dollar and Yen, shown by the former German Minister of Finance Lafontaine, has been rejected almost unanimously by politicians, experts, and central bankers; cf. the views of Presidents Greenspan (Federal Reserve) and Duisenberg (ECB) at the 8th European Banking Congress in Frankfurt, reported in *Süddeutsche Zeitung* No 269, 21–22 November 1998, 23.

[144] Cf. Selmayr, "Darf die EZB den Wechselkurs des Euro stützen?" [2000] *Europablätter* 209; and "Interventionen zwecks Preisstabilität. Die europarechtlichen Leitplanken für die EZB", *Neue Zürcher Zeitung* No 237, 11 October 2000, 11.

[145] To implement the intervention decided by the Governing Council of the ECB, the ECB made use of the Deutsche Bundesbank, the Banque de France and the Banca d'Italia. This is, again, an example of indirect implementation of a policy through the ESCB; on this, cf. *supra*, Ch. 3, p. 126 *et seq.*

[146] A previous meeting of the informal "euro group" in Versailles on 8 September 2000, which took place without a participation of ECB president Duisenberg, merely resulted in a communiqué declaring a strong euro to be in the interest of the euro area; cf. http://www.presidence-euro000. ./pagedossier3.htm?dossier=01078&nav=3&page=1&lang=.

Accord" of the G–7 finance ministers,[147] but based exclusively on the initiative of the ECB. It is interesting to note that on the other side of the Atlantic ocean, the concerted intervention was announced by a Statement of the United States Department of the Treasury,[148] not by the Federal Reserve System, while in Europe, it was the ECB itself which made public the first intervention in support of the euro on its website,[149] thereby demonstrating that in Europe, exchange policy falls, as a matter of principle, within the competence of the central bank, and not of finance ministers.

3.4. Implied external competences of the ECB

As shown above, the external competences of the ECB are not limited to those listed explicitly in the EC Treaty or in the Statute, but extend to competences which parallel the internal competences of the ECB, subject to the Community's competences under Article 111(1) and (3) EC.

3.4.1. Agreements on an exchange rate system for the euro in relation to Community currencies

A first clear case of an implied "external" competence of the ECB is its authority to decide on an exchange rate system for the euro with regard to the currencies of those EU Member States which have not (yet) adopted the single currency.[150] This competence belongs to the ECB for several reasons. First, as shown above, the Community's competence to conclude arrangements under Article 111(1) and (3) EC is limited to agreements with third countries. Secondly, it is the ECB's specific task to contribute to the abrogation of the existing derogations and exemptions inside the European Union. This task results from Article 2 of the Statute of the European Monetary Institute (EMI) according to which the EMI, the ECB's predecessor, had to contribute to the realisation of the conditions necessary for the transition to the third stage of economic and monetary union. Under Article 122(2) in conjunction with Article 121(1), third indent, EC, participation in an exchange rate mechanism is still a necessary prerequisite for such transition, and Article 111(2) EC provides that the ECB shall, if necessary, take over the tasks of the EMI. That the ECB has to contribute to full membership of Denmark, Sweden, and the United Kingdom in the

---

[147] Cf. the misleading report in *Süddeutsche Zeitung* No 220, 24–24 September 2000, 25. The G–7 only welcomed the intervention *a posteriori* when they met, on 23 September 2000, within the context of the annual meeting of the IMF and the World Bank in Prague. Cf. the G–7-communiqué, published in IMF Survey No. 19 of 9 October 2000, 328.

[148] Cf. http://www.ustreas.gov/press/releases/ps901.htm: "At the initiative of the European Central Bank, the monetary authorities of the United States and Japan joined with the European Central Bank in concerted intervention in exchange markets, because of their shared concern about the potential implications of recent movements in the Euro for the world economy". A parallel statement was published on the website of the Japanese Ministry of Finance.

[149] Cf. http://www.ecb.int/press/00/pr000922.htm.

[150] This view is shared by Slot, "The Institutional Provisions of the EMU" in Curtin and Heukels (eds.), *Institutional Dynamics of European Integration. Essays in Honour of Henry G. Schermers* (Dordrecht/Boston/London, 1994), ii, 229 (238).

third stage of economic and monetary union also results from Article 105(1), third sentence, EC which commits the ECB to the objectives of the Community, including the establishment of an economic and monetary union (Article 2 EC) with a *single* currency (Article 4(2) EC).[151]

Finally, the competence to conclude an exchange rate agreement as regards Denmark, Sweden and the United Kingdom belongs to the ECB because it is the ECB which is responsible, under Article 105(2) EC, for defining and implementing the monetary policy *of the Community*—a term that is all-encompassing and relates also to non-participants of the single currency in their continued capacity as full EU Member States.[152] As the ECB is not able to impose its monetary policy unilaterally on the central banks of the Member States with a derogation or with an exemption—by virtue of Article 43.2 of the Statute, they retain their power in the field of monetary policy—the only way to define and implement a monetary policy that takes into account the Community as a whole, i.e. also as regards Member States with a derogation or an exemption, is to negotiate and conclude exchange rate agreements with the central banks outside the euro area.

To promote the objective of a monetary union which one day will include all Member States of the European Union, an Agreement was concluded, on 1 September 1998, laying down the operating procedures for an exchange rate mechanism in the third stage of economic and monetary Union (the so-called *ERM 2 Agreement*).[153] The parties to this agreement are just the ECB and the three[154] national central banks of the non-participating Member States, acting under public international law by virtue of their (limited and derivative) international legal personality.

A matter of concern in this context is, however, the Resolution of the Amsterdam European Council on the establishment of an exchange-rate mechanism in the third stage of economic and monetary union.[155] Although the European Council fully acknowledges the competence of the ECB to lay down the operating procedures of the ERM 2 in an agreement with the national central banks of the Member States outside the euro area,[156] it tries to establish, in paragraph 2.3. of the Resolution, a specific procedure for decisions on central rates and the standard fluctuation band:

---

[151] It is clear that the ECB is bound to these objectives only as long as this is without prejudice to its primary objective, which is price stability. The ECB would thus not be obliged to favour the abrogation of the derogation of a Member State if it considered that participation of that Member State would, because of a poor performance of that Member State as regards the convergence criteria, endanger the proper functioning of economic and monetary union.

[152] Cf. *supra*, Ch. 4, p. 135 *et seq.*

[153] [1998] OJ C345/6

[154] The central bank of Greece ceased to be a party to the ERM 2 agreement with effect from 1 January 2001, the date on which the euro was introduced in Greece; cf. Art. 1 of the Agreement of 14 September 2000 between the European Central Bank and the national central banks of the Member States outside the euro area amending the Agreement of 1 September 1998 laying down the operating procedures for an exchange rate mechanism in stage III of economic and monetary union [2000] OJ C362/11.

[155] [1997] OJ C236/6.

[156] Third para. of the Resolution's introduction, para. 2.2 and 2.6.

Decisions on central rates and the standard fluctuation band shall be taken by *mutual agreement* of the ministers of the euro-area Member States, the ECB and the ministers and central bank governors of the non-euro area Member States participating in the new mechanism, following a common procedure involving the European Commission, and after consultation of the Economic and Financial Committee. The ministers and central bank governors of the Member States not participating in the exchange-rate mechanism will take part but will not have the right to vote in the procedure. All parties to the mutual agreement, including the ECB, will have the right to initiate a confidential procedure aimed at reconsidering the central rates.[157]

It is questionable whether such a new procedure, which is not foreseen by the EC Treaty, may be established by a Resolution of the European Council at all, and if so under what legal basis. The European Council as such neither has the competence to amend the EC Treaty—this can be achieved only via the amendment procedure under Article 48 of the Treaty on European Union—nor could it derogate from it by way of an international agreement between the Member States sitting in the European Council, even if it was considered that the Resolution amounts to such an agreement, nor has it—not being part of the institutional framework of the Community[158]—a power to act in a legally binding manner under the EC Treaty, to commit the Community institutions or even to give instructions to the ECB.[159] That the ECB, under this common procedure, has a right to veto any decision on central rates or fluctuation bands does not sufficiently reflect its implied (exclusive) external competence in relation to Community currencies. In this respect, it is striking that the ECB is not in a position to adapt autonomously the central rates to new economic developments, but has only the possibility of initiating a procedure for reconsidering these rates.

One might say that the ECB's competence is not really prejudiced by this arrangement as it always has, under paragraph 2.1 of the Resolution, the possibility of suspending interventions if these were to conflict with its primary objective of price stability. However, the distribution of internal and external competences under the EC Treaty permits the ECB to play a much more active and constructive role in the setting of central rates and fluctuation bands. In accordance with the doctrine of parallelism, the ECB has the exclusive external

---

[157] Emphasis added.

[158] The European Council is an institution of the European Union, but not a Community institution; see Art. 4 of the EU Treaty and Art. 7 of the EC Treaty; therefore, it is not competent to adopt Community legislation; cf. Martenczuk, "Der Europäische Rat und die Wirtschafts- und Währungsunion" [1998] *EuR* 151. Only two provisions of the EC Treaty foresee a role for the European Council in the field of EMU: Art. 99(2), according to which the (ECOFIN) Council has to adopt a recommendation setting out the broad guidelines of economic policy on the basis of the conclusions of the European Council in the field of EMU: and Art. 113(3), under which the annual report of the ECB has also to be addressed to the European Council.

[159] This is also the view expressed by Smits, *supra*, n. 74, 467 according to which the European Council's "competence", exercised already in the context of ERM 1, "cannot, legally, be continued". Regrettably, exactly this was tried by means of the European Council's ERM 2 resolution. See also the criticism by Martenczuk, *supra*, n. 158, 172 *et seq.*

competence for setting central rates and fluctuation bands in agreements with the central banks of the Member States outside the "euro area"—a competence which the ECB might want to co-ordinate with the Community institutions, but which it is not allowed, under the EC Treaty, to share or even to renounce completely, being the sole entity responsible for defining and implementing the monetary policy of the Community.

3.4.2. Agreements on payment systems

A further implied external competence of the ECB exists in the field of payment systems. According to Article 105(2), fourth indent, EC it is one of the tasks of the ESCB—and thus of the ECB—"to promote the smooth operation of payment systems".

This includes not only payment systems within the Community, but also has an external aspect, as is shown by Article 22 of the Statute which gives the ECB the competence to "make regulations, to ensure efficient and sound clearing and payment systems within the Community *and with other countries*".[160] This regulatory competence as regards payments systems implies a parallel external competence to negotiate and conclude, if necessary, international agreements on payment systems, if these involve the regulatory power of the ECB. An example would be international agreements on netting in the context of central banks' payment systems.

The legal situation is more complex as regards the technical side of payment systems. Article 22 of the Statute authorises both the ECB and the national central banks to provide payment systems facilities. As already mentioned in chapter 3 of this book,[161] this provision gives national central banks only some scope regarding the implementation of ECB Decisions; it has to be read in the light of the ECB's unfettered discretion to decide on direct or indirect implementation, in accordance with Article 9(2) of the Statute. Given the experience and the technical know-how of the national central banks, the ECB might find it appropriate to rely on the payment systems facilities already established by them, in particular the existing national real-time gross settlement systems.

This distinction between the ECB's exclusive competence to regulate on payment systems and its possibility to make use of the national central banks as regards payment systems facilities[162] explains why the Agreement on a Trans-European Automated Real Time Gross-Settlement Express Transfer System (the "TARGET Agreement")—an agreement which grants access to the TARGET System, established by the ECB and the participating national central banks—was concluded in autumn 1998 jontly by the ECB and the partipating

---

[160] Emphasis added.

[161] Cf. *supra*, Ch. 3, p. 115 and 127 *et seq*. Differently from the position taken in Zilioli and Selmayr, *supra*, n. 125, 313, we have come to believe that within the centralised organisational structure of the ESCB, there is no room for concurrent competences, not even limited to the technical side: it is always exclusively within the power of the ECB to decide for direct implementation of ESCB tasks.

[162] This distinction is also drawn by Smits, *supra*, n. 74, 301 *et seq*.

national central banks with the national central banks still outside the "euro area". The agreement is operated under the control and supervision of the ECB, while the technical implementation lies with the national central banks.

3.4.3. Administrative agreements

Like international organisations,[163] the ECB also has an implied competence to negotiate and conclude administrative agreements, in particular agreements concerning its relations with Germany as the country of its seat. Here again, one finds confirmation of the autonomous legal status of the ECB.

As regards the privileges and immunities of the ECB within the territory of the Member States of the European Union, the Preamble to the Protocol on Privileges and Immunities of the European Communities speaks of the privileges and immunities which the European Communities require for the fulfilment of their tasks. However, while agreements implementing this Protocol with the countries of the seat of the Community institutions need to be entered into by the Community—as the legal person entitled to privileges and immunities under the Protocol—the ECB itself has the capacity to enter such agreements with its country of the seat, as Article 291, second sentence, EC and Article 23 of the Protocol on Privileges and Immunities extends the privileges and immunities conferred under the Protocol to the European Communities to the ECB and its decision-making bodies.[164] For this reason, it was the President of the ECB, together with the German Minister for Foreign Affairs, who signed, on 28 September 1998, the Headquarters Agreement between the ECB and the Federal Government of Germany.[165]

The ECB would be able to make use of its implied external competence also as regards administrative agreements relating to the establishment of ECB representations or offices in third countries, whenever such representations or offices were required for the ECB's participation in international monetary organisations. To mention an example, the ECB is entitled to negotiate and conclude agreements with the United States of America, concerning the privileges and immunities of the ECB's observer at the IMF in Washington.

3.4.4. Agreements on banking supervision

A further implied external competence of the ECB exists in the field of banking supervision. The ECB's competence is, however, limited as its internal competence, under Article 105(5) EC, is only a power:

---

[163] Cf. the agreement between the Swiss Federal Council and the BIS to determine the Bank's legal status in Switzerland, dated 10 February 1987, published under http://www.bis.org/about/hq-ex.htm.

[164] The same is true for the EIB which concluded a Headquarters Agreement with Luxembourg on 24 February 1986; cf. Art. 22 of the Protocol.

[165] Cf. *supra*, n. 56. The same form and procedure had already been followed with the EMI Headquarters Agreement of 12 September 1995; see the German [1996] *Bundesgesetzblatt II* 654. Under Art. 291, second sentence, EC and Art. 23 of the Protocol on Privileges and Immunities, the EMI had the same legal status as the ECB.

to contribute to the smooth conduct of policies pursued by the competent authorities relating to the prudential supervision of credit institutions and the stability of the financial system.

This is further clarified by Article 25 of the Statute of the ESCB which gives the ECB not more than an advisory function as regards prudential supervision. The limitation of the ECB's internal competence takes account of the residual competence of most Member States in the field of banking supervision.[166] This competence cannot be disregarded in the external relations of the euro area. International agreements in the field of banking supervision would therefore be primarily within the national competence, although the ECB, by virtue of its advisory role, may contribute to the negotiation of such an agreement by offering advice or by participating in the negotiations with observer status; only exceptionally will such agreements need to be negotiated and concluded as "mixed agreements", with both the ECB and the Member States[167] as contracting parties with third countries or international organisations. In international fora, for example, the Basle Committee on Banking Supervision, the ECB would certainly not replace, but sit together with, the national central banks and national supervisory authorities which have traditionally assumed the role of participants in that body.[168] This situation would change only if and in so far as the Council, acting unanimously under Article 105(6) EC, conferred upon the ECB specific tasks in the field of banking supervision. The implied external competence of the ECB would increase accordingly.

3.5. Effects of ECB agreements

Under public international law, it is only the ECB which, as regards the euro area, becomes a party to an agreement concluded by the ECB on its own behalf. The effects of such an ECB agreement under Community law are more complicated to be qualified. This comes from the fact that there is no parallel provision to Article 111(3), second paragraph, EC which would say something on the binding effect of ECB agreements under Community law.

In our view, ECB agreements form an integral part of Community law, as they are negotiated and concluded by the ECB, which is a specialised organisation of Community law, independent of the Community, but established by the

---

[166] For Padoa-Schioppa, the institutional setting created by the EC Treaty results in a functional separation, between central banking and banking supervision, and in a geographical separation between the "euro area" jurisdiction of central banking and the "domestic" jurisdiction of banking supervision. In his view, this calls, first, for extensive co-operation among bank supervisors and, secondly, for increased monitoring of the development of the banking sector by the ECB. Cf. Padoa-Schioppa, "The Eurosystem and Financial Stability" (February 2000), published at http://www.ecb.int/key/00/sp/sp000210.htm,

[167] Or even national central banks if those should have autonomous competences in the field of banking supervision.

[168] This is also the view of Smits, *supra*, n. 74, 350.

EC Treaty and the Statute and thus legally acting under Community law.[169] An international agreement concluded by the Community is considered by the ECJ to be "an act of one of the institutions of the Community" in the sense of Article 234(1)(b) EC, which from the date it comes into force forms "an integral part of Community law".[170] The same must be true for an ECB agreement which represents "an act of the ECB" within the meaning of Article 234(1)(b) EC on the interpretation of which the ECJ has jurisdiction to give preliminary reference rulings, and also to decide on actions for annulment under Article 230(1) EC. ECB agreements thus enjoy the same level in the normative hierarchy of Community law as do Community agreements concluded by the Community institutions.

Inside the ESCB, ECB agreements have the same effect as regulations, decisions, opinions and recommendations adopted by the ECB's decision-making bodies[171]: they are binding on all national central banks which form an integral part of the ESCB under Article 14.3 of the Statute, provided that they are not central banks of Member States with a derogation or a special status which, for the moment, still retain their powers in the field of monetary policy[172]; but even these central banks will, as component parts of the ESCB by virtue of Article 107(1) EC, have to respect the obligations entered into by the other elements of the system under an ECB agreement. They therefore will, in line with the principle of System integrity, have to refrain from any acts which might prejudice the effects of an ECB agreement.[173]

Similarly, the principle of loyalty applies to the institutions and bodies of the Community and to the Member States which, though not being directly bound by an ECB agreement, still have to observe Article 10 EC. Article 10 EC has been interpreted by the ECJ as a provision which not only imposes mutual obligations of loyalty between the Member States and the Community, but has been extended to cover also the relationship between the institutions which "is subject to the same mutual duties of sincere cooperation as those which govern relations between Member States and the Community institutions".[174] The same has to apply in the relationship between the institutions and bodies of the Community on the one hand, and the ECB on the other hand. The institutions and bodies of the Community and all Member States are thus obliged to facilitate the fulfilment of the obligations stemming from an ECB agreement, and to abstain from any measure which could jeopardise their attainment by the ECB.

---

[169] Cf. cf. *supra*, Ch. 1, p. 29 *et seq.*
[170] Case 181/73, *Haegeman* v. *Belgium* [1974] ECR 449, para. 1.
[171] Cf. *supra*, Ch. 3, p. 103 *et seq.*
[172] Cf. *supra*, Ch. 4, p. 155 *et seq*
[173] Cf. *supra*, Ch. 4, p. 167 *et seq.*
[174] Case 204/86, *Greece* v. *Council* [1988] ECR 5323, para. 16; Case 65/93, *European Parliament* v. *Council* [1995] ECR I–643, para. 23. Cf. also Declaration No 3 on Art. 10 of the Treaty establishing the European Community, attatched to the Treaty of Nice, according to which the duty of sincere cooperation "also governs relations between the Community institutions themselves."

3.6. Residual competences of the Member States having adopted the single currency

It follows from the description of the encompassing competences of the Community and of the ECB in the field of monetary policy that there is only very little scope for residual competences of the Member States. However, they are not totally excluded as may be drawn from Article 111(5) EC which reads:

> Without prejudice to Community competence and Community agreements as regards economic and monetary union, Member States may negotiate in international bodies and conclude international agreements.

The insertion of such a paragraph in the last provision of the chapter on monetary policy can be interpreted only in the sense that there is still a certain competence of the Member States left in the field of monetary policy.[175] It cannot be interpreted as only referring to the national competence in the field of economic policy,[176] as Article 111(5) EC explicitly speaks of the competence "as regards economic and *monetary* union".[177]

However, Member States' competences in monetary policy shall also be without prejudice to the Community's external competence and—as one has to add—to the ECB's external competence. The exclusive competence of the ECB to define and implement the monetary policy of the Community, and of the Community to conclude formal agreements on an exchange rate mechanism for the euro, and agreements on monetary and foreign exchange regime matters, thus excludes any residual competence of the Member States in these fields of core monetary and foreign exchange policy. A closer look at the EC Treaty is therefore required to "discover" the few areas in which there are still national external competences as regards monetary union.

3.6.1. Agreements on foreign exchange working balances

According to Article 105(3) EC, the ESCB's competence to hold and manage the official foreign reserves of the Member States:

> shall be without prejudice to the holding and management by the governments of the Member States of foreign exchange working balances.

Such an autonomous holding and management of foreign exchange working balances is supposed to be required for efficient government functioning as it provides governments with day-to-day liquidity needs in respect of other, non-participating Member States and of third countries,[178] including financing requirements arising from foreign currency debt issues on the international

---

[175] Monetary policy in its broad sense, as contained in Part Three, Title VI, Ch. 2 of the EC Treaty.

[176] This is the view of Smits, *supra*, n. 74, 379, who points to the exclusive competence of the Community; however, he admits himself in n. 51 that there may be minor exceptions.

[177] See also Dehousse and Ghemar, *supra*, n. 62, 157, n. 3.

[178] Smits, *supra*, n. 74, 201.

capital markets. Under Article 31.2 of the Statute, only Member States' transactions with their foreign exchange working balance above a certain limit shall be subject to approval by the ECB, this limit being determined in an ECB Guideline addressed to the Member States and issued under Article 31.3 of the Statute.[179] This means that the Member States may autonomously conduct transactions with their foreign exchange working balances whenever the limit set by the ECB is not reached; this enables them also to conclude agreements as regards their foreign exchange working balances.

3.6.2. Agreements on banking supervision

Another residual competence of the Member States exists in the context of banking supervision. As already shown, the competence in the field of prudential supervision of credit institutions and other financial institutions (with the exception of insurance undertakings) only passes to the Community level—more precisely, to the ECB—if and in so far as the Council so decides in accordance with Article 105(6) EC. This means that as long as the Council has not taken such a decision, this competence remains a national competence exercised at national level. The competence to supervise insurance undertakings is even completely excluded from the scope of such a transfer, so that this competence will in any event remain a national competence.

The extent of the external competence of the Member States in the field of banking supervision depends on the internal legal order of the Member States. While in several Member States it is the national central bank,[180] or an institution depending on it,[181] which is responsible for banking supervision, other Member States have entrusted this task to a specific autonomous banking supervisory authority—for example, the Bundesaufsichtsamt für das Kreditwesen in Germany.[182] It depends very much on the independence and the competences

---

[179] Such Guideline was notified to the participating Member States on 31 December 1998. Cf. *supra*, Ch. 3, p. 102 and n. 107, where it is also explained that the true legal nature of this legal instrument is that of an "ECB Directive."

[180] This is the case of Banca d'Italia, Banco d'España, Banco de Portugal, Bank of Ireland, Nederlandsche Bank, and Bank of Greece.

[181] In France, the Commission bancaire is in effect an arm of the Banque de France, Cf. Louis (ed.), *Banking Supervision in the European Community—Institutional Aspects, report of a Working Group of the ECU Institute under the chairmanship of Jean-Victor Louis, Etudes Européennes, Editions de l'Université de Bruxelles* (Brussels, 1995). A similar situation exists in Finland.

[182] This authority however closely co-operates with the Bundesbank in agreement with which it has to lay down principles on solvency and liquidity; cf. ss. 7, 10 and 11 of the *Gesetz über das Kreditwesen*. Ironically, what once was a symbol of the functional independence of the Bundesbank—the clear separation between monetary policy and banking supervision—today is challenged by the Bundesbank itself which calls for handing over banking supervision to the Bundesbank. One could see a certain logic in such a move in view of the fact that the Bundesbank, on 1 January 1999, had to transfer all its decision making powers in the field of monetary policy to the ECB; this excludes that the traditional conflict between monetary policy decisions and banking supervisions could arise again at the level of the Bundesbank. However, the German government now seems to prefer the creation of a new independent agency to which the supervision of the financial markets shall be entrusted; on this matter cf. Berger, Gaddum, Henzler, Hesse, Hungenber, Nemitz, Pöhl, and Rudolph, *Bericht zur Strukturreform der Deutschen Bundesbank*, 4 July 2000,

granted to either supervisory authorities or central banks if they also have the power to act at the international level; however, it is current practice that international co-ordination of banking supervision takes place in international fora—for example, the Basle Committee on Banking Supervision—where sometimes supervisory authorities themselves agree on worldwide and regional standards.[183] One could therefore imagine that it is not the Member State itself, but its supervisory authority or national central bank which is also externally competent to negotiate and conclude international agreements relating to banking supervision.

3.6.3. Agreements on coins

As regards the issue of coins, the ECB's internal competence is limited to approving the volume of such issue, while the Community's competence is limited to harmonising, by means of a legal act to be adopted by the Council,[184] the denominations and specifications of euro coins. There is thus still a certain competence left to the Member States which internally have the competence to choose, with certain limitations, the design of the national side of the euro coins issued by them or the design and the specifications of commemorative coins to be issued within the volume approved by the ECB. One therefore could imagine a (rather limited) field of residual external competence of the Member States for international agreements on, say, a standard for minting commemorative coins. However, this covers only technical aspects and does not extend to agreements on the issue of normal euro coins in third countries; the latter is reserved to the Community under its competence to conclude agreements on monetary regime matters under Article 111(3) EC.

3.6.4. Old agreements under Article 307 EC

Agreements concluded before the entry into force of the EC Treaty represent the most important element of the Member States' residual external competence in the field of monetary policy. Despite the exclusive competence of the Community institutions and the ECB, Member States may continue to fulfil obligations stemming from so-called "old agreements" by virtue of Article 234(1) EC which allows Member States to continue to fulfil their obligations arising from agreements entered into before the entry into force of the Treaty. This provision incorporates into Community law the general principle of public international law that one cannot escape obligations stemming from an earlier Treaty by concluding a new Treaty with other parties—a rule which, ultimately, results from the principle *pacta sunt servanda*.

published at http://www.bundesfinanzministerium.de; and Herdegen, "Bundesbank und Bankenaufsicht: Verfassungsrechtliche Fragen" [2000] *WM* 2121.

[183] See Smits, *supra*, n. 74, 331.

[184] Cf. Council Regulation 975/98 of 3 May 1998 on denominations and technical specifications of euro coins intended for circulation [1998] OJ L139/6, amended by Council Regulation (EC) No 423/1999 of 22 February 1999 amending Regulation 975/98 on denominations and technical specifications of euro coins intended for circulation [1999] OJ L52/2.

There are essentially two conditions which an international agreement needs to fulfil to replicate the effects of Article 307(1) EC:

—First, the agreement in question must be *between one or two Member States and third countries*. This excludes all agreements which were concluded only between Member States; this is in accordance with Article 59 of the Vienna Convention on the Law of Treaties according to which an agreement terminates as soon as all its parties become members of a new agreement which derogates from the former. This is important also for the context of economic and monetary union where agreements on monetary or foreign exchange regime matters concluded only between participating and non-participating Member States would not fall under Article 307(1) EC, as all these Member States are today parties to the Treaty, despite the fact that they have been granted certain derogations or exemptions.

—Secondly, the agreement must have been concluded *"before the entry into force of this Treaty"*. This covers, from its wording, only agreements concluded prior to 1958, the entry into force of the EEC Treaty which already contained the provision of Article 307(1) or, for acceding States, prior to the date of their accession.[185] Even though the EEC Treaty was amended several times, and in the end even "re-baptised" as the EC Treaty by the Maastricht Treaty, it is legally still the same Treaty today, and it is "this Treaty" to which Article 307(1) EC refers[186]. This view is confirmed by the Amsterdam Treaty which specifies in Article 307 that this provision applies to "agreements concluded before 1 January 1958 or, for acceding States, prior to the date of their accession".

Only if the two conditions required by Article 307 EC are satisfied may an agreement on monetary or foreign exchange regime matters, concluded prior to 1958, remain in force in spite of the exclusive external competence of the Community and the ECB in this field. However, this is nothing more than a pure residual external competence of the Member States the scope of which is quite limited. In the first place, Member States may invoke old agreements only to justify the fulfilment of *obligations* stemming from such agreements. They are not allowed to rely on *rights* granted to them therein. Because the rationale of

---

[185] This was clarified by the Acts of Accession, e.g. Art. 5 of the Act of Accession relating to the accession of Denmark, Ireland and the United Kingdom, and Art. 6 of the Act of Accession concerning Austria, Finland and Sweden.

[186] Petersmann in Von der Groeben, Thiesing and Ehlermann (eds.), *supra*, n. 38, Art. 234, para. 6 and Vedder in Grabitz and Hilf, *supra*, n. 38, argue in favour of an analogous application of Art. 234(1) EC to agreements concluded in fields like monetary policy where Member States could not foresee, in 1958, that there would one day be a Community competence. However, one should note that already the original Treaty included in its Arts. 99 to 111 provisions relating to a co-ordination of the economic and exchange rate policies of the Member States, which were to be regarded as "a matter of common interest". It was in the context of these provisions that in the 1960s and in particular in the 1970s, legal acts were adopted to establish the Committee of Governors, a European Monetary Co-operation Fund, and finally the European Monetary System. In all these legal acts reference is made to the aim of the Community to achieve economic and monetary union.

Article 307 EC is that Member States should not be forced to breach previous international commitments by virtue of their membership of the Community, not to give them a better position than the other Member States. Therefore, "rights" referred to in Article 307(1) EC are those of third countries, while "obligations" are those of the Member States.[187]

Even more important, Member States are under *an obligation to amend or terminate old agreements which are incompatible with the Treaty.* This is stated in Article 307(2) EC:

> To the extent that such agreements are not compatible with this Treaty, the Member State or States concerned shall take all appropriate steps to eliminate the incompatibilities established. Member States shall, where necessary, assist each other to this end and shall, where appropriate, adopt a common attitude.

Article 307 EC not only creates obligations for the Member States. For the Community and its institutions, Article 307 EC imposes a duty not to obstruct the fulfilment of the obligations which result for the Member States from such old agreements. However, the Community is not bound by such agreements and does not become a party to it.[188] Although there is, of course, not yet case law on this issue, it is certainly not particularly daring to assume that the same applies to the ECB.

In one case, the ECJ nevertheless held that the Member States' obligations arising from an old agreement had passed to the Community. This was the case of the GATT 1947, which was an old agreement coming within the scope of Article 307 EC, but where the Community had successively taken over the obligations of the Member States—in parallel to the end of the transitional period on 31 December 1969[189]—became recognised by the other parties to the agreement as negotiating partner in the GATT rounds and finally became the sole object of GATT proceedings, instead of the Member States.[190] Today, this development is confirmed by the membership of the Community in the WTO and in the GATT 1994.[191]

The example of the GATT 1947 shows that an old agreement of the Member States may, by virtue of the expressed or implied intention of both the Community and the other parties to the agreement, be transformed into an agreement binding on the Community under public international law. In the context of monetary union, this could serve as a model for another old agreement:

---

[187] Cf. Case 10/61, *Commission* v. *Italy* [1962] ECR 1; Case C–324/93, *The Queen* v. *Secretary of State for Home Department, ex parte Evans Medical Ltd and Macfarlan Smith Ltd* [1995] ECR I–563, para. 32: "when an international agreement allows, but does not require, a Member State to adopt a measure which appears to be contrary to Community law, the Member State must refrain from adopting such a measure".

[188] See Case 812/79, *Burgoa* [1980] ECR 2787, para. 9.

[189] See Art. 17 EC. With the end of the transitional period, both the four freedoms of the common market became directly effective, and the Community could make full use of its exclusive external competence in the field of commercial policy under Art. 133 EC.

[190] See Joined Cases 21–25/72, *International Fruit Company* [1972] ECR 1219, paras. 14–18.

[191] A similar case is that of the FAO where the Community is today a member in parallel to its Member States; see *supra*, n. 40.

the Articles of Agreement of the IMF. This so-called Fund Agreement was concluded in Bretton Woods in July 1944 and entered into force on 27 December 1945. One may conclude that the surrender of monetary sovereignty by the Member States to the Community level has left them as "empty shell" IMF members which are no longer in a position to fulfil their obligations under the Fund Agreement.[192] However, as an old agreement, the legal situation of the Member States in the IMF does, in the beginning, not change by virtue of Article 307(1) EC. Nevertheless, there is an obligation on the Member States to terminate this situation in which they are no longer able to fulfil their obligations under the Fund Agreement without infringing the exclusive competence of the Community and the ECB in monetary and foreign exchange policy matters. This could take place by a renegotiation of the Fund agreement with the aim of enabling a membership of the Community[193] and the ECB in the IMF. At the moment, following the example of the GATT 1947, the ECB has been given the right to participate as observer in IMF meetings and negotiations.[194] Even though in the short run this represents a pragmatic alternative to a complete renegotiation of the Fund agreement, a clearer solution would be desirable in the future. A possible option would be parallel membership of the Community and the ECB in the IMF,[195] thereby following the example of parallel membership of the Community and the EIB in the EBRD.[196]

3.6.5. Agreements with countries and territories having a special status

There are a number of Protocols and Declarations attached to the Treaty which reserve external competences to specific Member States and thus enable them to continue their public international law relations with specific countries and territories. In addition, some territories have special status under the national law of the Member States. In what follows, these countries and territories are referred to as having a "special status".

3.6.5.1. *Monetary relations with the Republic of San Marino, the Vatican City and the Principality of Monaco*

San Marino, the Vatican City and the Principality of Monaco are three sovereign states outside the territory of the Community within the meaning of Article 299 EC.[197] They do not have currencies of their own. Instead, they have

---

[192] See Martha, *supra*, n. 19, 749.

[193] This is suggested by Petersmann in Von der Groeben, Thiesing and Ehlermann (eds.), *supra*, n. 38, Art. 234, paras. 8, 21.

[194] Cf. IMF, *Selected Decisions and Selected Documents of the International Monetary Fund* (24th edn., Washington, 1999), 551 *et seq.*

[195] This would require both the Community and the ECB to pay up their own IMF quotas. Member States will, however, keep a certain role inside the IMF as long as they contribute substantially to the finance of the IMF; this follows from *Opinion 1/78, International Agreement on Natural Rubber* [1979] ECR 2871, para. 52 *et seq.*

[196] Cf. *supra*, p. 180. On this possibility, cf. Selmayr "Die Mitwirkung der Europäischen Union in Internationalen Organisationen—unter besonderer Berücksichtigung der Rechtslage im Internationalen Währungsfonds" [2001] *ZEuS* (in press).

[197] They are not territories in the sense of Art. 299(4) EC as they alone are responsible for their

entertained for many years special monetary relationships with Italy and with France respectively:

—*San Marino* has a monetary link with Italy based on Article 47 of the Friendship and Good Neighbours Convention of 1939, as amended in December 1972. According to this Convention, the Italian lira is the currency of San Marino, and Italian lira banknotes and coins are the sole legal tender in San Marino with the exception of coins issued by the latter in accordance with a Monetary Convention which is renewed every 10 years—this happened the last time in December 1991. San Marino has thereby been granted permission to mint coins of a metal other than gold for a face value not exceeding a ceiling set annually. In practice, these coins are minted by the Italian mint, and their metal, chemical composition, denomination, size and intrinsic value are identical to Italian coins. They are also legal tender in Italy. In addition, gold coins may be minted by San Marino without any limitation, but have legal tender status only in San Marino itself.

—As with San Marino, the Italian lira is the currency of the *Vatican City* and Italian lira banknotes and coins are the sole legal tender in the Vatican City with the exception of coins issued by the latter in accordance with a Monetary Convention, along the same lines as that between Italy and San Marino, which is renewed every 10 years, which, again, happened the last time in December 1991. The Vatican City is authorised to mint a certain number of coins the metal, chemical composition, denomination, size and intrinsic value of which must be identical to Italian coins and which are legal tender also in Italy, and gold coins, which have legal tender status only in the Vatican City itself.

—Within the *Principality of Monaco*, only banknotes and coins denominated in French Francs have legal tender status. This results from a ruling of 1925, the Convention on the control of foreign exchange, dated 14 April 1945,[198] and an exchange of letters in 1963, which was amended in 1987.

The special monetary links of these three states can be qualified as old agreements under Article 307 EC, as they were all originally based on international agreements which predate the entry into force of the EEC Treaty on 1958. Although the numerous renovations of the agreements with San Marino and the Vatican City may be a reason to question this qualification, it is confirmed by Declaration No 6, attached to the Final Act of the Treaty at Maastricht, on monetary relations with the Republic of San Marino, the Vatican City and the Principality of Monaco. It reads as follows:

> The Conference agrees that the existing monetary relations between Italy and San Marino and the Vatican City and between France and Monaco remain unaffected by the Treaty establishing the European Community until the introduction of the ECU as the single currency of the Community.

external relations. Cf. Schrder in Von der Groeben, Thiesing and Ehlermann (eds.), *supra*, n. 38, Art. 227, para. 30 *et seq.*

[198] Published by Decree No 45–1006, dated 16 May 1945.

The Community undertakes to facilitate such renegotiations of existing agreements as might become necessary as a result of the introduction of the ECU as a single currency.

This Declaration goes even slightly further than Article 307(1) EC when stating that, during the second stage, these agreements would not be affected at all by the provisions on economic and monetary union. However, it also makes it clear that this situation has changed with entry into the third stage. Now, Italy and France may still fulfil their obligations stemming from these agreements; but, under Article 307(2) EC, they have to contribute to resolving the incompatibilities between these agreements and the EC Treaty, either by terminating these agreements or by supporting their renegotiation.

It was clear that, with the entry into the third stage, Italy and France had lost the competence to renew these agreements without authorisation by the Community.[199] Such renovation is from that moment a responsibility of the Community which is exclusively competent under Article 111(3) EC to negotiate and conclude "agreements on monetary . . . regime matters".[200] The effect of such agreements is that the Community becomes a party to them and both the Community institutions, the ECB and the participating Member States are bound by them by virtue of Article 111(3), second paragraph EC.

The EC Treaty does not oblige the Community to conclude such agreements with San Marino, the Vatican City or Monaco, but the second paragraph of Declaration No 6 obliges the Community to "facilitate" renegotiations. The Council therefore adopted, in December 1998, three decisions[201] under Article 111(3) EC which entrusted the negotiation and the conclusion of such agreements to Italy and France respectively, to take into account the historic character of these monetary links. All three decisions state in their Article 7 that these agreements are negotiated and concluded by Italy and France "on behalf of the Community",[202] while the ECB shall be fully associated to the negotiations. The latter has to be welcomed as these new monetary links of the Community may, despite the small size of the three countries involved, nevertheless have an

---

[199] Such authorisation is possible even in the field of the Community's exclusive competence; see Case 174/84, *Bulk Oil (Zug) AG* v. *Sun International Limited and Sun Oil Trading Company* [1986] ECR 559, para. 23, and *supra*, n. 127. It has the effect that a Member State may renew agreements under its sole responsibility, without any obligations being created for the Community or the ECB.

[200] The special procedure referred to in Art. 111(1) EC for the conclusion of an exchange rate system for the euro is not applicable, as all three states do not have their own currencies so that there is no possibility of determining a central rate.

[201] Council Decision 1999/96/EC of 31 December 1998 on the position to be taken by the Community regarding an agreement concerning the monetary relations with the Principality of Monaco [1999] OJ L30/31; Council Decision 1999/97/EC of 31 December 1998 on the position to be taken by the Community regarding an agreement concerning the monetary relations with the Republic of San Marino [1999] OJ L30/33; Council Decision 1999/98/EC of 31 December 1998 on the position to be taken by the Community regarding an agreement concerning the monetary relations with Vatican City [1999] OJ L30/35 .

[202] Cf. the fourth possibility for the conclusion of Community agreements under Art. 111(3) EC, mentioned *supra*, p. 198 *et seq.*

impact on the monetary amount circulating in the "euro area". In addition, as the Council is, when acting under Article 111(3) EC, obliged to observe the primary objective of price stability in accordance with Article 4(2) EC, the decisions require to make the volume of the issue of coins subject to the approval of the ECB, mirroring thus the internal competence of the ECB under Article 106(2) EC.

The agreements with San Marino and the Vatican City, signed by Italy on behalf of the Community on 29 November 2000 and 30 December 2000, respectively,[203] permit these states to issue euro coins which have legal tender in the whole "euro area".[204] The agreement between France, on behalf of the Community, and Monaco is still being negotiated.

3.6.5.2. *Monetary emission in French overseas departments (DOM)*

French overseas departments (DOM[205])—they include French Guyana, Martinique, Guadeloupe and Réunion—are, under the French constitution, an integral part of the French Republic[206] to which the EC Treaty applies according to Article 299(1) EC. There seems thus to be no reason to mention the DOM as a special case on the context of the *external* relations of the euro area.

However, some confusion may be caused by the fact that Article 299(2) EC seems to create a special regime for the French DOM. It draws a distinction between six titles of the EC Treaty which apply to the DOM as soon as the EC Treaty enters into force—for example, the chapter on free movement of goods—and the other provisions of the EC Treaty which apply only according to the conditions to be determined unanimously by the Council within two years of the entry into force of the EC Treaty.

Until today the Council has not decided on an encompassing regime for the DOM. From the wording of Article 299(2) EC one could conclude that, in the absence of a Council decision on the matter, only those titles mentioned explicitly in Article 299(2) EC would apply to the DOM. In the context of monetary union this would mean that Chapter 2 of Title VII of Part 3 of the EC Treaty does not apply to the DOM as long as the Council has not expressly extended its application to them. The ECJ, however, has taken a different view. In accordance with its jurisprudence granting direct effect to Treaty provisions with deadlines after the expiry of such deadlines,[207] the ECJ takes the deadline of two years allowed in Article 299(2) EC for a Council decision on the regime of the DOM as point of departure to conclude that:

---

[203] Cf. the Monetary Agreement between the Italian Republic, on behalf of the European Community and the Republic of San Marino [OJ 2001 C209/1].

[204] This was not prevented by Arts. 10 and 11 of Council Regulation 974/98 of 3 May 1998 on the introduction of the euro [1998] OJ L139/1 according to which euro coins issued by the participating Member States shall be the only coins which have legal tender status in these Member States. International agreements, by virtue of their binding effect on Community institutions, take precedence over secondary Community law: see *supra*, p. 199.

[205] Départements d'Outre Mer.

[206] Luchaire and Conac, *La constitution de la République française* (2nd edn., Pairs, 1987), 1248.

[207] Cf. on Art. 28 Case 74/76, *Iannelli & Volpi* [1977] 557, para. 13.

after the expiry of that period, the provisions of the Treaty and of secondary law must apply automatically to the French overseas departments inasmuch as they are integral part of the French Republic, it being understood, however, that it always remains possible subsequently to adopt specific measures in order to meet the needs of those territories.[208]

This means that today the whole EC Treaty applies, in principle without exceptions, to the DOM in the same way as it does to the European territories of the French Republic. The participation of France in the single currency therefore also includes the DOM, and so does the monetary law of the Community enacted by the Council under Article 123(4), third sentence, EC and aimed at the rapid introduction of the euro as the single currency of the participating Member States. There is thus no need for special agreements on the introduction of the euro in the DOM, as this is covered already by Council Regulation 974/98 which applies to France as participating Member State.[209]

The unrestricted application of the EC Treaty to the DOM means also that it is exclusively the ECB which, since 1 January 1999, may decide on the definition and implementation of the monetary policy of the Community as regards the DOM. This requires a change of the monetary regime in the DOM where there is a special institute, the Institut d'Emission des Départements d'Outre Mer (IEDOM), which, until recently, has had the responsibility of issuing banknotes and coins denominated in FRF. Since 1 January 1999, this competence has passed irrevocably to the ECB. It is of course possible for the ECB to delegate the implementation of its tasks to the Banque de France in accordance with Article 12.1 of the Statute. However, this provision does not mention the possibility of delegating these tasks also to the IEDOM. As there is no special Protocol or Declaration attached to the EC Treaty on this matter, the implementation of the monetary policy defined by the ECB in the DOM is only allowed through the Banque de France as a national central bank which is an integral part of the ESCB. For these reasons the French legislation has been amended[210] in this respect in order to make a sub-delegation by Banque de France to the IEDOM possible while ensuring at the same time the efficient and uniform implementation of the ECB's monetary policy by subordinating the IEDOM to the guidelines and instructions of the ECB.[211]

---

[208] Case 148/77, *Hansen* v. *Hauptzollamt Flensburg* [1978] ECR 1787, para. 11.

[209] [1998] OJ L139/1. Art. 1, first indent of this Regulation includes France within the definition of "*participating Member States*".

[210] By a convention between the Banque de France and the IEDOM, concluded on 22 January 2001.

[211] Another possibility of taking the specific needs of the DOM into account would have been a unanimous Council decision on a proposal from the Commission and based on Art. 299(2) EC (cf. Case 148/77, supra, n. 208) This is still possible today in spite of the expiration of the two-years period laid down in Art. 299(2) EC; on this see also Dewost in *Commentaire Mégret, Le Droit de la CEE* (Brussels, 1987), xv, Art. 227, 484 *et seq.* Such a decision could provide for the integration of the IEDOM into the ESCB. As such a decision would clearly relate to the field of competence of the ECB, both the Commission and the Council would be obliged to consult the ECB on such a (proposed) decision by virtue of Art. 105(4), first indent, EC.

3.6.5.3. *Monetary emission in overseas countries and territories, in particular in the French TOM*

Due to their colonial past, France, the United Kingdom and the Netherlands have overseas countries and territories which enjoy a special status both under national and Community law. In contrast to the EAEC Treaty,[212] the EC Treaty does not apply to the non-European territories of the Member States. This is confirmed by Article 299(4) EC which provides only for the application of the EC Treaty to certain European Territories controlled by the Member States. However, Article 299(3) EC takes into account the specific links between the Member States and their overseas territories by associating those overseas countries and territories which are expressly listed in Annex IV to the EC Treaty.[213] The legal status of these associated overseas countries and territories is defined in Articles 182–187 EC.

In the context of monetary union, the French overseas territories—the so-called TOMs[214]—deserve particular attention. According to Article 30 of Act 67–948 of 22 December 1967, banknotes and coins denominated in CFP[215] Franc have legal tender status in these territories. They are issued by the IEDOM, which exercises the monetary policy tasks which the Banque de France has delegated to it by means of a bilateral agreement, while the French Treasury guarantees a parity of 1 CFP Franc : 0,055 FRF.

The FRF now having been replaced by the euro, one would normally have to qualify this arrangement as an agreement on an exchange rate system for the euro, as it involves an obligation to guarantee the parity of the CFP Franc to the euro. France would thus have lost its competence irrevocably to the Community, which alone is competent for the conclusion of such agreements under Article 111(1) EC. However, according to Protocol No 27 on France, annexed to the EC Treaty at Maastricht:

> France will keep the privilege of monetary emission in its overseas territories under the terms established by its national laws, and will be solely entitled to determine the parity of the CFP Franc.

As Protocols form an integral part of primary Community law by virtue of Article 311 EC, this has thus to be considered as an express exception to the rule in Article 111(1) EC and thus as an exclusive residual external competence of France to determine the parity of a foreign currency to the euro.

As there is no such Protocol as regards the British and Dutch overseas countries and territories—this was not required in the absence of close monetary

---

[212] Cf. Art. 198 Euratom.

[213] The list has been changed many times in the past. A comprehensive and updated list of all overseas countries and territories is now to be found in Annex 1 to Council Decision 91/482/EEC of 25 July 1991 [1991] OJ L263/1.

[214] Territoires d'Outre Mer. They include New Caledonia and Dependencies, French Polynesia, French Southern and Antarctic Territories, Wallis and Futuna Islands. On the legal status of the TOM under the French constitution cf. Luchaire and Conac, *supra*, n. 206, 1282 *et seq*.

[215] Communauté financière du Pacifique.

links with these countries and territories—the introduction of the euro in these countries or the establishment of an exchange rate system for the euro with the respective local currencies[216] would require specific agreements to be concluded by the Community in accordance with Article 111(1) or (3) EC.[217]

3.6.5.4. *The special case of Saint-Pierre-et-Miquelon and Mayotte*

A very special case in the present context is that of the French islands of Saint-Pierre-et-Miquelon and Mayotte:

—*Saint-Pierre-et-Miquelon* were originally TOM and listed in Annex IV attached to the EC Treaty. They thus had the legal status of associated overseas countries and territories under Article 299(3) EC. In 1976,[218] they became DOM and thus became an integral part of the French Republic to which the EC Treaty applied in principle without any exceptions by virtue of Article 299(1) and (2) EC. In 1986,[219] their status was changed again; under the French constitution, they became territorial collectivities with a special status (*"collectivités territoriales à statuts particuliers"* or *"sui generis"*[220]) of the French Republic; in Community law, this had the effect of re-transforming them into associated overseas countries and territories within the meaning of Article 299(3) EC.[221] Since 1978, the IEDOM is responsible for issuing banknotes and coins denominated in FF in Saint-Pierre-et-Miquelon.

—*Mayotte* is also a territorial collectivity of the French Republic with a special status. It is mentioned in Annex IV attached to the Treaty.[222] Until recently, it was the Institut d'Emission d'Outre-Mer (IEOM) which issued banknotes in Mayotte which had legal tender status in continental France, i.e. banknotes

---

[216] It should be noted that the British overseas territories Anguilla and Montserrat are members of the East Caribbean Central Bank which issues the East Caribbean Dollar. In the British Cayman islands, the Cayman Dollar is issued by a currency board. The Netherlands Antilles and Aruba have their own currency, the Antillean guilder and the Aruban guilder, which is the sole legal tender in their respective territories. All these local currencies are currently pegged to the US Dollar.

[217] As overseas countries and territories are, by virtue of Art. 299(3) EC, not part of the Community, but only associated to it, they are legally in the same situation as third countries in the context of such agreements; this means that the conclusion of such agreements falls within the competence of the Community, and not of the ECB which is externally competent only in respect of Community currencies; cf. *supra*, p. 197 and p. 206. In so far as the UK and the Netherlands are responsible for the external relations of their overseas countries and territories, they may conclude such agreements on behalf of them with the Community. On this possibility see *Opinion 1/78, International Agreement on Natural Rubber* [1979] ECR 2871, para. 62.

[218] Loi No 76–664 of 19 July 1976, [1976] JORF 4523.

[219] Loi No 85–595 of 11 June 1985, [1985] JORF 1985.

[220] See Luchaire and Conac, *supra*, n. 206, 1225, 1229, and 1232 where it is stated that they are neither a DOM nor a TOM.

[221] As the reference to Saint-Pierre-et-Miquelon had not been deleted in Annex IV to the Treaty in 1976, this new change of legal status was possible without a Treaty amendment; on this, see Schröder in Von der Groeben, Thiesing and Ehlermann (eds.), *supra*, n. 38, Art. 299, para. 19.

[222] Annex IV mentions the Comoro Archipelago the members of which are no longer associated territories under Art. 299(3) EC with the sole exception of Mayotte. This is confirmed by Annex I attached to Council Decision 91/482/EEC, *supra*, n. 213, which mentions Saint-Pierre-et-Miquelon and Mayotte as territorial collectivities of the French Republic.

denominated in FRF. Since 1 January 1999, it has been the IEDOM, as in Saint-Pierre-et-Miquelon.

Both Saint-Pierre-et-Miquelon and Mayotte are today only associated with, but not integral parts of, the Community.[223] Their associated status is limited to the rights and obligations defined in Articles 182–187 EC. The provisions on monetary union therefore do not apply to these special territorial collectivities.

Despite this clear legal situation, the Council, acting unanimously on a proposal from the Commission, adopted a decision under Article 123(4), third sentence, EC to introduce the euro into Saint-Pierre-et-Miquelon and Mayotte.[224] It is recalled that Article 123(4), third sentence, EC enables the Council to take measures which are necessary for the rapid introduction of the euro as the single currency of the participating Member States. One might want to argue that the Council decision is a necessary measure for introducing the euro into these two French territorial collectivities. However, it is quite obvious that such measures, being institutional acts adopted on the basis of the EC Treaty, apply only to the same geographical area as the EC Treaty itself.[225] As Saint-Pierre-et-Miquelon and Mayotte are only associated with the Community, Article 123(4) EC does not apply to them. The Council decision—which in Recital 4 of its decision admits itself that Saint-Pierre-et-Miquelon and Mayotte do not form part of the Community—is thus void *ratione loci*.[226]

It is regrettable that the Council adopted its decision despite the fact that the ECB had, in its opinion,[227] explicitly questioned the choice of Article 123(4) as the legal basis for an introduction of the euro beyond the sphere of application of Community law. The correct legal manner of introducing the euro in Saint-Pierre-et-Miquelon and Mayotte would have been by a Community agreement under Article 111(3) EC with France acting as representative of its territorial collectivities.[228]

3.6.5.5. The "Zone Franc"

A final issue in the context of countries and territories with a special status is that of the so-called "Zone Franc".[229] It consists of:

—the six East African countries having formed the "Communauté économique et monétaire de l'Afrique Centrale" and established a common central bank,

---

[223] On the legal position of Mayotte under Community law cf. Gohin and Maurice, *Mayotte* (2nd edn., La Réunion, 1992), 378.

[224] Council Decision 1999/95/EC [1999] OJ L30/29.

[225] This was explicitly stated by Case 61/77, *Commission* v. *Ireland* [1978] ECR 417, para. 46.

[226] This view is shared by Krauskopf and Steven, "Einführung des Euro in außereuropäischen Territorien und währungsrechtliche Regelungen im Verhältnis zu Drittstaaten" [1999] *EuZW* 650 (653); and by Hafke, "Rechtliche Aspekte der Währungsbeziehungen zwischen Mitgliedstaaten der Europäischen Währungsunion und Territorien außerhalb des Geltungsbereichs des EGV" [2000] *ZEuS* 25 (29).

[227] [1999] OJ C127/5.

[228] Cf. *supra*, n. 217.

[229] See Olszak, *Histoire des unions monétaires* (Paris, 1996), 105 *et seq.*

the "Banque des Etats de l'Afrique Centrale" (BEAC), which issues the "franc de la Coopération financière en Afrique" (CFA Franc);
—the eight West African countries having formed the "Union économique et monétaire ouest-africaine" and established a common central bank, the "Banque Centrale des Etats de l'Afrique de l'Ouest" (BCEAO), which issues the "franc de la Communauté financière africaine", which is also called CFA Franc;
—the Comores which also have their own central bank issuing the *Comorian Franc*.

Since the 1970s, there have been agreements between France and what is now the Economic and Monetary Community of Central Africa,[230] the West African Monetary Union,[231] and with the Comores[232] according to which the two CFA Francs and the Comorian Franc are pegged to the FRF. Since 1994, the parity of 1 CFA Franc is 0.01 FRF, while 1 Comorian Franc is 0.013 FRF. Under these agreements, the parity with the FRF is guaranteed by the French Treasury.

Concluded after the entry into force of the Treaty in 1958, these arrangements cannot be regarded as old agreements under Article 307 EC. Today, the euro has legally replaced the FRF, and the competence for the conclusion of agreements providing for the pegging of a third country's currency to the euro has irrevocably passed to the Community level. As there is also no special Protocol or Declaration attached to the EC Treaty on the CFA Franc or the Comorian Franc, this would have meant that France was obliged, under Community law, to terminate these agreements by 1 January 1999.

This explains why the Council, acting under Article 111(3) EC, has meanwhile adopted a decision[233] relating to the CFA Franc and the Comorian Franc by which it authorises France to continue its present agreements with the 15 African states upon the substitution of the euro for the FRF. This decision explicitly stresses the fact that also in future it will be only the French Treasury, and not the Banque de France or even the ECB, which is required to support the parity of the CFA Francs and of the Comorian Franc.

One might wonder whether this manner of renovation will transform these agreements with the "Zone Franc" in Community agreements. This is quite important as this would imply that, by virtue of Article 111(3), second subparagraph, EC, these agreements were binding on the Community institutions, the ECB and the Member States. Such a continuation of the agreements on behalf of the Community could mean that in the (unlikely) event of a refusal by the

---

[230] Agreement signed on 23 December 1972 by France, Cameroon, Congo, Gabon, the Central African Republic, and the Chad. Equatorial Guinea joined on 1 January 1985.

[231] Agreement signed on 4 December 1973 by France, Benin, Burkina-Faso, Guinea Bissau, the Ivory Coast, Niger, Senegal, and Togo. Mali joined on 1 June 1984.

[232] The Comores joined the arrangements with France in 1979.

[233] Council Decision 98/683/EC of the 23 November 1998 concerning exchange rate matters relating to the CFA Franc and the Comorian Franc [1998] OJ L320/58. The choice of Art. 111(3) EC as legal basis contrasts with the answer given by Commissioner De Silguy in the European Parliament to written question 1812/96 [1996] OJ C365/37: "The CFA Franc is not concerned by Art. 109 of the EC Treaty".

French Treasury to support any longer the parity of the CFA Francs and the Comorian Franc, the African States concerned might turn to the Community or even to the ECB by reference to the new legal position of their agreements.

The Council, advised by the ECB,[234] has however avoided these legal consequences. On purpose, it did not authorise France to negotiate and conclude new agreements on behalf of the Community, as it had done in respect of France and Italy in its decisions relating to San Marino, the Vatican City and the Principality of Monaco. The Council simply authorised France *to continue its present arrangements* with the states in the "Zone Franc". This is in line with the jurisprudence of the ECJ, according to which even in the field of an exclusive Community competence, the Community institutions may authorise a Member State to continue to act on its own responsibility in a certain field.[235] In the case of the "Zone Franc", it was thus possible to authorise France to continue the present arrangements on its own behalf, without binding also, even in an indirect manner, the Community institutions, the ECB or other Member States. From this it follows also that any amendments of the agreements in future may be agreed upon by France only subject to authorisation by the Council under Article 111(3) EC, which would again require a consultation of the ECB.

3.6.5.6. Cape Verde

In the context of the historical ties of friendship and co-operation between Portugal and Cape Verde, the two countries concluded in July 1998[236] an exchange rate co-operation agreement linking the Cape Verde escudo to the Portuguese escudo at a fixed parity.[237] Clearly, this agreement is not covered by the provision of Article 307 EC; therefore, Portugal would have been obliged, under Community law, to terminate it by 1 January 1999.

---

[234] Opinion of the European Central Bank of 22 September 1998 at the request of the Council of the European Union on a recommendation for a Council Decision concerning exchange rate matters relating to the CFA franc and the Comorian franc (CON/98/37) [1999] OJ C200/6. See also Padoa Schioppa, "The Impact of the Introduction of the Euro on ACP Countries and Particularly on the CFA Franc Zone", published at http://www.ecb.int.

[235] This possibility of enabling the Member State to act is confirmed by Case 174/84, *Bulk Oil (Zug) AG v. Sun International Limited and Sun Oil Trading Company* [1986] ECR 559, para. 23; there, the ECJ upheld measures taken by the United Kingdom in trade relations with Israel despite the exclusive competence of the Community in the field of commercial policy because the Community had specifically authorised these measures in a Council regulation.

[236] *Acordo de cooperação cambial entre a República Portuguesa e a República de Cabo Verde* (Decreto No 24/98 of 15 July 1998), quoted in n. 3 of Council Decision 98/744/EC of 21 December 1998 concerning exchange rate matters relating to the Cape Verde escudo [1998] OJ L358/111. The conclusion of an agreement in the exchange rates field just before the beginning of Stage Three and the transfer of the competence from Portugal to the Community level seems to go against the duty of loyalty under Art. 10 EC, and may be seen as a tentative to prejudice Community competences.

[237] The Portuguese government provides a credit facility limited to PTE 9,000 million to the central bank of Cape Verde in order to reinforce its foreign-exchange reserves. Availability of the credit facility is conditional upon the existence of a stability oriented macroeconomic programme for Cape Verde, compliance with which is monitored by a joint exchange rate co-operation committee. See COM(1998)663 final, 3.

To avoid this, the Council, using the case of the "Zone Franc" as precedent, adopted, after consultation of the ECB,[238] a decision[239] under Article 111(3) EC authorising Portugal to continue its present agreement with Cape Verde, specifying that the two parties to the agreement will keep the sole responsibility for it. The present arrangement, therefore, is not binding on the Community institutions, the ECB or other Member States.

3.6.5.7. Agreements with other countries and territories

Other existing monetary links or relations of the Member States[240] are not explicitly referred to in the EC Treaty. This means that they will have to be dealt with in accordance with the new situation in Community law as from 1 January 1999:

—*Agreements predating the entry into force of the EEC Treaty in 1958* may, in the beginning, be allowed to continue their validity under Article 307(1) EC, but Member States are under an obligation, by virtue of Article 307(2) EC, to terminate such agreements as they are incompatible with the exclusive competence of the Community and of the ECB in this field. The Community may, however, authorise these Member States to continue such agreements on their own behalf.[241] Alternatively, it may also choose to become itself a party to such agreements in accordance with Article 111(3) EC.

—As regards *new agreements or the renovation of old agreements which have expired*, Member States have no competence any more to enter into such agreements, in view of the encompassing competence in this field exercised by the Community or the ECB. If Member States nevertheless enter into such new agreements which are incompatible with the EC Treaty, these agreements will, under Community law, not be applicable by virtue of the supremacy of Community law, and cannot be invoked by Member States to escape their obligations stemming from Community law.[242]

3.7. Residual (autonomous) competences of national central banks

As integral parts of the ESCB, the national central banks of the participating Member States are normally subordinated to the decision-making bodies of the

---

[238] Opinion of the European Central Bank of 17 December 1998 at the request of the Council of the European Union on a recommendation for a Council Decision concerning exchange rate matters relating to the Cape Verde escudo (CON/98/57) [1999] OJ C200/7.

[239] Council Decision 98/744/EC, *supra*, n. 236.

[240] As regards specific monetary links with central banks, see *infra*, p. 230 *et seq.*

[241] Cf. *supra*, n. 235.

[242] Under public international law, the validity of agreements is normally not affected by the violation of the internal rules of competences of one of the contracting partners; see Arts. 27, 46 of the Vienna Convention on the Law of the Treaties. However, there is an exception to the rule in the case of manifest infringements. See Brownlie, *supra*, n. 6, 613 *et seq.* As the creation of the euro and the passage of monetary sovereignty to the Community level are well-known facts today, it is suggested that an agreement relating to the euro, but concluded by a Member State, would also be void under public international law because of a manifest infringement of internal rules of competence.

ECB, which govern the ESCB,[243] and have to act in accordance with the guidelines and instructions of the ECB. They thus have, as a rule, no autonomous competences any more within the scope of the EC Treaty and the Statute, but may act only to fulfil the tasks of the ESCB as decided by the ECB in accordance with Article 9.2 of the Statute. This applies also externally where it is the ECB which decides on matters of external representation (Article 6.1 of the Statute). Even where such external representation would exceptionally be delegated to a national central bank, the latter would act, on the international level, not on its own behalf, but in the name of the legal person ECB and in accordance with the authorisation of the ECB.

However, both the EC Treaty and the Statute do not cover the whole field of central banking activities. In all fields not covered by the EC Treaty and the Statute, there thus remains room for a certain external competence of national central banks if such competence is given to them under the legislation of their respective Member State. Banking supervision has already been mentioned as one such possible field. Two others are expressly referred to in the EC Treaty: Article 31.1 of the Statute and the special monetary links of the National Bank of Denmark.

3.7.1. Article 31.1 of the Statute

As Article 307 EC covers old only agreements entered into by the Member States, the possibility of international agreements concluded by national central banks by virtue of their own international legal personality required a separate provision to avoid a breach of these obligations with entry into the third stage. This purpose is satisfied by Article 31.1 of the Statute which reads:

> The national central banks shall be allowed to perform transactions in fulfilment of their obligations towards international organisations in accordance with Article 23.

It should be noted that the scope of this provision is rather limited:

—First of all, from its wording ("perform transactions") it relates only to operational competences to fulfil obligations, but not to the competence to enter into such obligations themselves. Therefore, and in the light of Article 307 EC, Article 31.1 of the Statute applies only to existing obligations stemming from old agreements entered into by national central banks.

—Secondly, the provision covers only "obligations towards international organisations", but not obligations to third countries or central banks. This means that such international relations are, in principle, not allowed to continue in view of the exclusive competence of the ECB to decide how the ESCB is represented externally. This is confirmed by Article 31.2 according to which all other external transactions undertaken by national central banks are subject to the ECB's approval.

---

[243] Cf. *supra*, Ch. 2, p. 57 *et seq.*

The most prominent example falling under Article 31.1 of the Statute is the BIS, the Constituent Charter of which dates from 20 January 1930. Here, the national central banks are allowed to continue to fulfil the obligations resulting from their membership of the BIS. However, they also have to take into account that they are today no longer autonomous entities, but integral parts of the ESCB. They are thus bound by the objectives and tasks of the ESCB and have to observe the legal instruments adopted by the decision-making bodies of the ECB. Therefore, in accordance with the principle of System integrity,[244] national central banks had, first, to choose a co-ordinated approach in the BIS and always to closely associate the ECB. In addition, the obligation to amend international agreements to reflect properly the situation of competence under Community also applies to national central banks when they are parties to such agreements: this has led to a situation in which the ECB itself has become a member of the BIS[245]—this was possible by virtue of the international legal personality of the ECB, confirmed by Article 6.2 of the Statute and required by Article 8(3) of the Statute of the BIS.[246] In the long term, it is possible to imagine that the ECB could even replace[247] the individual national central banks as shareholders of the BIS.[248]

3.7.2. Monetary links between the National Central Bank of Denmark, the Faroe Islands and Greenland

A further residual autonomous external competence of national central banks is that of the National Bank of Denmark as regards the Faroe Islands and Greenland. Both the Faroe Islands[249] and Greenland[250] are autonomous regions within the Kingdom of Denmark which do not form part of the territory of the Community, as defined in Article 299(1) EC. Their respective monetary links are governed:

—in the case of the Faroe Islands by Act 137 of 23 March 1948, on home rule, and Act 248 of 12 April 1948, concerning notes in the Faroe Islands; these allow the Faroe Islands to have special banknotes—the *Faroese króna*—which are printed by the National Bank of Denmark, issued by the Prime Minister's representative on the Islands and there they have legal tender status. As regards size and denominations, the Faroese banknotes are identical

---

[244] Cf. *supra*, Ch. 2, p. 80 *et seq.*

[245] On 9 December 1999, cf. BIS, Press Release No 40/1999E of 8 November 1999. Cf. also *supra*, Ch. 1, p. 45 *et seq.*

[246] According to this provision, the Board of the BIS is obliged, in the process of issuing shares, to take into consideration "the desirability of associating with the Bank the largest possible number of central banks that make a substantial contribution to international monetary co-operation and to the Bank's activities".

[247] Smits, *supra*, n. 74, 423, mentions the additional possibility for the ECB to subscribe for preferential stocks available to some national central banks under Art. 8(2) of the Statute of the BIS.

[248] This view is shared by Bognar, *supra*, n. 41, 403.

[249] Cf. Art. 299(5)(a) EC.

[250] The application of the EC to Greenland was terminated by an Agreement dated 13 March 1984 which amended the Treaty and inserted Art. 188 EC. See Schweitzer and Hummer, *supra*, n. 38, 37.

to the Danish banknotes and are convertible 1:1; they are covered entirely by a specific account in Danish crowns with the National Bank of Denmark. There are no special Faroese coins, but Danish coins are in circulation on the Islands.

—in the case of Greenland by Act 577 of 29 November 1979, according to which Greenland is an integral part of the Danish currency area and Danish banknotes and coins are the sole legal tender in this autonomous region.

To avoid a legal situation in which these special monetary links would have to be given up in a future Danish move to the third stage of EMU, Protocol No 22 on Denmark, annexed to the EC Treaty at Maastricht, provides:

> The provisions of Article 14 of the Protocol on the Statute of the European System of Central Banks and of the European Central Bank shall not affect the right of the National Bank of Denmark to carry out its existing tasks concerning those parts of the Kingdom of Denmark which are not part of the Community.

This means that even when Denmark decides to terminate its special status as regards the third stage of EMU,[251] the National Bank of Denmark will be granted, by primary Community law, the competence to continue monetary links with the Danish autonomous regions, in spite of the explicit competence of the Community and the leading role of the ECB within the ESCB in this respect. To exercise this competence, the National Bank of Denmark thus needs special permission neither from the ECB nor from the Community institutions.

IV. EXTERNAL REPRESENTATION OF THE "EURO AREA" IN INTERNATIONAL ORGANISATIONS

Until this point, this chapter has dealt with the substance of competences in the external relations of the "euro area". Now we turn to a more practical point: the question of which entity is allowed to speak on behalf of the euro when external competences are at stake, in particular within the framework of international organisations and fora dealing with economic and monetary matters.

1. The rules on external representation in Article 111(4) EC and Article 6 of the Statute

Theoretically, one could imagine that, in spite of the division of competences as regards the conclusion of agreements, there would be only one institution or entity charged with speaking on behalf of the euro in international organisations and fora—on a case-by-case basis on behalf of the Community, the ECB, the Member States or even the national central banks.

---

[251] Cf. *supra*, Ch. 4, p. 137 *et seq.*

This idea of centralised representation was, despite its practical advantages, not chosen by the EC Treaty; on the contrary, the law on external representation exactly reflects the substantive competences of the different actors in the external relations of the euro area. This means that, as a rule, the euro must always be represented in international organisations and fora by the entity which has the external competence to conclude international agreements on the subject-matter to be discussed in the framework of that organisation.

This idea is, first of all, reflected in Article 111(4) EC which reads, in its relevant part, as follows:

> The Council shall, on a proposal from the Commission and after consulting the ECB, ... acting unanimously,[252] decide its (the Community's) representation in compliance with the allocation of powers laid down in Articles 99 and 105.

From this it follows that the Council has the competence only to decide on the representation *of the Community* in international organisations and fora. It has, however, to take into account that there are also other actors in the external relations of the "euro area": the Member States, which have a substantial concurrent competence with the Community as regards economic policy under Article 99 EC, and the parts of the ESCB, in particular the ECB, the competences of which cover monetary policy in a broad sense, as defined in Article 105 EC *et seq*.

That there is another actor to speak and act in international organisations and fora than the Community and the Member States is shown by the very existence of Article 6.1 of the Statute:

> In the field of international co-operation involving the tasks entrusted to the ESCB, the ECB shall decide how the ESCB shall be represented.

In addition, Article 6.2 of the Statute states:

> The ECB and, subject to its approval, the national central banks may participate in international monetary organisations.

It is clear that "international monetary organisations" has to be interpreted as including international organisations which deal also, but not exclusively, with monetary matters and thus allowing participation of the ECB in such organisations whenever they discuss matters falling within its field of competence. A more restrictive interpretation would create the (insurmountable) difficulty of identifing "pure monetary organisations"—even the IMF also deals with general matters of economic policy.[253] It would in addition be incompatible with Article

---

[252] The Treaty of Nice will shift the entire Art. 111(4) EC to decision by qualified majority.

[253] According to Art. I(ii) of its Artiles of Agreement, the purposes of the IMF include "to facilitate the expansion and balanced growth of international trade, and to contribute thereby to the promotion and maintenance of high levels of employment and real income and to the development of the productive resources of all members as primary objective of economic policy". See also Deutsche Bundesbank, *Sonderdrucke No 3, Internationale Organisationen und Gremien im Bereich von Währung und Wirtschaft* (4th edn., Frankfurt am Main, 1992), which deals without any distinction with all international organisations and fora relevant for international monetary and economic co-operation, as both cannot be separated strictly.

6.1 of the Statute which presumes international activities of the ECB whenever the tasks of the ESCB are involved.[254]

Of course, the competence of the ECB[255] to speak and act on behalf of the euro in international organisations and fora is, again, limited by the concurrent competence of the Community under Article 111 EC. Therefore, Article 6.3 of the Statute provides:

> Articles 6.1 and 6.2 shall be without prejudice to Article 111(4) of the Treaty.

This shows that both Article 111(4) EC and Article 6 of the Statute presuppose that the representational rights conferred by them are mutually exclusive in the sense that there are two strictly confined fields of competences, that of the Community and that of the ECB. Therefore, the following conclusions may be drawn from these two provisions:

—The Community is competent to speak and act in international organisations and fora whenever the external competences of the Community are involved. In the monetary field, this includes all areas covered by exchange rate agreements and by agreements concerning monetary or foreign exchange regime matters concluded by the Community under Article 111(1) and (3) EC. Its competence of representation also extends to matters which are of particular relevance to economic and monetary union and where the Community wants to take a position in accordance with Article 111(4) EC.

—The ECB[256] is competent to speak and act in international organisations and fora whenever the tasks entrusted to the ESCB are involved, in particular within the framework of international *monetary* organisations, but also of other international organisations whenever they deal with monetary or related matters (Article 6.1 and 6.2 of the Statute).

—The Member States remain, as a rule, competent to speak in international organisations and fora whenever they deal with economic matters which are not covered by the provisions on economic policy in Articles 98 *et seq.* EC. They also may participate in such organisations whenever their residual monetary competences are concerned.

2. The rules on external representation applied

The rules on external representation contained in the EC Treaty and in the Statute seem crystal clear, and at first glance one would not think that they could very easily give rise to conflicts or problems. However, the external

---

[254] This is also the view of Smits, *supra*, n. 74, 426, which justifies this interpretation of Art. 6.2 of the Statute both by the heading of Art. 6 ("International co-operation") and by the implied powers of the ECB.

[255] Or, in accordance with an ECB decision based on Art. 6.1 of the Statute, the ECB and/or one or more national central bank(s).

[256] See previous footnote.

representation of the "euro area" also has to observe the practice of international organisations. The fact that, according to the EC Treaty, there exists a specific division of competence in external relations has, in principle, no direct legal impact on other international organisations. They will normally consider this new division of tasks as an issue which is purely internal to the Community legal order. Therefore, there will be practical problems whenever the statutes or internal rules of such organisations do not reflect the division of competence between the Community, the ECB, the Member States and the national central banks.

The ECJ has always stated that in case of such conflicts, the guiding principle is *the requirement of unity* in international representation.[257] According to this requirement of unity:

> the Community institutions[258] and the Member States must take all necessary steps to ensure the best possible co-operation in that regard.

This best possible co-operation would have to take one of the following two forms:

—*The co-ordination model*: in international organisations and fora where different actors are allowed to take part on behalf of the "euro area" in negotiations and debates, the actors involved are obliged to co-ordinate their positions before such meetings and to agree which of them is entitled to speak and vote, and under which circumstances these rights will pass to the other actor. These arrangements should be laid down in inter-institutional or administrative agreements, as was done by the Arrangement concluded by the Commission and the Council and dated 19 December 1991 "regarding preparation for FAO meetings, statements and voting".[259] In addition, it may be required by the internal rules of an international organisation that the Community, the ECB and the Member States agree on a "declaration of competences" which lists the respective fields in which one of them is allowed to speak, to vote or to conclude agreements on behalf of the euro area.[260]

---

[257] *Ruling 1/78, supra*, n. 16, paras. 34 to 36; *Opinion 2/91, ILO-Convention No 170* [1993] ECR I–1061, para. 36; *Opinion 1/94, WTO* [1994] ECR I–5267, para. 108; Case C–25/94, *Commission* v. *Council (FAO)* [1996] ECR I–1469, para. 48.

[258] At the time of these rulings, opinions and judgments, the ECB did not exist. Therefore, the ECJ did not have to deal with potential conflicts of competence between the Community and a separate actor at Community level. However, as also the ECB has been established under the EC Treaty and thus falls within the framework of Community law, it seems evident that today the ECJ would not hesitate to extend this duty of co-operation also to the relationship between the Community and the ECB.

[259] See Case C–25/94, *Commission* v. *Council (FAO)* [1996] ECR I–1469.

[260] Such a declaration of competence was required by the Council of the FAO in accordance with Art. II.5 of the FAO's constituent charter. The Community attached such a declaration to its request for membership; see [1991] OJ C292/8. However, the difficulties of elaborating such a declaration should not be underestimated. The ECJ itself has stated in this respect in its *Ruling 1/78, supra*, n. 16, para. 35, that "it is not necessary to set out and determine, as regards other parties to the convention, the division of powers in this respect between the Community and the Member State, particularly as it may change in the course of time. It is sufficient to state to the other contracting parties that the matter gives rise to a division of powers within the Community, it being understood that the exact nature of that division is a domestic question in which third parties have no need to intervene".

—*The trustee model*: in international organisations and fora where only one type of actor from the "euro area" is admitted, this actor will be required to co-ordinate its positions with the other actors beforehand and to act as their trustee whenever their respective competences are at stake.[261] In the long run, this actor would have to initiate amendments of the internal rules of such organisations to make the participation of the appropriate actors legally possible and thus to permit representation in this organisation to mirror exactly the situation of external competences under Community law.[262]

In what follows, the most important international fora will be analysed to see whether there exist practical problems and by which form of co-operation they could be solved.[263]

2.1. IMF

The IMF is both the most prominent and also—in the context of the present analysis—the most problematic international organisation.[264] This comes from the fact that under Article 2 section 2 of the Fund Agreement, only "countries" are permitted membership. From the point of view of public international law—and this is the relevant point of view for interpreting international agreements like the Fund Agreement—it seems not possible to consider the Community or the ECB as countries in this sense. Despite their far-reaching competence in monetary policy matters, both the Community[265] and the ECB lack the three essential characteristics of countries required under public international law: a defined territory, a permanent population, and the *plenitudo potestatis*, i.e. the competence to create new competences for itself.[266] Therefore, membership by the ECB and/or the Community of the IMF will depend on an amendment of the Fund Agreement which will raise a number of delicate issues, in particular the redistribution of quotas and of constituencies. This means that, for the foreseeable future, the only workable solution seems to be a trustee model where the Member States are under an obligation to act jointly in the interest of the Community, and in particular of the ECB in the IMF decision-making bodies. Successively, the ECB may also participate in talks and negotiations, first as an

---

[261] This was stated by the ECJ in *Opinion 2/91, ILO-Convention No 170* [1993] ECR I–1061, para. 5. In view of the fact that the statutes of the ILO did not allow the EC to become a member, Member States were held to be under an obligation to act jointly in the interest of the Community.

[262] In the case of old agreements, which are the most prominent example of where such problems could arise, this obligation results from Art. 307(2) EC.

[263] Cf. also ECB, "The ECB's Relations with International Organisations and Fora", *Monthly Bulletin* (Frankfurt am Main, January 2001), 57.

[264] See on these issues Smits, *supra*, n. 74, 429; Martha, *supra*, n. 19, 749.

[265] Smits, *supra*, n. 74, 442 *et seq.* nevertheless argues in favour of considering the Community as a country.

[266] See Brownlie, *supra*, n. 6, 72 *et seq.* The "territory" of the Community is that of the Member States (Art. 299 EC), "its" population is composed of the nationals of the Member States, and its competences are limited to those enumerated in the EC Treaty, as stated in Art. 5(1) EC. For the ECB, the same principle is mentioned in Art. 8 EC.

observer—as is already the case at present[267]—in the future possibly as a member in its own right, which would substitute the participating Member States whenever monetary matters are on the agenda.[268]

2.2. BIS

The case of the BIS has already been mentioned as that of an international organisation established under an old agreement in which national central banks may continue to participate by virtue of Article 31.1 of the Statute. National central banks have to act jointly, in accordance with the decisions of the ECB, whenever the tasks of the ESCB are involved.

2.3. OECD

The Convention on the Organisation for Economic Co-operation and Development (OECD), dated 14 December 1960,[269] provides for a relatively easy solution. Although the OECD was founded by states and thus normally permits only states as members, Article 12(b) of the Convention already foresees the possibility for the OECD to establish and maintain relations with organisations, and Article 12(c) of the Convention even enables the OECD to invite organisations to participate in the activities of the OECD. This would permit simultaneous participation both of the Community and of the ECB in their respective fields of competence.

In addition, the case of the European Communities is explicitly envisaged by Article 13 of the Convention and, more particularly, by Supplementary Protocol No 1 to the OECD Convention which reads as follows.

> 1. Representation in the Organisation for Economic Co-operation and Development of the European Communities established by the Treaties of Paris and Rome of 18 April, 1951, and 25 March, 1957, shall be determined in accordance with the institutional provisions of those Treaties.
>
> 2. The Commissions of the European Economic Community and of the European Atomic Energy Community as well as the High Authority of the European Coal and Steel Community shall take part in the work of that Organisation.

It should not be forgotten that this text dates from 1960 and therefore can hardly be said to be up-to-date with the current development in the Community law on external relations, in particular in the context of economic and monetary union. However, it is of utmost importance that paragraph 1 of this Protocol refers to "the institutional provisions of those Treaties" as regards representation in the OECD, as this is clearly to be understood as a reference to the inter-

---

[267] Cf. *supra*, Ch. 1, p. 46.

[268] Cf. Selmayr, "Unabhängigkeit gegenüber Finanzministern sichern. Die Europäische Zentralbank muß im Internationalen Währungsfonds für den Euro sprechen (Gastkommentar)", *Financial Times Deutschland,* 16 October 2000, 29.

[269] Published at http://www.oecd.org/about/origins/convention/conventn.htm.

nal distribution of competences. The OECD Convention is thus open to enable all potential actors of the "euro area" to make use of their representational rights inside the OECD. While the Commission is explicitly referred to in paragraph 2, the other actors can rely on the first paragraph. This is the avenue which has been followed in practice: since 1999, the Community has been represented jointly by the Commission and by the ECB in the groups in which central banking and financial issues are discussed.

The ECB could, in addition, also have relied on Article 12(c) of the Convention as it qualifies, without any doubt, as an "organisation" within the meaning of this provision. Although the OECD is chiefly an organisation for economic co-operation, the ECB would be entitled to take part, as an autonomous organisation, in Working Party 3 of the OECD which consists of representatives of central banks and finance departments.[270]

In view of the alternative participation of the Member States, Community institutions, the ECB and even national central banks (when authorised by the ECB under Article 6.2 of the Statute[271]), there is clearly a strong need for co-ordination. All actors involved, therefore, have to find a specific OECD "co-ordination model" to ensure unity in the international representation of the euro.[272]

2.4. G–7

The G–7[273] comprises the United States, Japan, Canada, Germany, France, Italy and the United Kingdom and organises regular meetings of central bank governors and finance ministers. The matters discussed are thus both economic and monetary. Here, the realisation of the "co-ordination model", which has been envisaged by the Council,[274] depended on the agreement of the non-Community G–7 members. If they had not agreed to participation of the ECB, the national central banks invited would have had to act jointly as trustees for the ECB, while the national finance ministers would have had to act jointly as trustees of the Community, and both groups would also have had to co-ordinate with each other to satisfy the requirement of unity. Fortunately, such complicated co-ordination has been avoided as in the meantime non-European G–7 partners

---

[270] This view is shared by Smits, *supra*, n. 74, 427.

[271] See *supra*, p. 176 *et seq*. Of course, when national central banks are performing functions outside the ESCB tasks, they need not be authorised by the ECB, subject to Art. 14.4 of the Statute.

[272] The best possible co-operation, as required by the ECJ, would certainly be achieved by creating a common Community delegation at the OECD which would include representatives of the Community institutions, in particular of the Commission, the ECB and the Member States and which will have agreed on rules, compatible with the division of external competences established by the Treaty, specifying which entity is allowed to speak and vote in the respective Working Groups and other fora inside the OECD.

[273] See Deutsche Bundesbank, *supra*, n. 253, 346 *et seq*.

[274] See the Press Release of the ECOFIN meeting of 1 December 1998, No 13462/98, published at http://ue.eu.int/Newsroom.

have accepted that the President of the ECB attends meetings of the Group which relate to EMU.[275]

2.5. G–10

The G–10[276] is a further informal group of highly industrialised countries which discusses economic and monetary policy and fulfils a certain co-ordinating role, but goes beyond the sphere of central banking. Its members are the United States, Japan, Canada, Germany, France, Italy, the United Kingdom, Belgium, the Netherlands and Sweden.[277] Here, the same applies as in the case of the G–7; however in view of the greater importance of economic matters, more weight will have to be given to the interest of the Community, as represented jointly by the finance ministers.

2.6. G–20

The G–20[278] is a new informal forum set up by the G–7 on 25 September 1999. It comprises the finance ministers and central bank governors from Argentina, Australia, Brazil, Canada, China, France, Germany, India, Indonesia, Italy, Japan, Korea, Mexico, Russia, Saudi Arabia, South Africa, Turkey, the United Kingdom and the United States. The mandate of the G–20 is to involve key emerging market countries in the dialogue on international economic and financial policy issues and thus to promote consensus-building on issues discussed by the relevant decision-making bodies of international organisations, such as the IMF or the World Bank. The ECB participates as twentieth member of this informal group, alongside the respective EU presidency, with which it co-ordinates its contributions to the extent appropriate.[279] It goes without saying that on all issues related to monetary policy, only the ECB may speak within the G–20, and not the EU presidency or even the finance ministers or central bank governors from individual EU Member States.

V. LEGAL REMEDIES

The complexity of the division of competences in the external relations of the "euro area" will without any doubt often provoke legal disputes. Such disputes

---

[275] The President of the ECB has already participated in the G–7, in Washington, DC, 3 October 1998, in Bonn, 20 February 1999 and in Tokyo, 22 January 2000; cf also *supra*, Ch. 1, p. 46, n. 205. The non-European G–7 partners have rejected (at least for the moment) the proposal to invite also the President of the Commission and the President of the "Euro 11" (now the "euro group") to their meetings, as suggested by the European Council in Vienna on 11–12 December 1998. It is in fact questionable whether such an "over-representation" would really be helpful for efficient co-operation among the G–7.

[276] See Deutsche Bundesbank, *supra*, n. 253, 344 *et seq.*

[277] Today, Switzerland also participates in the G–10.

[278] On the G–20, f. the information on their website: http://www.g20.org/.

[279] Cf. *Monthly Bulletin*, *supra*, n. 263, 65.

arose a number of times before the entry into force of the Maastricht Treaty when there were just two main actors which claimed competence to negotiate and conclude international agreements or to participate in international organisations: the Community and the Member States.[280] With the ECB and the national central banks being added to these actors, each having international legal personality and autonomous external competences, the likelihood of legal conflicts has been multiplied. Although many conflicts may be settled by mutual co-operation between these actors, the experience of the past shows that sometimes recourse to the ECJ cannot be avoided. This did, however, not weaken the position of the Community at the international level, as the ECJ took the opportunity to issue rulings, opinions and decisions in such cases most of which became landmark rulings in the Community law on external relations. In the end, these rulings all promoted the standing of Community at the international level and guaranteed that it there speaks with one voice.

In the law on external relations, there are essentially two devices for giving the ECJ the chance to intervene and to clarify the legal situation, in particular regarding the proper distribution of competences:

—First, the usual possibility of challenging the conclusion of an international agreement or a decision on external representation either directly by an action for annulment under Article 230 EC, or indirectly in the context of a national court case in combination with a preliminary reference to the ECJ under Article 234 EC (*judicial control a posteriori*).

—Secondly, the exceptional possibility to request an opinion of the ECJ before international agreements are signed (*judicial control a priori*).

1. Judicial control *a posteriori*

After the entry into force of an international agreement or a decision on external representation, the action for annulment under Article 230 EC permits challenges of legally binding acts adopted by Community institutions (Parliament, Council, Commission) and by the ECB. International agreements concluded on behalf of the Community are traditionally considered by the ECJ to be acts of the Community institutions,[281] because Article 230 EC treats as acts open to review by the ECJ all measures adopted by the institutions which are intended to have legal force.[282] *Mutatis mutandis* this reasoning would also apply to international agreements entered into by the ECB, which then would have to be qualified as acts of the ECB.

---

[280] One could add the EIB which, however, has made use of its international legal personality in areas in which conflicts could hardly be foreseen. Conflicts were also avoided by the very fact that the members of the EIB were identical to the Member States of the Community; see Art. 251 EC and Art. 3 of the Statute of the EIB.

[281] Case 181/73, *Haegeman* v. *Belgium* [1974] ECR 449, para. 4.

[282] Case 22/70, *Commission* v. *Council (ERTA)* [1971] ECR 263, para. 39.

Possible grounds for challenges are: lack of competence, infringement of an essential procedural requirement, infringement of the Treaty or of any rule of law relating to its application, or misuse of powers. The first ground (lack of competence) will need to be argued whenever one of the four actors acting internationally for the "euro area" takes the view that either the wrong actor has negotiated and concluded an agreement (for example, Community instead of ECB), or that the wrong decision-making body acted on behalf of one of these actors (for example, Executive Board of the ECB instead of Governing Council of the ECB). The second ground (infringement of an essential procedural requirement) could be argued whenever the consultation requirements under Article 111 EC have not been observed, for example, when the Council has concluded a formal agreement on an exchange rate system for the euro under Article 111(1) EC without properly consulting the ECB or the European Parliament. The third ground (infringement of the Treaty) is the broadest of all four grounds and would come into play whenever none of the three others applies; a possible example would be the infringement of general principles of Community law, in particular fundamental rights. The fourth ground (misuse of powers) has extremely rarely been accepted by the ECJ in the past. This might come from the fact that the EC Treaty normally endows the Community institutions with a broad discretion without specifying priorities to be given to specific Community aims; however, this has somewhat changed with the insertion of economic and monetary union into the EC Treaty which makes price stability a primary objective of monetary and foreign exchange policy for the Community and the Member States (Article 4(2) EC) and of the ECB (Article 105(1) EC). As Article 111(1) EC requires "an endeavour to reach a consensus consistent with the objective of price stability" in the consultation procedure between the Council and the ECB before the establishment of an exchange rate system for the euro, "misuse of power" could be argued successfully if no proof of such an endeavour may be found in the preparatory work or in the recitals of such an agreement.

Proceedings under Article 230 EC may be started by the Member States, the Council and the Commission, which are privileged applicants and thus do not need to prove that they are concerned by the challenged act or another form of *locus standi* (Article 230(2) EC). In addition, the action for annulment is open to the European Parliament and the ECB which are semi-privileged applicants[282a] and may start proceedings for the purpose of protecting their prerogatives (Article 230(2) EC). Exceptionally, individuals as non-privileged applicants may challenge Community acts if they are of direct or individual concern to them (Article 230(4) EC).

One could therefore imagine a Member State challenging a Community agreement under Article 111 EC—regardless of whether the respective Member State itself voted in favour of the conclusion of such an agreement in the

---

[282a] The Treaty of Nice will change the status of the European Parliament to that of a privileged applicant.

Council[283]—or an ECB agreement which it considers to undermine its residual national competence. Similarly, it would be open to the Council or the Commission to challenge an ECB agreement which it considered to be within the Community's competence under Article 111(1) or (3) EC, while Article 230(3) EC would give the ECB the capacity to challenge a Community agreement which, in its view, infringed the ECB's prerogatives, either for lack of competence or for lack of proper consultation of the ECB, the latter being an infringement of an essential procedural requirement just like an illegal non-consultation of the European Parliament, as it disturbs the institutional balance established by the EC Treaty.[284] Finally, national central banks may protect their residual competences under the EC Treaty by challenging international agreements concluded by the Community or the ECB under Article 230(4) EC; in spite of the restrictive interpretation given by the ECJ to the requirement of *locus standi* in that provision, it cannot be denied that a national central bank could be directly and individually concerned by an agreement which has been concluded in violation of this central bank's external competence.[285]

2. Judicial control *a priori*

In the context of external relations, judicial control *a posteriori* has disadvantages. A court case in an action for annulment in which the ECJ strikes down an agreement concluded by the Community or the ECB would result in the ECJ declaring such an agreement to be void (Article 231 EC). In the Community legal order, such an agreement would thus not have any effect any more. However, in public international law, the agreement, which was properly concluded according to the rules of public international law, the Community or the ECB would still remain bound by the agreement; as under public international law, it is not permissible to point to internal legal difficulties to escape the binding effect of a properly concluded agreement: *pacta sunt servanda*.

Therefore, there exists in Community law the exceptional procedure of a *prior reference to the ECJ* in the case of international agreements. This

---

[283] See Case 166/78, *Italy v. Council* [1979] ECR 2575, para. 6.

[284] See Case 138/79, *Roquette Frères v. Council (Isoglucose)* [1980] ECR 3333, para. 33. The obligation to consult the European Parliament is considered by the ECJ to be an *essential* procedural requirement as "it is the means which allows the Parliament to play an actual part in the legislative process. Although limited, it reflects, at Community level, the fundamental democratic principle that the peoples should take part in the exercise of power through the intermediary of a representative assembly". Similar reasoning could be said to apply to the ECB: the obligation to consult the ECB is essential for the institutional balance established by the EC Treaty, as it is a means which allows the ECB to play an actual part in the legislative process and thus to ensure the proper functioning of economic and monetary union. It reflects, at Community level, the primacy of the principle of price stability the maintenance of which has been entrusted to the ECB as an organisation distinct from the Community to ensure that short-term politics do not take precedence over the long-term benefits of a stable single currency, and thus to maintain the value of individual property rights.

[285] In favour of an extensive interpretation of the *locus standi* of national central banks see Di Bucci, "La Corte di Giustizia, l'Unione Economica e Monetaria ed il Passaggio alla Moneta Unica" in *Scritti in Onore di Giuseppe Federico Mancini* (1998), ii, 307 (332 *et seq.*).

procedure is mentioned in Article 300(6) EC according to which the Council, the Commission or a Member State may obtain an opinion of the ECJ on whether an agreement envisaged is compatible with the provisions of the Treaty.

The purpose of this prior reference procedure is to avoid a potential conflict between Community law and public international law. As the ECJ stated, the procedure is intended:

> to forestall complications which would result from legal disputes concerning the compatibility with the Treaty of international agreements binding upon the Community. In fact, a possible decision of the Court to the effect that such an agreement is, either by reason of its content or of the procedure adopted for its conclusion, incompatible with the Treaty could not fail to provoke, not only in a Community context but also in that of international relations, serious difficulties and might give rise to adverse consequences for all interested parties, including third countries.[286]

2.1. Application of Article 300(6) EC to Community agreements concluded under Article 111(1) and (3) EC and to ECB agreements

There is no specific prior reference procedure in the context of economic and monetary union. The question therefore arises whether it is legally possible to use the procedure under Article 300(6) EC also for *a priori* control of international agreements concluded under Article 111 EC, i.e. agreements on monetary and foreign exchange regime matters, including formal agreements on an exchange-rate mechanism for the euro with regard to non-Community currencies, and of agreements concluded by the ECB using its explicit or implied powers.

At first glance, the principle *lex specialis derogat legi generali* seems to exclude any recourse to Article 300 EC for agreements in the context of monetary union. The fact that the authors of the EC Treaty did not insert into Article 111 EC a provision paralleling Article 300(6) EC seems to indicate their intention not to allow a prior reference procedure for agreements concerning the field monetary union.[287]

However, in legal reasoning the derogating effect of a special provision extends only as far as this provision itself. Article 111 EC mentions in two places that it derogates from Article 300 EC: in Article 111(1) and (4) EC, where it is always stated at the beginning of the paragraph: "*By way of derogation from Article 300 . . .*". As a consequence, paragraphs (1) to (4) of Article 300 EC—which deal with the procedure for concluding international agreements—do not apply in the context of monetary union agreements. The same is true for Article 300 (7) EC according to which agreements "*concluded under the conditions set*

---

[286] *Opinion 1/75, Local Cost Standard* [1975] ECR 1355.

[287] This result is supported by Stadler, *Der rechtliche Handlungsspielraum des Europäischen Systems der Zentralbanken* (Baden Baden, 1996), 181 *et seq.*, who argues with the history of the negotiations on Art. 111 EC—an argument that is hardly convincing in view of the jurisprudence of the ECJ which has never given much attention to the intentions of the authors; see only Case 26/62, *Van Gend en Loos* [1963] ECR 1 where the ECJ held that Art. 12 EEC was directly effective although all Member States involved in that case and the AG had argued that this had not been the intention of the Member States which had concluded the Treaty of Rome.

out in this Article" are binding on the Community institutions and the Member States; Article 111(3) EC, second paragraph, foresees that *"agreements concluded in accordance with this paragraph"* are also binding on the ECB and leaves unaffected by such agreements Member States with a derogation by virtue of Article 122(4) EC. In all these cases there can be no doubt that the provisions contained in Article 300 EC are not applicable to monetary union agreements.

But what about the remaining paragraphs of Article 300 EC? Article 300(5) EC, to start with, imposes an obligation on the Council first to initiate the amendment procedure under Article 48 of the Treaty on European Union before it may conclude agreements which call for Treaty amendments. It is extremely unlikely that the authors of the EC Treaty, by not inserting this provision into Article 111 EC, wanted to enable the Council to conclude international agreements in the field of monetary union which could amend the EC Treaty without having recourse to Article 48 of the Treaty on European Union.[288] The wording of Article 300(5) supports the contrary as it speaks in general terms of "agreements" which the Council envisages concluding; in contrast to Article 300(7) EC, it does not refer only to "agreements concluded under the conditions set out in this Article". Furthermore, the derogating effect mentioned in Article 111(1) and (3) EC does not extend to the question whether the Council may conclude agreements which modify the EC Treaty; there is no derogating paragraph on this issue in Article 111 EC. Therefore, it is both logical and supported by the wording and the spirit of Articles 300 and 111 that Article 300 EC applies to all agreements concluded under the EC Treaty where the EC Treaty does not foresee derogations. This means that Article 300(5) EC also applies to all Article 111(1) and (3) agreements.[289]

This reasoning is also valid as regards the prior reference procedure under Article 300(6) EC which is also applicable to agreements concluded in the context of monetary union, for the following reasons. First, the wording of Article 300(6) EC mentions as subject-matter of a prior reference procedure *"an agreement envisaged"*; it is not limited to agreements concluded in accordance with Article 300 EC, as is the case of Article 300(7) EC, but extends to all agreements to be concluded under Community law. Secondly, there is *no derogating paragraph* in Article 111 or elsewhere in the EC Treaty which would state that Article 300(5) was not applicable to international agreements in the field of monetary union. Thirdly, the *aim of the prior reference procedure* is identically relevant for international agreements in the field of monetary union. Here, it proves at least[290] similarly necessary to avoid divergence between the legal position of an agreement under Community law and under international law

---

[288] See, however, the view of Smits, *supra*, n. 74, 385, according to whom "the derogation in Art. 111(1) is from Art. 300 *in toto*".

[289] This is also the view of Di Bucci, *supra*, n. 285, 348.

[290] One could even argue that the specific sensitivity of international monetary agreements requires *a fortiori* a possibility of prior judicial review.

before the entry into force of such an agreement. One cannot imagine why the authors of the EC Treaty would have wanted to exclude the possibility of verification just in the case of agreements concluded in the context of monetary union; if they had wanted to override this procedure of constitutional import-ance,[291] they would have needed to state this explicitly.

In conclusion, the prior reference procedure may, in accordance with the wording of Article 300 EC, also be used by the Commission, the Council and the Member States in the case of agreements on monetary or foreign exchange regime matters (Article 111(3) EC), including agreements on an exchange rate mechanism for the euro, and in case of agreements concluded by the ECB by virtue of its explicit or implied external powers.[292]

2.2. The ECB as applicant in the prior reference procedure

The application of Article 300(6) EC to agreements in the context of monetary union leads to a further problem. Article 300(6) EC mentions as possible appli-cants of a prior reference procedure the Council, the Commission and the Member States. The ECB is not mentioned. This limited wording results in a considerable imbalance: while the Council, the Commission and the Member States are able to question the legality of an agreement already prior to its entry into force, the ECB is limited to legal remedies *a posteriori*. This would create a situation in which the Council, the Commission or a Member State could always check the legality of agreements concluded by the ECB by virtue of Article 300(6) EC, while the ECB would have to wait to challenge agreements concluded by the Community or by the Member States until they had entered into force—a serious disadvantage which might cause the ECB not to challenge such agreements at all, even if they infringed its prerogatives, in order not to cause a divergence between Community law and public international law.

Such an institutional imbalance is not compatible with the system of legal remedies created by the EC Treaty. When the European Parliament, in 1990, challenged a directive of the Council because it was, in its view, based on the wrong Treaty provision, the ECJ decided to grant *locus standi* to the Parliament, although at that time it was not mentioned among the possible applicants in Article 230 EC:[293]

> The absence in the Treaties of any provision giving the Parliament the right to bring an action for annulment may constitute a procedural gap, but it cannot prevail over the fundamental interest in the maintenance and observance of the institutional balance laid down in the Treaties establishing the European Communities.

---

[291] According to the ECJ, "Art. 300 EC constitutes, as regards the conclusion of treaties, an autonomous general provision of a constitutional nature"; cf. Case C–327/91, *France* v. *Commis-sion* [1994] ECR I–3641, para. 28.

[292] The same conclusion is drawn by Di Bucci, *supra*, n. 285, 349.

[293] Case C–70/88, *European Parliament* v. *Council (Chernobyl)* [1990] ECR I–2041, para. 26 *et seq.*

Consequently, an action for annulment brought by the Parliament against an act of the Council or the Commission is admissible provided that the action seeks only to safeguard its prerogatives and that it is founded only on submissions alleging their infringement.

This reasoning applies *mutatis mutandis* also to the role of the ECB under Article 300(6) EC. As the institutional relationship between the ECB, the Community and the Member States would otherwise be seriously imbalanced, and as otherwise the ECB would not have an efficient remedy at its disposal to protect its prerogatives in the field of external relations, the fact that the ECB is not mentioned as a possible applicant in Article 300(6) EC constitutes only a procedural gap which cannot prevail over its legitimate interest to protect the prerogatives entrusted to it by the EC Treaty. Therefore, the ECB may also request a prior reference ruling by the ECJ under Article 300(6) EC whenever agreements are at stake which could prejudice the prerogatives of the ECB.[294]

VI. CONCLUSION

The law governing the international relations of the ECB confirms that, with the beginning of the third stage of EMU on 1 January 1999, a new chapter of Community law has begun. The main characteristic of this new chapter is its complexity which is, however, not a consequence of badly drafted legal provisions or an ill-devised concept of law, but of the increasing complexity of the real world itself which has to be taken into account also by the legal order. In this sense, the EC Treaty and the Statute establish a new and perhaps unusual interaction in the external relations of the "euro area" between the ECB, the Community, the Member States and sometimes even the national central banks. However, the general principles of Community law, as laid down in the case law of the ECJ, ascertain that the European Union will cope with the challenge to co-ordinate the diverging interests related to the single currency at the international level.

---

[294] This view is also favoured by Di Bucci, *supra*, n. 285, 349.

A final word

In the Preface to this book on the law of the European Central Bank, our starting point was the reduced importance of the rule of law for central banks in the past—a phenomenon which we explained by the exceptional reputation of central banks like the Federal Reserve System and the Bundesbank.

The *leitmotif* of the five chapters of this book has been the constitutional importance of the rule of Community law for the ECB and the single currency for which it is responsible. We have reflected on the way in which the law excludes any interference with the tasks of the ECB by the Community institutions and the Member States, always keeping in mind the primacy of the legal objective of price stability as *ratio* behind the far-reaching independence of the ECB. We have explored the legal construction of the ESCB and revealed that Community law has organised the ESCB in a clearly centralised manner, thereby creating the preconditions for a strong "monetary government" in Frankfurt. We have discovered the legal peculiarities of the decision-making process inside the ECB and analysed the different types of ECB law which results therefrom, including its effects and its implementation in the Member States. We have seen that the law also serves as a bridge to overcome and attenuate the inevitable differentiation of a European Union in which only 12 of 15 Member States have transferred monetary sovereignty to the ECB. Finally, we have made a *tour d'horizon* through the complex field of international relations where we could identify the ECB as natural bearer of monetary sovereignty also in relation to third countries and international organisations.

In the end, the law of the European Central Bank leaves hardly any room for central banking activities exempt from the rule of law; Community law appears to be all encompassing. In our view, this new importance of the rule of law for the new supranantional central bank in Frankfurt does not make reputation, as it was traditionally enjoyed by central banks in the past, superfluous, on the contrary: the continuous observance of and adherence to the law will create legal certainty around the single currency, which in turn will be the best ground for the establishment of a new kind of central bank reputation—a credibility based not so much on quasi-religious mystery, but much more on the rule of Community law. Unlike the famous dollar notes, euro banknotes therefore will not need the inscription "In God we trust". From a lawyer's point of view, the secular words "a creation of Community law" would be much more appropriate for the euro.

Bibliography

AMTENBRINK, F., *The Democratic Accountability of Central Banks* (Oxford/Portland, 1999).

ARNDT, N., "Engere Zusammenarbeit und Flexibilität im Vertrag von Amsterdam—Eine neue Entwicklungsstrategie im Hinblick auf die Vertiefung und Erweiterung der Europäischen Union?" in Scholz and Ruprecht (ed.), *Europa als Union des Rechts— eine notwendige Zwischenbilanz im Prozeß der Vertiefung und Erweiterung* (Cologne, 1999), 179.

ASPETSBERGER, A., and SCHUBERT, A., "Möglichkeiten und Grenzen der Subsidiarität in einer Europäischen Währungsunion" [1993] *Berichte und Studien der Österreichischen Nationalbank* 110.

ASSO, B., "Le contrôle de la décision économique devant la Cour européenne de justice" [1976] *RTDE*, 21 and 177.

AUBIN, P., *Die Haftung der Europäischen Wirtschaftsgemeinschaft und ihrer Mitgliedstaaten bei gemeinschaftsrechtswidrigen nationalen Verwaltungsakten* (Baden Baden, 1982).

BAILLEIX BANERJEE, C., *La France et la Banque Centrale européenne* (Paris, 1999).

BARRO, R.J., and GORDON, D.B., "Rules, Discretion and Reputation in a Model of Monetary Policy" [1983] *Journal of Monetary Economics* 101.

BERGER, M., *Vertraglich nicht vorhergesehene Einrichtungen des Gemeinschaftsrechts mit eigener Rechtspersönlichkeit* (Baden Baden, 1999).

BERGER, R., GADDUM, HENZLER, H., HESSE, H., HUNGENBERG, H., NEMITZ, K., PÖHL, K.O., and RUDOLPH, B., *Bericht zur Strukturreform der Deutschen Bundesbank* (4 July 2000), published at http://www.bundesfinanzministerium.de.

BERNHARDT, R. (ed.), *Encyclopedia of Public International Law* (Amsterdam, 1983), v.

BICKERICH, W., *Die D-Mark. Eine Biographie* (Berlin, 1998).

BLECKMANN, A., *Europarecht* (6th edn., Cologne/Berlin/Bonn/Munich, 1997).

BLEICHER, S., "UN v IBRD: A Dilemma of Functionalism" [1970] *International Organization*.

BLINDER, A.S., "Central Banking in a Democracy" in Federal Reserve Bank of Richmond, [1996] *Economic Quarterly* 1.

—— Contribution in *Kauppalehti*, 8 December 1999, 7.

BLOKKER, N., and HEUKELS, T., "The European Union: Historical Origins and Institutional Challenges" in N. Heukels, T. Blokker, and M. Brus (eds.) *The European Union after Amsterdam. A Legal Analysis* (The Hague/London/Boston, 1998), 26.

BOGNAR, Z., *Europäische Währungsintegration und Außenwirtschaftsbeziehungen* (Baden Baden, 1997).

BROWNLIE, I., *Principles of Public International Law* (4th edn., Oxford 1990).

BURDEAU, G., "Indépendance des banques centrales et droit international" in Weber, A. (ed.), *Währung und Wirtschaft. Das Geld im Recht. Festschrift für Hugo J. Hahn* (Baden Baden, 1997), 17.

CAFARO, S., "I primi accordi della Comunità in materia di politica monetaria e di cambio" [1999] *Il Diritto dell'Unione Europea* 243.

CASSESE, S., "L'aquila e le mosche. Principio di sussidiarietà e diritti amministrativi nell'area europea" [1995] *Il Foro Italiano* 375.

—— "Remarks on Scelle's Theory of Role Splitting (*dédoublement fonctionnel*) in International Law" [1990] *EJIL* 210.

CHÉMAIN, R., *L'Union économique et monétaire. Aspects juridiques et institutionnels* (Paris, 1995).

CLOOS, J., REINESCH, G., and VIGNES, D., and WEYLAND, J., *Le Traité de Maastricht. Genèse, Analyse, Commentaires* (Brussels, 1994).

COLLIGNON, S., and MUNDSCHENK, S., "Die internationale Bedeutung der Währungsunion" [1998] *Integration* 77.

CONSTANTINESCO, V., "Who's Afraid of Subsidiarity?" [1991] *YEL* 33.

CURTIN, D., "The Constitutional Structure of the Union: A Europe of Bits and Pieces" [1993] *CML Rev.* 17–69.

—— and DEKKER, I.F., "The EU as a 'Layered' International Organization: Institutional Unity in Disguise" in P. Craig and G. de Búrca (eds.), *The Evolution of EU Law* (Oxford, 1999).

—— VAN OIK, R., "Denmark and the Edinburgh Summit: Maastricht without Tears" in D. O'Keefe and P.M. Twomey (eds.), *Legal Issues of the Maastricht Treaty* (London, 1994), 349.

DEHOUSSE, R., "European Institutional Architecture after Amsterdam: Parliamentary System or Regulatory Structure?", *RSC Working Paper No 98/11*.

—— and GHEMAR, K., "Le traité de Maastricht et les relations extérieures de la Communauté européenne" [1994] *EJIL* 151.

DE KOCK, M.H., *Central Banking* (Pretoria, 1954).

DEMARET, P., "Le Traité de Maastricht ou les voies diverses de l'Union" in J. Monar, W. Ungerer, and W. Wessels (eds.), *The Maastricht Treaty on European Union* (Brussels, 1993), 37.

DE WITTE, B. "The Pillar Structure and the Nature of the European Union: Greek Temple or French Gothic Cathedral?" in N. Heukels, T. Blokker and M. Brus (eds.), *The European Union after Amsterdam. A Legal Analysis* (The Hague/London/Boston, 1998), 6.

DI BUCCI, V., "La corte di giustizia, l'unione economica e monetaria ed il passaggio alla moneta unica" in *Scritti in onore di Giuseppe Federico Mancini, vol. II: Diritto dell'Unione Europea* (Milan, 1998), 307.

DÖRR, O., "Zur Rechtsnatur der Europäischen Union" [1995] *EuR* 334.

DUISENBERG W.F., and SASZ, A., "The Monetary Character of the IMF" in J.A. Frenkel, and M. Goldstein (eds.), *International Financial Policy: Essays in Honour of Jacques Polack* (Washington, 1991), 254.

DUNNETT, D.R.R. (Head of Division at the EIB), "The European Investment Bank: Autonomous Instrument of Common Policy?" [1994] *CML Rev.* 721.

EUROPEAN CENTRAL BANK, "The Eurosystem and the European System of Central Banks", *Monthly Bulletin* (Frankfurt am Main, January 1999), 7.

—— "The Stability-orientated Monetary Policy Strategy of the Eurosystem", *Monthly Bulletin* (Frankfurt am Main, January 1999), 9.

—— "The Institutional Framework of the European System of Central Banks", *Monthly Bulletin* (Frankfurt am Main, July 1999), 55.

—— "Legal Instruments of the European Central Bank", *Monthly Bulletin* (Frankfurt am Main, November 1999), 53.

—— "The Eurosystem and EU Enlargement", *Monthly Bulletin* (Frankfurt am Main, February 2000), 41.

—— "The Two Pillars of the ECB's Monetary Policy Strategy", *Monthly Bulletin* (Frankfurt am Main, November 2000), 37.

—— "The ECB's Relations with International Organisations and Fora", *Monthly Bulletin* (Frankfurt am Main, January 2001), 57.

EICHENGREEN, B., "Designing a Central Bank for Europe: A Cautionary Tale from the Early Years of the Federal Reserve System" in M.B. Canzoneri (ed.), *Establishing a Central Bank: Issues in Europe and Lessons from the US* (Cambridge, 1992), 13.

EMMINGER, O., *D-Mark, Dollar, Währungskrisen. Erinnerungen eines ehemaligen Bundesbankpräsidenten* (Stuttgart, 1986).

FALKNER, G., "Das Maastrichter Sozialprotokoll: Differenzierte Intergration wider Willen" in F. Breuss and S. Griller (eds.), *Flexible Integration in Europa. Einheit oder Europa "à la carte?"* (Wien, 1998), 79.

FELDHAHN, M. *Die Rechtsnatur der Diskontsatzfestsetzung der Deutschen Bundesbank und der dagegen gegebene Rechtsschutz* (München, 1991).

FERNANDEZ MARTIN, R., and TEXEIRA, P.G., "The Imposition of Sanctions by the European Central Bank" [2000] *EL Rev.* 391.

FRIEDMAN, Milton, *A Program for Monetary Stability* (New York, 1960).

—— "A Case for Floating Rates", *Financial Times*, 18 December 1989, 21.

FRID, R., "The European Economic Community. A Member of a Specialized Agency of the United Nations" [1993] *EJIL* 239.

FROWEIN, J., "Integration in the Federal Experience in Germany and in Switzerland" in M. Cappelletti, M. Seccombe and J. Weiler (eds.), *Integration Through Law: Europe and the American Federal Experience* (Berlin, 1986), 586.

GAJA, G., "How Flexible is Flexibility under the Amsterdam Treaty?" [1998] *CML Rev.* 855.

GIAVAZZI, "Il banchiere debole di Francoforte", *Corriere della Sera*, 29 October 1998, 1.

GIOVANOLI, M., "The Role of the BIS in International Monetary Cooperation and its Tasks Relating to the ECU" in R.C. Effros (ed.), *Current Legal Issues Affecting Central Banks* (Washington, 1992), i, 39.

GLESKE, L., "Organisation, Status und Aufgaben der zweistufigen Zentralbanksysteme in den Vereinigten Staaten von Amerika in der Bundesrepublik Deutschland in der künftigen Europäischen Währungsunion" in A. Weber (ed.), *Währung und Wirtschaft. Das Geld im Recht. Festschrift für Prof. Dr. Hugo J. Hahn zum 70. Geburtstag* (Baden Baden, 1997), 123.

GLOMB, W., and LAUK, K.J. (eds.), *Euro-Guide: Handbuch der Europäischen Wirtschafts- und Währungsunion* (Cologne, 1998).

GOLD, J., "On the Difficulties of Defining International Agreements. Some Illustrations from the Experience of the International Monetary Fund" in P.L.N. Simha (ed.), *Economic and Social Developments. Essays in Honour of Dr. C. D. Deshmukh* (Bombay, 1972), 25.

GORMLEY, L., and DE HAAN, J., "The Democracy Deficit of the European Central Bank", [1996] *EL Rev.* 95.

—— "Independence and Accountability of the European Central Bank" in M. Andenas, L. Gormley, C. Hadjiemmanuil and I. Harden (eds.), *European and Monetary Union: The Institutional Framework* (The Hague/London/Boston, 1997).

GRABITZ, E., and HILF, M., *Das Recht der Europäischen Union, Kommentar* (Munich, December 1999).

GRAMLICH, L., *Bundesbankgesetz, Währungsgesetz, Münzgesetz*. Kommentar (Munich, 1988).

GROS, D., "Euro-Zentralbank ist eine Schönwetterkonstruktion", *Frankfurter Rundschau*, 6 October 1998, 13.

—— "Mehr Gewicht für die Europäische Zentralbank", *Frankfurter Allgemeine Zeitung*, 2 May 1998, 15.

GROSS, J., "Abgespeckt", *Capital No 5* (1998), 3.

GROUX, J., "Le parallelisme des compétences internes et externes de la CEE" [1978] *CDE* 3.

GUILLIEN, R., and VINCENT, J., *Lexique de termes juridiques* (8th edn., Paris, 1990).

GUSTAVSSON, S., "Reconciling Suprastatism and Democratic Accountability" in C. Hoskyns and M. Newman (eds.), *Democratizing the European Union. Issues for the 21st Century* (Manchester, 2000).

HÄDE, U., "Die Europäische Wirtschafts- und Währungsunion" [1992] *EuZW* 171.

—— "Währungsintegration mit abgestufter Geschwindigkeit" in A. Weber (ed.), *Währung und Wirtschaft. Das Geld im Recht. Festschrift für Hugo J. Hahn zum 70. Geburtstag* (Baden Baden, 1997), 123.

HAFKE, H.C., "Rechtliche Aspekte der Währungsbeziehungen zwischen Mitgliedstaaten und Territorien außerhalb des Geltungsbereichs des EGV" [2000] *ZEuS* 25.

HAHN, H.J., "Europe: A Single Currency and A Single Central Bank?" (1990) *Michigan Journal of International Law* 121.

—— *Währungsrecht* (Munich, 1990).

—— "The European Central Bank: Key to Monetary Union or Target" [1991] *CML Rev.* 783.

—— *Der Vertrag von Maastricht als völkerrechtliche Übereinkunft und Verfassung* (Baden Baden, 1992).

—— "Berichtspflichten und Informationsmöglichkeiten der Europäischen Zentralbank" [1999] *JZ* 957.

HAWTREY, R.G., *The Art of Central Banking* (London, 1970).

HAYEK, F.A., *Denationalisation of Money—The Argument Refined. An Analysis of the Theory and Practice of Concurrent Currencies* (2nd edn., Lancing, 1978).

HASSE, R., *Die Europäische Zentralbank. Perspektiven für eine Weiterentwicklung des Europäischen Währungssystems* (Gütersloh, 1989).

HENRION, R., "La Banque européenne d'investissement" in W. Ganshof van der Meersch (ed.), *Droit de communautés européennes* (Brussels, 1969).

HERDEGEN, M., "Price Stability and Budgetary Restraints in the Economic and Monetary Union: The Law as Guardian of Economic Wisdom" [1998] *CML Rev.* 9.

—— "Bundesbank und Bankenaufsicht: Verfassungsrechtliche Fragen" [2000] *WM* 2121.

HERTNER, P., "Modern Banking in Italy" in M. Pohl (ed.), *Handbook on the History of European Banks* (Hants, 1994), 561.

HEUN, W., "Die Zentralbank in den USA—das Federal Reserve System" [1998] *Staatswissenschaft und Staatspraxis* 241.

HILF, M., *Die Organisationsstruktur der Europäischen Gemeinschaften* (Berlin, 1982).

HOLDER, W., "The Relationship Between the International Monetary Fund and the United Nations" in R.C. Effros (ed.), *Current Legal Issues Affecting Central Banks* (Washington, 1997), iv, 16.

HOWARTH, D., "The Compromise on Denmark and the Treaty on the European Union" [1994] *CML Rev.* 765.

JANZEN, D., *Der neue Artikel 88 Satz 2 des Grundgesetzes* (Berlin, 1996).

INTERNATIONAL MONETARY FUND, *Selected Decisions and Selected Documents of the International Monetary Fund* (24th edn., Washington, 1999).

IPSEN, K., *Völkerrecht* (Munich, 1990).

ISSING, O., "Geldpolitik im Spannungsfeld von Politik und Wirtschaft" in H. Albeck (ed.), *Wirtschaftsordnung und Geldverfassung. Symposium zum 65. Geburtstag von Norbert Kloten* (Göttingen, 1992).

—— "Hayek-Currency Competition and European Monetary Union", Annual Hayek Memorial Lecture Hosted by the Institute of Economic Affairs (London, 27 May 1999) published at http://www.ecb.int/key/sp990527.pdf.

—— "European Integration at the Beginning of the New Millenium", the Morgan Stanley Dean Witte conference "Germany-Structural Revolution" (Berlin, 26 January 2000), published at http://www.ecb.int/key/00/sp000208.htm.

—— "Should We Have Faith in Central Banks?", St. Edmund's College Millenium Year Lecture, Cambridge, 26 October 2000, published at http://www.ecb.int/key/00/sp 001026_2.htm.

JESTAEDT, T., and HÄSEMEYER, T., "Die Bindungswirkung von Gemeinschaftsrahmen und Leitlinien im EG-Beihilfenrecht" [1995] *EuZW* 787.

KÄSER, J., "The European Investment Bank: its Role and Place within the European Community System" [1984] *YEL* 303.

KLAU, T., "Heißes Eisen Außenvertretung", *Börsenzeitung*, 26 July 1998, 4.

KORTENBERG, H., "Closer Cooperation in the Treaty of Amsterdam" (1998) *CML Rev.* 833.

KOENIG, C., "Die Europäische Union als bloßer materiellrechtlicher Verbundrahmen" [1998] *EuR* 139.

KÖLZ, A., "Bundestreue als Verfassungsprinzip?" [1980] *Schweizer Zentralblatt für Staats- und Gemeindeverwaltung* 145.

KÖNNEKER, W., "Vom Zentralbanksystem zur Deutschen Bundesbank" [1957] *Zeitschrift für das gesamte Kreditwesen* 796.

KOVAR, R., *Le pouvoir réglementaire de la Communauté européenne du Charbon et de l'Acier* (Paris, 1964).

KRAL, F., and KURM-ENGELS, M., "Die nationalen Zentralbanken haben im EZB-Rat Übergewicht", *Handelsblatt*, 10 June 1998.

KRAMER, H.-R., *Die Rechtsnatur der Geschäfte des Internationalen Währungsfonds* (Berlin, 1967).

KRAUSKOPF, B., and STEVEN, C., "Immunität ausländischer Zentralbanken im deutschen Recht" [2000] *WM* 269.

—— "Einführung des Euro in außereuropäische Territorien und währungsrechtliche Regelungen im Verhältnis zu Drittstaaten" [1999] *EuZW* 650.

KUHL, L., and SPITZER, H., "Das Europäische Amt für Betrugsbekämpfung (OLAF)" [2000] *EuR* 671.

LAGAYETTE, P., "Répartition des rôles au sein du SEBC", *Aujourd'hui l'écu/The ecu today*, special edition, June 1992, 4.

—— "In Maastricht Subsidiarität vereinbart", *Deutsche Bundesbank, Auszüge aus Presseartikeln*, No 22, 20 March 1992.

LA MARCA, L., "Il controllo giurisdizionale sulla Banca centrale europea e sull'Istituto monetario europeo" [1996] *Il diritto dell'unione europea* 773.

LEANZA, U., "Commento all'articolo 129" in *Commentario del Trattato CEE* (Milan, 1965), ii, 999.

LÉGER, P. (ed.), *Union européenne. Communauté européenne. Commentaire article par article des traités UE et CE* (Basel, 2000).

LENAERTS, K., "Regulating the Regulatory Process: 'Delegation of Powers' in the European Community" (1993) *EL Rev.* 23.

—— "Federalism: Essential Concepts in Evolution—The Case of the European Union" [1998] *Fordham Int. LJ* 747.

—— and VAN YPERSELE, P., "Le principe de subsidiarité et son contexte: étude de l'article 3B du traité CE" [1994] *CDE* 3.

LOHMANN, S., "Olaf hat keine Zuständigkeit für die Europäische Zentralbank", *Vereinigte Wirtschaftsdienste*, 1 December 1999.

LOUIS, J.-V., "Differentiation and the EMU" in *The Many Faces of Differentiation in EU Law* (Antwerp, 2000).

—— "Union monétaire et Union politique, Le rôle du juge" in *La tutela giurisdizionale dei diritti nel sistema comunitario—Congresso di Venezia dell'U.A.E.* (Brussels, 1997).

—— "Le lien entre les conférences intergouvernementales sur l'Union économique et monétaire et sur l'Union politique" in J. Monar, W. Ungerer and W. Wessels (eds.) *The Maastricht Treaty on European Union* (Brussels, 1993), 163.

—— "L'évolution du Conseil européen à la lumière de la réalisation de l'Union économique et monétaire" in V. Starace (ed.), *Divenire sociale e adeguamento del diritto. Studi in onore di Francesco Capotorti* (Milan, 1999).

—— "Le Fonds européen de co-opération monétaire" [1973] *CDE* 255.

—— "Les relations internationales de l'Union économique et monétaire", *Working Paper LAW No 99/10* of the European University Institute (San Domenico (Florence), 1999).

—— "L'Union économique et monétaire" [1992] *CDE* 251.

LUCHAIRE, F., and CONAC, G., *La constitution de la république française* (2nd edn., Paris, 1987).

MAJONE, G., "The European Community—an 'independent fourth branch of government'?" in G. Brüggemeier (ed.), *Verfassungen für ein ziviles Europa* (Baden Baden, 1994), 23.

MANCINI, G.F., "The Making of a Constitution" (1989) *CML Rev.* 595.

MANN, F.A., *The Legal Aspects of Money* (5th edn., Oxford, 1992).

MARCHEGIANI, G., [2000] *RMC* 690.

MARGER, U., "Das Europäische Amt für Betrugsbekämpfung (OLAF)—Rechtsgrundlagen seiner Errichtung und Grenzen seiner Befugnisse" [2000] *ZEuS* 177.

MARTENCZUK, B., "Der Europäische Rat und die Wirtschafts- und Währungsunion" [1998] *EuR* 151.

MARTHA, R., "The Fund Agreement and the Surrender of Monetary Sovereignty to the European Community" (1993) *CML Rev.* 749.

MAURER, H., *Allgemeines Verwaltungsrecht* (13th edn., Munich, 2000).

MAZZAFERRO, F., "Unity through Diversity. Banknotes and Coins in the European Monetary Union", *ECU Newsletter*, June 1992, 29.

MÉGRET, J., *Commentaire Mégret, Le Droit de la CEE* (2nd edn., Brussels, 1998).

MENG, W., *Das Recht der Internationalen Organisationen—eine Entwicklungsstufe des Völkerrechts* (Baden Baden, 1979).

MIGLIAZZA, A., *Le Comunità europec in rapporto al diritto internazionale e al diritto degli Stati membri* (Milan, 1964).

MITRANY, D., *The Progress of International Government* (New Haven, Conn., 1933).

—— *A Working Peace System* (London, 1943).

MUNRO, C., *Studies in Constitutional Law* (London, 1987).

NICOLAYSEN, G., *Rechtsfragen der Währungsunion* (Berlin/New York, 1993).

—— "Der rechtliche Status Griechenlands als Mitgliedstaat mit einer Ausnahmeregelung" in M. Papaschinopoulou (ed.), *Greece on Course Toward the European Economic and Monetary Union. Lessons to be Learnt from the German Experience* (Athens, Baden Baden, 1999), 39.

NIEHANS, J., *The Theory of Money* (Baltimore, 1978).

NOYER, C., "Some ECB Views on the Accession Process" (Vienna, 17 January 2001), published at http://www.ecb.int/key/01/sp010117.htm.

—— "The International Impact of the Euro" (United States, January 2000), published at http://www.ecb.int/key/00/sp000113.htm.

NOVAK, R., "Ist ein 'Vollzugsföderalismus' noch föderalistisch?" in R. Novak, B. Sutter and G.D. Hasiba, *Föderalismus-Studien, vol. 1: Historische und aktuelle Probleme des Föderalismus in Österreich* (Vienna/Cologne/Graz, 1977), 27.

OLSZAK, N. *Histoire des unions monétaires* (Paris, 1996).

PACHE, E., "Die Kontrolldichte in der Rechtsprechung des Gerichtshofs der Europäischen Gemeinschaften" [1998] *DVBl* 380.

PADOA-SCHIOPPA, T., "The External Representation of the Euro Area", introductory statement at the Sub-Committee on Monetary Affairs of the European Parliament (Brussels, 17 March 1999), published at http://www.ecb.int/key/st990317.htm.

—— "The Impact of the Introduction of the Euro on ACP Countries and Particularly on the CFA Franc Zone", published at http://www.ecb.int.

—— "The Eurosystem and Financial Stability" (February 2000), published at http://www.ecb.int/key/00/sp/sp000210.htm.

PATRIKIS, E., "Sovereign Immunity and Central Bank Immunity in the United States" in *Current Legal Issues Affecting Central Banks* (Washington, 1992), 159.

PERNICE, I., "Das Ende der währungspolitischen Souveränität Deutschlands und das Maastricht-Urteil des BVerfG" in O. Due, M. Lutter and J. Schwarze (eds.), *Festschrift für Ulrich Everling* (Baden Baden, 1995), ii, 1057.

PERNTHALER, P., *Der differenzierte Bundesstaat* (Vienna, 1992).

PETERS, H., *Lehrbuch der Verwaltung* (Berlin, 1949).

PETERSON, J., "Subsidiarity: A Definition to Suit Any Vision?" [1994] *Parliamentary Affairs* 116.

PIPKORN, J., in C. Starck (ed.), *Erledigung von Verwaltungsaufgaben durch Personalkörperschaften und Anstalten des öffentlichen Rechts* (Baden Baden, 1992), 227.

—— "Der rechtliche Rahmen der Wirtschafts- und Währungsunion—Vorkehrungen für die Währungspolitik" [1994] *EuR* 85.

—— "Legal Arrangements in the Treaty of Maastricht for the Effectiveness of the Economic and Monetary Union" (1994) *CML Rev.* 263.

PIRIS, J.-C., "Does the European Union have a Constitution? Does it need one?" (1999) *EL Rev.* 557.

POTACS, M., "Nationale Zentralbanken in der Wirtschafts- und Währungsunion" [1993] *EuR* 31.

PROST, G., "Zur Rechtsnatur des Zentralbanksystems der Bundesrepublik (Bank deutscher Länder und Landeszentralbanken)" [1952] *DöV* 237.

RADICATI DI BROZOLO, L., "Some Legal Aspects of the European Monetary System" (1980) *Rivista di Diritto Internazionale* 330.

REMSPERGER, H., "Subsidiarität in der Zentralbankpolitik: Erfahrungen und Perspektiven" in W. Filc and C. Köhler (eds.), *Integration und Desintegration der Weltwirtschaft?* (Berlin, 1994).

RENGELING, H.-W., *Rechtsgrundsätze beim Verwaltungsvollzug des Europäischen Gemeinschaftsrechts* (Cologne/Berlin/Bonn/Munich, 1977).

REUTER, D., *La Communauté européenne du Charbon et de l'Acier* (Paris, 1953).

RIVAIS, R., "Le Parlement européen et la jurisprudence Le Pen", *Le Monde*, 13 February 2001, 23.

SACK, J., "Die Europäische Gemeinschaft als Mitglied internationaler Organisationen" in *Gedächtnisschrift für Grabitz* (Munich, 1995), 631.

SAINZ DE VICUÑA, A., "Legal Consequences of the Single Currency" in M. Giovanoli (ed.), *International Monetary Law* (Oxford, 2000), 161.

—— "The Lawyer at the ECB: A Description of the Legal Services of the European Central Bank" [1999] *Euredia* 591.

SANDHOLTZ, W., "Monetary Bargains: The Treaty on EMU" in A. Cafruny and G.C. Rosenthal (eds.), *The State of the European Community, vol II: The Maastricht Debates and Beyond* (Harlow, 1993), 125.

SANNUCCI, V., "The Establishment of a Central Bank: Italy in the Nineteenth Century" in M. De Cecco and A. Giovannini (eds.), *A European Central Bank?* (Cambridge, 1988), 244.

SAUERZOPF, B., and SELMAYR, M., "Das Europäische System der Zentralbanken als Hüter eines stabilen Euro" [1998] *Der Wirtschaftstreuhänder* 12.

SCELLE, G., "Le phénomène juridique du dédoublement fonctionnel" in Schätzel and Schlochauer (eds.), *Rechtsfragen der Internationalen Organization, Festschrift für Hans Wehberg zu seinem 70. Geburtstag (* Frankfurt, 1956), 324.

SCHELLER, H.K. in W. Glomb and K.J. Lauk (eds.), *Euro-Guide: Handbuch der Europäischen Wirtschafts- und Währungsunion* (Colgogne, 1998), 2.

—— *Die Europäische Zentralbank* (Frankfurt am Main, 2000).

SCHERMERS H.G., and O'KEEFFE, D. (eds.), *Mixed Agreements* (Deventer, 1983).

—— "International Organisations as Members of Other International Organisations" in *Festschrift für Mosler* (Berlin etc., 1983), 82.

—— and BLOKKER, N.M., *International Institutional Law. Unity within Diversity* (3rd edn., The Hague/London/Boston, 1995), 22.

SCHILLER, K.V., "Weisungsrechte der EG nach dem EWG-Vertrag bei nationalem Verwaltungsvollzug von EG-Recht?" [1985] *RIW* 36.

SCHMAHL, S., "Ungereimtheiten und Rechtsschutzlücken bei der außervertraglichen Haftung der Europäischen Gemeinschaft" [1999] *ZEuS* 415.

SCHMIDT-LOSSBERG, A., *Kontrolldichte im EG-Wirtschaftsrecht. Eine Untersuchung am Beispiel der Rechtsprechung des EuGH zu den Verordnungen im Währungsausgleich* (Frankfurt am Main, 1992).

SCHÖNFELDER, W., and THIEL, E., *Ein Markt—Eine Währung. Die Verhandlungen zur Europäischen Wirtschafts- und Währungsunion* (Baden Baden, 1994).

SCHROEDER, W., "Die Rechtsnatur der Europäischen Union und verwandte Probleme" in W. Hummer and M. Schweitzer, *Österreich und das Recht der Europäischen Union* (Vienna, 1996), 3.

—— and SELMAYR, M., "Der EuGH, das GATT und die Vollzugslehre. Warum der EuGH manchmal das Völkerrecht ignoriert" [1998] *JZ* 344.

SCHUSTER, G., "Rechtsfragen der Maastrichter Vereinbarung zur Sozialpolitik" [1992] *EuZW* 178.

SCHUSTER, G., "Der Sonderstatus Dänemarks im Vertrag über die Europäische Union" [1993] *EuZW* 177.

SCHWEITZER, M., and HUMMER, W., *Europarecht* (5th edn., Neuwied/Kriftel/Berlin, 1996).

—— *Staatsrecht III* (6th edn., Heidelberg, 1997).

—— and FIXSON, O., "Subsidiarität und Regionalismus in der EG" [1992] *Jura* 579.

SEIDEL, M., "Die Wirtschafts- und Währungsunion im rechtlichen und politischen Gefüge der Europäischen Union" in R. Caesar and H.E. Scharrer (eds.), *Ökonomische und politische Dimensionen der Europäischen Wirtschafts- und Währungsunion* (Baden Baden, 1999), 215.

—— "Probleme der Verfassung der Europäischen Gemeinschaft als Wirtschafts- und Währungsunion" in J.F. Baur (ed.), *Europarecht, Energierecht, Wirtschaftsrecht. Festschrift für Bodo Börner* (Cologne, 1992), 417.

—— "Die Euro-Zentralbank ist nicht nach dem Vorbild der Bundesbank gestaltet", *Frankfurter Rundschau*, 8 October 1998, 12.

—— "Im Kompetenzkonflikt: Europäisches System der Zentralbanken (ESZB) versus EZB" [2000] *EuZW* 552.

SEIDL-HOHENVELDERN, I., and LOIBL, G., *Das Recht der Internationalen Organisationen einschließlich der Supranationalen Gemeinschaften* (7th edn., Cologne/Munich, 2000).

SELMAYR, M., "Die Europäische Währungsunion zwischen Politik und Recht" [1998] *EuZW* 101.

—— "Die Wirtschafts- und Währungsunion als Rechtsgemeinschaft" [1999] *AöR* 357.

—— "Die EZB als Neue Gemeinschaft—ein Fall für den EuGH?" [1999] *Europablätter* 170.

—— "Wie unabhängig ist die Europäische Zentralbank? Eine Analyse anhand der ersten geldpolitischen Entscheidungen der EZB" [1999] *WM* 2429.

—— "Gefahr für die Europäische Zentralbank?" [1998] *Europablätter* 39.

—— "Intervention zwecks Preisstabilität. Die europarechtlichen Leitplanken für die EZB", *Neue Zürcher Zeitung* No 237, 11 October 2000, 11.

—— "Darf die EZB den Wechselkurs des Euro stützen?" [2000] *Europablätter* 209.

—— "Unabhängigkeit gegenüber Finanzministern sichern. Die Europäische Zentralbank muß im Internationalen Währungsfonds für den Euro sprechen (Gastkommentar)", *Financial Times Deutschland,* 16 October 2000, 29.

—— "Die Grenzen der Geldpolitik der Europäischen Zentralbank—eine Fallstudie" in A. Rohde and C. Köhler, *Geldpolitik ohne Grenzen* (Berlin, 2001—in press).

—— "Die Rechtssache T–33/99 und ihr gemeinschaftsverfassungsrechtlicher Hintergrund" [2001] *EWS* (in press).

—— "Die Mitwirkung der Europäischen Union in Internationalen Organisationen— unter besonderer Berücksichtigung der Rechtslage im Internationalen Währungs- fonds" [2001] *ZEuS* (in press).

—— and BRAND, T., "Die Euro-Bank", *Oberösterreichische Nachrichten*, 7 January 2000, 3.

—— and KAMANN, H.-G., "Streit um die Unabhängigkeit", *Frankfurter Allgemeine Zeitung* Nr. 86, 11 April 2000, 14.

—— and PROWALD, N., "Abschied von den 'Solange-Vorbehalten'—Die wahre Bedeutung des 'Kooperationsverhältnisses' des BVerfG zum EuGH" [1999] *Deutsches Verwaltungsblatt* 269.

SHAPIRO, M., *Who Guards the Guardians? Judicial Control of Administration* (Athens (Georgia), 1988).

SLOT, P.J., "The Institutional Provisions of the EMU" in D. Curtin and T. Heukels (eds.), *Institutional Dynamics of European Integration. Essays in Honour of Henry G. Schermers* (Dordrecht/Boston/London, 1994), 229.

SMEND, R., "Ungeschriebenes Verfassungsrecht im monarchischen Bundesstaat" in *Festgabe für Otto Mayer* (1916), 247.

SMITH, C., "On Central Bank Independence" in A." Weber (ed.), *Währung und Wirtschaft. Das Geld im Recht. Festschrift für Hugo J. Hahn* (Baden Baden, 1997).

SMITS, R., *The European Central Bank. Institutional Aspects* (The Hague/London/Boston, 1997).

—— "Positie en bevoegdheden van een Europese Centrale Bank" in *Een Economische en Monataire Unie (EMU) in Europa—Juridische en Institutionele Consequenties, Asser Instituut Colloquium Europees Recht* (1990), 25.

SNYDER, F., "EMU—Metaphor for European Union? Institutions, Rules and Types of Regulation" in R. Dehousse (ed.), *Europe after Maastricht. An Ever Closer Union?* (Munich, 1994), 63.

—— "EMU Revisited: Are We Making a Constitution? What Constitution Are We Making?" in P. Craig and G. de Búrca (eds.), *The Evolution of EU Law* (Oxford, 1999), 417.

SOLANS, E.D., "Should the ECB have Broader Objectives Beyond Price Stability", Speech of 24 May 1999, published at http://www.ecb.int.

STADLER, R., *Der rechtliche Handlungsspielraum des Europäischen Systems der Zentralbanken* (Baden Baden, 1996).

STARCK, C. (ed.), *Erledigung von Verwaltungsaufgaben durch Personalkörperschaften und Anstalten des öffentlichen Rechts* (Baden Baden, 1992).

STEIN, E., *Staatsrecht* (14th edn., Tübingen, 1993).

STERN, K., *Das Staatsrecht der Bundesrepublik Deutschland* (Munich, 1988), ii.

STREINZ, R., *Europarecht* (4th edn., Heidelberg, 1999).

TEMPLE LANG, J., "The Duties of National Courts under Community Constitutional Law" (1997) *EL Rev.* 3.

—— "The Duties of National Authorities under Community Constitutional Law" (1998) *EL Rev.* 109.

TIETMEYER, H., "Ein dezentrales Umsetzen der gemeinsamen Geldpolitik sichert nahtlosen Übergang auf europäische Ebene", *Frankfurter Rundschau*, 9 October 1998, 13.

TIMMERMANS, C., "The Uneasy Relationship Between the Communities and the Second Union Pillar: Back to the 'Plan Fouchet" [1996] *LIEI* 61.

—— "Editorial Comment, Executive Agencies within the EC: The European Central Bank—a Model?" (1996) *CML Rev.* 623.

TIZZANO, A., "Contratti 'strumentali' e contratti d'impiego delle Comunità europee" [1978] *Rivista di diritto europeo* 481.

—— "La personnalité internationale de l'Union européenne" [1998] *RMC* 11.

TORRENT, R., "Whom is the European Central Bank the Central Bank of?: Reaction to Zilioli and Selmayr" (1999) *CML Rev.* 1229.

—— "Droit et pratique des relations économiques extérieurs dans l'Union européenne" (Brussels/Barcelona 1998) published at http://www.ub.es.dpecp/ep/livretorrent.html.

TUYTSCHAEVER, P., *Differentiation in European Union Law* (Oxford, 1999).

ULLRICHT, H., and DONNELLY, A., "The Group of Eight and the European Union", G 7 Governance No 8 (November 1998) published at http://www.library.utoronto.ca/ g7/governance/gov.5

USHER, J.A., *The Law of Money and Financial Services in the European Community* (Oxford, 1994).

VANTHOOR, W.F., *European Monetary Union since 1948—A Political Historical Analysis* (Cheltenham, 1996).

VIGNERON, P., and MOLLICA, M.R., "La différenciation dans l'Union Economique et Monétaire" [2000] *Euredia* 197.

VIRALLY, M., "Definition and Classification of International Organizations: a Legal Approach" (1997) 29 *Int. Soc. Sci. J.* 58.

VOCKE, W., "Schwieriger Start der neuen Zentralbank" [1973] *Zeitschrift für das gesamte Kreditwesen* 549.

VON BOGDANDY, A., "The Legal Case for Unity: The European Union as a Single Organization with a Single Legal System" (1999) *CML Rev.* 887.

—— "Die Europäische Union als einheitlicher Verband" [1998] *EuR* 165.

—— "Organizational Proliferation and Centralisation under the Treaty on European Union" in N. Blokker and H.G. Schermers (eds.), *Proliferation of International Organisations. Legal Issues* (The Hague, 2001), 177.

—— and NETTESHEIM, A., "Die Verschmelzung der Europäischen Gemeinschaften in der Europäischen Union" [1999] *NJW* 2324.

VON BORRIES, R., "Die Europäische Zentralbank als Gemeinschaftsinstitution" [1999] *ZEuS* 281.

—— "Die Fortentwicklung der Europäischen Wirtschaftsgemeinschaft zur Wirtschafts- und Währungsunion" in H.-W. Rengeling and R. von Borries (eds.), *Aktuelle Entwicklungen in der Europäischen Gemeinschaft* (Cologne, 1992),105.

VON DER GROEBEN, H., THIESING, J., and EHLERMANN, K.-D., *Kommentar zum EU/EG-Vertrag* (5th edn., Baden Baden, 1997/1999).

VON HAGEN, J., "Die EZB ist keine Superbundesbank", *Vereinigte Wirtschaftsdienste*, 11 August 1998.

—— and SÜPPEL, R., "Central Bank Constitutions for Federal Monetary Unions" (1994) 38 *European Economic Review* 774.

VON WEIZSÄCKER, R., DEHAENE, J.-L., and SIMON, D., "The Institutional Implications of Enlargement" (the so-called "Three Wise Men-Report"), Brussels, 18 October 1999, published at http://europa.eu.int/igc2000/repoct99_en.htm.

WAGENHÖFER, C., "Der Föderalismus und die Notenbankverfassung" in H. Seidel (ed.) *Festschrift zum 70. Geburtstag von Dr. Hans Ehard* (Munich, 1957), 97.

WALTER, C., *The European*, 5 May 1998.

WEBER, A., "Die Wirtschafts- und Währungsunion nach dem Maastricht-Urteil des BVerfG" [1994] *JZ* 53.

—— *Währung und Wirtschaft. Das Geld im Recht. Festschrift für Hugo J. Hahn* (Baden Baden, 1997), 93.

WEBER, M., *Die Kompetenzverteilung im Europäischen System der Zentralbanken bei der Festlegung und Durchführung der Geldpolitik* (Munich, 1995).

WEBER, M., "Das Europäische System der Zentralbanken" [1998] *WM* 1465.

WEILER, J., "Neither Unity nor Three Pillars—The Trinity Structure of the Treaty on European Union" in J. Monar, W. Ungerer and W. Wessels (eds.), *The Maastricht Treaty on European Union* (Brussels, 1993), 49.

WEILER, J., *Il Sistema Comunitario Europeo* (Bologna, 1985).

WEINBÖRNER, S., *Die Stellung der Europäischen Zentralbank (EZB) und der nationalen Zentralbanken in der Wirtschafts- und Währungsunion nach dem Vertrag von Maastricht* (Frankfurt, 1998).

WEINRICHTER, N., "The World Monetary System and External Relations of the EMU— Fasten your Safety Belts!" [2000] *EIoP* No. 10.

WELTEKE, E., "Die Rolle der nationalen Zentralbanken im europäischen System der Zentralbanken", speech of 10 September 1998, published at http://www.bundes bank.de/lzb-h/index.html.

WELLENSTEIN, E.P., "Unity, Community, Union—What's in a Name?" (Guest Editorial) (1992) *CML Rev.* 205.

ZEHETNER, F., "Völkerrechtliche Außenvertretungsbefugnisse der Oesterreichischen Nationalbank?" in *Festschrift für F.A. Mann* (1977), 470.

ZILIOLI, C., "L'applicazione del principio di sussidiarietà nel diritto comunitario dell'ambiente" [1993] *Rivista Giuridica dell'Ambiente* 533.

—— and SELMAYR, M., "The External Relations of the Euro Area: Legal Aspects" (1999) *CML Rev.* 273.

—— and —— "The European Central Bank, its System and its Law" [1999] *Euredia* 187 and 307.

—— and —— "The European Central Bank, its System and its Law" [1999–2000] *YEL* 347.

—— and —— "The European Central Bank: An Independent Specialized Organization of Community Law" [2000] *CML Rev.* 591.

ZULEEG, M., *Das Recht der Europäischen Gemeinschaften* (Cologne/Berlin/Bonn/ Munich, 1969).

Index